Promoting
Sexual Responsibility
and Preventing
Sexual Problems

Primary Prevention Psychopathology

George W. Albee and Justin M. Joffee, *General Editors*

Promoting Sexual Responsibility and Preventing Sexual Problems

George W. Albee,
Sol Gordon, and
Harold Leitenberg, editors

Published for the University of Vermont
and the Vermont Conference on
the Primary Prevention of Psychopathology
by University Press of New England
Hanover and London, 1983

University Press of New England

Brandeis University

Brown University

Clark University

Dartmouth College

University of New Hampshire

University of Rhode Island

Tufts University

University of Vermont

Copyright ©1983 by the Vermont Conference
on the Primary Prevention of Psychopathology

"Self-Esteem and Knowledge: Primary Requisites to Victimization" copyright ©1981
by Gloria J. Blum; "Childhood Sexuality: Approaching the Prevention of Sexual
Dis-ease" copyright ©1981 by Mary S. Calderone; "Nonsexist Sexuality" is adapted
from *Growing Up Free* copyright ©1980 by Letty Cottin Pogrebin and is included
by permission of McGraw-Hill Book Company.

Printed in the United States of America

LIBRARY OF CONGRESS CATALOGING IN PUBLICATION DATA

Vermont Conference on the Primary Prevention of
  Psychopathology (7th: 1981: University of Vermont)
  Promoting sexual responsibility and preventing sexual problems.

  (Primary prevention of psychopathology; 7)
  Papers presented at the Seventh Annual Vermont Conference
held in June 1981 at the University of Vermont.
  Includes bibliographies and index.
  1. Psychosexual disorders—Prevention—Congresses.
2. Sexism—Congresses. I. Albee, George W.
II. Gordon, Sol, 1923-   . III. Leitenberg, Harold.
IV. Title. V. Series: Vermont Conference on the Primary Prevention
of Psychopathology. Primary prevention of psychopathology; 7.
[DNLM: 1. Sex behavior—Congresses. 2. Sex disorders—Prevention
and control—Congresses. PR 945CK v. 7/WM611 V527 1981p]
RC454.V46 1977 vol. 7 [RC556] 616.85'8s 82-40474
ISBN 0-87451-248-4   [616.85'83]

Contents

Introduction

George W. Albee

The Seventh Annual Vermont Conference on the Primary Prevention of Psychopathology was held at the University of Vermont in June 1981. Each year, beginning in 1975 with a conference focused specifically on identifying the essential issues in primary prevention (Albee and Joffe, 1977), we have examined in depth the theoretical and research knowledge relevant to a specific aspect of the prevention of emotional disturbances and of the promotion of human competence. Each year the conference has resulted in a volume (Bond and Joffe, 1982; Bond and Rosen, 1980; Forgays, 1978; Joffe and Albee, 1981; Kent and Rolf, 1979).

For our seventh conference we chose to consider issues in fostering mature and responsible sexuality and preventing sexual problems. This topic arose from discussions with those who attended previous conferences and from an examination of the clinical literature. Clearly, sexual problems are a major source of stress, and disturbances generated from sexism are a major form of psychopathology. One of the organizers of the conference, Harold Leitenberg, has done research and clinical work with atypical sexual behavior and sexual dysfunction for the past 15 years. Currently he is co-authoring a text on human sexuality. Another conference organizer, Sol Gordon, has spent many years writing and speaking out for more rational and humanistic attitudes toward sexual education and sexuality in general. I have attempted to relate the rise of the Protestant ethic, with its emphasis on sexual repression, to the development of new forms of psychopathology (Albee, 1977).

Clearly there is no need to defend the choice of human sexuality, and problems of sexuality, as a topic for a conference on primary prevention of psychopathology. Sexual relations are a major source of anxiety; teenage pregnancy is epidemic; marital disruption and divorce are major sources of stress; the traditional family is the exception rather than the rule; rape and the sexual abuse of children are endemic. Meanwhile books on sexuality and on solving sexual problems are best sellers, and personal advice columns and radio programs are attended to by millions. Moreover, after years of effort an attempt has failed to pass an amendment to the Constitution that guarantees equal rights for women.

Our society is characterized by hierarchical power relations of all kinds, but especially between men and "their women and children." Madonna Kolbenschlag (1979) has argued that all social oppressions are ultimately reflections of the power relations that exist between men and women in a society. From the ancient days of the Greeks, when slaves and women were considered irrational species, to modern religious androlatry, she sees social violence preserving and sustaining hierarchical relations that emphasize male power. When an agency of the federal government recently classified jobs according to social desirability, nuclear physics was at the top and child care was at the bottom. Recent changes in the economic power structure further advance the process of the "feminization" of poverty and the "masculinization" of war and medicine. The federal government now proposes that it retain responsibility for war, weapons, and medical care and that it relinquish to the states the responsibility for block grants that reduce the level of support for welfare programs which most heavily involve women and children.

According to Catherine Ross (1982) one of the many consequences of the decentralization of welfare programs—pushing them back to the states from the federal government—will be the decreasing effectiveness of child advocacy groups. In the past, while the federal government was largely responsible for support programs for children, families, and the poor, groups advocating support for these populations could focus their efforts on members of Congress and the executive agencies in Washington. By returning these programs to the individual states, advocacy efforts will have to be repeated in every state by groups less well organized, less well funded, and less articulate than those that represented the have-not groups in the past.

The so-called Family Protection Act proposed by conservatives in the Senate is not really an act at all, but a list of rules that seem to have as their goal the legislation of conservative social values. Among the grab bag of contents of the act are proposals to end the life of the Center on Child Abuse and Neglect, to abolish all standards (except fire control) for daycare centers throughout the country, to forbid any state legislation aimed at banning corporal punishment in the schools, and to require that parental consent be obtained before birth control materials are distributed to persons under 18 years of age. This is patriarchy with a vengeance!

Looking for the Cause of the Causes

Joffe (1982) has suggested an important concept that we should consider in the current context as well as in broader efforts at primary prevention of behavioral problems. He has asked us to seek *the cause of the causes*. Very often in examining a particular phenomenon or condition that we want to prevent, we halt our efforts when we have found one or more apparent specific proximate causes. Thus if we are interested in preventing premature pregnancy and low birthweights among the infants of young teenage women, we may discover that early pregnancy is common among unemployed or underemployed and undernourished inner-city young women with inadequate sexual knowledge, many of whom are doing poorly in school. We conclude that we have identified some conditions that may represent causes. This discovery may lead us to institute preventive programs involving sex education and/or nutritional counseling. But we fail to take the critical step of trying to identify the *cause of the causes*. We should ask ourselves what causes poverty, unemployment, low self-esteem, boredom, and hopelessness in inner-city teenagers? If we do not ask what are the conditions that are responsible for slums and unemployment, then we are not dealing with the important cause. If we focus only on counseling to change self-esteem and sexual knowledge, we may fail to examine the causes of the poor life prospects facing these youths that lead them to attach a low value to themselves and to want a baby to love.

In a similar way, we may identify specific epidemiological factors associated with rape and the sexual abuse of children. But we may neglect to search for the larger causes. Some of these causes may appear to be the sexist nature of our society with its emphasis on the importance of male dominaton of females, the emphasis in the mass media on male violence and female passivity, and the pervasive, subtle sexism that is as present as the air we breathe and the water we drink — and as polluted. What is the cause of the cause? What causes sexism and what can we do about sexism? We must first examine the epidemiology of sexism and its relation to the power structure of our society, a power structure rooted in an economic philosophy that survives through exploitation and militarism.

Like programs to reduce or eliminate other forms of psychopathology, effective prevention programs ultimately require changes in social values and a redistribution of power. When Joffe and I (1981) edited a book on an earlier conference, *Prevention through Political Action and Social Change*, we suggested that a major source of psychopathology in this society is powerlessness and that the logical remedy is the redistribution of power. But the distribution of power between men and women in contemporary society is not a result of chance. Those with power benefit from the status quo and will go to great lengths to maintain things the way they are. Simply pointing out the fact that we are a patriarchal, militaristic, and sexist society is not enough. Perhaps consciousness raising is a first step in the journey, but it is not enough to make us feel we have solved the problem. Teenage girls, for example, may develop low self-esteem, together with ignorance and shame about their bodies. But anatomy lessons and exhortations to feel positively about themselves do not change the realities of restrictions on career choice, the prospects of low-paying menial jobs or unemployment and welfare, low social status, and powerlessness. Again we see, as Joffe (1982) showed us earlier, that the causes have causes that we should be focusing on. He says:

> When we do this, we find that our best predictors are global and complex variables like ethnic group and socioeconomic status....
> An interesting question arises, however. Since the broad demographic variables seem to encompass something closer to ultimate causes, and since we seem to be better able to design prevention programs when we deal with causes of causes, why do we choose the middle ground? Why do we ask: What is it about poverty that produces increases in birth defects, prematurity, perinatal death [and, in the current context, low self-esteem in women, the experience of abuse, and premature parenting] instead of designing programs to prevent poverty? Why do we ask, what is it about powerlessness that produces breakdown, misery, and violence [and low self-esteem in women] instead of trying to redistribute power? (p. 147-148)

We might also ask, if women are exploited as powerless sex objects and cheap labor, and if their lower self-esteem results from this exploitation, and if all this results from an economic system whose purpose is to maximize the profits of the powerful, where should prevention efforts be directed?

If sexual guilt, anxiety, and pathology all result from religious and economic forces that benefit from sexism and the repression of pleasure, then there is a compelling logic that supports attempts to change the system.

(The widespread repression of sexuality is reflected in the pornography industry, which profits from male sexual neuroses that require the depersonalization of women as objects of sex and aggression.)

It may not be too farfetched to see efforts at sex education as contributing to the undermining of the system. Clearly conservatives recognize the threat posed by the liberalization and enjoyment of sex. As Pogrebin, Calderone, and other authors in this volume point out, sex should be regarded as a source of pleasure, not just as a means of procreation. Obviously, this message is a threat to the establishment power structure and to the religious fundamentalists, who oppose women's rights, the ERA, freedom of choice, and sensuality.

Prescott (1979) argues from cross-cultural studies that societies that are strongest in their opposition to women's rights are also strongest in their opposition to abortion. They are also more likely to treat their enemies with cruelty, and they tend to practice slavery. These patriarchal cultures also tend to place a great deal of emphasis on the importance of female virginity, and they oppose expression of sexual and physical pleasure. Prescott says, "In this context it is perhaps not surprising to discover that cultures that enslave women to the bondage of compulsory pregnancy also practice other forms of human slavery" (p. 317). He observes that there is a relationship between punitive attitudes toward those who advocate or practice abortion and the support of capital punishment. He reports that every culture that punishes abortion is patrilineal while nearly three quarters of those cultures that do *not* punish abortion are matrilineal.

Prescott also considered the voting record of senators in the United States on such matters as abortion, providing family nurturance, and capital punishment. He divided senators into different groups based on their support or rejection of bills on these subjects, and he concluded that the votes showed that senators "clearly and unequivocally link opposition to abortion with the support of human violence legislation, opposition to civil liberties, and the absence of family nurturance" (p. 337). As a current joke has it, those who claim to believe that human life begins at conception distribute federal dollars as if it ends at birth. The fundamental question, as Prescott points out, is whether human sexuality is perceived as an equalitarian sharing of mutual pleasure, or as a necessary evil for the purpose of reproduction only.

Origins of Sexual Pathology

If we are to seek to prevent sexual problems in our own society, we must identify some of the powerful cultural forces in which these exploitative patterns of sexual behavior develop (Albee, 1977). Let me try to summarize the relationship of the dominant Protestant ethic to sexual attitudes and behavior for the light this may cast on the social forces that contribute to sexual exploitation of women and children and to sexual problems in general in our society.

Before the Industrial Revolution, and in many parts of the world today where people continue to live in agrarian village societies, sexual activity, marriage, and childbearing begin shortly after puberty. Margaret Mead (1964) taught us about relaxed adolescent and adult sex in the South Seas cultures. Whether we investigate the villages of Africa, India, or rural China, or the Indian cultures of Central America, we find sexual activity and childrearing the norm among teenagers. This pattern of early marriage began to change during the Industrial Revolution in certain parts of the world, particularly in Western Europe and the United States. The demands of industrial production, of work in the manufacturing centers, were very different from the demands of life in the agrarian village. As Max Weber (1904-1905/1958) pointed out in his classic essay, *The Protestant Ethic and the Spirit of Capitalism*, it became urgently important for work to become the most important source of satisfaction. Punctuality and hard labor offered the opportunity for upward mobility and escape from serfdom or poverty. The development of the ability to read and write and to do sums also could lead hard-working men into middle-class clerical occupations. In short, it became important to postpone childbearing and marriage, especially for males, in order to allow time for an education to be acquired, or for an individual to accumulate sufficient capital resources to go into business for himself (*sic*). This meant that in order to gain entrance into the middle class, sex, marriage, and childbearing had to be delayed. In the absence of any effective, widely available method of contraception, aside from infanticide, the best method to ensure delay was abstinence, and so the middle-class ideals of female chastity and male continence became part of a broader religious proscription against the pleasures of the flesh and self-indulgence of all kinds that informed the rigorous and repressive theology of the Protestant reformers. There is little question but that phenomenal industrial growth in the Protestant countries, both during and following the

Industrial Revolution, was made possible by a theology that stressed the importance of upward striving, sexual continence, and the repression of sexual pleasure. Hard work, frugality, and sexual control provided the motivational power. The theology of John Calvin clearly differentiated the "saved" from the "damned." Those who were saved were most likely to be those people who were "successful in their calling." And the damned were those who were failures, either economically or morally. Clearly, sexual pleasure was a subversive force that could distract men aspiring to the middle class from their central purpose in life—hard work and success. But the picture was not entirely as repressive as it sounds. While women of the middle class were expected to be chaste and not subject to sexual feelings, the women of the lower classes were fair game for men. As Steven Marcus (1964) has demonstrated, servant girls and sweatshop women employees, along with destitute women in general, were available for the predatory male. Despite the incredible sexual confusion engendered by repressive religion, some sexual relief was available to men with the power and inclination to exploit the defenseless women of the society. Many men, of course, were inhibited by their fear of discovery or of eternal damnation. One instructive consequence was the flowering of the florid sexual pathologies described by Havelock Ellis (1897-1928/1936) and others.

We are the inheritors of the sexual pathologies of the Calvinists, the Puritans, and their successors, the latter-day fundamentalists. In developing plans for primary prevention programs to prevent sexual anxiety, perverse outlets, rape, and child sexual abuse and in attempting to help people enjoy sexual relations, we will have to face the urgent need for a wholesale sexual reorientation of the society—a reorientation that will be threatening to the basic values of many religions and to industrial societies and their supporting patriarchal values.

Calvinism and Victorian Sexuality

Let me quote a few passages from my earlier essay to illustrate the social and cultural origins of disturbed sexuality leading to psychopathology and the consequent relevance of efforts at prevention through sex education and social change.

To facilitate this whole process [industrial capitalism] it is necessary to develop a *guilt* culture, in which impulse control no longer comes from outside, from the long-familiar members of the individual's own village society, but rather from a strict and tyrannical internalized conscience. In order to associate anxiety and guilt with adolescent sex, *all* sexual behavior and impulses, especially sexual interest and curiosity in children, must be severely forbidden. Eventually, as generation succeeds generation and as religious proscriptions support and rationalize social practices, sexual impulses acquire such a load of anxiety and guilt that they are widely repressed, avoided, denied, or otherwise twisted into unrecognizable forms....

An important point for psychopathologists, parenthetically, is the interaction between the imposition of the cultural controls essential for industrialization and the appearance of new and widespread forms of psychopathology. As behavioral scientists interested in the prevention or alleviation of disturbed behavior, we must understand the essential relationship between social sanctions of strong human drives and resulting patterns of emotional disturbance....

Calvinist asceticism, as Weber pointed out, was an inhumane religious doctrine producing intense loneliness and chronic anxiety. The central message of the Puritan culture was the elimination of sensuousness and emotionality of every kind. The Puritans taught that no one was to be trusted, that each person was alone, that each was to seek personal salvation, that each was to consider him- or herself as one of God's chosen and to have a high level of confidence in the possibility of personal salvation. Raw feelings and emotions were suspect, and so self-control was all important. Calvin's God demanded a lifetime of dedication and service. Weber noted that there was no place in this religion for the sequence of sin-and-repentance, of atonement and forgiveness, found in other religions. One's life had to be guided by constant vigilance, by planning and thought, by fierce self-control; if one's neighbor sinned, one did not tolerate and forgive—rather one saw in the neighbor's imperfection the signs of damnation and evidence of a fatal defect. Restraint, control, suppression of spontaneity, rejection of mysticism, and elimination of magic were the rules.

Sexual asceticism was an important, if not all-important part of the religion. As Weber (1904-1905/1958) said, "For sexual intercourse is permitted even within marriage, only as the means willed by God for the increase of His glory, according to the commandment, 'Be fruitful and multiply'" (p. 158). Along with a moderate vegetable diet and cold baths, the prescription given for all sexual temptations was the same one used against religious doubts and a sense of moral unworthiness: "Work hard in your calling" (p. 159).

Weber demonstrated how Protestant asceticism "turned with all its force against one thing: the spontaneous enjoyment of life and all it had to offer" (p. 166). Sunday amusements, sports, and impulsive living were all forbidden, but so was anything magical or festive including spontaneous religious art, the theatre, and fancy clothes. Eroticism and nudity simply were not tolerated, of course....

One of the most influential purveyors and reflectors of Victorian attitudes about sexuality was William Acton (cited in Marcus, 1964), a gifted, able, and productive physician and surgeon of the time. He wrote extensively on diseases of the urinary tract. But Acton was also a social moralist, and his description of diseases was interspersed with observations, social commentary, advice, and dire warnings on the subject of sexual behavior. Marcus describes some of the contents of Acton's book as "a world part fantasy, part nightmare, part hallucination, and part madhouse" (Marcus, 1964, p. 13).

Acton certainly was not mad. He was in many respects extremely capable. But being the son of an English clergyman and growing up in middle-class Victorian England, he reflected as well as influenced the attitudes of his class and his day. For Acton, in discussing children, stressed the importance of not permitting any "sexual impression" to reach the child. The child was to be raised in total ignorance of anything sexual. Acton assured parents that by keeping children from any exposure to sexual matters, the children would be free of all sexual notions and feelings. He assured his readers that proper English women were not troubled with sexual feelings: their only passions involved domestic things such as home and children. Because men, in Acton's view, were far more likely to succumb to passion, his book is a veritable compendium of warnings, advice, platitudes, and downright nonsense. He urged parents to spy on their children and to force boys to engage in strenuous physical exercise. In fearful warnings he painted the horrible consequences of masturbation, which in his view, were invariably physical deterioration and the most horrible forms of insanity. (He puzzled over the fact that the forms of insanity resulting from this practice—characterized by ideas of guilt and religious delusions—occurred primarily among fallen members of good families in which religious training had been strict and the moral upbringing had been the most rigorous.)

Nor would all of the many dire consequences of childhood and adolescent sexuality be solved with marriage. Acton issued dire warnings about the effects of sexual excesses even in monogamous marriage. The only safe course, he advised, was continence, brought about by the constant exercise of will power and control. (pp.152-156)

It will become clear to the reader of this volume that Victorian and Calvinist attitudes are still very much present in the American culture and that they create much irrational guilt and emotionally disturbed behavior.

Recently I wrote an article (Albee, 1981) for a special issue of *Professional Psychology* concerned with mental health and women. At the invitation of the editors, Nancy Russo and Suzanne Sobel, I focused my article on the prevention of sexism. In the course of extensive background reading and preparation for the article, I discovered the depths of the sexist attitudes of several of the world's major religions. I observed what most feminists already know, that Christianity, Judaism, Islam, and Buddhism all

were and are patriarchal in their orientation and all share powerful negative attitudes toward females. In many ways and in many diverse cultures, patriarchy supports embedded economic structures that profit from
the exploitation of women. I concluded that the prevention of sexism
would be difficult as long as these major religions and economic systems
flaunt and practice both subtle and overt forms of sexism. Inevitably, so-
ciobiologists, among others, raise the question about whether all of this
may not reflect the "natural order."

My friend and former student Marie Miranti Burnett directed my attention to another of the world's major belief systems—one that seems
to be a significant exception to the rule. She introduced me to Taoism,
an ancient and major Eastern belief system that expresses restraint and
balanced love, that is not sexist, that "seeks the harmony of the Yin and
Yang." Unlike many religions Taoism does not demand renunciation of
sexual joy and desire; indeed, the Taoist seeks actively to enjoy both
heavenly and earthly peace and joy—including the area of human sexuality.

Taoism is somewhere between a religion and a philosophy. Because it
stresses moderation and harmony, it de-emphasizes formal rules and doctrines, ceremonies and images. It stresses physical and spiritual harmony.
And the Taoist holds that women and men who are sexually fulfilled and
who have a harmonious sex life will act with kindness and sympathy toward
each other and toward others.

In dramatic contrast to most other major religions, the Taoist writings
provide detailed and unselfconscious instructions for achieving sexual
pleasure through the prolongation of intercourse and the mutual sharing
of sexual pleasure. Gulik (1961/1974), discussing sexual life in ancient China,
points out that (unlike Judaism and Christianity) attitudes toward Taoist
sexuality were not associated with feelings of guilt or sinfulness and, apparently, the lack of repression resulted in an absence of most sexual aberrations.
The "Tao of loving" differs from practically all historic Western views
on sexuality; throughout the centuries this Tao has been a frequent guide
to sexual relations among the Chinese. It stresses the importance of the
prolongation of intercourse through regulation and control of male ejaculation, the importance of sexual satisfaction in the female, and the belief
that health and longevity both result from successful adherence to Taoist
principles. (A good introduction to Taoist views about sexuality is contained in Chang (1977), *The Tao of Love and Sex: The Ancient Chinese Way
to Ecstasy.*) The point is that hatred and denigration of female sexual pleas-

ure is not a universal human phenomenon and so is not the "natural" human state. Neither is the patriarchal mode of sexual exploitation so common in many traditional agrarian societies a universal phenomenon. It is difficult to imagine a Taoist culture practicing female circumcision, for example. (But for a thousand years the Chinese upper classes bound and deformed the feet of girls to make them "more attractive"—a practice similar to more familiar Western devices such as the spike heel, silk stockings, long fingernails, and so on—which, as Veblen (1899/1973) explains, made women incapable of manual labor and therefore a luxury, a form of conspicuous waste for the male partner.)

The Field of Primary Prevention

The field of primary prevention is sometimes seen as distinct from the field of competence promotion and the search for wellness. The present volume clearly illustrates the interdependence of prevention efforts aimed at reducing sexual pathology and efforts to enhance mature, responsible, and pleasurable sexuality. The following formula (Albee, 1979) has been used to categorize prevention efforts:

$$\text{Incidence} = \frac{\text{stress} + \text{organic factors}}{\text{competence} + \text{self-esteem} + \text{support networks}}$$

Reducing guilt and anxiety over sexuality is a way of reducing stress and the incidence of sexual pathology; correcting or compensating for organic factors (myocardial infarction, mental retardation, physical handicap) also reduces incidence. On the positive side, improved sexual competence and self-esteem, and support groups also reduce incidence. All of these approaches are covered in this volume.

The main tools and models for primary prevention are provided by education, social engineering, and social change. Primary prevention efforts are based on the assumption that reducing stress and giving people better resources for coping are effective ways to prevent social difficulties; so are helping them find support groups and developing good self-esteem.

Clearly our efforts must focus on primary prevention if we are ever to reduce the incidence of sexual psychological damage. Efforts at primary prevention intended to reduce the incidence of sexual anxiety and undesirable behavior are not aimed directly at specific individuals but at all members of specified groups. Our purpose in primary prevention is to reduce the rate of the undesirable condition or behavior in the entire specified group.This often means sex education in the family, the schools, and the society. And it means protecting potential victims from sexual abuse by those already damaged.

The papers in this volume do not deal, except occasionally and indirectly, with individual treatment (which is usually called secondary prevention or tertiary prevention). There are several arguments to support our focus on primary prevention.

One of these arguments involves recognition of the unbridgeable gap between (1) the large number of persons with sexual problems—for example, the large number of men exhibiting pathological sexual behavior leading to the exploitation of and damage to victims—and (2) the small number of persons prepared to provide individual therapeutic intervention to reduce the psychopathology of the perpetrator and/or to provide therapeutic support and assistance for the victim. This imbalance is exacerbated because a very large proportion of rapes and child molestations go unreported; thus, neither the perpetrator nor the victim is available for intervention.

Sexual problems of individuals who are inhibited by guilt and anxiety— lack of pleasure, lack of drive, lack of performance capability—are also so numerous in the society as to defy efforts at one-to-one intervention. And here another serious problem complicates the treatment picture. Although this problem is rarely discussed, it is quite real. Physicians and mental health professionals, as a class, have a high level of ignorance and emotional discomfort about the subject of sexuality. For better or for worse, medical schools have long insisted that their entering neophytes must be obsessive overachievers in the hard sciences to the neglect of the humanities; as a consequence, first-year medical students have been shown (Lief, 1976) to be more poorly informed about sexual matters, more anxious about sex, and less experienced—that is, likely to be virgins—when compared with their intellectual peers of the same age. Yet it is physicians to whom society assigns the responsibility of treating people with sexual problems. The reluctance or inability of surgeons to see their patients as whole human beings with perfectly human fears and anxieties is more than matched by the reluctance or inability of many other physicians to apply a caring and humane approach to sexual victims. But physicians are not alone. Members of other helping professions have been selected largely for intellectual achievement rather than for emotional maturity. And the long, drawn-out pattern of professional education results in the selective survival of those most able to repress impulses and postpone pleasure—those most observant of the reality principle—those most imbued with the Protestant ethic!

Sexual Exploitation

The problem we face in attempting to prevent rape and the sexual abuse of children becomes an instructive paradigm that helps us clarify our thinking about the more general problem of the prevention of psychopathology. Rape is a specific form of exploitation of women and children by the more powerful male for his own gratification. It often occurs in the context of a family situation where there is no escape. A wife without the skills to be economically independent and unable to support herself and her children may acquiesce hopelessly to her fate and fail to protest the sexual abuse of her children. She may have no support system and no hope of rescue. This pathological form of culturally sanctioned exploitation and oppression is characteristic of a social system that supports patriarchy. The victims suffer a variety of damaging consequences to their personhood and their self-esteem. Too frequently the society, supporting patriarchal myths, blames the victims. Sometimes the victims, not the perpetrators, are stigmatized. Certainly they learn to regard themselves as persons of low worth.

But so it is with many other forms of emotional disorder. I suggest to you that most forms of emotional disturbance are interpersonal in origin, and that the process begins with the exploitation of persons when they are defenseless and powerless (often during infancy and childhood). As in the instance of rape, we often blame the victim—he or she was flawed by bad genes or bad chemistry.

Less overt, more symbolic, rapes occur with great frequency in our patriarchy. Our society provides a subtle but nurturant climate for the exploitation of the weak by the powerful. Unequal pay for equal work; sexual harassment in the workplace, the kitchen, and the bedroom; the endless media depiction of women as mindless sex objects adorning automobiles, or chortling with glee over whiter washes or shinier floors; the constant media modeling of males as warriors, as powerful manipulators of machines and people (often women); the portrayal of males on the TV screen as lawgivers, priests, overpaid sports gladiators, diplomats and judges, outlaws and sheriffs—all of these images put social pressure on marginal men, susceptible men, psychopathic men, to buttress their shaky self-esteem by brutalizing a woman or a child. Only a small proportion of men who are potential rapists actually carry out the overt act with a stranger. A larger number act out in their families and help produce the next generation of hysterics, obsessives, and schizophrenics. But an even larger number of men carry out "little rapes" in their daily lives—exploiting women as objects, as nonpersons—and the cumulative effects on the victims may be as destructive as overt assault.

References

Albee, G. W. The Protestant ethic, sex, and psychotherapy. *American Psychologist*, 1977, *32*, 150-161.

Albee, G. W. The prevention of prevention. *Physician East*, 1979, *4*, 28-30.

Albee, G. W. The prevention of sexism. *Professional Psychology*, 1981, *12*, 20-28.

Albee, G. W., and Joffe, J. M. (Eds.). *The primary prevention of psychopathology: The issues*. Hanover, N.H.: University Press of New England, 1977.

Bond, L. A., and Joffe, J. M. (Eds.). *Facilitating infant and early childhood development*. Hanover, N.H.: University Press of New England, 1982.

Bond, L. A., and Rosen, J. (Eds.). *Competence and coping during adulthood*. Hanover, N.H.: University Press of New England, 1980.

Chang, J. *The Tao of love and sex: The ancient Chinese way to ecstasy*. New York: E.P. Dutton, 1977.

Daly, M. *Gyn/ecology: The metaethics of radical feminism*. Boston: Beacon Press, 1978.

Ellis, H. *Studies in the psychology of sex* (4 vols). New York: Random House, 1936. (Originally published, 1897-1928.)

Forgays, D. (Ed.). *Environmental influences and strategies in primary prevention*. Hanover, N.H.: University Press of New England, 1978.

Gulik, R. H. van. *Sexual life in ancient China* (Rev. ed.). Atlantic Highlands, N.J.: Humanities Press, 1974.

Joffe, J. M. Approaches to prevention of adverse developmental consequences of genetic and prenatal factors. In L. A. Bond and J. M. Joffe (Eds.), *Facilitating infant and early childhood development*. Hanover, N.H.: University Press of New England, 1982.

Joffe, J. M., and Albee, G. W. (Eds.). *Prevention through political action and social change*. Hanover, N.H.: University Press of New England, 1981.

Kent, M. W., and Rolf, J. E. (Eds.). *Social competence in children*. Hanover, N.H.: University Press of New England, 1979.

Kolbenschlag, M. *Kiss Sleeping Beauty good-bye*. New York: Doubleday, 1979.

Leitenberg, H. Sexual victimization of children: Pedophilia and incest. In J. Geer, J. R. Heiman, and H. Leitenberg (Eds.), *Human sexual behavior*. Englewood Cliffs, N.J.: Prentice-Hall, in press.

Lief, H. I. Medical students' life experiences and personalities. In H. I. Lief and

A. Karlen (Eds.), *Sex education in medicine.* New York: SP Books, 1976.

Marcus, S. *The other Victorians.* New York: Basic Books, 1964.

Mead, M. *Anthropology, a human science: Selected papers, 1939-1960.* Princeton, N.J.: D. Van Nostrand, 1964.

Prescott, J. W. Appendixes 3 and 4. In S. Gordon, P. Scales, and K. Everly (Eds.), *The sexual adolescent: Communicating with teenagers about sex* (2nd ed.). North Scituate, Mass.: Duxbury Press, 1979.

Ross, C. Speech to Chittenden County Child Protection Network, Trinity College, Burlington, Vermont, 1982.

Veblen, T. *The theory of the leisure class.* Boston: Houghton Mifflin, 1973. (Originally published, 1899.)

Weber, M. *The Protestant ethic and the spirit of capitalism.* (T. Parsons, Trans.). New York: Charles Scribner's Sons, 1958. (Originally published, 1904-1905.)

PART I

Defining and Fostering Mature Sexuality— In a Nonsexist Society

Introductory Notes

The first section of the book includes nine papers that deal in a variety of ways with the problems of defining and fostering mature and meaningful sexuality in a Western industrial society in the 20th century. The problems, everyone agrees, are made especially difficult because of the endemic sexism that pervades this society. Each author focuses on different components of the overall interaction pattern, but each concludes that cultural, social, attitudinal, and behavioral changes must be accomplished.

In the first three papers, Heiman, LoPiccolo, and Pogrebin present complementary reviews dealing with the sexual problems and gratifications of women and men and with ways of reducing the problems and increasing the satisfactions. Each focuses on different aspects of the interventions, but it is interesting to observe the several similarities in their attention to historical, cultural, social, and religious causes. All three papers rely on scientific evidence and historical analysis.

Julia R. Heiman stresses the uniqueness of human female sexuality—how it differs from male sexuality and from the sexuality of females of other species. In the latter aspect, the human female does not have periods of heat but is eroticized throughout her monthly cycle and life-span. Heiman examines the implications of this fact: the evidence that the female is capable of frequent responsiveness, and the male jealousy and suspiciousness that is evoked by potential uncertainty regarding paternity. She considers the implications of confusing multiple roles, including double binds, for women, variously symbolized as Lilith, Eve, Mary, a witch, and Victoria. She sees the images of women, and the relations of women to men, as reflecting political forces that shape the meanings of sex and sexuality. Interestingly, the research data reflect both a high degree of sexual conflict and dissatisfaction, and a relation between sexual gratification and healthy reactions in pregnancy, especially when the quality of the sexual interaction is equalitarian. Nor are we surprised to learn that the research supports the relation between self-esteem and sexual competence. What is to be done to change the pattern for those suffering from the double bind (be good *and* be sexy) in Western culture? Heiman is not enthusiastic about specific classes in sexuality but suggests integrating sex education into "natural media," making it part of biology, art, religion, literature, and social studies. She also wants appropriate sex information to appear in the mass media—a suggestion that is repeated many times in this book.

Joseph LoPiccolo reports a high incidence of male sexual dysfunction—comparable to women's reports—and observes the dearth of research literature on prevention of male sexual problems. What data exist tend to be focused on treatment. (Again, the chapter deals with men in our Western industrial society.) And because behavioral treatment of male dysfunction tends to be effective (for the small number who seek help), little attention is paid to the need for research in prevention. LoPiccolo sees an almost unbroken 2,000-year-long repetition of the religious message that sex is for procreation, not for pleasure. As a consequence men, like women, suffer from the "princess and prostitute" role conflict. The culture also concentrates male attention on the "primacy of the penis" and defines the male's role in sex as the intromissor, whose inability to perform is seen as a shameful failure. Other forms of loving may be quite acceptable to the partner (who may enjoy "outercourse" as much as or more than intercourse), but these do not conform to the macho self-image. Men cannot ever be too tired, too worried, or too uncomfortable; performance is demanded and failure is a tragedy. Obviously a change in cultural values (and religious values) would be effective prevention. LoPiccolo also argues that good quality sexual information must be made part of the mainstream of American literature, films, and especially television, in order to reach young people. He notes wryly that the average American child, by age 18, will have witnessed 15,000 murders on television, but very few instances of tender, caring love making. He is critical, as are many other authors in this volume, of the errors of Freud and the analysts. Underlying his whole approach is a consistent theme: change the stereotypic macho sex role and the result will be meaningful prevention of male sexual dysfunction and increased shared sexual pleasure.

Letty Cottin Pogrebin stresses certain important messages that must be transmitted from parents to their children if the children are to grow up feeling sexually comfortable and sexually healthy. These include: permission to feel sexual pleasure; a positive attitude toward the body—their own and others'; the right to accurate sexual knowledge without sex role distortion; and protection from sexual abuse. Her paper elaborates these themes in some detail with wise and thoughtful guidance to parents. She stresses the importance of being certain that sexual information is not sexist. She gives numerous examples of ways that stereotypic sexist roles are implicit in many of the sexual messages transmitted to children and warns against subtle expressions of sexist attitudes. She recognizes that a very large proportion of teenagers in our society will have sexual experiences and that it is important to provide them with birth control information. She denies the frequent allegation that giving birth control information encourages sexual experimentation. She and Sol Gordon are in agreement on this question. Wanting children to postpone sexual experience until they are more able to handle it, while at the same time giving them birth control information, "is not a double message to our young people; it means simply that we respect them enough to give them our best advice, and love them enough to help them if they choose not to listen."

The Boston Women's Health Book Collective is a group of 11 women who have been meeting, talking together, exploring sexual issues, and writing books in English and Spanish that have changed the lives of millions. The paper "Reclaiming Our Bodies: A Feminist Experience in Sex Education" was presented by collective members Paula Brown Doress and Wendy Coppedge Sanford. It is a powerful statement of the politics of sexual relationships, a theme sounded repeatedly during the conference: the patriarchal culture creates, supports, and demands the attitudes that perpetuate itself. The Boston Women's Health Book Collective paper accuses the religious fundamentalists, exemplified by the Moral Majority, of impeding responsible sexuality in America. It suggests that a most urgent prevention task confronting us is to devise strategies to defeat the views of the Moral Majority, to prevent the further imposition of this ideology on our communities and our children. Again, it is important for us to look for a cause of the cause. Conservative evangelical religionists are the inheritors of the Puritan and Calvinist ideology that Max Weber identified as the "spirit of capitalism." If, indeed, it is true that the "ruling ideas of a society are the ideas that support the ruling class," then we begin to see why the fundamentalists have such cozy relations with political conservatives, and we get more clues to underlying causes of sex role conflicts and sexual problems.

By way of contrast, the conference heard the ideas of a theologian who occupies a space quite some distance from the fundamentalists. James B. Nelson presents the views of an enlightened religionist on the subject of sexuality. He identifies seven deadly sins characteristic of religion's approach to human sexuality and traces many of our contemporary sexual anxieties and pathologies to religious errors. One of the deadly sins he identifies is guilt over self-love. He argues that self-love or self-acceptance is essential for a mature sexual relationship or indeed any relationship. How can we love our neighbors *as* ourselves if we do not love ourselves?

Using evidence from the Bible, Nelson counters these sins with seven virtues of the Judeo-Christian tradition. Since most of us are aware, especially with the upsurge of fundamentalism, of the problems organized religion has caused and is causing, this more liberal interpretation gives us useful ammunition of the chapter-and-verse kind. His paper echoes the theme of primary prevention espoused by Albee in the Introduction: we must rid ourselves of the misconceptions of the Victorian era and the harsh dogma of the Calvinists and those of their ilk, and we must embrace the life-exalting, self-esteem-promoting aspects of religion.

Brian R. McNaught identifies self-hate as the greatest obstacle for gay people to overcome, and the opportunity for a mature love relationship as their major goal. This obstacle and this aspiration are reminders that oppressed people have the same needs as all human beings—but in addition must bear the burden of stigma and discrimination. We are reminded of Shylock's anguished query: "If you prick us, do we not bleed? if you tickle us, do we not laugh? if you poison us, do we not die? and if you wrong us, do we not revenge?" McNaught describes his own anguish at coming to terms with his homosexuality, and his early attempts to reconcile his personal sexual identity with his religion. Ashamed and frightened, unable to confide in anyone, unable to find anything meaningful to read on homosexuality, he attempted suicide. This experience was the beginning of his liberation and his dedication to a career devoted to public education for gays, for their parents, and for society.

We believe many of the strategies and the guidance McNaught gives to gays are useful to us all: being honest and open, seeking honest relationships, sharing equally, encouraging creativity, standing firm for the rights of others, daring to trust our feelings, and daring to be different.

Carol Cassell's paper undertakes to define responsible sexuality and examines how changing rates in divorce, teenage sexual experimentation, cohabitation, and age at first marriage are helping to modify the ways responsibility is perceived. Cassell aptly negotiates the slippery philosophical/social issue of what constitutes responsible sexuality from a societal/personal perspective. She concludes that there is more than one definition of responsible sexuality and that the definition is often a matter of cultural and personal choice. She does argue for more open discussion and debate and for a social climate in which learning about sexuality can occur easily and naturally. Cassell makes a strong case for working to guide sexual learning more effectively and positively by providing better opportunities for learning about sex roles and behaviors. The author may disappoint those who were hoping for a nugget of wisdom in the form of a definitive definition of responsible sexuality; instead she offers common sense and historical perspectives on a difficult question.

In his paper, John H. Gagnon examines sexual change over the last 40 years in the United States and finds that superficially there appear to have been great changes: pornography and erotica are easily obtainable; the media reflect a more permissive attitude toward sex and nudity. The social science media bombard us with surveys, results of polls, and "how to" articles—magazines abound in columns dealing with everything from amenorrhea to zoophilia. The abnormal has become normal through a process of familiarization. Yet parents still tell—or fail to tell—their children much the same sort of thing about sex that they told them 30 years ago.

On the other hand, there is more premarital sex, and it begins at an earlier age; more homosexuals live openly. Information and even contraception are easily obtainable but sex education is still not presented adequately in most schools; parents and children and married couples have problems communicating about sex; teenage pregnancies increase each year. For some understanding of these conflicting attitudes and behaviors, Gagnon suggests we look beyond the field of sexology because "the domain of sexual acts is not a singular and well-connected set of activities which mutually influence each other and which have a common set of causes."

Instead, one broader cause that Gagnon examines in some depth is television. Television has become for many people what the family and community once were: "the replacement for values and attitudes." What exactly does television do in this role? It continues to reinforce sexual stereotypes; it pushes consumerism and waste. It offers the goods and services of the upper middle class as background to nearly all the shows. These goods, in backgrounds, advertisements, and giveaways, are the potential rewards for conformity.

One might go one step further than Gagnon and point out that children learn from a very early age through cartoons that outwitting others (no matter how violent the means, for example, Tom and Jerry) is more important than cooperating. Contests, the craze for setting records by bizarre and incredible means, the soap operas, the detective and macho-man programs, all promote the age-old message of success through competition— proving that the roots of puritanism go deep. No female watching the nightly news should be in any doubt as to who rules the world—it is still men. It is not surprising after all to find that things have not changed that much in the field of sexology.

Paul H. Gebhard, director of the Kinsey Institute, from his perspective of years of research in the field of human sexuality, offers an overview of the problems confronting us if we seek to do serious work in preventing sexual pathology. Like Gagnon, Gebhard finds that changes in norms have brought about changes in what any given community feels needs to be prevented.

He takes a commonsense look at what is sexual pathology and what is not, and he comes to the conclusion that the criteria for intervention must be based on what is harmful to self and to others. He advocates providing useful knowledge, trying to increase competence, and increasing tolerance for imperfections in others as the best we can do. At the same time, he makes a plea for more objective empirical sex research on which to base judgments, predictions, therapies, and educative efforts. He concludes, as do most of the other authors, that widespread attitudinal and ideological changes represent a first step toward the goal of prevention of sexual pathology and the promotion of human competence.

Women and Sexuality: Loosening the Double Binds

Julia R. Heiman

To talk about female sexuality, by culture or by generation, is to discuss contradictory extremes. Woman as sexual or chaste, whore or goddess, carnal or divine, utterly insatiable or hopelessly inhibited—these images have been connected to female sexuality since human consciousness created symbols.

We all, women and men, live in the midst of these opposing images, whether or not our particular historical period is labeled as sexually conservative or sexually liberal. A liberal or conservative period lives with and remembers the ghost of its opposite. Individuals face the tasks of coming to terms with and reconciling these opposing images. This is not easy. Religious, scientific, and artistic discussions have made attempts to explain the complexities. Woven into each type of discussion have been myths, both in the colloquial sense of making assumptions about and in the academic sense of finding the structural meaning of, our past, present, and future.

In light of the topic of this volume, prevention and sexual responsibility, I would like to diverge from the perhaps expected categorization of rules to live by in order to be a sexually satisfied and happy female. Instead, I will pursue a global theme encompassing the contradictory images of female sexuality as both powerful and vulnerable. Women's power and vulnerability are part of our mythological, cultural, religious, and scientific knowledge, affecting one-to-one interactions within and between the sexes. I would like to point out several major sources of women's sexual power, to use this theme to account for sexual malaise by way of a double-bind model, and, finally, to outline the tasks of prevention.

The Uniqueness of Female Sexuality

Female sexual functioning can be viewed from the perspective of its uniqueness or from that of its similarity with respect to male sexuality. Historically, at any given time, one perspective has been favored over the other. For the first half of the 20th century, the sexuality of men and women was seen as separate, and what was true for male sexuality was not and could not be true for females. Kinsey and Freud, among others, provided support for this emphasis. Since the 1960s, and marked by the appearance of Masters and Johnson's (1966) book on human sexual response, there has been a tendency, if not a mandate, to stress the similarity between the sexes and to dismiss the differences in anatomical, response, and psychological factors in sexuality. Either extreme position omits information and complexities that are crucial for conceptualizing the human experience of being sexual. However, since the similarities have been so emphasized in the literature, I would like to balance that with a discussion centered on the uniqueness of female sexuality and the power and vulnerability therein.

The Uniqueness of the Female Body and Its Meaning

Sexuality for women is distinctive in two essential and related ways, namely, reproductive functioning and sexual responsivity.

Menstruation

Approximately 50 percent of a woman's life is spent in the cyclical throes of menstruation. There are several clear effects that menstruation has upon women. One is that menstruation signals fertility potential and does so in a very special way. A woman's fertile period, ovulation, is not connected to any easily observable signs, such as the swelling and coloration of the genitals occurring in species with estrus cycle. Sherfey (1973) has called this "silent ovulation."

This fact has several consequences. One is the "eroticization of time" (Thompson, 1981). In other words, if sexual receptivity is not ruled by fertility, women's (and men's) lifetimes are eroticized. Sexual contact is possible at any time, including the time following the cessation of menses. Two, knowledge of who is the father of a given child is primarily in the woman's keeping, an issue that has varying degrees of social relevance but which is quite critical to central arguments in sociobiology (see Symons, 1979), including justifications of female parental investment in offspring, male jealousy, and the degree of effort needed to produce successfully surviving offspring.

Another general feature of menstruation is that it is a periodic reminder to women about their bodies, their reproductive capability, and, to a lesser extent, their sexuality. Although the most observable sign of menstruation is blood flow, there are also a variety of congestive symptoms (breast swelling, edema, fullness in the abdomen) and spasmodic symptoms (muscle tension, more intense uterine contractions). These body changes and their psychological correlations (that is, whether they are perceived as positive or negative) differ among women and among the cycles of an individual woman. The signs and symptoms of menstruation essentially become rehearsals for pregnancy. A woman's body swells, her hormones shift, and at some point her body lets go with often noticeable and painful contractions.

Women then are connected to cyclical time. Prescientific generations were more aware of the meanings of these cycles. Australian and Hottentot tribes have long believed in a moon spirit-woman connection and according to Briffault (1977), this idea is pervasive in primitive thought. He quotes a Maori, "According to the knowledge of our ancestors and elders, the marriage of a man and a wife is of no moment; the moon is the real husband" (p. 252). Pregnant Siberian women keep lunar calendars to calculate childbirth, a pregnancy taking 10 lunar months. Even more striking is the emphasis Thompson (1981) gives to Upper Paleolithic artwork, in which there is evidence of lunar counting and crescent moons associated with the Great Mother/Goddess figures, such as the Venus of Laussel.

To most of us dealing with practical therapeutic and research issues, connections between a natural (moon) time and women's (body) time may seem inconsequential or even irrelevant. I suggest that it is merely a sign that we have lost our connection to the mystery, awe, and power of female sexuality. Women particularly have lost the connection with their mythological female images. Menstruation is hardly seen as a celebrated event. More likely it is an unpleasant and sometimes painful nuisance and tends to be viewed as such by scientists, clinicians, and educators, as well as by the general public.

The ways in which physiological and emotional changes during the menstrual cycle have affected sexuality have been examined in a variety of studies. Premenstrual distress, labeled the *premenstrual syndrome* (see Dalton, 1964), includes psychological symptoms that have been estimated to affect between 25 percent and 100 percent of all women (Moos and Leiderman, 1978). The premenstrual syndrome has not clearly been shown to be connected to physical symptoms and is characterized by a wide variety of symptoms including headaches, irritability, depression, and nausea. Thus, a principal area of research has been mood states and their relation to sexual arousal.

The results of studies of mood state variability during the menstrual cycle have suggested that women who experience premenstrual tension scored higher on tests measuring anxiety, depression, and aggression during *all* phases of their cycles (Moos, Kopell, Melges, Yalem, Lunde, Clayton, and Hamburg, 1969). Moos (1969) also found that mood was more variable premenstrually and menstrually than at other times and that the cycle-to-cycle variation was less consistent for mood states like depression and irritability than for sexual arousal. It seems possible that the premenstrual phase may place women in a sensitive psychological or physiological condition that can augment the effects of external events.

An interesting attempt to clarify the interaction between body (menstrual) time and social (calendar week) time was done by Rossi and Rossi (1977). They asked 67 women and 15 men to fill out daily rating forms on mood and sexual activity. Overall, moods were more related to the calendar week for men. For women, psychological and body positive moods were associated with weekends; for men only body positive mood, primarily sexual arousal, was associated with weekends. Additionally, the social week did not affect negative moods. However, social time did interact with the menstrual cycle; positive moods were enhanced if ovulation or menstruation occurred on the weekend. An analysis of the individual mood patterns in women suggested that women whose positive moods were responsive to the menstrual cycle were physically active, socially assertive, orgasmic women who saw the maternal role as important but were neither strongly attracted to men nor socially ambitious. In general, these women seemed more comfortable with themselves as women and with their own bodily processes (Rossi and Rossi, 1977).

One might suspect that fluctuations in mood would bear on fluctuations in sexual desire and behavior. This is true if we keep in mind that mood fluctuations are somewhat inconsistent. Depending on the investigator and the method, peaks of sexual arousal and activity have been reported at *each phase* of the menstrual cycle.

The most frequently mentioned surges of erotic interest have been reported to be around ovulation (see Udry and Morris, 1968), premenstrually, and immediately after menstruation (Cornor, 1952; Davis, 1929; Kinsey, Pomeroy, Martin, and Gebhard, 1953; Masters and Johnson, 1966;

Terman, 1938). Approximately 90 percent of Kinsey's (Kinsey et al., 1953) sample of 5,940 women had greater sexual interest and preferred sexual activity premenstrually and in the early menstrual phase. A higher orgasm rate was also characteristic of this phase. Similarly, using laboratory studies of physiological response, Masters and Johnson (1966) demonstrated that women showed greater genital vasocongestion and more copious lubrication of the vagina during the pre- and early menstrual phases. Greater sexual awareness and responsivity have been associated with increased vascularity of the genital area (Masters and Johnson, 1966; Sherfey, 1973). Fifty-two percent of the Masters and Johnson sample preferred intercourse on the last 2 menstrual days.

Sherfey (1973) attaches a great deal of importance to female physiology during the luteal or premenstrual phase of the cycle. Using Kinsey's and Masters and Johnson's results as supporting evidence, Sherfey claims that because of the increased genital congestion, women are in a mild, though often unrecognized, state of sexual excitement throughout the luteal phase. Frequent coitus or masturbation, if these include orgasm, can temporarily relieve premenstrual tension symptoms. Orgasms are easier, and multiple orgasms more likely at this time. While the theory is interesting, it is unclear how much and what type of psychological factors can mitigate the physiological condition. While acknowledging this complexity, Sherfey claims that the body knows best.

Several qualifications need to be attached to the above studies on sexual changes throughout the menstrual cycle. First of all, *libido* is defined differently, depending on the particular investigator. Sexual desire differs from frequency of sexual intercourse or consistency of orgasm. The intensity of sexual desire may have little to do with the actual frequency of behavior. This is especially true for women, since they have not traditionally taken on the role of initiating sexual interactions. Desire, behavior, and satisfaction are rarely differentiated within a single study.

A related problem is that most of the research is based on self-reports, which are often unreliable and, more important, influenced by social expectations. Few studies actually evaluate hormone levels, leaving the actual cycle phase in some doubt. The menstrual cycle duration is sensitive to external factors, including stress and tension. Many cycles are also anovulatory, which cancels premenstrual tension symptoms (Melody, 1961). Measures of additional physiological variables would help elucidate the psychological and physiological effects of the menstrual cycle. Phasic changes have been found to occur in blood pressure, pulse rate, and acoustical and optical reaction time (Engel and Hildebrandt, 1974). These changes may correspond to informal reports of differences in smell, sight, and hearing in the premenstrual and early menstrual phases. All of these changes may have an influence on women's sensitivity to and interest in sexual activity.

Studies on how menstrual cycle changes affect sexual interest must address the cultural context. Menstruation has traditionally, in this society and many others, been surrounded with taboos. Its association with uncleanliness has historical and cultural roots. It is also connected with sexuality, another traditionally taboo topic. This negative context has two effects.

First, individual attitudes toward menstruation may influence sexual patterns in that many women and men will exclude the menstruation days as possible days to have sexual contact. Thus, the days before and the days after menses show more sexual behavior, though there is no physiological reason to avoid sex during menstruation. Furthermore, orgasm during menstruation decreases cramps for some women (Clifford, 1978a). However, social norms, combined with the physical discomfort a number of women feel at the onset of their periods, are enough to reduce sexual contact during menstruation (Kinsey et al., 1953).

The second effect of negative sociocultural attitudes toward menstruation is that researchers seem to spend more time and questionnaire space on the negative consequences than on the positive consequences of menstruation. Many researchers only look for pathology and neglect to evaluate possible positive concomitants of the menstrual phases. Moos's (1968) menstrual distress questionnaire, a widely used symptom questionnaire, is slightly more inclusive of positive factors and includes scales for evaluating water retention, pain, negative affect, behavior changes, concentration, autonomic revelations, control, and arousal. A study by Brooks, Ruble, and Clark (1977) found that out of a sample of 191 college women, 77 percent rated menstruation as a positive experience, 59 percent claimed it was bothersome, and 32 percent claimed it was psychologically and physically debilitating (women could respond to more than one factor, thus the total percentage exceeds 100 percent). The inclusion of a positive dimension to evaluate cycle changes would similarly benefit our understanding of sexual changes, since it would be more likely that women would be asked about their degree of enjoyment of general and genital physical touching, in addition to questions on desire and frequency.

A predominance of statements on the negative impact of menstruation comes from the psychoanalytic literature as well as from the more behavioral studies just mentioned. Deutsch (1944) has related menstruation to reproduction and its implication that women take on the demanding and stressful roles of being both nurturant and an object of dependency. Reproductive potential also evokes fears of body damage and death. Additionally, blood is usually associated with being hurt and wounded. Abraham (1966) linked menstruation with fears of castration. Menstruation can also seem dirty, especially during the first menstruation, owing to the proximity of the other elimination sites (Benedek and Rubenstein, 1939; Deutsch, 1944).

Some positive comments about menstruation have been made by the analytically oriented writers. It may be welcomed as a "satisfying step" along the road to adulthood (Deutsch, 1944), as a symbol of youth and fecundity or as a sign of being a normal female (Drellich and Bieber, 1958). Hysterectomized and postmenopausal women have been reported to miss the experience of menstruation; according to the authors, the behavioral and social patterns of these women, which are "organized within the periodicity of the menstrual month," are unconsciously disrupted (Drellich and Bieber, 1958, p. 324).

The conflicting attitudes, positive and negative, toward menstruation are probably just one example of conflicts over broader issues with respect to the body, women, and sexuality. De Beauvoir (1953) claimed that the female body has always been seen in some way as mysterious, powerful, fertile and capable of instilling awe, fear, disgust, or sometimes rage in men. Thus women must be confined and ritually segregated, as has been reported in less westernized societies (Mead, 1949). There is no doubt about the association between women and the image of the "dirty goddess," to use Dinnerstein's (1976) phrase.

And yet, images create reactions that result in new searches to confirm the old images. For example, we must ask ourselves if the observation of a ritual, such as isolation during menstruation, is all we *see* it to be, namely, degrading and dehumanizing. This may not always be the case.

Writing of the rituals of the Yurok Indians in northwestern California, Buckley (1979) noted that when a girl menstruates for the first time, she withdraws for a 10-day period of seclusion and ritual activity, a more expanded version of a routine she will follow until menopause:

One side of her menstruation is seen as polluting and dangerous, even poisonous. The other, balancing side is seen to be that of great, female energy, menstruation marking the time at which a woman is at the peak of her powers, closest to realizing her full potential. (p. 34)

The young woman uses her solitude for reflection and self-definition. She is at some point given an abalone shell. In its pattern, she is to see her own unique, individual life's direction. Scratching sticks are used if she wants to touch her body, as she is not permitted to touch herself while menstruating.

The standard anthropological explanation of this practice, widespread in Native North America, is that one is so highly charged with pollution that, touching one's self, one poisons oneself. The analysis of Yurok women makes a more satisfying logic: one makes scratching and touching difficult, keeping it conscious and intentional, they say, so that a woman is encouraged to perceive all of her body exactly as it is, every itch included. Coming to know the body more intimately during this time of heightened access to the truth, the facts, one comes to know one's self more intimately. (p. 34)

When menstruation stops

There are two hormonal conditions during which menstruation ceases: pregnancy and menopause. During pregnancy, the few reports that exist show that there is as much variation in sexual patterns as during non-pregnancy. Furthermore, the studies done on problems during pregnancy show little correlation between sexual satisfaction and pregnancy disorders. Grimm (1967), for example, found no relationship between consistent sexual dissatisfaction and problems such as prolonged labor, toxemia, infertility, or habitual abortions. Fisher (1973) found several interesting correlations including:

The greater a woman's orgasm consistency, the greater was her total pregnancy discomfort (pain, illness, and discomfort), the fewer were her body image distortions, and the less time she spent in the hospital following delivery.

The more satisfied a woman felt 5 minutes after orgasm, the less disturbance she experienced during pregnancy or after delivery.

The less ecstatic a woman feels during orgasm, the greater her disturbance during delivery.

The less tired a woman feels during orgasm, the less her disturbance during pregnancy.

Women who felt happier after orgasm were less disturbed 1 week after delivery.

Women feeling less relaxed after orgasm were more likely to experience disturbance during pregnancy.

Women feeling less guilty after orgasm felt less disturbed during pregnancy, and their hospital stay was shorter after delivery.

The more a woman continued to be interested in sexual activity during pregnancy, the less her disturbance 1 week after delivery.

The more a woman saw sex as one of life's most important experiences, the less she experienced delivery disturbance and postdelivery disturbance.

Pregnancy disturbance was correlated with menstrual pain and irregularity.

Although Fisher (1973) does not make any extensive comments on these results, they do suggest that sexual satisfaction, the emotional enjoyment of orgasm and sex, corresponds to fewer problems surrounding the pregnancy experience. It should be noted that this was not true if only the frequency of orgasm was examined. There is also some suggestion that menstrual distress and pregnancy distress, but not delivery problems, are associated.

Masters and Johnson's (1966) research on sexual responsiveness during pregnancy has shown several interesting results. They have reported two sources of data, one set from 6 women whose physiological sexual response cycle was observed at various points during the pregnancy, and one from 111 women (101 who carried a full-term pregnancy) who were interviewed at selected intervals during the pregnancy. During the first trimester, increased vaginal lubrication begins, and it continues throughout pregnancy. Lubricants are produced more copiously during sexual stimulation. Many women experience severe breast tenderness. Sexual activity during this period is often lower due to the woman's discomfort from nausea, fatigue, or other early symptoms of pregnancy. Women with first pregnancies are more likely to notice a decrease in sexual interest. Intercourse and masturbation, while permissible for some women, may be harmful for those women who have a history of miscarriage.

During the second trimester, most women feel generally healthier and, coincident with their pelvic area being more vasocongested, begin to show increasing interest in sex. Of the 101 women Masters and Johnson interviewed, 82 showed markedly improved sexual interest. Masters and Johnson (1966) also observed several changes surrounding orgasm: the rhythmic contractions of orgasm were subjectively felt but not observable (in non-pregnant women the contractions are observable); during orgasm the uterus may tonically contract for about 1 minute, instead of rhythmically contracting for a shorter duration; the orgasmic platform, the additional vasocongestion of the distal third of the vaginal barrel, is more pronounced and grips the penis tighter during intercourse; and fetal heart rate sometimes slows during the woman's orgasm. Resolution, the time it takes the genital area after orgasm to return to the prearousal condition, takes longer and is less complete, and some women have abdominal and lower back cramping after orgasm. Furthermore, orgasm does not seem to reduce sexual tension for very long. Many of these latter changes in the sexual response cycle may be related to the increased vasocongestion of the genitals. This also fits in with Sherfey's (1973) idea of the increased "insatiation" of sexual interest associated with edema and pelvic vasocongestion.

During the third trimester, many women again feel fatigued and uncomfortable with the increasing bulkiness of the pregnancy and are thus less interested in sex. The majority of women interviewed (74 out of 101) reported less interest in sex (Masters and Johnson, 1966). Orgasm is not likely to result in premature birth, though intercourse may be harmful if the baby's head engages into the cervix and the cervix distends into the axis of the vagina.*

Women who have no reason to be suspicious of a problematic pregnancy are usually advised to continue whatever sexual activity is comfortable for them during the pregnancy, with some physicians advising restrictions in the last 6 weeks. Some clinicians claim that premature delivery can be induced by the female's orgasm or by the prostaglandin in the man's ejaculate. However, this association has not been clearly established in research (Jensen, Benson, and Bobak, 1977).

In spite of the long assumed safety of intercourse during pregnancy, a recent report (Naeye, 1979) has cast doubt on this assumption. This study reported on 26,886 pregnancies between 1959 and 1966. The results suggest that intercourse early in pregnancy may be more likely to result in infections (possibly carried by male semen) in the amniotic fluid; moreover, women who had intercourse one or more times a week during the

---

* It should be noted, however, that recent research findings reflect considerable differences of opinion in this area.

last month of pregnancy showed higher infection rates (156 per 1,000 pregnancies) than women who abstained (117 per 1,000). Infections were more serious in infants born prematurely, and infants whose mothers had had intercourse the month before delivery were more likely to die as a result of these infections. More careful analyses of these data are necessary before any authoritative conclusions are drawn. To be abstinent throughout pregnancy is probably too conservative, too maritally stressful, and unlikely to be adhered to even if recommended.

Pregnancy indeed influences the physiology and emotional reactions of the woman as well as the dyadic interaction with a woman's partner. Pregnancy seems to affect women and men differently. For some couples, it solidifies their sexual relationship and roles; for others it is disruptive. Pregnancy challenges a woman's view of her body, her role, and the meaning sexuality has for her and for her male partner. For those women who are conflicted about their sexuality—in other words, those who are struggling to reconcile the contradictory images surrounding being a sexual person—the experience of pregnancy may heighten these conflicts. Perhaps some postnatal problems could be avoided if more attention were devoted to dealing with pregnancy as a psychologically and physiologically sensitive period.

Menopause also begins a series of changes in the physical sexual response patterns of women. Menopause is marked by a large decrease in ovarian hormone production. Since almost all of women's estrogen is produced by the ovaries, estrogen levels decrease. The result is that the rapidity and intensity of physiological responses during sexual stimulation are reduced (Masters and Johnson, 1966). Among the 61 women between 41 and 78 who Masters and Johnson studied, the following changes were noted as they passed through menopause and advanced along the aging process: some decrease in the degree of breast vasocongestion during sexual stimulation; more delayed loss of nipple erection after orgasm (a sign of continued arousal); less separation and elevation of the major labia; less minor labial vasocongestion; decreased width and length of the vagina; and thinning of the vaginal mucosa. Gradually, as aging occurs, it takes many women more time to show vaginal lubrication and sexual arousal. Fewer contractions occur during orgasm. However, the entire sexual response cycle remains intact—it just slows and alters over the years. Masters and Johnson also observed and emphasized that the sexual health of the genitals (lubrication, ease of response, lack of pain) is helped by having regular opportunity for coital contact. Unfortunately, many women do not have continuously available partners. The social problems associated with older women finding mates are probably as difficult as the tremendous hormonal changes and aging process itself.

Menopause often results in various intensities of physical symptoms such as excessive fatigue, nervousness, irritability, headaches, flushing, or pelvic pain. These symptoms can last from several weeks to several years and can be alleviated by low doses of artificial hormones, though these preparations are currently under review. What must be kept in mind is that menopause has many of the complementary positive and negative psychological features that menarche does. Because menopause signals the end of the woman's fertility, it may be particularly difficult for a woman who has attached a great deal of her self-esteem to her image as a mother or sexually productive person. It also may be difficult for those women who were unable or elected not to have children. For some women, menopause may also signal the beginning of old age and the end of sexual attractiveness.

Alternatively, this period can be the start of a new phase. Free from concerns about pregnancy, and freer from the demands of children, the woman who passes 50 may be able at last to feel more sexually relaxed.

Menopause and sexuality in the advanced years is a fairly recent evolutionary phenomenon, particularly in humans. Most other species die before their reproductive abilities end. Yet, the slow social adjustment to the postreproductive period in women is difficult to see as purely a problem of recency. In our culture, women are viewed as most useful for their seductive or reproductive (including childrearing) capabilities. When those years have passed, women's roles and their value in our society have no clear definition. The social message is indeed a sexless one.

In summary, females are sexually responsive after menopause, and there is evidence to suggest that maintaining some kind of consistent sexual activity is more psychologically and physically healthy than abandoning sex. Furthermore, sex interest postmenopausally is best predicted by sex interest premenopausally (Kinsey et al., 1953). Sexual desire rarely stops or even experiences a sudden drop for either sex (George and Weiler, 1981). It remains to be seen if some of the negative attitudes toward age and sexuality can be constructively altered (see Hotvedt, in press, for an interesting review of this topic).

Genitals and sexual functioning

Much has been said in the last 2 decades about the homologous (similar and parallel) structuring of the male and female genitals (see Money and Ehrhardt, 1972) and functioning in sexual response (Masters and Johnson, 1966). Homologous does not mean identical, however. For example, there are differences in vasocongestive structures. Vasocongestion is one of the two major physiological responses during sexual arousal (the other being myotonia, or muscle tension) and is the first observable sexual response (Masters and Johnson, 1966). Vasocongestive erectile tissue exists on various parts of the body, though most of it is concentrated in the breasts and genitals. In the genital area, men have three erectile bodies: two corpora cavernosa, and one bulb with its corpus spongiosum shaft. Women have five erectile bodies: two corpora cavernosa and their crura (rootlike structures), muscular attachments to the clitoral shaft, two vestibular bulbs that attach to the clitoral shaft, and the plexus (network of veins) surrounding the vagina. The blood capacity of the female clitoris and crura is negligible when compared to the male penis. However, with the addition of the female erectile bodies, women have a greater generalized vasocongestion capacity of the entire pelvic area (Sherfey, 1973). This is particularly true if they have borne children.

What implications does this anatomical differentiation demonstrate? First, it suggests that the anatomical uniqueness of a woman is based on the fact that she has not only a clitoris, but a *clitoral system,* plus a large venous and muscular system surrounding the vagina. Despite the conclusions reached by much of the psychoanalytic literature (Deutsch, 1944; Freud, 1905/1963) male and female sexual differences cannot be reduced to penis versus the lack of a penis (or rudimentary castrated representation of penis), or even vagina versus the lack of a vagina. The penile system and clitoral vaginal systems are different, and different in ways that may be important to sexual response.

Second, the anatomical genital capacity of the female suggests that men and women may differ in their expressions of sexual response. Indeed they do. While both sexes show vasocongestion as the earliest observable sign of reaction, for women this is manifested in the appearance of transudate vaginal lubrication. The first sign of male vasocongestion is penile erection. The parallel clitoral erection and retraction occurs much later in the arousal cycle, usually within 1 to 2 minutes of orgasm (Masters and Johnson, 1966). Thus, the earliest sign of vasocongestion in women is a more generalized vaginal reaction; in men it is a more specific penile reaction.

Orgasm is also different for the two sexes. Masters and Johnson (1966) noted that men usually show 3 to 4 very strong contractions at 0.8-second intervals followed by numerous irregular contractions. Women show a range of anywhere from 3 to 5 to 10 to 15, with the first 5 or 6 being the strongest. Additionally, a number of women (estimates range from 25 percent to 100 percent, depending on the definition of "multiple") are capable of multiple orgasms, that is, several orgasms in succession without loss of high arousal and vasocongestion between orgasms. All of Masters and Johnson's (1966) sample was multiply orgasmic, an unusually high figure compared to other researchers (for example, Kinsey et al., 1953). Nevertheless, Sherfey (1973) has argued that the capacity for multiple orgasm is a universal phenomenon in women. She notes that women's greater genital vasocongestive capacity and edema, combined with the luteal phase increase in congested tissues, are important clues to the necessity for multiple orgasms in order to allow complete sexual release. Consequently, the more orgasms a woman has, the stronger they become and the more a woman is able to have since the supply of blood and edema fluid to the pelvis is unlimited. Sherfey (1973) has said:

Continuous labial congestion and edema constitute a paramount factor in maintaining the sensation of intense perineal and pelvic congestion and of sexual tension. Consequently, the more inexperienced woman with undistended labia majora can feel more satisfied with one orgasm or two; for the woman who has borne many children, no matter how many "fully satisfying" orgasms she may have, she will not feel completely satiated until she is physically exhausted. (p.108)

The picture painted by Sherfey then is of women being physiologically sexually insatiable.

Sherfey's theory, which is indeed a theory only partially substantiated with biological data, is interesting. It allows us to address the idea of physiological satiation versus psychological satisfaction. Some women will be satisfied with one orgasm. Perhaps this is a result of the limits of their physiological vasocongestive capacity. But satisfaction may be determined by the emotional or psychological meaning that orgasm has for a woman. It is this psychological appraisal that provides feedback to the nervous system which, in turn, affects the venous distension of the genitals. Since clinicians suspect that one's expectations affect whether or not orgasm occurs at all, it is likely that expectations also affect how satisfactory one orgasm is to any one woman. This psychological difference in orgasm satisfaction may parallel or even override the physiological capacity.

Sherfey's theory and Masters and Johnson's research sensitize us to other aspects of female sexual response. First, sexual response, particularly orgasm capacity, is physically enhanced by the experience of pregnancy (the psychological effects on sexual response are less consistent). There are other reports that some women experience their first orgasm after they have had one child (Luria and Rose, 1979). Thus, it may be that the sexual needs of childbearing women are different from those of women who have never had children. Along this dimension, older, or more orgasmically experienced women may be different in their sexual satisfaction needs from the younger or less orgasmically experienced. Second, women report certain symptoms that may relate to insufficient orgasmic release. These symptoms include chronic pelvic pain, nausea or cramping after orgasm, and, in some cases, lack of satisfaction from orgasm. Finally, cultural theorists and feminists might well wonder whether the expected pattern of the singular female orgasm is related to the expectation of one male orgasm. In this culture, we have become fairly accustomed to using the male as the standard of sexuality, psychoanalytic theory being one example of that tendency. This may influence the psychological satisfaction females feel after one orgasm.

It is hoped that the preceding data and theory will not make uniorgasmic women feel sexually dysfunctional or cheated. Women's bodies and minds show tremendous variety, and changes occur throughout their lifetimes. To interpret these data to mean that every woman should be multiorgasmic would be a disservice. Psychological and physical satisfaction are not necessarily in tune with one another. Researchers have found that women who experience multiple orgasms do not find them more satisfactory than single ones (Clifford, 1978b; Hite, 1976). More important, just as the genitals are only one site of sexual response, so is orgasm only part of the definition of sexual satisfaction.

Meanings Associated with Images of the Feminine Body

If we examine the Stone Age fertility goddess figures of Willendorf, we will see faceless forms with wide hips, heavy flesh, swollen bellies, and thick bosoms. There have been moments in cultural evolution when the representation of the female body has been connected to, and made representative of, the reproductive, life-giving components of sexuality. Sumerian culture, for instance, includes early (3,000-1,000 B.C.) examples of women who were connected not to earth mother symbols of fertility but to erotic symbols. With that view came a focus on the youthful, thin, sleek, feminine image (Leroi-Gourhan, 1967; Margueron, 1965).

During the 20th century, women in Western cultures have generally lived with a physical ideal image of female sexuality that equates sexual attractiveness with slender, youthful, sometimes pubescent, features. Whether or not women intellectually "buy" this image, emotionally it does register. The cultural message of sexual beauty is difficult to resist. One outcome of this restricted sexual attraction criterion is that it furthers competition among women, adding to the distance between, rather than cooperation among, individuals who belong to a less powerful class (if we consider males to be the first and more powerful class, as does de Beauvoir, 1953). More directly relevant is the tendency for women to be in competition with themselves, fighting wrinkles, weight, age, and making their bodies their adversaries. Conflict results from battling one's body and, at the same time, expecting it to give sexual pleasure.

Such conflict can become expressed in a variety of sexual problems. It may create a discrepancy between what a woman thinks she wants sexually and what she can actually express, such as arousal and orgasm (Barbach, 1975; Heiman, LoPiccolo, and LoPiccolo, 1976). Or, a woman may take out her own perfectionistic demands on her partner by being critical of his body and by being suspicious and resentful of his sexual interests. In the latter situation, the woman may become disinterested in sex, since sex becomes defined as his lusty and indiscriminate arousal toward a physical self that she hates. For some women, a countercultural body appearance is safer than having to deal with sexuality and sexual attractiveness. To be svelte and sexually attractive in a conventional sense means being vulnerable to sexual advances.

Another aspect of body image is a woman's feelings with regard to her genitals. A woman's genitals are less visually available than a man's, thus denying a woman a visual sense of her body's genital responsiveness, and perhaps encouraging sexual feelings to be experienced more kinesthetically and diffusely. This may be important in early self-exploration, which boys do far more often than do girls. Girls are most likely to become aware of their genitals by way of menstruation, which at best is a reproductive introduction to sexuality and, at worst, is associated with an untouchable, dirty, and sometimes pain-producing area. Furthermore, the clitoris is not as frequently mentioned as the vagina. It is not surprising that females often have to learn to feel positive about their genital areas or that they connect sexuality with genitals at a later time than do males (Gagnon and Simon, 1973). It is also not surprising that men tend to be more oriented toward visual triggers of early arousal and that much of pornography feels to women like an invasion of their privacy—showing to others what women themselves cannot see.

Psychoanalytically oriented therapists have concentrated on other aspects of the development of body concept. Freud (1959) and others (Fenichel, 1945) believed that the primary core of self formed from sensations a person has about his or her own body. Psychosexual development, in fact, was seen as a progression of stages during which psychogenic energy becomes invested in different parts of the body (oral, anal, and genital). Each stage colors a person's interpretations and perceptions of experience. From this basic conceptualization, a variety of studies have suggested the importance of body attitudes in affecting behavior (Fisher, 1970; Fisher and Cleveland, 1968). Theorists have suggested that disturbance in body image may negatively affect women as a result of fears of penetration (Barnett, 1966; Horney, 1967); a sense of being defiled due to the proximity of the vagina to the rectum (Bonaparte, 1953; Freud, 1905/1963); or a sense of body distortion during sexual response that results in fear if the woman is insecure about her body (Fried, 1960). Women's feelings about sex being connected with pregnancy are also hypothesized as influencing her sexual response: if pregnancy is feared a woman may turn off sexually (Benedek, 1968).

Underlying the belief that women tend to be insecure about their bodies is the assumption, now doubted in many analytic circles, that the woman considers her genitals to be a castrated version of the male's. She has a rudimentary phallus and a vagina and therefore is chronically doubtful and fearful about her body. Using males as the standard from which to judge male-female differences is typical of the earlier psychoanalytic writings (Freud, 1905/1963) but less accepted now in the light of new evidence of anatomy and physiology (Sherfey, 1973), as well as reworkings of psychoanalytic theory (Tooley, 1977).

Empirical findings suggest that women may actually feel more secure and more identified with their bodies than do men (Fisher, 1970). Fisher (1973) has suggested that women are taught to be socially aware of the impression their bodies are making on others, and from an early age they are encouraged to experiment with body "decorations." Women are also regularly made aware of their bodies through menstruation. Actually, body awareness seems to be a positive characteristic in women, correlated with aggressiveness and activity, and a negative characteristic in men, correlated with being maladjusted or ineffectual (Korchin and Heath, 1961; Mordkoff, 1966). In Fisher's (1973) words:

Her harmonious relationship with her body may reflect that a woman can, more easily than a man, see a direct connection between her body and her important life goals. A man's body tends to be alienated from his prime social roles that typically embrace his achievement and success. (p. 79)

Let us return to the Stone Age image of the fertility goddess that was raised earlier. The femaleness that this figure represents has more to do with what the body does in its connection to life. By contrast, the current image of women, as idealized in the more commercial arts, suggests that the body is for the use of others: to sell high fashion, to entice men's sexual interest, to provide pleasure for another. The consequences of certain images on sexuality are important in this context. One consequence already mentioned is that females feel they have to conform to a standard image in order to feel sexual. Another consequence is that a restricted and nearly unattainable image makes sex more scarce. Slater (1970) claims:

The root of sexual dissatisfaction is the capacity of man to generate symbols which can attract and trap portions of his libido.

The fundamental mechanism for generating sexual scarcity is to attach sexual interest to inaccessible, nonexistent, or irrelevant objects; and for this purpose man's capacity to symbolize is perfectly designed. (p. 85)

One could argue that our current attraction to the eroticized view of the female body is indeed a trap that keeps women uneasy and insecure about being sexual (since the image is difficult to achieve), makes women more "irrelevant" by focusing on stereotypical physical characteristics, and feeds into the isolation of sex from its general emotional power. The common practice of valuing sexuality for pleasure rather than procreation fits into this image of women, as does the fact that men often have difficulty combining love and sex in one relationship (LoPiccolo and Heiman, 1978).

Attempting to achieve an earth mother ideal will not solve our sociosexual malaise, and wanting to be slim and young is not merely capitulating to the social system. The point is that the image of women—and women's implicit relationships to men—is tied into social and political forces that, in turn, shape the meaning of sexuality. Freud long ago saw the struggle between social order and the chaotic power of sexuality (Freud 1905/1963).

Given these conflicts and restraints, reconciling a woman's body-image with her body, a woman's image of sexuality with her own sexuality, in such a way as to foster her individual, personally healthy development becomes an important task. The first step in achieving this reconciliation is taken up in the following section.

The Double Binds in Female Sexuality

The State of Sexual Dysfunction

Despite the clear power of women's bodies to respond sexually, they often do not, or if they do, they do not enjoy it. For example, a recent study (Frank, Anderson, and Rubinstein, 1978) of 100 predominantly white, happily married couples revealed that 63 percent of the women and 40 percent of the men reported having a sexual dysfunction (arousal or orgasm problems). Additionally, 77 percent of the women (and 50 percent of the men) reported a sexual difficulty, with significantly more wives complaining of inability to relax, disinterest in sex, too little foreplay, and feeling "turned off." These figures were in sharp contrast to the reported satisfaction with the sexual relationship (86 percent) and marital happiness (83 percent). While this study does not necessarily represent a norm and other research has found higher sexual satisfaction in couples, one could conservatively estimate one-third to one-half of all married couples are experiencing sexual problems.

Looking beyond the mere percentages of the Frank et al. (1978) study, an interesting pattern emerges between partners. For wives, the more dysfunctions and particularly the more difficulties, the less satisfied they were with their sexual relationships. This was not true for the husbands, whose ratings of sexual dissatisfaction were instead significantly correlated with their spouses' dysfunctions and difficulties. For women, sexual dissatisfaction was particularly affected by their difficulties with becoming aroused, disinterest, feeling of being turned off, and, to a lesser extent, having difficulty reaching orgasm, the inability to relax, the lack of sufficient foreplay, and having the partner choose an inconvenient time. The presence of dysfunction in the wife did not affect frequency of intercourse.

One picture that emerges from these data is that of married women as more aware of (or more easily admitting to) sexual problems and dysfunctions than their husbands, more focused on problems in becoming aroused, and having husbands who underestimate the extent of their difficulties. At the same time,

Among all possible kinds of sexual problems, it is clearly the wives' sexual "difficulties" that were the least well tolerated. Indeed, they seem to have a ripple effect on all sexual relations. (Frank et al., 1978, p. 115)

So, despite husbands' underestimation of their wives' difficulties, the message did get across. One wonders whether women are generally more dissatisfied in sexual relationships. One also wonders how there can be so many sexual complaints from people who still rate their sexual and marital relationships as happy and satisfying. Either there is a high tolerance for sexual problems or a low expectation for sexual bliss, or there are other factors that are more important than those studied in determining the quality and meaning of sexual satisfaction.

What factors are associated with sexual satisfaction? One might suspect that orgasmic response is a factor. Indeed, the Frank et al. (1978) study showed that sexual dissatisfaction was related to orgasmic frequency, though orgasm was less strongly related than was ease of becoming aroused. Whether or not orgasm is considered important to general sexual satisfaction seems to be related to other variables. One questionnaire study of 370 women, of whom 44 percent were single, found three basic "styles" of sexual expression (Hoon and Hoon, 1978). One style was characterized by women who had frequent intercourse and orgasms, lived with someone, but did not necessarily report satisfaction with their current sexual responsivity. A second style was noted in older women who were dissatisfied with their sexual responsivity and currently without partners, who liked erotic literature and films, and liked direct genital stimulation and frequent masturbation. The third style was characterized by women who were aware of physiological changes during sexual arousal and enjoyed gently seductive erotic activities, breast and genital stimulation, and were more satisfied with their sexual responsivity. In short, women who were more satisfied with their sexual responsivity experienced frequent intercourse and orgasm and enjoyed gently seductive erotic activities and breast stimulation, but were unresponsive to erotic literature and media.

A consistent pattern that emerges is that sexual satisfaction may be more related to the overall quality of the interaction, which may include tenderness, sensuality, and consideration, and it is this interactional framework that makes arousal and orgasm more likely. Other relationship factors may also be important. Fisher (1973) found that high-orgasmic and low-orgasmic women differed in that low-orgasmic women have anxiety about losing what they love. These women feel that love objects are not dependable and may leave. Although Fisher sees this as a personality trait, often established by a history of a distant, absent, or disinterested father, it is also a very realistic fear for women in certain types of relationships. In some cases, the male may maintain psychological or physical distance to the extent that some women will fear his eventual withdrawal from the relationship.

Clearly, sexual satisfaction is also determined by factors outside of the sexual interaction itself. How one sees oneself—self-esteem—is important (Barbach, 1975; Heiman et al., 1976; Kaplan, 1974). Thus, if there is conflict about being a good person and being sexual, sexual responsiveness and satisfaction may suffer. Women who dislike their bodies, for whatever reason, often find themselves at odds with their sexuality. Similarly, women who dislike themselves often report less sexual satisfaction (Frank, Anderson, and Rubinstein, 1979). One study that looked at couples in sex therapy and marital therapy, and those in no therapy at all found that in all groups individuals dissatisfied with their roles in their marriages were more likely to experience sexual dissatisfaction (Frank et al., 1979). This "role strain," the tension between the perception of one's current role in the marriage and one's ideal role, was far more apparent in the women in marital therapy and sex therapy.

Thus, sexual satisfaction is not a universal concept that can be applied to all women in the same way. Satisfaction can exist despite sexual dysfunctions and difficulties, which probably occur frequently in the general population. Sexual responsiveness seems to be related to satisfaction, in some cases directly and in other cases because of indirect qualities of the relationship. Both individual and relationship characteristics can be important to sexual responsiveness, and there is some evidence that self-esteem, or *self*-satisfaction, positively influences and is influenced by *sexual* satisfaction.

From this unsettled concept of satisfaction, let us go one step further and summarize several reported differences between functional and dysfunctional samples. First, compared to functionals, sexually dysfunctional women and men have been shown to have less sexual information, higher scores on tests measuring depression, anxiety, and interpersonal sensitivity, generally more negative and fewer positive affects, less self-confidence, less self-assurance, more depression, and more irritability (Clement and Pfafflin, 1980; Derogatis and Meyer, 1979). Additionally, dysfunctional women are more likely than functional women to describe themselves as shy, timid, distrustful, and likely to conceal their feelings; dysfunctional women have lower scores on femininity and masculinity scales and more sex fantasy themes than functional women (Clement and Pfafflin, 1980; Derogatis and Meyer, 1979). Finally, after sex therapy, women gain self-confidence, are more relaxed, become more permissive and realistic about sex, feel less depressed and irritable, and have fewer stereotypical attitudes about sex roles. There are similar changes for males and also similar changes in the partners of dysfunctional individuals (Clement and Pfafflin, 1980).

If we distill this information further and complement it with other research in the area, there seem to be two broad characteristics differentiating women who experience sexual dysfunction and women who do not. Sexually dysfunctional women have a more limited and less positive concept of their own self-worth. This may be evident in a definition of self-worth that has extremely high standards, extremely rigid categories, or great sensitivity to external evaluations, especially those of a sexual partner. Dysfunctional women have either markedly undefined, rigid, or stressed sex-role identities. This is in sharp contrast to functional women who seem to incorporate both masculine and feminine role characteristics.

The Double-Bind Analysis

The classical double-bind hypothesis, developed by Bateson, Jackson, Haley, and Weakland (1956), may seem an unusual strategy for conceptualizing female sexual dysfunction. It was, after all, aimed at understanding schizophrenia and the communication patterns within a family structure. But I would like to entertain the model as a heuristic device to evoke the conflicting messages, indeed the nearly schismogenic processes, associated with female sexuality.

The ingredients for a double-bind process include: the involvement of two or more persons; repeated exposure to the messages; a primary negative injunction (do/do not do something, or you will be punished); a secondary negative injunction conflicting with the first; a tertiary negative injunction prohibiting the victim from escaping from the situation (Bateson et al., 1956).

First, let us look at double-bind messages to women, mindful of the fact that these messages to women are clearly perceived by men. In the broadest form:

Primary injunction: *Do not be sexual because:* you will not be a nice woman; men will not respect/like/love you.

Secondary injunction: *Do be sexual because:* you will not be a real and complete woman; men want sex.

Tertiary injunction: Your value is determined by how you handle your sexuality; you must try to please others or they will not care about you; men will not care about you unless you are sexual; it is terribly important to be loved and liked.

A very natural type of response to these double messages would be not to ask, obtain, or admit to sexual satisfaction. Lack of arousal, disinterest, lack of desire, and difficulty in reaching orgasm hardly seem like abnormal resolutions to the no-win situation.

Perhaps the most difficult issue from a prevention perspective is that these messages have been woven throughout Western culture since its beginnings. If we take Levi-Strauss (1958) to heart, looking for the structural consistency across myths, we see clear archetypes separating women into sexual and nonsexual categories. The earth mother was a symbol of fertility and fecundity; her power was located in her sexual nature and connected to earthly events and religious rites. When times changed and male power replaced female power, as in the Sumerian epic of Gilgamesh, we see women reduced from fertility symbols to erotic objects. For example, in the story of Gilgamesh (dated from about 1,600 B.C.), Inana, the goddess of love and war, is slighted by the male heroes. In addition, her complement, a harlot, traps Enkidu, the human who is more comfortable with and akin to the beasts in the wilderness. The harlot traps Enkidu in his humanness by making love with him for 6 days and 7 nights, after which the animals no longer roam and feed with him. Sex then brings about his fall from a natural state to a civilized one (see Thompson, 1981, for further development of this theme).

Perhaps the most familiar creation theme, again focused on woman as sexual temptress, is that of Adam and Eve. But even in the Garden of Eden, there are many versions. The midrashim, folk tales surrounding the more formal biblical stories, tell us of Lilith, Adam's first mate. Lilith was not created from Adam's rib but from the filth and sediment of the earth. She was his equal and quite furious, so one midrash goes, at being forced to submit to Adam's dominance. Cursing Adam with God's name, Lilith forever vanished, but her archetypal image is the one that still taunts men with nocturnal emissions. With Lilith remains the image that female sexuality cannot be clearly and rationally controlled by men; women will ultimately exert their power.

Eve, created from the same flesh as Adam, disobeys God by sampling the apple; she is the vehicle for the fall from the garden into the world of human birth and death. She also offers her "ripeness" to Adam. Eve symbolizes many things but, as an archetype, she is the purely sexual, the source of human confrontation with mortality, the decline of spirituality, the irresistibly delectable, the demise of all men.

Within the chain of archetypes it is the Virgin Mary who restores the balance. Mary symbolizes chastity, reserve, obedience, service to God, and the source of man's hope for everlasting life. Indeed the cross on which Christ died is hewn from the world trees, the same material from which Eve plucked the fruit (Travers, 1981). Her sexuality is as purely spiritual as Eve's is purely carnal.

Historically, this balance of contrasting female images has been repeatedly evident. For example, toward the end of the 11th century courtly love was born. The female objects of courtly love were usually adored, served, and praised in poetry. However, sex—at least intercourse—was not part of the ideal of courtly love, which was of a purer, almost Platonic nature. Meanwhile marital relationships encompassed duty, which included sex but not love. Even so, sex was highly restricted in marriage, and sexual intercourse outside of the purpose of conception was considered by confessors to be a venial sin (Hunt, 1959).

An even more dramatic contrast occurs in the 15th and 16th centuries. It is at this time that images of the Renaissance lady and the witch were juxtaposed. On the one hand, women were regarded as creatures of beauty and goodness, awe inspiring to a nearly religious extent, who required men to seduce and conquer them. In the witches' manual of Sprenger and Kramer, however, women were evil, carnal, obsessed with lust, dangerous to man, and accused of having had intercourse with the devil (Hunt, 1959).

Similarly, in the Victorian period, the purity and chastity of the married woman were preserved by and balanced by the simultaneous explosion of prostitution (Foucault, 1979).

All of these images suggest that female sexuality has indeed been seen as powerful, a life-giving force and an irrational attractant to which men give over their power. If we look just at the archetypical relationships of men adoring women on a pedestal, or men despising women in the gutter, they are hardly egalitarian. The only equivalence is in the superimposition of the images, a blending of the angelic and animalistic. This is the clue that leads us to the next challenge: how are we to start working on the resolution of problems in female sexuality?

Problems of Resolution, Pathways of Change

To review the major themes addressed thus far: (a) while men and women have many similarities, it must be acknowledged that women's bodies are unique both in terms of sexual response and reproductive functioning; (b) many women, perhaps more than men, experience sexual problems that women may either accept and be sexually satisfied, or that they may see as a core difficulty in their relationships; (c) sexual problems have been shown to be associated with anxiety, depression, social sensitivity, and the lack of self-esteem. However, theory and clinical experience suggest that a precondition for good sexual functioning in women is a positive self-image; for men, the arrow is reversed—a positive self-image seems to require good sexual functioning. Sexual functioning is more peripheral to a woman's self-concept and identity while it is more central for a man (Tooley, 1977); (d) mythological, religious, and historical images of female sexuality are manifested in contrasting extremes that carry moral (good or bad) overtones. Today, these images force a choice between being sexual or nonsexual, or between feeling good or bad about feeling sexual; and (e) essentially the expectation for women to be sexual or not is a double bind, with no best solution, and the threatened cost is the loss of love, respect, and emotional satisfaction of a relationship.

The structure within which we try to interpret these cycles is important. Education seems to be the major vehicle for enlightenment. The primary focus of education still seems to be parents who deal with their children in the early years and meet their children's daily social crises more directly. Sex education in schools is a big question mark, since we really do not know the goals and effects of the programs. School sex education that is conducted at the expense of parental antagonism and makes little effort to address parental concerns and fears seems doomed to truncation and eventual failure.

An alternative, consonant with the themes of this paper, is to abandon sex education as a separate, isolated topic, and instead let sex be integrated into its natural environment. To encompass the multiple meanings of sexuality in an educational framework, sex would be best taught as a *part* of biology, art, religion, mythology, literature, and a social studies course on marriage and the family. College courses, public service courses, degree or professional requirement credits could and do usefully include a class on sexuality. However, these reach only a handful of people.

As for those of us who are involved in sex research, education, or therapy, my assessment is that, quite frankly, we tend to talk more to each other than to the potential targets for prevention. Rarely do we reach out to popular magazines, radio, or television. And not without justification, as our personal and professional status can be threatened by going public. Yet how many typical readers of *McCalls,* or *Playboy* would leap at the chance to read a *Journal of Consulting and Clinical Psychology* article on sexual satisfaction or plod through a *Psychophysiology* article on human sexual arousal? The messages go nowhere without a proper medium. We at least have to meet our audience halfway, and not all of our audience is made up of our colleagues.

In closing, I would like to discuss six pathways for change, foci of content to consider in planning for prevention and sexual responsibility.

Strategies for loosening the double binds

Some men and women do not experience sexuality as a double-bind situation. Others do, but like children in a family with double-bind communication, they can ignore it, which is a good strategy. Alternatively, one can hear both conflicting messages, accept both as partly true, and go beyond them to create a personalized sexual standard. In reconciling the opposites, one can view them as necessary parts to the whole, a yin/yang image, one giving meaning and balance to the other. Thus, we can make use of Eve's carnal, disobedient sexual essence to complement Mary's spiritual, reverent sexuality. Mary conveys more than chastity; she also conveys the part of sexuality that goes beyond the body and time. We, women and men, need Mary to balance Eve, who wisely reminds us of our earthliness.

Exploring consequences of different values of sexuality

If we take our role of promoting sexual responsibility seriously—that role being one of consolidating rather than splitting and rejecting opposing images—then we must acknowledge the variety of values that sexuality can have. Too often, at least in the writing of sex therapists and educators, there is an attempt to substitute an Eve value—pleasure—as the antidote to obliterate a Mary value—sex as an obligation. Is it any wonder that our clients seem resistant? I would propose that we look again at the deeper meanings of what seem to be restrictive values before we force-feed our clients an equally restrictive alternative. One deeper value of sex as obligation could be a need for sacred meaning, devotion, and the unselfish side of love. The task is to respect these values while trying to find ways to integrate them into a balanced whole. We must do the same for other values that sex has for people: intimacy, tension release, integrity, self-worth, bonding, security, comfort, and reproduction are all worthy components of a sexual exchange. The solution to fragmentation is integration.

Sexual responsibility is partly a personal issue

This is an important point for women, whose sexuality does tend to be reactive rather than autonomous. Women will invite more often than initiate, try to stir their desire rather than say no, and see their body and genitals as possessions of their partners rather than parts of themselves. These beliefs are strongly reinforced by society. It is important for a woman to feel that she owns her body and her own sexual feelings if she is to give them freely. It is also important for her to respect herself and feel she deserves to be treated as someone who is valued, if she expects her partner's respect and consideration. Thus part of the work and effort is indeed up to the women.

Sexual responsibility is partly an interactional issue

Interactional here refers to the societal effects, particularly as conveyed through one's sexual partner. The degree to which the woman's partner believes in the split between femininity and sexuality will affect her ability to feel comfortable about being sexual. This split may be manifested in a man's fear of a woman's sexuality or in his own inability to consolidate love and sex in one relationship. The task again becomes one of integration of opposing images.

Sexuality is connected to both life and death

Single-celled organisms retain a meiotic immortality. Where there is sexual reproduction, there is biological death, and women have taken the blame for this dilemma. Note that the contrasting images of female sexuality revolve around both the life meanings (earth mother, Virgin Mary, Inana as the goddess of love) and death meanings (Eve, witches, Inana as the goddess of war). Men are excluded from this duality, victimized into the periphery where they seem assigned to seeking immortality by their heroic but mortal deeds. In truth it is our humanity, not our maleness or femaleness, that is distinguished by our sexuality and our ability to perceive our own deaths through language (Dinnerstein, 1976; Thompson, 1981). There are no individuals to blame for this condition, though women are tempting targets since they bear children, and, especially, since they have a disproportionate amount of the daily contact with children. Other writers have eloquently described the social and sexual consequences of bringing the fathers into the nurseries (e.g., Dinnerstein, 1976; Tooley, 1977).

The psychological impact of death and sexuality has been extensively discussed, usually as an adversary dualism. Freud's position, that sexuality, not death, is the major determinant of psychic development, is well known. Conversely, Becker (1973) viewed most of life's energies as being focused on the avoidance of death terror, which reminds us that we are only expendable and interchangeable links in the chain of being. It is Lifton (1979) who pursues a dialectical rather than a dualistic view: "sexual transcendence and death awareness are part of the dialectic bequeathed in human evolution, a dialectic that, perpetually unresolved, lies at the heart of human energies" (p. 123). Again, a shift is necessary away from the view of women as the evil guardians of the life/death force, the light and dark sides of sexuality. The term *femme fatale* is no accidental label.

A revision of images of both female and male sexuality is in order
Our present era has been hailed as a period that demands (Janeway, 1980) or at least challenges new models of sexuality (Campbell, 1980). There are, as Campbell has pointed out, no models for the individual woman's quest, nor for a man's response to that woman. The biological, mythological, and historical archetypes no longer fit.

In sexuality the role of the male as well as the female deserves to be reevaluated. Power and vulnerability, for example, are part of the meaning of sexuality for both sexes, though not necessarily expressed in the same way. For example, one current view of men presents them as random, nonselective fertilizers:

If anthropomorphic and anthropocentric propensities are held in check...one should not flinch from the assumption that the primordial role of the male was highly specialized as no more than a temporary and ephemeral appendage to life. (Zilboorg, 1973, p. 110)

Zilboorg proceeds to explore how the realization of the male's position with respect to his ancillary role in childbearing combined with his greater (than female) size helped create hostility toward females and social conditions that protected his power over females. Sherfey's (1973) work is in agreement with this position.

If we accept this line of thinking for the moment, then we must realize that the sexual power relationships between men and women are in a dangerous equilibrium. The power of one sex feeds off the vulnerability of the other. This suggests that to make both sexes more humanly equal, we must acknowledge vulnerability as well as power in symmetrical aspects of the sexual expression of each gender. Dinnerstein (1976) has offered an intriguing example of this direction:

We already recognize, though so far in principle only, the symmetry between man's peculiar procreative magic and woman's. Her breast, her hidden womb and the dark grotto that leads to it, are dramatic, in a sense sacred: powerful, yet vulnerable, violable. Her superfluous clitoris, vividly alive on its own, is uncannily moving. But so are his superfluous nipples strangely moving. His proud, vulnerable, untamable external genital is no more and no less dramatic than the belly it fertilizes and the breasts that need it to make them flow. And it is no more or less a sacred carnal truth, for his burst of fertile fluid is as powerful, and at the same time as vulnerable and violable, as the part of her it bursts into: the fragility of his tie to the seed that he buries in her for so many months in the dark center of another, independent, body balances the fragility of her claim on him to help take responsibility for the child she carries. (pp. 150-151)

This is not to say that the emotional tie between women and men is based on procreative sex. It is to say that the emotional balance between the sexes, expressed in sexuality, is bound up with our perceptions of the most basic meanings of sexuality.

References

Abraham, K. On character and libido development. New York: Basic Books, 1966.
Barbach, L. G. For yourself: The fulfillment of female sexuality. New York: Doubleday, 1975.
Barnett, M. C. Vaginal awareness in the infancy and childhood of girls. Journal of

the American Psychoanalytic Association, 1966, *14*, 129-141.

Bateson, G., Jackson, D. D., Haley, J., and Weakland, J. H. Toward a theory of schizophrenia. *Behavioral Science*, 1956, *1*, 251-264.

Becker, E. *The denial of death*. New York: Free Press, 1973.

Benedek, T. Discussion of Sherfey's paper on female sexuality. *Journal of the American Psychoanalytic Association*, 1968, *16*, 424-448.

Benedek, T., and Rubenstein, B. The correlations between ovarian activity and psychodynamic processes: I. The ovulation phase. *Psychosomatic Medicine*, 1939, *1*, 245-270.

Bonaparte, M. *Female sexuality*. New York: International Universities Press, 1953.

Briffault, R. *The mothers*. New York: Atheneum, 1977.

Brooks, J., Ruble, D., and Clark, A. College women's attitudes and expectations concerning menstrual-related changes. *Psychosomatic Medicine*, 1977, *39*, 288-297.

Buckley, T. Doing your thinking. *Parabola*, 1979, *4*, 29-37.

Campbell, J. Joseph Campbell on the Great Goddess. *Parabola*, 1980, *5*, 74-85.

Clement, U., and Pfafflin, F. Changes in personality scores among couples subsequent to sex therapy. *Archives of Sexual Behavior*, 1980, *9*, 235-244.

Clifford, R. Development of masturbation in college women. *Archives of Sexual Behavior*, 1978, *7*, 559-573. (a)

Clifford, R. Subjective sexual experience in college women. *Archives of Sexual Behavior*, 1978, *7*, 183-197. (b)

Cornor, G. W. The events of the primate ovarian cycle. *British Medical Journal*, 1952, *2*, 403-409.

Dalton, K. *The premenstrual syndrome*. Springfield, Ill.: Charles C. Thomas, 1964.

Davis, K. B. *Factors in the sex life of twenty-two hundred women*. New York: Harper, 1929.

de Beauvoir, S. *The second sex*. New York: Alfred A. Knopf, 1953.

Derogatis, L. R., and Meyer, J. K. A psychological profile of the sexual dysfunctions. *Archives of Sexual Behavior*, 1979, *8*, 201-224.

Deutsch, H. *Psychology of women* (Vol. 1). New York: Grune and Stratton, 1944.

Dinnerstein, D. *The mermaid and the minotaur: Sexual arrangements and human malaise*. New York: Harper and Row, 1976.

Drellich, M. G., and Bieber, I. The psychologic importance of the uterus and its functions. *Journal of Nervous and Mental Disease*, 1958, *126*, 322-336.

Engel, R., and Hildebrandt, G. Rhythmic variations in reaction time, heart rate, and blood pressure at different durations of the menstrual cycle. In M. Farin, F. Halberg, R. Richart, and R. L. Van de Wiele (Eds.), *Biorhythms and human reproduction*. New York: John Wiley and Sons, 1974.

Fenichel, O. *The psychoanalytic theory of neurosis*. New York: W. W. Norton, 1945.

Fisher, S. *Body experience in fantasy and behavior*. New York: Appleton-Century-Crofts, 1970.

Fisher, S. *The female orgasm*. New York: Basic Books, 1973.

Fisher, S., and Cleveland, S. E. *Body image and personality*. New York: Dover Press, 1968.

Foucault, M. [*The history of sexuality*] (Vol. 1) (R. Hurley, Trans.). New York:

Random House, 1979.

Frank, E., Anderson, C., and Rubinstein, D. Frequency of sexual dysfunction in "normal" couples. *New England Journal of Medicine,* 1978, *229,* 111-115.

Frank, E., Anderson, C., and Rubinstein, D. Marital role strain and sexual satisfaction. *Journal of Consulting and Clinical Psychology,* 1979, *47,* 1096-1103.

Freud, S. *Collected papers* (Vol. 5). J. Strachey (Ed. and trans.). New York: Basic Books, 1959.

Freud, S. *Three essays on the theory of sexuality.* New York: Basic Books, 1963. (Originally published, 1905.)

Fried, E. *The ego in love and sexuality.* New York: Grune and Stratton, 1960.

Gagnon, J., and Simon, W. *Sexual conduct: The social sources of human sexuality.* Chicago: Aldine, 1973.

George, L. K., and Weiler, S. Sexuality in middle and late life. *Archives of General Psychiatry,* 1981, *38,* 919-923.

Grimm, E. R. Psychological and social factors in pregnancy, delivery, and outcome. In S. A. Richardson and A. F. Guttmacher (Eds.), *Childbearing: Its social and psychological aspects.* Baltimore: Williams and Wilkins, 1967.

Heiman, J., LoPiccolo, L., and LoPiccolo, J. *Becoming orgasmic: A sexual growth program for women.* Englewood Cliffs, N.J.: Prentice-Hall, 1976.

Hite, S. *The Hite report.* New York: Macmillan, 1976.

Hoon, E. F., and Hoon, P. Styles of sexual expression in women: Clinical implications of multivariate analyses. *Archives of Sexual Behavior,* 1978, *7,* 105-116.

Horney, K. *Feminine psychology.* New York: W. W. Norton, 1967.

Hotvedt, M. The cross-cultural and historic context. In R. Weg (Ed.), *Sexuality in the later years.* New York: Academic Press, in press.

Hunt, M. *The natural history of love.* New York: Minerva Press, 1959.

Janeway, E. Who is Sylvia? On the loss of sexual paradigms. *Signs,* 1980, *5,* 573-589.

Jensen, M. D., Benson, R. C., and Bobak, I. M. *Maternity care: The nurse and the family.* St. Louis: C. V. Mosby, 1977.

Kaplan, H. *The new sex therapy.* New York: Brunner/Mazel, 1974.

Kinsey, A. C., Pomeroy, W. B., Martin, C. E., and Gebhard, P. H. *Sexual behavior in the human female.* Philadelphia: W. B. Saunders, 1953.

Korchin, S. J., and Heath, H. A. Somatic experience in the anxiety state: Some sex and personality correlates of "autonomic feedback." *Journal of Consulting Psychology,* 1961, *25,* 398-404.

Leroi-Gourhan, A. *Treasures of prehistoric art.* New York: H. N. Abrams, 1967.

Levi-Strauss, C. *Structural anthropology.* New York: Basic Books, 1958.

Lifton, R. J. *The broken connection.* New York: Simon and Schuster, 1979.

LoPiccolo, J., and Heiman, J. The role of cultural values in the prevention and treatment of sexual problems. In C. B. Qualls, J. Wincze, and D. Barlow (Eds.), *The prevention of sexual disorders: Issues and approaches.* New York: Plenum Press, 1978.

Luria, Z., and Rose, M. D. *Psychology of human sexuality.* New York: John Wiley and Sons, 1979.

Margueron, J. *Mesopotamia.* New York: World, 1965.

Masters, W. H., and Johnson, V. E. *Human sexual response.* Boston: Little, Brown, 1966.

Mead, M. *Male and female.* New York: William Morrow, 1949.

Melody, G. F. Behavioral implications of premenstrual tension. *Obstetrics and Gynecology,* 1961, *17,* 439-446.

Money, J., and Ehrhardt, A. *Man and woman: Boy and girl.* Baltimore: Johns Hopkins University Press, 1972.

Moos, R. H. The development of a menstrual distress questionnaire. *Psychosomatic Medicine,* 1968, *30,* 853-867.

Moos, R. H. Typology of menstrual cycle symptoms. *American Journal of Obstetrics and Gynecology,* 1969, *103,* 390-402.

Moos, R. H., Kopell, B. S., Melges, F. T., Yalem, I. O., Lunde, D. F., Clayton, R. B., and Hamburg, D. A. Fluctuations in symptoms and moods during the menstrual cycle. *Journal of Psychosomatic Research,* 1969, *13,* 37-44.

Moos, R. H., and Leiderman, D. B. Toward a menstrual cycle typology. *Journal of Psychosomatic Research,* 1978, *22,* 31-40.

Mordkoff, A. M. Some sex differences in personality correlates of "autonomic feedback." *Psychological Reports,* 1966, *18,* 511-518.

Naeye, R. L. Coitus and associated amniotic fluid infections. *New England Journal of Medicine,* 1979, *301,* 1198-1200.

Rossi, A. S., and Rossi, P. E. Body time and social time: Mood patterns by menstrual cycle phase and day of the week. *Social Science Research,* 1977, *6,* 273-308.

Sherfey, M. J. *The nature and evolution of female sexuality.* New York: Vintage Books, Random House, 1973.

Slater, P. *The pursuit of loneliness: American culture at the breaking point.* Boston: Beacon Press, 1970.

Symons, D. *The evolution of human sexuality.* New York: Oxford Press, 1979.

Terman, L. M. *Psychological factors in marital happiness.* New York: McGraw-Hill, 1938.

Thompson, W. I. *The time falling bodies take to light.* New York: St. Martin's Press, 1981.

Tooley, K. M. "Johnny, I hardly knew ye": Toward revision of the theory of male psychosexual development. *American Journal of Orthopsychiatry,* 1977, *47,* 184-195.

Travers, P. L. What the bees know. *Parabola,* 1981, *6,* 42-50.

Udry, J. R., and Morris, N. M. Distribution of coitus in the menstrual cycle. *Nature,* 1968, *220,* 593-596.

Zilboorg, G. Masculine and feminine: Some biological and cultural aspects. In J. Miller (Ed.), *Psychoanalysis and women.* Baltimore: Penguin Books, 1973.

The Prevention of
Sexual Problems in Men

Joseph LoPiccolo

This paper will focus on the prevention of sexual dysfunctions in men, and on the facilitation of a more satisfying sexual life for all men, including those men who do not suffer from a specific sexual dysfunction. Consideration will be given to ways in which the factors of cultural and religious values, parent-child relationships, sex education, sex laws, sex roles, the mass media, the writings of mental health professionals, and physical health problems contribute to the development of male sexual dysfunctions and interfere with attainment of a maximally satisfying sex life for most, if not all, men. Discussion of the role of these factors will be primarily speculative and discursive and not tied to existing research data. In the area of male sexual problems, there has been little empirical work done on the issues of causality and prevention. Much of the published work on male sexual problems is oriented toward treatment procedures, and even here anecdotal accounts outweigh controlled experiments by a large margin (Hogan, 1978).

The male sexual dysfunctions referred to throughout this paper include problems of desire (low sexual drive, aversion to sex), problems of arousal (difficulty in achieving and/or maintaining erection, lack of subjective feelings of arousal and pleasure), problems of orgasm (premature ejaculation, anhedonic orgasm, orgasm with flaccid penis), and disagreement about frequency of sex between male and female members of a couple. In the absence of any such specific dysfunctions, many men's sexual relationships are still negatively affected by the factors to be considered below. What is not included in this paper is a discussion of prevention of sexual deviations such as pedophilia, sexual assaultiveness, rape, transvestism, and so on. The scope of this paper is also limited to heterosexual dysfunctions and problems. Homosexual orientation per se is no longer considered to be pathological, according to DSM-III of the American Psychiatric Association,

Preparation of this paper was supported in part by a grant from the National Institute of Mental Health, U.S. Public Health Service.

and much research indicates normal psychological adjustment among non-patient homosexuals (see Hart, Roback, Tittler, Weitz, Walston, and McKee, 1978, for a review of this literature). Thus prevention of the "problem" of homosexual orientation could be considered to be a contradiction in terms. Dysfunctions in homosexual couples seem, on the basis of available evidence (Masters and Johnson, 1979), to be remarkably similar to heterosexual dysfunctions, and so will not be considered separately.

In discussing male sexual problems, the first issue is the incidence of such problems. Although it would be difficult to quantify how much the factors mentioned above interfere with the overall quality of men's sex lives, there is some evidence available on the quantity or incidence of specific symptomatic sexual dysfunctions. A recent study (Frank, Anderson, and Rubinstein, 1978) of 100 happily married couples found that 40 percent of the men reported having experienced specific dysfunctions such as premature ejaculation or erectile dysfunction, and 60 percent reported sexual difficulties such as inability to relax, lack of sufficient foreplay, partner choosing inconvenient time, and so forth. Obviously, the incidence of male sexual dysfunctions and dissatisfaction is high.

If our knowledge of incidence of sexual dissatisfaction and dysfunction is limited, empirical evidence on specific etiology is virtually nonexistent. The available literature is composed of collections of case histories (see Masters and Johnson, 1970), which indirectly reason that since certain life history events are commonly reported by dysfunctional males, the dysfunctions must have been directly caused by these events. For example, Masters and Johnson (1970), in discussing premature ejaculation, see patterns among adolescents who engaged in rapid, furtive masturbation, and whose initial experience of sexual intercourse was a rushed, conflict-filled event that occurred in a semipublic setting where discovery by parents, peers, or police was possible. Although this reasoning is appealing because it makes a kind of intuitive sense, work in progress at the Sex Therapy Center at Stony Brook presents a more complicated view. In comparing dysfunctional patients with normal control subjects, it appears that the occurrence of these supposedly crucial causal events is just as common in men who are *not* premature ejaculators. These events are apparently common, high base rate occurrences for men in our culture. Thus, if these events are related to being dysfunctional as an adult, there must be some mediating intervening variables that account for why, given the same life history events, some men become dysfunctional and some do not.

It is somewhat ironic that it is the very effectiveness of the behavioral sex therapy procedures that accounts for this lack of focus on etiology of sexual dysfunction. Since the directive, here-and-now physical training procedures are generally effective (Hogan, 1978), research on both etiology and prevention has not been emphasized. Given that most men do have some experience of sexual dysfunction, and that sexual dissatisfaction is perhaps even more common than supposed (Frank et al., 1978), it is clearly time for a focus on prevention of sexual problems.

The Role of Cultural and Religious Values

The Judeo-Christian ethic that shapes our culture's view of sexuality has remained remarkably consistent over the last 2,000 years. From the writings of the Apostle Paul, St. Augustine, and the 1976 Vatican Council statement on sexuality to Pope John Paul II's recent statements, the message has been clear: procreation, not pleasure, justifies sexuality; birth control, masturbation, premarital sex, and homosexuality are anathema (Taylor, 1970). Protestant views are generally similar, both Calvin and Luther argued that even marital sexuality was shameful, unclean, and sinful (Bailey, 1970).

These religiously based negative views of sexuality are especially severe in regard to women's sexuality. While the view of the good woman as asexual and virginal certainly creates dilemmas and problems for women, this view also has negative effects on men. Many men find it difficult to accept sexuality as part of the personality of the sort of woman that one loves, marries, and chooses as the mother of one's children. For these men, there is a dichotomy between good women and sexual women. This dichotomy is often referred to by clinicians as the "princess and the prostitute" syndrome.

The effects of this syndrome are disastrous for both men and women. One aspect of the syndrome is that the man gives subtle (and sometimes not so subtle) cues to the woman that he does not really want her to be too sexual. Thus the man who perhaps was initially attracted to his future wife at least partially by her sexual responsiveness, finds himself, after marriage, feeling uncomfortable with it. Alternatively, such a man, when seeking a future wife, chooses someone who is not particularly sexually responsive. Clinicians specializing in sexual dysfunction see many such cases: the complaint presented is that the wife is not very interested in sex, does not get very aroused or have orgasms during sex, and has a low desired frequency of sex. Often, the husband has convinced her to come to therapy by threats of divorce or having an affair if she does not change. In sex therapy, the positive benefits of sex for women are stressed, not as a way to please her husband, but as something highly pleasurable for herself that she is now missing. What we often see, if therapy is successful, is that as the woman becomes more sexually expressive and responsive, the male begins to undermine therapeutic progress. Although his stated reason for entering therapy was for his wife to enjoy sex more, once this begins to happen, he feels vaguely uneasy and uncomfortable. In some of these cases, the man refuses to find the time for the assigned sex therapy homework procedures. Other men become threatened if their wives now attempt to initiate sex with them, which, typically, was one of their pretherapy goals. As a more direct example of this ambivalence about female sexuality, one of our patients told his wife, after she had had a particularly intense orgasm, "I don't like it when you act that way."

In discussing this ambivalence about female sexuality with the male client, we try to reassure him that his wife will not have an affair, become promiscuous, or become insatiable as a result of discovering and expressing her own sexuality. Neither will she have a personality change and become a different sort of woman. In dealing with these fears, however, we are confronted with rather basic, powerful cultural and religious values about female sexuality that men have learned. Obviously, these sorts of profound changes in attitude are not easily produced, and prevention of the development of the negative attitudes would be worthwhile.

Another variation of the princess and the prostitute syndrome more directly affects the man's own sexuality. In this case, the man is unable to reconcile his feelings of love and respect for a woman with his sexual feelings for her, since, after all, decent women are not sexual. Such a man has no sexual difficulties in functioning adequately with prostitutes and other women that he does not love, respect, and value, but finds himself, to his bewilderment, unable to function with his wife. In one of our cases, the male had had intercourse with some 200 different women before his marriage at age 26. Most of these women had been prostitutes; the others he described variously as "whores, party girls, and one-night stands." He married a very attractive woman with whom he did not have intercourse before marriage. Actually, during one of their heavy petting sessions before marriage, she suggested they have intercourse, but he refused. He explained that, since her parents were being very good to them and helping them out financially, he "couldn't do that to them." Yet after marriage, his sex drive toward her actually declined, and he found himself unable to have an erection. At first this was attributed to financial pressures and other worries, and it was only in therapy that his difficulty in experiencing both love and sexual feelings toward the same woman became evident.

Another way in which our culture's religiously based view of sexuality causes problems for men concerns what might be called the "primacy of the penis." That is, since sex is only legitimized by procreation (and only then if you do not enjoy it too much), only penile-vaginal intercourse is truly legitimate. This value, of course, places considerable pressure on the man to have an erection sufficient for intromission and to ejaculate in the vagina. If he cannot accomplish either of these culturally prescribed (and religiously based) goals, he is a failure. Thus, in trying to treat men whose inability to get an erection or ejaculate in the vagina is caused at least in part by anxiety about failure, we run up against a culturally induced set of values that stresses that *real* sex *is* "penis in the vagina plus ejaculation." Furthermore, in working with physically disabled men who cannot attain these goals (men who are diabetic and cord injured), we find it difficult to convince them that other types of sexual expression can be equally valid and pleasurable. Again, our cultural and religious values block therapeutic progress.

In trying to treat the problems caused by these values, rather than to prevent them by changing the values, there are two common but different problems. One problem concerns the male patient whose religious values are central to his whole life. Any attempt to change his sexual values may be seen as an attack on his religion, and this will probably result in resistance to therapeutic suggestions and may even result in his leaving treatment. Obviously, it is presumptuous and intrusive for a therapist to try to change a patient's religious beliefs when the patient only contracted for help with his erection. Yet what is the clinician to do when it is the religious value that is contributing to the problem? Our treatment approach at Stony Brook is to attempt to separate for the patient—sometimes with pastoral assistance—religious views about sex in general from the particulars of the marital relationship and sexuality as an expression of love within marriage. Sometimes this works, but prevention would probably be more effective.

The second type of problem is more subtle. In these cases, the man has already, at a cognitive level, rejected what his religion taught him about sex. Yet emotional "gut level" changes do not come as easily, and an emotionally powerful residue of the values that were developed in child-hood and adolescence remains. Such cases are especially difficult, as in the face of the patient's statement that his religious values are no longer active, it is hard to focus on the role of these values in causing his dys-function.

A set of values that views sex positively is not necessarily incompatible with religion. As numerous religious scholars have pointed out, there is remarkably little in the Bible and other scriptures to justify the antisexual stand of the Judeo-Christian ethic (Taylor, 1970). This antisexual bias actually reflects the sexual values of the lower-middle-class society in which organized Christianity and Judaism developed, rather than being inherent in the religions themselves. Thus, a change in sexual values does not have to be at the expense of religion per se. There is nothing neces-sarily incompatible between a positive view of sexual expression and a belief in God.

Another concern about changing values to a sex positive ethic concerns the effect on society. From Freud (1930) to your local police chief, there is agreement that allowing unrestrained sexual expression leads to the downfall of civilization. This belief persists despite the existence of stable, family-centered cultures—for example, Mangaia, in the South Seas, as described by Marshall (1971)—that allow virtually total sexual freedom. Furthermore, cross-culturally, it has been found that the level of sexual permissiveness is uncorrelated with the amount of intra- or extracom-munal violence present in a culture (McConahay and McConahay, 1977). In the absence of evidence that sexual permissiveness has negative effects on cultural stability, the viability of the family, or level of violence, perhaps advocating a change in cultural values is not such a terribly rad-ical proposal.

The Male Sex Role: "My Only Sex Problem Is That I Can't Get Enough of It"

A comprehensive review of American sex role stereotypes and their psy-chological effects is provided by Hochschild (1973). In our American sex roles, women are put in a double-bind situation and are expected to be beautiful, sexy, and seductive, while remaining chaste, celibate, and preferably virginal until marriage. Men, on the other hand, do not have such a contradictory and confusing sex role model to follow. Our culture gives a clear and unambivalent message to men about sex, but it is a demanding one. The content of this message includes several directives that create problems for men, lead to development of dysfunctions, and interfere with the attainment of optimum sexual gratification for both men and women.

Bem (1972) has presented evidence that children have learned to behave in accordance with sex role stereotypes by the time they enter nursery school. The male role, in general, stresses achievement, power, skill, competitiveness, strength, endurance, aggression, and success, while devaluing vulnerability, emotional expressiveness, dependency, and affiliation (Goldfried and Friedman, in press). When carried into the sexual area, this role model creates a number of different problems for men, and problems in relationships between men and women (Zilbergeld, 1978).

One major problem is that the male sex role requires a man to want sex always, to seek it out actively, and to define his masculine worth in terms of sexual conquest. This "always on" role, of course, places enormous demands on men. Men are not allowed to have fatigue, worry, or physical discomfort interfere with their sexual drive and ability to perform. To illustrate how strong this expectation for a constantly high male sex drive is, one need only examine the content of sex jokes. For example, consider the large number of jokes that have as the punch line the woman refusing sex by saying, "Not tonight, dear, I have a headache." If one reverses the sexes in these jokes, so that the man is refusing, do the jokes make any psychological sense to us? Almost without exception, they do not. We are simply not programmed by our cultural sex role stereotypes to think of a man as not wanting sex and needing to find an excuse not to have it.

What this model suggests is that men often attempt to have sex when at some level they do not really feel like it. Male patients often report that their problems of erection began at a time of increased stress, worry, or depression when they continued attempting intercourse despite these interfering emotional factors. Similarly, in working with single men (often postdivorced or widowed males), it is surprising to discover how often these men initiate sex or respond to partner initiation when in actuality they are not sexually or emotionally attracted to the woman. Not surprisingly, under these circumstances, arousal, pleasure, and erection are absent.

If you ask these men why they initiated sex or accepted a partner's initiation when they really felt no desire, the common response is that men are supposed to want sex all the time, and the need to maintain this image (both in the partner's eyes and the man's own self-image) makes refusal impossible.

Another aspect of the male sex role that has negative consequences concerns the demand that a man be a skilled, highly experienced, and competent lover. In adolescent male culture, this ethic leads to a good deal of competitive boasting, most of which is usually highly exaggerated. For adult men, this role as the expert has three main negative effects.

First, this role perpetuates sexual ignorance. Since men are supposed to know everything about sex, they cannot bring themselves to buy books, attend classes, or expose themselves to any source of sexual information. After all, if you do so, you are admitting that you could learn something. As an example, in the author's several years of teaching a very large undergraduate course in human sexual behavior, the male-female sex ratio of enrollees was about 60 percent female, despite the fact that the overall university sex ratio was the opposite.

A second negative aspect of the expert role is that men are not comfortable discussing sex with their partners. Since the man knows all about sex, he cannot ask the woman what she enjoys and indeed may be threatened by her attempts to communicate to him what it is that she likes. Men supposedly know what women like, and the idea that there are individual differences in preferences between women that require the man to take the role of learner, rather than expert, is unsettling to the traditional male.

A third negative aspect of the male role as sex expert is that when a sexual problem occurs, men find it extraordinarily difficult to seek out help. Goodman (1960) has noted that among men, "To boast of actual or invented prowess is acceptable, but to speak soberly of a love affair or sexual problem in order to be understood is strictly taboo" (p. 124). This attitude keeps many men with dysfunctions from coming to therapy, or indeed from talking to anyone about their problem. Unfortunately, men's fears about the consequences of revealing their vulnerability are not totally groundless. A study by Derlega and Chaikin (1976) found that males who do not disclose any problems are rated by both men and women as better adjusted than males who do admit to the normal problems we all experience. The opposite pattern, interestingly enough, was found for disclosure of problems by women.

There are other damaging messages in our culture's role model for male sexuality. Another aspect of the male role is that the man must not be emotionally expressive, especially in regard to any tender, intimate, dependent, and therefore unmasculine feelings. The model for male sexuality is conquest, with orgasm, but with as little tenderness, intimacy, and emotionality as possible. Obviously, this lack of emotional expressiveness impoverishes the quality of the sexual relationships for both men and women. Fortunately, with the advent of the women's movement, fewer women are willing to accept this sort of sexual encounter as satisfying and are supplying both pressure and permission for men to drop this unemotional facade.

If the ideal male sex role stresses high drive, expertise, and the lack of emotional expression, it also demands that men function adequately. Lack of erection, on even one occasion, is an emotionally shattering experience for many men. The more strongly the culture values male sexual competence, of course, the more susceptible the man becomes to having his ability to have an erection blocked by anticipatory performance anxiety. There is nothing like worrying about getting an erection for interfering with arousal to the extent that erection becomes impossible. The clearest example of this syndrome occurs in the South Sea Island culture mentioned earlier, Mangaia (Marshall, 1971). Although this culture is extremely free and permissive with regard to sex, a man's social standing is determined not by his wealth or wisdom, but by his sexual prowess, his ability to attain erection. Not surprisingly, with these sorts of stakes on the outcome, the incidence of erectile problems on Mangaia is high. In our culture, the sanctions are more private and internal, yet the demand that a man *always* function perfectly is clearly an unrealistic and damaging aspect of the male sex role.

As one aspect of the double standard, male competence has traditionally been defined only as having an erection and ejaculating. With the women's movement, the acceptance of female sexuality, and the focus on women's needs for sexual satisfaction, another demand for sexual competence has been added to the male sex role. Now the male must not only have an erection and ejaculate, but he must also make sure his partner has at least one and preferably several orgasms. Thus we see patients who put enormous pressure on their female partners to have orgasms, to reassure themselves about their adequacy as males. Again, this sort of pressure is damaging for both men and women. Given these unrealistic demands that men must meet if they are to satisfy the male sex role, it is not surprising that some men find it all a bit overwhelming and prefer to drop out and leave the battlefield. The incidence of complaints of male lack of interest in sex seems to be rising across many different sex therapy programs around the country (Kaplan, 1979; Zilbergeld and Ellison, 1980). In our center, 39 recently completed cases included 27 with complaints of low sexual interest; in 17 (63 percent) of these cases, it was the male who had the lack of interest.

Obviously, a good deal of therapeutic time is currently spent trying to undo these four negative aspects of the male sex role: constant high drive, expertise, emotional inexpressiveness, and flawless functioning. It would certainly be a positive change, and one likely to effect primary prevention, if we could redefine the male role in our culture.

We must attribute major blame for the perpetuation of the current role to advertising, television, and the mass media. If we look at the type of male who is used as a status model to sell everything from cars to beer, he is clearly an achieving, strong, unemotional, expert, and highly competent man. Many of the male role models we see in novels and television similarly do not include men who cry, who are vulnerable, need help, and have egalitarian, communicative relationships with women, especially in regard to sex. Instead, we see the image of masculinity as extremely "macho," dominant, aggressive, or, in short, suffering from what might be called testosterone poisoning.

The Effects of Sex Laws: Inhibitions from Prohibitions

Laws regarding sexual conduct in the United States have been in a state of flux for many years. The Supreme Court continues to struggle with the problems of defining what is obscene or pornographic. In many states husbands and wives break the law if, in the privacy of their own bedroom, they engage in oral or anal sex. Rape laws in many jurisdictions punish the victim rather than the offender. Given our culture's basically antisexual bias, it is not surprising that our sex laws tend to prohibit behaviors that virtually everyone engages in (Kinsey, Pomeroy, and Martin, 1948; Kinsey, Pomeroy, Martin, and Gebhard, 1953), forbid access to erotica in the absence of any evidence of negative effects of exposure to erotica (*Report of the U.S. Commission on Obscenity and Pornography*, 1971), and are especially severe in regard to sexual behavior in adolescence and outside of marriage.

There are three ways in which our sex laws contribute to sexual problems. One major negative effect of censorship and antipornography laws is to limit access to educational material and contraceptive devices and to generate media material that contains a suggestive rather than an open and honest approach to sex. If access to educational material were easier, especially for adolescents, we presumably would see fewer sexual problems caused by ignorance about sexual physiology and sexual technique. Of course, even many small towns have their local "X-rated" bookshops and movie theaters, but such places do not really address the problem. For one thing, people under the ages of 18 or 21 are typically forbidden to patronize these shops and movies. Additionally, the adults who are so lacking in information that they could benefit are also, of course, those likely to be too embarrassed or inhibited to enter such establishments. The quality of material found in "X-rated" books and movies is also problematic, in that it is often factually inaccurate, exploitive of women, and depersonalizing and mechanical in its approach to sex.

What is needed is legislation that would allow sex to enter the mainstream of American literature, film, and television, so that sexually explicit material of good quality would become widely available. Such a change would also have the positive effect of eliminating the titillating and suggestive approach to sex now common in mainstream media productions, especially those on television. Presenting sex as something that is exciting but cannot be discussed openly or portrayed honestly on TV probably contributes to the development of negative or ambivalent attitudes about sexuality and, in particular, women's sexuality, that are common in men with sexual problems.

Someone has worked out that the average American child, by age 18, will have seen 15,000 explicit murders on television. How many explicit, caring, and tender instances of making love will this 18-year-old have seen on TV? This difference is especially remarkable when one remembers that we have recently had separate presidential commissions conduct massive amounts of research on the effects of televised violence and pornography on children. The results of this research demonstrated overwhelmingly that exposure to media violence was harmful in a number of ways and that there was no negative effect of exposure to implicit erotica (*Report of the U.S. Commission on Obscenity and Pornography*, 1971; *Report of the U.S. Commission on Effects of Television Violence*, 1974). Yet violence is allowed in the mainstream of American visual media, whereas erotica are forbidden.

A second problem with our current sex laws concerns the legislation against premarital sexual activity, especially among teenagers under the "age of consent," which ranges from 12 to 21 in various states. These laws, aside from being out of touch with reality, as evidenced by recent research on teenage sexual behavior (Chilman, 1979), serve to legitimize parental attempts to inhibit the expression of sexuality in adolescence, as well as to support police harassment of adolescents at the local parking spot. It is unreasonable to have a law that forbids sexual activity until a certain age, and then expect people to have positive and healthy attitudes about sex after reaching this magic, highly variable age.

The presumed intent of age-of-consent laws is to prevent statutory rape—sexual exploitation of children by adults—which is a worthwhile motive. To prevent these laws from being used in problematic ways, all that would be necessary would be to specify that statutory rape does not apply when the sexual act is between two persons of similar age.

A third negative aspect of our sex laws concerns the laws against sodomy, which in many states includes anything other than penile-vaginal intercourse, even between husband and wife. As previously discussed, the belief that "real" sex consists of getting an erection to put in the vagina places men under considerable pressure to perform and is an especially severe problem for men with physical disabilities or illnesses that interfere with erection. The sodomy laws and the values they reflect are also a problem for the elderly couples now being seen in increasing numbers in sex therapy. Although the aging changes in sexual response are relatively minor and nonproblematic, one change is that as the male ages, it typically takes more direct physical stimulation of the penis for longer periods of time to produce erection. Although this can be a positive change, especially for men who previously had a problem with rapid ejaculation, it is often distressing for elderly couples who have not been comfortable with engaging in lots of foreplay prior to coitus, especially manual or oral stimulation of the male's penis. Prior to entering therapy, these couples typically had a history of many years of adequate functioning, focused exclusively on penile-vaginal intercourse, until the man began to have erectile difficulties. In some cases, direct stimulation of the penis had never been part of their sexual repertoire, and in others it had occurred but was of only brief duration before beginning intercourse.

Suggestions by the therapist to restore sexual functioning by engaging in manual and oral stimulation of the penis and continuing this for some time, often raise concerns about sodomy. One patient, a 77-year-old woman, said, "I've never touched that thing or put it in my mouth in over 50 years of marriage, and I'm certainly not going to commit sodomy now." A similar reaction often occurs when the therapist suggests the man bring the woman to orgasm manually or orally, to reduce the pressure on him to get an erection. Of course, the therapist tries to deal with these negative attitudes by citing the incidence of manual and oral sex, discussing its normality, self-disclosure, and so forth. Yet the fact remains that in many states the therapist is advocating that the patient commit a felony, and the patient may well be aware of this. Adoption of the American Bar Association's model legal code, which decriminalizes all sexual activity performed in private between consenting adults, might help prevent this type of sexual problem.

Preventing Iatrogenic Problems

> We have met the enemy and he is us.
> —Pogo

Lest it seem that all sexual problems can be blamed on religion, sex roles, and sex laws, it must be noted that a good many sexual problems are actually iatrogenic diseases, caused by the things we experts in human behavior have written over the years. Indeed, it would appear that many of the pronouncements on sexuality made by experts (psychiatrists, psychologists, and sexologists) over the years have been little more than translation of cultural biases into pseudoscientific jargon (LoPiccolo and Heiman, 1977).

The first real sex experts of the modern era, Havelock Ellis and Richard von Krafft-Ebbing noted that masturbation was the direct cause of epilepsy, eye disease, acne, asthma, feeblemindedness, headaches, warts on the hands, deafness, cardiac murmurs, insanity, criminality, mammary hypertrophy, painful menstruation, "neuroses of the sexual apparatus," and "weakness of the center governing erection, ejaculation, and pleasure in coitus." Not surprisingly, the views of these experts gave rise to a lively commerce in devices to prevent masturbation, including metal mittens for children and an alarm that rang in the parents' bedroom if the child's bed was moving. Sex advice books written around the turn of the century abounded in warnings of the dire effects of "excessively frequent" marital coitus, or the use of "unnatural and studiously licentious" practices in marital sexual relations (Haller and Haller, 1974; LoPiccolo and Heiman, 1977). Thus many of the sexual problems of that era were simply behaviors that we now accept as normal and healthy. For the person who believed these experts and sought treatment, the cure was clearly worse than the disease: Krafft-Ebbing (1899) reported treating young girls who were brought in by their parents for masturbation by applying a white-hot iron to the child's clitoris.

The writings of Freud have had a particularly disastrous effect in creating sexual problems, especially for women. Freud's views on female sexuality, developed in the absence of any empirical work on the physiology of female sexual response, created severe problems for those women who only had immature, neurotic, masculine, clitoral orgasms as opposed to mature, healthy, feminine vaginal orgasms (Freud, 1925/1959). A large volume of empirical evidence has been accumulated to indicate that virtually all of Freud's inspired guesses about sexuality were wrong (Kinsey et al., 1948; Kinsey et al., 1953; Masters and Johnson, 1966; Sherfey, 1973). Yet we continue to see couples applying for sex therapy with concerns that reflect this Freudian view of female sexuality.

Freud's views on male sexuality (1905/1962) have also been influential in producing iatrogenic problems for men. For Freud, real sex occurred only when the penis was in the vagina. Men who enjoyed manual or oral stimulation of the penis, or who perhaps required such stimulation to reach erection, were said to be fixated at some pregenital level of sexual development and to have an infantile polymorphous perverse personality defect (Freud, 1905/1962; LoPiccolo and Heiman, 1977). Thus the ethic of the primacy of the penis, with all its pressure for the man always and spontaneously to have an erection for intercourse, was strongly supported by the writings of Freud. It has been suggested that Freud's ideas simply reflected traditional Jewish attitudes toward sex. In Gordon's (1972) words: " 'Infantile,' 'immature,' 'personality defect' is just name calling and the substitution of Freudian pseudoscientific language for the prohibitions of the Talmud" (p. 27).

In the last few years, there has been a turnaround in professional writing about sexuality. Freudian theory about sex is no longer accepted, except by some die-hard analysts whose allegiance verges on the religious in that it is not susceptible to change by evidence. The present generation of sex therapists' writings stress the values of sensual pleasure, giving and receiving, communication, flexibility, and experimentation with a wide range of sexual activities (LoPiccolo and Heiman, 1977). This is in marked contrast to Freudian theory's rigid focus on organs and orgasms. Although the presumed intent of the current literature is to enable people to relax, to enjoy whatever works for them, and to accept female sexuality as legitimate, the media have somehow managed to subvert this message. That is, instead of reflecting the nondemanding, nonperformance-oriented model stressed in today's sex therapy, the recent flood of popular books, magazines, and advice columns has done quite the opposite. Much of this material is pejorative, and it demands that a woman be aroused, multiorgasmic, and skilled at a wide variety of lovemaking techniques. Similarly, a man must be hypersexual and must be able to produce all sorts of orgasms in large numbers in his wife, or he is an inadequate lover.

This pressure for a man to keep track of his own and his partner's arousal and orgasm, and to define his adequacy by the number of orgasms she has, tends to have a disastrous effect on the couple's sexual relationship. We now see couples seeking therapy, after reading current literature, for complaints such as desire for the wife to have multiple orgasms, occurrence of female coital orgasm on only 3 or 4 out of 5 weekly lovemaking sessions, or failure of the man to get multiple erections. Somehow the popular media have transformed "sex is a legitimate activity for men and women" into "sex is a required activity, and you must be very, very good at it." Hopefully, present-day therapists will not treat such cases but will instead reassure such therapy-seekers that they are functioning normally and not in need of therapy. Although the therapist can give this permission to relax and enjoy what was satisfying to the couple before reading some pejorative article, the preventive impact of simply changing the media approach to sexual competence would certainly be much more widespread. Ultimately, this change in the popular media will not occur until the writings of sex therapy professionals contain much less emphasis on functioning and orgasm and much more emphasis on pleasure. As Comfort (1972) has noted, "In writing descriptively about sex, it is hard not to be solemn however unsolemnly we play in bed" (p. 14).

Physical Health, Nutrition, and Life-Style

In the discussion of the male sex role earlier in this chapter, the focus was on the elements in this role that have negative effects on sexuality. Other aspects of the male role, not directly related to sex, appear to lead to a variety of physical problems that then affect sexual function.

In recent years, there has been much attention devoted to the "type A" life-style, which carries with it an increased risk of coronary heart disease (Roseman and Friedman, 1974; Jenkins, 1976). Type A behavior is much more typical among men than among women and is largely responsible for the vastly higher death rate from heart disease for men than for women (Waldron, 1976, 1978). The type A pattern reflects the highly instrumental, goal-oriented, nonemotional approach to life expected of men in our culture and includes excessive competitiveness, impatience, and involvement in multiple activities while under a tight deadline, an overcommitment to vocation, an accelerated pace of living, and the need to strive for achievement and responsibility. Since the type A behavior pattern is associated with coronary artery disease, it can be argued that it also affects male sexuality in three ways.

First, for those men who survive a coronary incident, problems of sexual adjustment are very common (Friedman, 1978). These problems include fears that sexual activity will trigger another heart attack, restriction of sexual activity because of angina during exertion, and inhibition of sexual interest because of the stress and depression that typically follow a heart attack. Second, both for survivors of a heart attack and for men with arteriosclerosis resulting in lowered cardiac output, there may be insufficient blood supply available to the penis for erection to occur (Kempczinski, 1979; Zorgniotti, Rossi, Padula, and Makovsky, 1980). Although there are some surgical techniques for revascularization of the penis in cases of coronary disease, applicability is limited, as are success levels among those men for whom the techniques are suitable (DePalma, Levine, and Feldman, 1978; Michal, Kramar, Pospichal, and Hejhal, 1977). Third, for men with high blood pressure, treatment with antihypertensive beta-blocking agents commonly leads to loss of erection and also inability to ejaculate (Forsberg, Gustavii, Hojerback, and Olsson, 1979; Kolodny, Masters, and Johnson, 1979). Clearly, a change in the type A male life-style would have some effect on reducing the frequency of these three types of male sexual problems.

Reducing the incidence of smoking could prevent some male sexual problems. Current advertising supports the notion that the *real* man is a smoker—the Marlboro man. Unfortunately, some recent evidence tends to indicate that heavy smokers have markedly reduced penile blood pressure, with concomitant difficulties in erection (Forsberg et al., 1979). In other words, though Marlboro man may be macho, he may also be impotent.

Another aspect of the male sex role that has negative consequences as far as sexuality is concerned involves the use of alcohol. It has been noted that heavy drinking in men is socially sanctioned both as an acceptable, nonthreatening social context for contact with other men and as a response to emotional stress (Goldfried and Friedman, in press). Yet even one drink interferes immediately with arousal and erection (Wilson, 1977). For long-term drinkers, especially clinical alcoholics, the effects are quite serious. A number of studies have shown that about 50 percent of heavy drinkers and as many as 80 percent of men with alcoholic liver damage have impaired sex drive, erection, or ejaculation (Lemere and Smith, 1973; VanTheil, Sherins, and Lester, 1973). In one study, about 40 percent of alcoholic men were found to be unable to get an erection and another 10 percent had retarded ejaculation; abstention from alcohol for months or even years led to a return of function in only about half of the cases (Lemere and Smith, 1973). There are several physiological effects associated with alcoholic sexual dysfunction, including liver damage, endocrine abnormalities, changes in pituitary and hypothalamic regulation of the gonads, peripheral neuropathy, and a variety of autoimmune mechanisms (Kolodny et al., 1979). In its most severe form, male alcoholic sexual dysfunction includes testicular atrophy, gynecomastia, diminished sex drive, erectile and ejaculatory failure, and sterility (Kolodny et al., 1979). Education about the negative effects of alcohol on sexuality might have some effect on men's drinking and help prevent this type of male sexual dysfunction.

Yet another life-style issue leading to physical problems that affect sexuality is diet. Obesity does not usually have direct effects on sexuality, except in cases where there is so much adipose tissue in the stomach, thighs, and perineum that coital positioning and penile intromission become problematic. More generally, however, obesity is associated with both high blood pressure and diabetes. The negative effects of antihypertensive medication were discussed previously; diabetes also has very negative effects on sexuality (Ellenberg, 1978; Renshaw, 1978). The major effect of diabetes is to produce erectile dysfunction, which occurs in about 40 percent of younger diabetic men, 70 percent of older diabetic men, and 80 percent of men with diabetic complications such as neuropathy or vascular damage (Kolodny et al., 1979). Diabetic erectile failure typically develops gradually and is apparently caused primarily by vascular damage and by neuropathy. The neuropathy consists of demyelination and defective myelin synthesis in autonomic nervous tissue that regulates erection (Faerman, Glover, Fox, Jadzinsky, and Rapaport, 1974). Retrograde ejaculation, caused by damage to the autonomic fibers that control the urinary bladder neck, is also present in some cases of diabetes (Ellenberg and Weber, 1966). Unfortunately, good control of diabetes, through proper diet and insulin, does not appear to influence the long-term development of erection problems in diabetic men, and the problem is not amenable to surgical or other medical interventions (Kolodny et al., 1979). Thus, prevention of diabetes, inasmuch as diabetes is partially related to diet, obesity, and exercise, is especially important. Diabetic sexual problems are an example of a disorder where only a preventive approach can directly affect the problem.

Finally, the life-style issue of general physical condition might be noted. Aside from lowering the risk of coronary disease and diabetes, and increasing testosterone levels (Remes, Kuoppasalmi, and Adlercreuty, 1979), being in good physical condition increases enjoyment of sex as well. The large muscle movements associated with exercise seem to lead to increased body awareness and increased kinesthetic pleasure during sexual activities. Clinical experience shows that the man who is out of shape and chronically tired does not seem to enjoy sex as fully as he might, and his drive level seems to be suppressed.

Prevention of sexual problems related to health and life-style issues would be facilitated by family physicians trained in this area. If a discussion of sex and and health were part of routine physical examination and history taking, male awareness of the roles of life-style and health in sexuality would be increased.

Parent-Child Interactions

It has been noted that sex education by parents "has indeed been preventative—of healthy, fulfilling sexual lives!" (Calderone, 1978, p. 146). Although this statement is a bit extreme, it is true that the case histories of our patients abound with parents who made sexuality a frightening, threatening, negative, and punitive concept for their developing children. As previously mentioned, many nondysfunctional adults have similar histories, and the actual role of parent-child interactions in the etiology of dysfunction is unclear. Therefore, rather than focus on the negative histories of our patients, this section will attempt to specify what sort of parent-child interactions might facilitate later sexual adjustment. As before, much of this material will be speculative, since research in this area is virtually nonexistent (Calderone, 1978). Clearly, parental discomfort interferes with much parent-child interaction on the topic of sexuality, as evidenced by a study in which over 70 percent of adolescents reported that their parents did not ever talk with them about sex (Sorenson, 1973).

One important feature of parent-child interaction is simply education. A fairly standard recommendation regarding the "right age" for parents to discuss sex with their children is to "wait until they ask" (Crooks and Bauer, 1980). Although this advice is appropriate for "where did I come from" sorts of questions from toddlers, it is obviously not appropriate for older children. If one waits until an 11-year-old girl is terrified by menarche to explain menstrual bleeding, one has obviously waited too long. If one waits for an adolescent boy to inquire about masturbation, ejaculation, and "wet dreams," one will probably wait forever, as relatively few boys will ask parents about these matters. What boys and girls *will* do is ask their peers, who function as the major source of sex information—more accurately termed sex misinformation—in our culture (*Report of the U.S. Commission on Obscenity and Pornography*, 1971). Obviously, the ideal situation would be for parents to spontaneously offer sex education to their children and to create the sort of atmosphere in which children will ask questions of their parents rather than of their peers. Given that this is probably not something many parents will be able to do, at the very least parents should give their children good books appropriate for their age and indicate a willingness to read the books themselves, and then discuss them with the children.

Although education for children is probably important, parental modeling is probably more crucial to the development of healthy sexuality. Seeing a loving and physically affectionate relationship modeled between mother and father is almost certain to facilitate later sexual adjustment, and there is at least some evidence that seeing the lack of such leads to sexual dysfunction (Fisher, 1973). If we move beyond the need for children to see their parents express physical affection for one another, however, the issues become more difficult. Should children see their parents actively involved in sex, or is this a damaging experience? Freudian theory suggests that the experience of viewing the primal scene is a shattering one for children, as it activates castration fears, penis envy, and other aspects of the Oedipal conflict (Freud, 1905; 1962). It has also been argued that children who observe their parents having intercourse are likely to misinterpret arousal as pain, coital movement as aggression, and moans of pleasure as cries of injury (Crooks and Bauer, 1980, p. 377). Yet many children, from anecdotal accounts, respond to observing parental intercourse merely with curiosity, interest, or, in the case of young adolescents, surprise that their ancient and "out of it" parents are still "getting it on." Rather than terror, the reaction of one four-year-old to viewing the primal scene was the delighted comment, delivered with a broad grin upon walking into his parents' bedroom, "Attaboy, Daddy, ride 'em cowboy!" This is not to argue that parents should routinely engage in sex in front of their children but, rather, to suggest that a phobic avoidance of all nudity, physical affection, and sexual expression around children is clearly not necessary and, indeed, may be harmful in that good models for adult relationships are not provided. Certainly, we do have evidence from other cultures where nudity and sexual activity are *not* private behaviors that healthy sexual adjustment can flourish in such an atmosphere (Ford and Beach, 1951; Marshall, 1971). If parents choose to keep their sexual behavior private, perhaps they should somehow indicate that this is the way they choose to enjoy a wonderful experience, rather than conveying that sex is somehow a nasty business that must be hidden.

Another ideal change would be for parents to become more comfortable in dealing with their children's masturbation and sex play and with the sexual behavior of adolescents. Masturbation is virtually universal, and childhood sex play is only slightly less common (Kinsey et al., 1948; Kinsey et al., 1953). Yet the typical parental response to these entirely normal, harmless behaviors is to attempt to eliminate them. Even enlightened childcare manuals typically advise parents to respond to early childhood masturbation by distracting the child and providing him or her with another toy. Along with the typically punitive parental response often given to discovering children "playing doctor," the parental response to masturbation sets the stage for the development of sex negative attitudes.

In the area of masturbation, it is difficult to arrive at a rational reason for discouraging or even distracting children from genital exploration. At most, a simple statement that this should not be done in front of other people would be sufficient for parents concerned about social conventions. Such a statement should, however, be coupled with the information that masturbation is normal, healthy, pleasurable, and that everyone does it.

Any child who is toilet-trained can probably understand that some things are good but should only be done in private.

The question of childhood sex play poses a more difficult question. Here, whatever the enlightened parents' feelings, the feelings of another set of parents are typically involved as well. Perhaps a sensible approach would be for a parent to tell the child that while sex play reflects normal curiosity and is exciting and fun, it is something that some parents get upset about. It can be stressed that this is a belief some people have, like racial prejudices or religious taboos, which is emotionally loaded to an extent that is out of proportion with the reality of what children do when playing with each other. However, since the parent does not want the child to be considered bad, the child must respect these feelings and not do something that is upsetting to other people.

Adolescent sexual behavior raises even more emotional issues. Even liberal and accepting parents often have difficulty applying these values to their own teenage children. There is a real difference in how parents feel about sexual behavior on the part of their teenage sons and daughters, as illustrated by Simone de Beauvoir's (1956) comment that "Girls are weighted down with restrictions, boys with demands" (p. 378). Indeed, the adolescent male is faced with a number of demands for meeting the male sex role, with all its negative implications previously discussed. Given that teenage peer culture is almost certainly going to support male hypersexuality, conquest of women as a status symbol, and the good woman-sexual woman dichotomy, parents need to work actively to counter their sons' socialization into this sex role stereotype. However, one more often sees fathers of adolescent boys adding to the pressure to be "macho," and taking great pride and vicarious pleasure in their sons' acting out the male sex role, thus reinforcing the peer socialization process.

If this discussion has focused on a lack of sexual openness and interaction between parents and male children, it should be noted that the opposite pattern is also disastrous for the development of healthy sexuality, especially in regard to the effects of incest on female sexuality (Meiselman, 1978). Although actual incestuous intercourse is much rarer with sons than with daughters, we are seeing a pattern of an eroticized, quasi-incestuous relationship between mother and son in many of our current cases of male low sex drive (LoPiccolo, 1980). These patterns include mothers who slept in the same bed with their late adolescent sons, who had their sons give them highly erotic leg and buttock massages every night, ostensibly for their muscle aches, and who were sensually and passionately affectionate with their sons. Our clients report being aroused by these behaviors, but upset and anxious as they were aware that sexual feelings toward one's mother are forbidden. In cases where there was a father present in the home, the boys were also typically both frightened of his jealous reaction and unable to relate to him positively as a role model. This pattern is common enough in men with low drive, and rare enough in both normal control subjects and in patients with other sexual dysfunctions that it appears to be a genuine example of a life history event that leads directly to a dysfunction.

In conclusion, parents can help prevent development of male sexual problems in a number of ways. Good sex education should be provided, and a loving, sensual, physically affectionate relationship of the parents can be modeled. Childhood masturbation can be treated as the harmless event it is, and childhood sexual exploration responded to in terms of sex positive but culturally realistic values. Attempts can be made to prevent the media and peer culture from leading the adolescent to accept uncritically the traditional male role in regard to sex; additionally, the mother-son relationship should not be eroticized. While these suggestions do add to the already demanding and difficult parental role, the cost-benefit ratio is attractive.

Formal Sex Education

If sex education by parents is often inadequate, the job done by the schools is often worse. One feels somewhat guilty about being critical of formal sex education curricula, as it is comparable to shooting sitting ducks with a 155-mm howitzer. Given the enormous conservative and religious scrutiny brought to bear on a school's sex education program, to say nothing of the outright opposition to *any* form of sex education by the far right, it is not surprising that school officials design sex education programs that are so far removed from the reality of childhood and adolescent sexuality. In light of how strongly many people feel about sex education, it is surprising that there is such a small amount of research data available on the controversy (Calderone, 1978). Opponents of sex education argue that it will increase premarital permissiveness, which is supported by one study (Carton and Carton, 1971), but another study did not find this to be true (Weichman and Ellis, 1969). Research on the effects of sex education is hard to do, perhaps because people are afraid of what the results will show. James Elias, of the Institute for Sex Research, for example, spent 2 years looking for a school that would permit their sex education program to be researched on this issue (Calderone, 1978). The proponents of sex education often counter the permissiveness argument by stating that education will reduce premarital pregnancy and venereal disease, but the little available research on this point also does not support this claim (Bidgood, 1973).

The obvious flaws of most, if not all, current sex education programs in the schools include the following:

1) Sex education occurs too late. The average age of menarche is now under 12 years (Chilman, 1979), but school sex education programs often do not occur until the ninth grade or later, where the students average from 14 to 15 years of age.

2) Sex education is rarely taught by someone with any special training in human behavior. More commonly, the biology teacher or the physical education teacher is responsible.

3) Sex education actually covers plumbing—the anatomy and physiology of reproduction—rather than sexuality. Values, techniques, skills, and communication are noticeably absent in most curricula.

4) Sex education rarely includes any preventive material, such as education about normal adolescent sexual fears and concerns, sexual dysfunctions, changes in sexuality with aging, or the effects of having children on the sexual relationship in marriage.

5) Often, children are segregated by sex for the sex education program, which hardly fosters a positive view of male-female relationships.

6) Finally, and perhaps most important, because of fears about community reaction, sex education curricula often take care to present sexual behavior in a negative, unappealing light. Rather than stressing the positive values in sex, there is an emphasis on unwanted pregnancy, venereal disease, and so forth. As an example of this sort of thinking, here is a partial list of the reasons one high school and college level text cites for young women to have premarital intercourse: "to hold her popularity; she is confused; she feels obligated; she is frightened, lonely, bored, or insecure; she desperately needs affection and is willing to purchase it by being sexually compliant; she is hostile and wishes to use sex as a means of defying her

parents" (Saxton, 1968, p. 185). Nowhere is the positive value of sex as an expression of love and closeness discussed, nor is there acceptance of the notion that normal women have a sex drive.

Because of the extremely conservative nature of school sex education programs, it may well be the case that school is where men learn sex negative attitudes and learn to have difficulty in accepting female sexuality. Given the current state of affairs, male sexual problems might be prevented if the right wing is successful in eliminating school sex education. At least in that case parents who do a good job building positive values in their children will not have them undercut by the school curriculum.

Conclusion

The theme of this paper has been that there are major problems in the way our society thinks about sex in general, and about male sexuality in particular. It is easy to specify what is wrong, and even to suggest how things ought to be changed. The problem, of course, is that massive change in areas where people have very strong opinions and biases has been suggested. As the reaction to the report of the Commission on Obscenity and Pornography demonstrated, when facts conflict with cherished beliefs, the facts are ignored. The experience in Denmark after legalization of pornography was a large drop in sex crimes, yet the idea that liberalization of pornography laws would lead to an increase in sex crimes is still cherished by our lawmakers (Wilson, 1978). The prospect for any rapid change in our social institutions and general cultural values regarding sex is dismal at best. However, in the area of how individual sets of parents raise their children, and how we ourselves as adults relate to each other, change is possible.

References

Bailey, D. S. Sexual ethics in Christian tradition. In J. C. Wynn (Ed.), *Sexual ethics and Christian responsibility*. New York: Association Press, 1970.

Bem, S. L. *Psychology looks at sex roles: Where have all the androgynous people gone?* Paper presented at a symposium on women, University of California, Los Angeles, May 1972.

Bidgood, F. The effects of sex education. *SIECUS Report*, 1973, *1*, 11-14.

Calderone, M. S. Is sex education preventative? In C. B. Qualls, J. P. Wincze & D. H. Barlow (Eds.), *The prevention of sexual disorders*. New York: Plenum Press,

1978.

Carton, J., and Carton, J. Evaluation of a sex education program for children and their parents. *Family Coordinator*, 1971, *20*, 377-386.

Chilman, C. S. *Adolescent sexuality in a changing American society*. Washington, D.C.: U.S. Government Printing Office, 1979.

Comfort, A. *The joy of sex*. New York: Crown, 1972.

Crooks, R., and Bauer, P. *Our sexuality*. San Francisco: Benjamin Cummings, 1980.

de Beauvoir, S. *The mandarins: A novel*. New York: Penguin Books, 1956.

DePalma, R. G., Levine, S. B., and Feldman, S. Preservation of erectile function after aortoiliac reconstruction. *Archives of Surgery*, 1978, *113*, 958-963.

Derlega, V. J., and Chaikin, A. L. Norms affecting self-disclosure in men and women. *Journal of Consulting and Clinical Psychology*, 1976, *44*, 376-380.

Ellenberg, M. Impotence in diabetes: The neurologic factor. In J. LoPiccolo and L. LoPiccolo (Eds.), *Handbook of sex therapy*. New York: Plenum Press, 1978.

Ellenberg, M., and Weber, H. Retrograde ejaculation in diabetic neuropathy. *Annals of Internal Medicine*, 1966, *65*, 1237-1246.

Ellis, H. *Studies in the psychology of sex* (7 vols.). Philadelphia: F. A. Davis, 1899-1928.

Faerman, I., Glover, L., Fox, D., Jadzinsky, M. N., and Rapaport, M. Impotence and diabetes: Histological studies of the autonomic nervous fibers of the corpora cavernosa in impotent diabetic males. *Diabetes*, 1974, *23*, 971-976.

Fisher, S. *The female orgasm*. New York: Basic Books, 1973.

Ford, D., and Beach, F. *Patterns of sexual behavior*. New York: Harper and Row, 1951.

Forsberg, L., Gustavii, B. A., Hojerback, T., and Olsson, A. M. Impotence, smoking, and Beta-blocking drugs. *Fertility and Sterility*, 1979, *31*, 589-603.

Frank, E., Anderson, C., and Rubinstein, D. Frequency of sexual dysfunction in "normal" couples. *New England Journal of Medicine*, 1978, *299*, 111-115.

Freud, S. [*Civilization and its discontents*] (J. Riviere, Trans.). London: Hogarth Press, 1930.

Freud, S. [Some psychological consequences of the anatomical distinction between the sexes.] In J. Strachey (Ed. and trans.), *Sigmund Freud: Collected papers* (Vol. 5). New York: Basic Books, 1959. (Originally published, 1925.)

Freud, S. [*Three essays on the theory of sexuality*.] (J. Strachey, Ed. and trans.). New York: Basic Books, 1963. (Originally published, 1905.)

Friedman, J. M. Sexual adjustment of the postcoronary male. In J. LoPiccolo and L. LoPiccolo (Eds.), *Handbook of sex therapy*. New York: Plenum Press, 1978.

Goldfried, M. R., and Friedman, J. M. Clinical behavior therapy and the male sex role. In K. Solomon and N. B. Levy (Eds.), *Men and mental health: Changing male roles*. New York: Plenum Press, in press.

Goodman, P. *Growing up absurd*. New York: Random House, 1960.

Gordon, D. G. *Self-love*. Baltimore: Penguin Books, 1972.

Haller, J. S., and Haller, R. M. *The physician and sexuality in Victorian America*. New York: W. W. Norton, 1974.

Hart, M., Roback, H., Tittler, B., Weitz, L., Walston, B., and McKee, E. Psychological adjustment of nonpatient homosexuals: Critical review of the research literature. *Journal of Clinical Psychiatry*, 1978, *39*, 604-608.

Hochschild, A. R. A review of sex role research. *American Journal of Sociology*, 1973, 78, 1011-1029.

Hogan, D. R. The effectiveness of sex therapy: A review of the literature. In J. LoPiccolo and L. LoPiccolo (Eds.), *Handbook of sex therapy*. New York: Plenum Press, 1978.

Jenkins, C. D. Recent evidence supporting ecologic and social risk factors for coronary disease. *New England Journal of Medicine*, 1976, *294*, 987-994, 1033-1038.

Kaplan, H. S. *Disorders of sexual desire*. New York: Brunner/Mazel, 1979.

Kempczinski, R. F. The role of the vascular diagnostic laboratory in the evaluation of male impotence. *American Journal of Surgery*, 1979, *138*, 278-282.

Kinsey, A. C., Pomeroy, W. B., and Martin, C. E. *Sexual behavior in the human male*. Philadelphia: W. B. Saunders, 1948.

Kinsey, A. C., Pomeroy, W. B., Martin, C. E., and Gebhard, P. H. *Sexual behavior in the human female*. Philadelphia: W. B. Saunders, 1953.

Kolodny, R. C., Masters, W. H., and Johnson, V. E. *Textbook of sexual medicine*. Boston: Little, Brown, 1979.

Krafft-Ebbing, R. von. *Psychopathia sexualis*. Brooklyn, N.Y.: Physicians and Surgeons Books, 1899.

Lemere, F., and Smith, J. W. Alcohol-induced sexual impotence. *American Journal of Psychiatry*, 1973, *130*, 212-213.

LoPiccolo, J., and Heiman, J. Cultural values and the therapeutic definition of sexual function and dysfunction. *Journal of Social Issues*, 1977, *33*, 166-183.

LoPiccolo, L. Low sexual desire. In L. A. Pervin and S. R. Leiblum (Eds.), *Principles and practice of sex therapy*. New York: Guilford Press, 1980.

Marshall, D. S. Sexual behavior on Mangaia. In D. S. Marshall and R. C. Suggs (Eds.), *Human sexual behavior: Variations in the ethnographic spectrum*. New York: Basic Books, 1971.

Masters, W. H., and Johnson, V. E. *Analysis of human sexual response*. Boston: Little, Brown, 1966.

Masters, W. H. and Johnson, V. E. *Human sexual inadequacy*. Boston: Little, Brown, 1970.

Master, W. H. and Johnson, V. E. *Homosexuality in perspective*. Boston: Little, Brown, 1979.

McConahay, S. A., and McConahay, J. B. Sexual permissiveness, sex role rigidity, and violence across cultures. *Journal of Social Issues*, 1977, *33*, 134-143.

Meiselman, K. C. *Incest*. San Francisco: Jossey-Bass, 1978.

Michal, V., Kramar, R., Pospichal, J., and Hejhal, L. Arterial epigastricocavernous anastomosis for the treatment of sexual impotence. *World Journal of Surgery*, 1977, *1*, 515-524.

Remes, K., Kuoppasalmi, K., and Adlercreuty, H. Effect of long-term physical training on plasma testosterone, adrostenedione, globulin capacity. *Scandinavian Journal of Clinical Laboratory Investigation*, 1979, *39*, 743-749.

Renshaw, D. C. Impotence in diabetes. In J. LoPiccolo and L. LoPiccolo (Eds.), *Handbook of sex therapy*. New York: Plenum Press, 1978.

Report of the U.S. commission on effects of television violence. Washington, D.C.: U.S. Government Printing Office, 1974.

Report of the U.S. commission on obscenity and pornography. Washington, D.C.: U.S. Government Printing Office, 1971.

Roseman, R. H., and Friedman, M. Neurogenic factors in pathogenesis of coronary heart disease. *Medical Clinics of North America,* 1974, *58,* 269-279.

Saxton, L. *The individual, marriage, and the family.* Belmont, Calif.: Wadsworth, 1968.

Sherfey, M. J. *The nature and evolution of female sexuality.* New York: Vintage Books, Random House, 1973.

Sorenson, R. *Adolescent sexuality in contemporary America.* New York: Vintage Books, Random House, 1973.

Taylor, G. R. *Sex in history.* New York: Harper and Row, 1970.

VanThiel, D. H., Sherins, R. H., and Lester, R. Mechanism of hypogonadism in alcoholic liver disease. *Gastroenterology,* 1973, *65*(A-50), 574. (Abstract)

Waldron, I. Why do women live longer than men? *Social Science and Medicine,* 1976, *10,* 349-362.

Waldron, I. The coronary-prone behavior pattern, blood pressure, employment, and socioeconomic status in women. *Journal of Psychosomatic Research,* 1978, *22,* 79-87.

Weichman, G. H., and Ellis, A. L. A study of the effects of sex education on premarital petting and coital behavior. *Family Coordinator,* 1969, *18,* 231-234.

Wilson, G. T. Alcohol and human sexual behavior. *Behavior Research and Therapy,* 1977, *15,* 239-252.

Wilson, W. C. Can pornography contribute to the prevention of sexual problems? In C. B. Qualls, J. P. Wincze, and D. H. Barlow (Eds.), *The prevention of sexual disorders.* New York: Plenum Press, 1978.

Zilbergeld, B. *Male sexuality.* Boston: Little, Brown, 1978.

Zilbergeld, B., and Ellison, C. R. Desire discrepancies and arousal problems in sex therapy. In L. A. Pervin and S. R. Leiblum (Eds.), *Principles and practice of sex therapy.* New York: Guilford Press, 1980.

Zorgniotti, A. W., Rossi, G., Padula, G., and Makovsky, R. D. Diagnosis and therapy of vasculogenic impotence. *Journal of Urology,* 1980, *123,* 674-677.

Nonsexist Sexuality

Letty Cottin Pogrebin

Children, even infants, are sexual in their own fashion (Simon and Gagnon, 1969). Not only do they respond with pleasure to warm baths and baby oil, but one of the earliest things a boy baby does after the first cry is to have an erection; the girl baby's vagina lubricates within 24 hours of birth. Masturbation and almost unmistakable signs of orgasm have been identified by observers for boy and girl babies under one year (Calderone, 1974, pp. 338-339). Many men and some women testify that their first remembered masturbation to orgasm was at 4 or 5 years of age (Kinsey, Pomeroy, and Martin, 1948; Kinsey, Pomeroy, Martin, and Gebhard, 1953).

Recent research shows that the clitoris is physiologically analogous to the penis and that the female sex drive and orgasm are as strong as the male's, if not more so (Fisher, 1971; Gadpaille, 1975a; Masters and Johnson, 1966; Money and Tucker, 1975; Sherfey, 1972). Despite these and other similarities, "the lessons taught each sex regarding sexuality and love are opposite and contradictory" (Faunce and Phipps-Yonas, 1978).

To countermand sexist sex education, your child needs:

permission to feel sexual pleasure;

a positive attitude toward the body—her or his own and others';

the right to sexual knowledge without sex role distortion;

protection from sexual abuse.

Permission to Feel Sexual Pleasure

About 40 percent of Americans still believe masturbation is immoral and harmful (Roberts et al., 1978) even though it is openly discussed in the media, endorsed by diverse experts (Fass, 1969; Sarnoff and Sarnoff, 1979) and known to be an "all but universal habit" (Mead, 1973). Nevertheless, most of us were raised to feel guilty about it. Our parents' anger and disgust, or their less than casual attempts to distract us from our bodies, told us that "when you feel good, you are bad." Like it or not, many of us have inherited that negativism. Regardless of all the research and sex surveys attesting to the normal and beneficial nature of masturbation (Fisher, 1973; Kline-Graber and Graber, 1976), people still find it difficult to remain enlightened when it comes to their children—especially their daughters.

Today's parents punish girl babies more than boy babies when erotic activity is discovered, and, as is clear from an important Cleveland study of sexual attitudes in the family, parents think masturbation is more acceptable for sons (ages 3 to 11) than for daughters (Roberts et al., 1978).

Apparently, attitudes have not changed much in 20 years. A typical 1950s mother scolded her daughter, "Your eyes are to see with, your mouth is to eat with and that part of your body is to go to the toilet with" (Sears, Maccoby, and Levin, 1957). In the 1970s a Cleveland woman told her 5-year-old "that she would get the germs on her fingers and I would appreciate it if she would wash her hands after she was playing with herself because she could get sick from it" (Roberts et al., 1978).

Parents' discomfort arises not only from their own upbringing or their reaction to unbridled sexual expression in such small "innocent" humans, but also from the notion that it is their responsibility to civilize the child's body and teach control of its "animal" leanings. Thus, taming masturbation is lumped together with toilet-training, teaching acceptable eating habits and other social controls (Fisher and Fisher, 1976).

Whatever its origins, parents in general cannot conceal their discomfort from their children or overcome it by sheer force of will. It needs to be reasoned away. Since science has no definite answers about the effects on children of their parents' responses to masturbation (Sears, 1979), we must be guided by experience and common sense.

Girls who do not masturbate at all are unlikely to discover that they have a clitoris, "the small organ of erectile tissue that plays an important role in every female orgasm" (Boston Women's Health Book Collective, 1973). In most families, the clitoris is never seen and rarely even named. Not one parent in the Cleveland survey reported mentioning the clitoris to either daughter or son. Boys experience their genitals differently, partly because the penis is held and observed during urination, and easily stimulated, and partly because of the masculine stereotype.

Only after their sons are old enough to be expected to make heterosexual connections do parents begin to object to male masturbation, because they associate it with homosexuality (Simon and Gagnon, 1976). Until then, boys are believed to have pent-up "animal" sexual energy for which childhood masturbation is an acceptable outlet—so acceptable, in fact, that many boys are comfortable masturbating in front of their friends (Gagnon, 1979; Gagnon and Simon, 1973).

For the boy, then, self-stimulation is seen as a phase, a socially validated, parentally condoned rehearsal for eventual heterosexual activism. By the time he teams up with a girl, a boy has learned that male sexuality needs no object, is its own subject, and delivers its own orgasmic payoff. As a result, sexologists maintain, boys have "a capacity for detached sexual activity, activity where the only sustaining motive is sexual; this may actually be the hallmark of male sexuality in our society" (Simon and Gagnon, 1976).

If detached sexuality is the negative side of masturbation, the positive side is sexual self-sufficiency—and for the libido, that is like money in the bank (Faunce and Phipps-Yonas, 1978).

Girls have no such luck. First, because the clitoris is unknown or unacknowledged by parents and peers, a girl who has found the "magic button" keeps it a secret, often thinking herself a freak of nature. She does not boast or masturbate communally because, crazy as it sounds, the female orgasm seems shamefully "unfeminine." Anything that autonomous must be "masculine."

Second, since the clitoris has no function in reproduction, and the female is so totally associated with reproduction ("girls are meant to be mothers"), the very idea of a girl's being sexual when she is not yet fertile is hard to accept. (That is why premenstrual girls and postmenopausal women are considered neuter to nearly the same degree.)

Third, parents intent on training a girl for the female role imagine their young daughter poised between two historical archetypes: the modern version of the lustful siren, the multiorgasmic "libber," whose aggressive sexuality makes men impotent; and the innocent maiden—virtuous and properly indifferent to sex. Boys as well as girls are made aware of the distinction: "We were brought up to believe that nice girls—the goddess next door—did not like sex, or at the very best would permit us to 'use' their bodies after we got married" (Barclay, 1975; Wetzsteon, 1977).

In some American communities in the 1980s, the alternatives are slightly less polarized. Most girls, even "good girls," are expected to have sex (when they are older)—but they still are not being raised to enjoy it, and certainly not all by themselves (Faunce and Phipps-Yonas, 1978).

Since traditional parents still believe chastity is a girl's only bargaining chip (college students listed it *last* among 18 criteria wanted in a mate [Meuli, 1972]) they discourage masturbation in order to reduce her libido, to assure her chastity, and to make her eligible for a good marriage, which, in turn, is necessary for legitimate female sexuality.

A "good girl" is supposed to be good at servicing others, not the self. A good girl is flirtatious, not carnal; sexy, not sexual; affectionate, not orgasmic. Twisting Daddy around her little finger is "feminine," but putting that little finger to erotic uses is not.

Once a daughter completes puberty, however, parental policies change. Now, promiscuity is the calamity for girls and homosexuality the stigma for boys. Therefore, whereas parents would rather their sons fornicate than masturbate, they prefer masturbation to premarital intercourse for their daughters (Roberts et al., 1978). After all, the sexually self-sufficient virgin can still be a madonna.

Girls' sexuality has been sabotaged with unfortunate success. While nearly 100 percent of American boys (virgin or not) have experienced orgasm by age 18, only 40 percent of American girls have had the same pleasure. To live two decades of one's life without ever utilizing the body's hormonal fuel and orgasmic fervor is like having healthy eyes and never opening them.

The consequences are not minor. Early sexual deprivation may cause physical damage in the sensory system and parts of the central nervous system (Money, 1980). If she has little or no masturbatory outlet, and if her sexual activity is confined to petting, the young girl is prone to vasocongestion, which has been found to cause cystic changes in the breasts, ovaries, and uterus (Vaughter, 1976). Sexual deprivation after puberty has been correlated with adult inability to reach orgasm (Kinsey et al. 1953; Rook and Hammen, 1977). Socialized from infancy to inhibit and repress their sexuality, women cannot just switch to uninhibited enjoyment as the changing culture or their husbands dictate (Rubin, 1976).

Wardell Pomeroy, coauthor of the Kinsey reports, prescribes masturbation as a matter of health routine:

Girls who have orgasm when they are young—as early as three or four—but anywhere along in preadolescence, have the easiest time having orgasm in marriage, or as an adult. It's a real learning experience. (Pomeroy and Arnow, 1977)

To give your children permission to feel pleasure, be matter-of-fact about masturbation; stay silent if your personal style makes that the most comfortable positive response, or be affirmative and comment, "I'll bet that feels good." Either reaction says, "It's all right. We approve."

Later you can attach the word to the act. Explain what is happening in the child's body. Talk, point, draw pictures, identify your son's erection by name, differentiate your daughter's clitoris, urethra, and vagina. (Some women illustrate anatomical discussions with their own bodies. It is my feeling that, though a mother should never hide her body, mature female genitalia are too different from those of a young girl to serve as a relevant educational model.) Under age 5, girls seem comfortable opening their own labia (vaginal lips) to inspect the vulva and have their questions answered. Older girls can be encouraged to examine their own genitals with the aid of a hand mirror in the privacy of their rooms, and to ask questions later. For children of all ages, make available books that show or discuss the clitoris as well as other genital parts (see Appendix A for a list of books).

Many parents believe it is wrong to volunteer sex information. I find it absurd *not* to. How can we expect kids to raise these sensitive topics themselves in our repressed culture? They may not know what they should know, or they may already be too ashamed to admit what they *do* know. They need us to initiate discussion and give guidelines; tell them where and when children can feel free to masturbate and when it will lead to embarrassment; establish that pleasure seeking is a private but normal activity—so normal that it even has a code of appropriate locales; teach the wisdom of discretion, since some people are upset by masturbation and might even punish the child for it; talk about how orgasms are good for the human body and how everyone is entitled to have them.

For girls, especially, your talk can be their ticket to sexual sanity. Sex counselors were amazed when a group of 13-year-old girls submitted a long list of questions about sex of which the first two were "Do any girls masturbate" and "Does masturbation harm intercourse" (Calderone, 1978).

Perversely, masturbation—one of the biggest subjects on kids' minds along with V.D., wet dreams, and menstruation—is among the last subjects parents discuss with their children (Thornburg, 1974). Do not be one of those who would rather explain pregnancy and birth to a 6-year-old than talk about the penis, clitoris, and orgasms that refer directly to the sexuality of the child (Roberts et al., 1978).

A Positive Attitude toward the Body—His or Her Own and Others'

The second contribution you can make to children's libidos is to teach them to accept and like the human body as conscientiously as you teach them to conceal it. "Children want to know what the other sex looks like. Children want to know what bigger people look like...and they want to know for sure" (Hymes, 1977). By 18 months of age, babies show great interest in anatomy. They inspect one another during diaper changes or in the nursery school bathroom (Galenson and Roiphe, 1976). They check out the bottoms of their dolls, pets, and stuffed animals. Before long, they are asking impertinent questions in loud voices on crowded buses. With their friends they play "doctor" or "marriage." They experiment: girls try to urinate standing up; boys squat. They pretend: boys puff out their tummies and say, "I'm having a baby;" girls put a stick between their legs and sing, "I have a pee-nus." Such "preoccupation" with male and female anatomy is natural and good. If a child was as actively inquisitive about architecture or horticulture, you would think you had a genius in the family. Why not be as positive about sexual curiosity?

Use children's "mistakes" and malapropisms as conversation openers. Create opportunities for comparative anatomy lessons. Let girls and boys peek at one another, have sleep-over dates, and bathe together when they are small. Arrange visits so they can watch a baby being changed or watch their friends going to the toilet or getting undressed. "Your aim is not to keep children apart because they might become curious. Your aim is to bring them together because you know they are" (Hymes, 1977, p.6). Children are students, not voyeurs. Do not panic if you happen upon show-and-tell between a brother and sister. (Why should pornographers be able to co-opt the genitals? Looking and learning from one another need be no more obscene than listening to each other's heartbeats through a stethoscope.)

Visual familiarity in the very young years, when children are matter-of-fact about their bodies and unconcerned about privacy, might make the vulva less frightening or "funny looking" than it has been for past generations, and might establish that what girls have is just as substantial as what boys have. Keep an ear tuned for phallocentric bias. If a girl says, "He has a penis and I don't," you might answer, "Right. But you have a vulva, clitoris, and vagina, and he doesn't." Define the female by what is there, not by what is not. We do not say the face has eyes, a nose, and a nonnose; we name the mouth and all its wondrous properties. "Mostly inside," like the mouth and female genitalia, and "mostly outside," like the nose and male genitalia, should be facts, not judgments.

Girls actually learn the correct anatomical labels for the male sex organs sooner than they learn their own. Only 8 women in 100 remembered knowing the right names for female genitalia when they were children; the rest learned euphemisms or nonsense names (like "your nasty" or "down there"), or inaccurate designations, such as calling the entire genital area the vagina (Gartrell and Mosbacher, 1979; Roberts et al., 1978). (If she learns that the tiny urinary opening is the vagina, a girl may well be appalled when someone tells her babies come out of the vagina.) Parents' failure to acknowledge female genitals, says Harriet Lerner (1975), is a key cause of female sexual difficulties:

Because neither girl nor boy [is] informed that the clitoris is an important part of "what girls have," this organ may unconsciously (and even consciously) be experienced as a small and inadequate penis rather than a valid, feminine part of the growing girl's sexuality…an unconscious message that her parents do not want her to achieve sexual pleasure and genital fulfillment. It is as if mother and father are saying "The vulva (including the clitoris) is not important, must not be spoken of nor thought about; it does not exist." (pp. 5-6)

Lerner concludes that what makes girls devalue their sex and diminish their sexuality is not the "mysterious and concealed nature of the female anatomy" but the mysterious and concealed nature of our communication about it.

Family Nudity

Healthy acceptance of the body would be more likely for children if nudity were less a problem for their parents. In the Cleveland study, the majority of parents said, "Nudity is bad." They tell their children, "You should be careful of who sees your body," a warning fathers most often gave to daughters (Roberts et al., 1978). Parents more readily leave boy babies naked (often admiring their "equipment") but cover up girls in the presence of strangers, as if "to instill in them from the start a so-called innate sense of modesty" (Belotti, 1976, p. 43).

That modesty is made, not born. From the time the chest of a 2-year-old is covered with a bikini bra, through years of instruction to keep her legs crossed, girls learn to show enough skin and contours to keep boys interested, but not so much that they think her the wrong kind of girl. She learns the paradox of female existence: her body incarnates both innocence and evil—and a millimeter of exposed flesh can make the difference. Good girl/bad girl. Good girls show themselves only to their husbands, and good women teach the rules to their daughters; thus does modesty keep female sexuality in check from one generation to the next.

The boy, on the other hand, is allowed to display his favored male body in infancy, but not as he grows older. Admiring one's own image is "feminine," nonproductive, unmanly. After all, Narcissus was a weakling. Only in homosexual subcultures is male nakedness overtly appreciated, and then usually in its more glorified forms. For most males, it is as if the adult penis is too prized and too vulnerable to be exhibited—as if men fear comparison, exposure, and judgment, even from their kids.

A friend of our daughter's confessed her father has never been unclothed in the presence of his children, and says she is terrified of the time when she will "have to" see a naked man. A 6-year-old boy who asked to look at his father to satisfy a question about the penis met the man's uneasy refusal. Looking might "cause trouble," said the father. The boy might "get the wrong idea" (Roberts et al., 1978, p. 26).

Actually, boys get the wrong idea from concealment: "I never saw his cock, limp or hard. I wish I had. For lack of a real look-see, I substituted a vision in which it became a monstrous engine, a veritable battering ram." (Herndon, 1978, p. 12). The fig leaf is passed from father to son. The once proud, naked boy joins the secret fraternity of men whose oath demands that the presence of the penis be heralded but the proportions of the penis be shrouded in awe and mystery.

Children of both sexes are confused by parents' ambivalence. Fathers who read *Playboy* and mothers who wear low-cut dresses are often shy violets about their own natural, naked bodies. Well over half of the surveyed parents said they have trouble undressing or using the bathroom in front of a child (Roberts et al., 1978). Many admit they avoid nudity specifically to evade their children's questions about sex (Roberts et al., 1978).

A century of Victorian, religious, and psychological prohibitions have left a mark on parents and experts alike (Kinsey et al., 1948). Many fear that parent nudity may overstimulate children (Dodson, 1974; Fass, 1969; Spock, 1976), that a child's castration anxieties may be aroused (Selzer, 1974), or that the Oedipal attraction to the parent might inhibit children's heterosexual development (Coplan, 1978; Salk, 1972; Weissberger, 1979).

Little boys may feel small and weak in comparison with their big fathers....To be repeatedly reminded by the sight of the father's naked body that they are smaller may emphasize over and over again inner feelings of inferiority and resentment despite reassurances that they will grow up to be as big as daddy. (Selzer, 1974, p. 9)

How familiar. Rather have them imagine the battering ram than expose the real organ. In the guise of protecting children, are we merely protecting ourselves from being seen on a human scale? Are we also unwittingly perpetrating the myth of the modest maiden and the phallic god?

Despite the highly charged connotations of the sexual portions of our bodies, seeing one's father's penis and testicles need not necessarily make a little boy feel hopelessly inferior, any more than seeing Daddy's larger hands or feet makes his son feel doomed to lifelong littleness. Children understand that they grow larger with age. Boys assume their sex organs will grow along with the rest of them, unless *we* isolate the penis and make it mythic. Alayne Yates (1978) comments, "As a culture we remain preoccupied with penis size and penis envy. When will we begin systematically to develop penis pride in our boys and feelings of clitoral worth in our girls?" (p. 30).

If taboos against parent-child nakedness are supposed to guard against incest, sexual deviation and turmoil, why do Western societies have so much incest and sexual deviation, and so many crowded mental institutions?

Among 250 cultures studied, ours is one of the three most restrictive (Murdock, 1960). Millions of us have honored the taboo against family nudity, and yet we are not a generation of psychosexually healthy people. It is time for an alternative.

Many experts (Flaste, 1976) dispute the standard warnings about family nudity: Gloria Friedman (personal communication) says, "If a kid is overstimulated it's because the parents are sending out sexual vibes, not because they're naked on the way to the shower. Children raised in more permissive cultures, or even in American nudist colonies where the body is natural and accepted, seem to suffer no unusual sexual problems. It isn't nudity but our *attitude* toward the body, or parents' sexual hanky-panky with their children, that creates the problems."

Robert Gould (personal communication) blames popular culture for making nudity prurient. "Pornography, X-rated movies, and popular indoctrination that isolates breasts or buttocks make it difficult to normalize nudity in natural family settings," he says. "But a parent who gets coy or tries to hide the body when children happen upon him or her dressing or coming from the bathroom indicates that there is something dirty or wrong about it." Warren J. Gadpaille (1975b), himself a conservative psychoanalyst, says this about parental nudity:

Data from other cultures [do] not support the fear of emotional damage, nor does information gathered informally from sexually well-adjusted Western adults, who frequently recall the bodily freedom of their parents during their early years as a major source of their comfortable acceptance of their own physical sexuality....

Both common sense and authoritative reasoning lead to the conclusion that casual and natural parental nudity is not only harmless but beneficial. (pp. 101-102)

Common sense tells us that concealment negates body positivism, and mystery makes for estrangement. If our bodies are to be lovable to one another, females and males must become physically familiar and unfrightening. This can happen most easily if parents are comfortable in their nakedness. If a mother's body is concealed during a child's observant years, he or she is left with only those exaggerated memories of her body as it appeared in an infant world, when mother was the nurturing-denying, omnipotent "center of everything the infant wants and feels drawn to, fears losing and feels threatened by" (Dinnerstein, 1976, p. 93).

Instead, the casual occasional sight of her body year after year may help children make a more gradual transition from mother-as-manna to mother-as-woman to woman-as-human. By the same token, the sight of the father's body demythologizes the penis. Together and in contrast, the truth of both parents' bodies spares children upsetting fantasies and fears.

I am suspicious of a culture that hides from children the factual evidence that girls and boys are different but spends so much energy embellishing the sex *role* differences. Why not let our bodies speak for themselves, instead of making pink and blue or dolls and trucks define our genders? Casual but observable family nudity gives children a physical reality check for their own gender identity clarification process. Parental nudity invites young children to ask questions and draw conclusions about differences and samenesses (Church, 1973; Neill, 1960; Pomeroy, 1974) and guarantees the older child that puberty comes to all who wait, that sexual maturity runs in your family. Family nudity gives children a nonsexual, nonthreatening context within which to get used to what the other sex looks like in finished form, and what they might look like fully grown.

Nudity is not just for learning; it creates good feelings too. From the time my children crawled until about age 6, they enjoyed a daily 15-minute period before their baths when they could run around the house, play, or lounge while completely undressed. "Naked time," as we called it, was a time for joyful sensual abandon, and we were kind of sorry when it gave way to their sense of privacy (and to the demands of homework).

When that moment of modesty arrives, you will know it by a clear signal: the sound of doors closing (Flaste, 1976). During the middle school years, most children begin to need privacy just as they need space in which to define the boundaries of the self (Boston Women's Health Book Collective, 1973; Neill, 1960). They will refuse to let parents bathe them, or to be seen naked by brothers and sisters. They might ask everyone in the family to be more circumspect about nudity. Honor their wishes. Privacy is not the same as secrecy. Privacy means you can close the door of your own bedroom; secrecy means refusing to acknowledge that parents make love or kids masturbate behind that closed door. Secrecy is founded on sexual shame, but privacy recognizes individual needs and respects them. It is important that everyone in your family knows the difference.

If you can accept healthy sexual curiosity and family nakedness, your child should be well on the way to a positive body image. But the issue of good looks introduces a sexist stumbling block.

Beauty and Body Pride

In our culture, "what is beautiful is good" (Hildebrandt and Fitzgerald, 1979). That is, attractive individuals are believed to have more good qualities than unattractive individuals. As a result of their looks, they receive better treatment from parents, teachers, and friends, which in turn helps them feel better about themselves.

Since people expect girls to be more attractive than boys (Rosenbaum, 1979), a girl has to be even more attractive, on a scale of 1 to 10, in order to enjoy the same treatment that accrues to a boy who is less attractive according to that same scale. In other words, to be called "cute" and to be treated with special adoration, a baby boy might be average looking, but a baby girl must be exceptionally attractive. Therefore, right from birth, say researchers, "Male and female infants may receive differential treatment as a function of the interaction between their sex and their perceived attractiveness" (Hildebrandt and Fitzgerald, 1979, p. 480). Subliminally, girls learn how important it is to be pretty, but boys learn that sheer good looks are not enough, nor quite appropriate. ("Such gorgeous eyes belong on a girl.")

A boy's appearance is not for others. A girl is told, "Look pretty for daddy" and by inference, "Look pretty for men." Sons are never haunted by a parent's admiration for the handsomeness of the boy around the corner, but daughters hear raves about this beauty or that, about how homely so-and-so's daughter is, or how stunning a niece looked in her party dress.

Day after day, year after year, female appearance is what wins notice and approval. It does not take long for a little girl to ask herself not "How do I feel?" but "How do I look?" To wonder not "Who do I like?" but "Who will like me?" To become so completely an object of erotic focus that her "female sexuality gets twisted into narcissism." So relentlessly is she trained to think of her physical surface as both target and source of all sexual interest that in the sex act the adult female almost makes love to herself vicariously, through the excitement she arouses in a male (Firestone, 1970; Stannard, 1972).

The girl's preoccupation with her face, figure, and clothing comes with other previously mentioned risks and burdens: the retreat from intellectual success, dread of aging, and obsession with body weight. Body pride and self-esteem are nearly unattainable for someone whose inner voice is always gnawing: "Will they like me? Am I too fat? Is this skirt too short? Should I curl my hair? Should I shave my legs? Am I as pretty as other girls?" (Rubin, 1978, p. 64).

Comparisons and envy poison female friendship as surely as the apple poisoned Snow White (Pogrebin, 1972). While boys compete for honor and achievement, girls compete for boys' admiration.

Before puberty, girls seem self-accepting—"as if they had not yet turned an observing eye to their own body" (Rosenbaum, 1979, p. 240). But between 11 and 18, most white, middle-class girls learn to dislike their weight, complexion, nose, ears, body hair, and breasts (Rosenbaum, p. 242).

When asked what they *did* like about their bodies, many girls answered that their hair was their best feature, their eyes were second, and hardly anything was in third place. In contrast, a 14-year-old boy liked these things about his body: "It's alive, it's smart, it moves; I can talk, I can see, I have all the senses" (Rosenbaum, p. 241).

Such reactions reflect the different conditioning of female and male physicality—"girls in the direction of being observed, boys in the direction of action, of the body as machine, in keeping with our cultural stereotypes" (Rosenbaum, 1979, p. 241).

It is almost a blatant quid pro quo: "feminine" upbringing yields cosmetic beauty and sexual polish without core body image, while "masculine" upbringing with its emphasis on athletics and activity "seemingly goes hand in hand with healthy ego development" and a realistic body image. The girls who were active in sports or who danced regularly generally felt better about their bodies than did the nonathletic girls (Rosenbaum, 1979, p. 243).

Long-term studies have found that people who are most satisfied with their bodies tend to have the most confidence, self-esteem, and satisfying sex lives (Latorre, 1975; LoPiccolo and Heiman, 1977). People who feel good about themselves "are not available for exploitation" (Jerome, 1978). Every girl might be unavailable for exploitation if the feminine stereotype did not stand in the way of her self-esteem.

The masculine stereotype also impinges on some boys' self-images, though to a far lesser extent. Boys may want to be tall, to have a muscular physique, and to have a large penis (Dwyer and Mayer, 1968-1969; Frazier and Lisonbee, 1950; Mussen and Jones, 1958a). If this ideal goads your teenager, he should know that in the estimation of most females, the least important physical attributes for a male are height, muscles, and penis size (Safilios-Rothschild, 1974).

As a parent you alone cannot defeat the "he-man" ideal or beauty contest mentality, but you can accept your child's appearance for what it is. Compliment girls and boys profusely, but keep your adjectives genderless and free of stereotype. "You look great!" or "Your hair is so marvelously healthy looking!" or "That shirt is terrific with your coloring!" endorses the total person far better than "You look so manly in that suit," or "That coat makes you look so dainty and feminine."

Compliment a daughter for her radiant health and physical *effectiveness,* not for her physical *effect* on others. Tell her she is beautiful when no one else will—when she is concentrating intensely, or working up a sweat. Tell your son he looks wonderful when he is gently rocking the baby to sleep or when he is feeling tired and small. In the presence of both sexes, express your admiration for women and men in public life who fall short of the body beautiful but whose dynamism or humanity eclipses the wan and sexist American ideal.

The Right to Sexual Knowledge without Sex Role Distortion

The usual answer to "How do you make a baby?" goes something like this: "When a man and woman love each other, they get married and the daddy puts his penis inside the mommy's vagina and plants a seed and it grows inside the mommy's tummy and 9 months later, a baby comes out." Although it sounds right, this tale is rife with misinformation.

Regardless of how young the child, no basic sex education conversation should give the impression that the anatomical sex differences are solely for making babies. This is not just a half-truth, it is a lie. People have sex without love, marriage, or procreational intent as kids learn soon enough from news about rapes in the neighborhood, or from witnessing a friend's mother share a bedroom with a man who is not her husband.

People make few babies in a lifetime, but they make a lot of love. Let your children think of their parents as lovers. Let them know that male-female sex is primarily for fun. You can add your own morality to that, but do not misrepresent the physical truth. Ask yourself whether, in hiding your sexual intercourse from your children (which I happen to believe wise), you may also be inadvertently hiding gestures of affection, a stroke of a wife's or lover's cheek, or a hug that communicates the warmth of adult physical love without its clinical detail. When was the last time your children saw their parents kiss?

A few more suggestions: do not call the uterus a "tummy," or give Daddy all the moves and let his seed upstage her egg. Instead of father "puts," it could be that mother "takes" the penis into her vagina. A verb can change the whole dynamic of the act.

What happens when your children ask for sexual rather than reproductive information? Do your moral standards have double standards? Most parents say they want their children to know about erotic activity by the time they are teenagers. Yet only 12 parents in 100 have ever talked about sexual intercourse to their children, and fewer than 4 in 100 have ever discussed contraception (Roberts et al., 1978).

What have they discussed? They have "cautioned their sons about not acting like a sissy and their daughters about not acting like a tomboy, or warned their children about sex play and child molesters. On most other aspects of sexual learning...parents are remarkably silent" (Roberts et al., pp. 67, 79). Not because they are prudish, I think, but because they are confused, uncertain, and limited by their own upbringing. They want to have heart-to-heart talks but they are not sure what they believe, and what they fear (Roberts et al., pp. 51, 60). They want their children to know more but not to *do* more (Roberts et al., p. 63).

They believe their daughters should have sexual and emotional fulfillment, but are afraid they'll become promiscuous and unmarriageable. They want their sons to be gentle, open and emotionally expressive but are afraid the boys will become sissies or homosexuals. (White, 1978)

You cannot have it both ways. You must give up sex role stereotypes if you want to help your children prepare for happy, healthy, and responsible sex lives. You cannot hope your daughters will find emotional fulfillment if other parents are not raising sons who can give it. You cannot tell your daughter to be good and your son to be careful.

A mismatch is fated for women and men in the future if girls continue to be programmed for romance without sex and boys for sex without emotion. (Or as one boy put it, "To me, fucking *is* feeling.") A boy will not learn to be open and affectionate if his father is not (70 percent of men rarely or never hug anyone), or if his parents stand ready to call him a sissy (Roberts et al., 1978), or if affection does not win any points from his friends.

Friends become the sex experts when parents offer little more than silence. Like the blind leading the blind, kids teach each other (Elias and Gebhard, 1969; Gordon and Dickman, 1977; Hopkins, 1977):

masturbation gives you pimples or brain damage;

virgins cannot use tampons;

girls cannot urinate when wearing a diaphragm;

boys get "blue balls" if they get excited but do not reach orgasm;

no one gets pregnant the first time;

you cannot get pregnant standing up;

you can get pregnant from a toilet seat;

you can only get pregnant if you do it during your period;

a girl loses her virginity when she masturbates to orgasm;

if there is penetration but no ejaculation, you are still a virgin.

Friends misrepresent sex. Parents repress sex. The culture exploits sex. How can children make sense of their bodies, especially when such sensitive issues as puberty, menstruation, and contraception are involved?

Puberty

Boys who mature early tend to become self-confident adults. Girls who develop early become self-conscious, but late-maturing girls grow up to be more active, buoyant, cheerful, sociable, and prone to leadership (Landis, 1973; Mussen and Jones, 1958b; Nicholi, 1978).

The discrepancy makes sense. Physical manhood gives a boy more power, size, and sexual agency. But the arrival of physical womanhood seems bereft of bonuses. Menstruation is seen as a burden. Breasts are always too big or too small, the butt of jokes or the object of obsession. As soon as a daughter is capable of maternity, many parents limit her activities and oversee her friends and her whereabouts as never before (Katz, 1979). No wonder girls are less than ecstatic about early sexual development.

By inverse sexist reasoning, the late-maturing boy child suffers the agonies of hell. In a world that expects male superiority in all things, it is bad enough that girls are *normally* 2 years ahead of boys in physical development during adolescence. If, on top of that, a boy's growth is slower than average, his "emasculation" is compounded.

How can parents cushion the blows of puberty's capricious timetable without patronizing sex stereotypes?

Compliment your children's appearance no matter how awkward or clumsy they appear. Reassure them that almost *everything* is temporary or transitional. Tell stories of your own adolescent experience.

Avoid comparisons with other children. Renounce sarcasm or teasing about puberty-related phenomena. Shaving 22 whiskers, losing his voice mid-sentence, or waking up to wet bedsheets: all are serious matters to an adolescent boy. Advise and explain without laughter.

Characterize puberty as maturity, "a consolidation of your mental, emotional, and physical powers." Do not present it to your daughter as "Now your body can make a baby." Puberty should enhance your children's feelings about themselves in the present. Why make it into a utilitarian event with relevance only to a girl's future?

Find a sensitive (preferably female) gynecologist to answer your daughter's puberty-related questions in the privacy of the doctor's office. I gathered a group of four girls—Abigail and Robin and their best friends—for a 2-hour session with Dr. Marcia Storch, and the girls reported how relieved they were to learn how *normal* they were, no matter what "horrible" truth they confessed about their bodies or their sexual fantasies and fears.

Do not penalize your daughter for becoming a woman. That means do not withdraw your affection and trust. A father should neither avert his eyes nor fixate on a girl's physical development; only admiration and casual acknowledgment are appropriate. A mother should not sigh that a woman's body is a "sacred vessel," *or* "a vale of tears." Do not make puberty the occasion to object to a daughter's clothes or to restrict her social life. Do not assume every boy is after her body, or she may wonder if that is all she has going for her.

Menstruation

Although girls may begin menstruating as early as age 9, by 12 (the average age of menarche [Zacharias, Rand, and Wurtman, 1976]), about half still have learned nothing about this major physiological event (Roberts et al., 1978). Even among mothers who remembered how frightened they had been by menstruation, few had explained it to their 12-year-old daughters ("Moms Are Still Mum about Sex," 1979). One young woman remembers: "My mother said to me, 'Well, dear, you're going to be going through a change.' That was the end of the subject. I had no idea what kind of change...whether I was going to turn into a frog or what."

When menstruation is discussed, it is often in derogatory terms: getting sick, unwell, the curse, on the rag (Ernster, 1975). It is packaged with myths—menstruating women attract reptiles, kill wildlife, give babies cramps, bring bad luck in coal mines (Snow and Johnson, 1978)—prohibitions—against baths, shampoos, swimming, sports, and sexual intercourse (Paige, 1977)—and other frightening or debilitating misinformation—blood loss is weakening; every woman gets premenstrual tension, and so on (Weitz, 1977).

The impressions given to both boys and girls about menstruation are predictably in keeping with stereotypic feminine sex role socialization (Ernster, 1975): girls are physically vulnerable, emotionally moody, and mentally irrational; pain is the lot of a woman; hormones will triumph.

"What you expect is often what you get," notes one scientist. Women who are told they are premenstrual have been found to suffer from more severe distress than those who are made to believe they are between periods. What is more, female socialization propaganda has a measurable somatic effect: girls who test highest on conventional femininity scales also report the most menstrual discomfort (Douvan and Adelson, 1966). Therefore,

Do not give your daughter any ideas. Although many adolescents experience menstrual cramps, many do not. Do not condition your daughter for fragility or suffering. Cope with her symptoms, not your expectations.

Make it clear that physical and sexual activity, baths, and sports are not only possible but beneficial. Let her know that "an American Olympic swimmer recently broke a world record and won three gold medals during the height of her period" (Brody, 1978), and that life can go on as usual for her, too.

Explain everything when your daughter is 8 years old, and review the whole subject at least once a year thereafter if she does not ask about it again. When her breasts and pubic hair seem to be developing is the time to prepare her for the logistics of getting her period in public and for the use of sanitary protection. She should know that virgins can wear tampons; and for the sake of her mobility and comfort, persuade her to give them a try. Help her experiment with the various tampon styles and offer to assist in learning how to insert them. (It can dramatically change a girl's life to wear her protection on the inside, where it is forgettable.)

Fathers can describe menstruation as well as mothers, though mothers add that "I know how it feels" element. But fathers must show an accepting attitude toward menstruation—not gag at the sight of a bloody panty and not insist that tampons or napkins be kept out of his view.

Menstruation should be explained to boys, too. The more time they have to get used to the facts of female physiology, the more likely they will develop the same casual, accepting attitude exhibited (one hopes) by their fathers.

I am always glad when one of my children notices me taking a tampon with me in my briefcase, or hears Bert remind me to pack the tampons in my tennis bag. The unspoken message to children is, "Mommy has her period but it is no big deal—it is nothing to be afraid of, it is nothing to hide."

Of course, menstruation *is* a big deal. It marks sexual maturity and reproductive fertility, awesome realities in a girl's life. Many women experience premenstrual syndrome (tension, headaches, pain, irritability), and cramps (dysmenorrhea), usually on the first day of their periods (Dalton, 1969). One gynecologist estimates that just under 50 percent of his patients report symptoms of real discomfort (Debrovner, 1979), which matches the national data (Gomez, 1972). No one should suggest that these are imaginary or psychosomatic reactions. They are hormonally determined and the more painful ones may require special adaptation or medication. But the start of 3 or 4 decades of ovulation need not be the end of freedom. If your daughter feels menstruation is a sickness or a mystery, dirty or weakening, it can adversely affect her body image, her sexuality, her dietary habits, even her adult attitudes toward medication, contraception, and family planning (Larsen, 1963; Snow and Johnson, 1978).

The notion of menstruation as a mystery is a profoundly androcentric (male-centered) notion—one might just as well speak about the mystery of the dry male body if one took the female body as the norm rather than the deviation. (Eichler, 1975, p. 922)

One psychologist insists, "It is an extraordinary jump for women to accept the idea that bleeding means health" (Bardwick, 1971). I have not found that to be true. "Health" is an ever changing concept. It is also remarkably responsive to cultural values. (A century ago, the "healthy" people were fat, not slim.) Bleeding *can* mean health if female body equals human norm. Bleeding can mean health if our daughters understand the physiology of menstruation, if they control it rather than let it incapacitate them, and if we help them celebrate it both as proof of nonpregnancy now and potential for childbearing later. Can anything be healthier than that?

Sexual Activity and Contraception

"That male adolescents may 'sow their wild oats' premaritally while females save themselves for marriage is one of the most durable aspects of sexual polarization" (Gallatin, 1975, p. 260). That double standard is also laced with hypocrisy: whether or not mothers themselves had sex before marriage, they still disapprove of it for girls up to three times more often than for boys (Cannon and Long, 1971). One mother was barely joking when she quipped that her son could have sex at 18, but her daughter should "wait until she's 43" (Roberts et al., 1978, p. 59). Another mother defended having never told her 12-year-old daughter about intercourse and birth control because "she's not into that yet" (Roberts et al., 1978,

p. 57). Of course, when she is "into" sex it may be too late for a parent to help her out of it without scars.

Fact: In a representative group of 100 teenagers, 3 girls and 10 boys will have intercourse for the first time before age 12. Nearly 40 percent of all 13- to 15-year-olds are no longer virgins (Gadpaille, 1975a; Reinhold, 1977).

Fact: The younger a girl is at first intercourse, the more likely she is to become pregnant (*New York Times* study, 1979).

Fact: At least 1 teenager in 10 (about a million girls) will become pregnant this year (30,000 of them will be under 15 years old). Half of these pregnancies will occur during the first 6 months of sexual activity (Alan Guttmacher Institute, 1979; Sackman-Reed, 1979), activity that parents often believe does not exist.

Fact: Eight out of 10 unwanted pregnancies happen to girls who use no contraception (Brody, 1978).

Fact: Up to 95 percent of all parents have *never* discussed contraception with their children prior to puberty (Roberts et al., 1978).

Let me be blunt. Parents who fail to provide contraceptive information to both girls and boys are guilty of child abuse. Having a child while still a child abuses a girl's body and ruins her life. "Teenage pregnancy is not only a health risk for the mother and the child, it is a major cause of high school drop-outs, unemployment, and poverty" (Jaffe, 1978).

Why are Americans willing to tolerate an epidemic of teen pregnancies rather than provide their children with simple contraceptive information? Why are parents unable to face the truth of a daughter's sexual activism even at the risk of destroying her future? Because virginity—chastity as an institution—helps men assure their paternity, which is essential to the patriarchal transfer of power. But making contraception openly available to girls removes the threat of pregnancy that previously policed female chastity and instead accepts nonreproductive sex as a female prerogative. This weakens the links between virginity and "femininity" and between female sexuality and maternity, effectively destroying that sex role imperative: girls are meant to be mothers.

Rather than break the back of the patriarchy, we allow one million girl children to become mothers each and every year (Fosburgh, 1977).

Suppose you agree with Calderone (1978) that "Babies should not be used as a 'punishment' for sexually active girls." But you also disapprove of sex before marriage, or sex without love, or sex before a certain age, or whatever. Then, I think, there are several points for you to ponder:

If most young people subscribe to a single standard and disregard female virginity, why do you care about it? Might you be using your daughter's chastity as a mark of your own virtue?

Have you taught your children technical virginity but neglected sexual ethics? A respected sex educator writes: "Instead of worrying about the distinctions between necking, petting, heavy petting...and real intercourse, young people would be better advised to examine their motives. After all, a boy can do wrong even by simply kissing a girl, if he knows that she is not ready for it and that it upsets her. In other words, it is not the type of sexual activity that counts, but the intentions behind it" (Haeberle, 1978, p. 172).

Are you unconsciously programming your daughter for the kind of "feminine" passivity that leads to just the promiscuous behavior you fear most? Raise a girl on romantic notions of being swept off her feet, and she may be prey to any sweet-talking seducer. If premeditated sex (using contraception) strikes her as incompatible with the female role, but being "taken" excuses her sexual activity, she is the perfect potential victim of early pregnancy. It is the "good girl" who does not ask her parents for birth control advice and who believes only boys should be ready for sex.

Do you know that sexual sophistication reduces rather than increases teen sex activity? "Young people who talk with their parents about sex and contraception tend to delay sexual intercourse and to use contraception. When they do enter into relationships, they tend to be more mature and less exploitive" (Gordon and Snyder, 1978, p. 32).

Have you objectified your daughter's body? Warnings such as "No boy will buy the cow if he can get the milk free" imply that a girl is a piece of property with finite and depleting value. Parents cannot constantly monitor boys' access to a daughter's body. They can only make her strong enough to define her own boundaries and self-respecting enough to think herself more valuable than a cow.

Eventually you will find that truth unavoidable—as well as nonsexist: the sex drive is comparable for both sexes and their levels of heterosexual activity (kissing, necking, petting) show "remarkable similarity" (Currier, 1977; Klemesrud, 1978; Vener, Stewart, and Hager, 1972). Although girls, as well as boys, are "doing it," they need not do themselves damage to pay for their sexuality. They can know about sex—and be prepared for sex—and still decide not to *have* sex.

Certainly, they can refuse to be premature mothers. Girls raised to play a meaningful role in life do not "turn to a baby as a source of identity....instant adulthood, an instant role and instant femininity" (Fosburgh, 1977, p. 32). Girls raised to take responsibility for themselves are not likely to be victimized; they want more from a boy—and from a relationship—than the assurance that they satisfy.

The best sex education you can offer your children, therefore, is an anti-sex-role education. For a girl, dignity, self-respect, and unabashed authority over her own well-informed, authentic sexual self; for your daughter, goodbye to Sleeping Beauty, or "I only did it because I was drunk," or "What kind of girl will he think I am?" For a boy, good-bye to Mr. Macho, Don Juan, "Get any lately?" For your son, who is growing up alongside girls who will expect equality in the bedroom as well as in the boardroom, the new sexual ideology affirms that:

"scoring" is stealing unless a girl is as willing, as risk-free, and as sexually satisfied as he is;

"knocking up" a girl is a sign of stupidity, not virility;

"It isn't any fun that way" is no excuse for not wearing a condom;

if the responsibility for birth control is not shared, the responsibility for the pregnancy will be;

"losing respect" for a girl after sex signifies contempt for female sexuality, not morality (Kirkendall, 1970);

it is not a girl's job to restrain a boy's sex drive, or her fault if he cannot restrain himself;

his sexuality is neither so wild it cannot be controlled, nor so vulnerable it can be ruined by rejection;

he does not always have to know what to do or take charge or perform; he is masculine when he follows, as well as when he leads.

If you can communicate these ideas to your son throughout his childhood, he should be able to tell you what a 14-year-old boy told Mary Calderone after three days of discussion: "You sure taught me that there is more to sex than just doing it!" (Calderone, 1978, p. 28).

Finally, for parents who are still troubled by the issue of morality versus the risk of pregnancy, Sol Gordon seems to offer the best summation: wanting children not to have sex while at the same time giving them birth control information "is not a double message to our young people; it means simply that we respect them enough to give them our best advice, and love them enough to help them if they choose not to listen" (Gordon and Snyder, 1978, p. 33).

Protection from Sexual Abuse

After giving your child permission to feel sexual pleasure, a positive body image, and sexual knowledge without sex role distortion, the last guarantee is the hardest to make good on. Children inevitably leave the house and go out into the world. We do the best we can issuing cautions, warning children about suspicious situations, dangerous neighborhoods, not taking candy from strangers (Gordon and Dickman, 1977; Levine and Seligmann, 1973). Unfortunately, however, child abuse often begins at home where those whom children love most take advantage of their weakness and dependency.

Incest, the greatest of all family secrets, has been brought out of the closet. Books, surveys, and confessional seminars (Brady, 1979; DeFrancis, 1967; Herman and Hirshman, 1977; Rush, 1980; Thomas, 1977; Weber, 1977; Weinberg, 1955) have begun to delineate a veritable epidemic of child molestation in the home setting. The subject is far too complex and serious to explore here; however, an understanding of sexual abuse as a by-product of misogyny and male supremacy may be illuminating for the nonsexist parent (Malamuth, Feshbach, and Yaffe, 1977; Russell and Griffin, 1977).

People (usually men) sexually abuse children (usually girls) when sex becomes confused with power. As more grown women refuse to be passive and innocent, some men move to little girls who are still powerless, who can still be controlled and used, who cannot assert their will.

Frequently, when little girls complain about molestation by their brothers, uncles, neighbors, but most often by their own fathers, their reports are dismissed. This is the legacy of Freud's denial of his women patients' accounts, one after another, of having been seduced or abused by their fathers. He attributed their reports to wishful fantasy, the Electra complex of adoring daughters. To accept that all those fathers molested their little girls would have been too unspeakable, too damning of *Man*—and, by inference, of Freud's own father (Rush, 1977).

On the heels of Freud, generations of parents and doctors have discounted children's accusations, and blamed little girls for "wanting it." Like blaming the rape victim, like firing the woman member of the couple who has sex on the job, like punishing the teenage girl with pregnancy for the intercourse a boy engineered, it is always the female who pays twice—once with the original abuse, and again for "allowing" the loss of her own innocence.

I do not know how to prevent sexual molestation of children in the home or on the streets. But I believe deeply and surely that such abuse is intrinsic to gender inequality. It is a short step from the infantilized, "baby doll" woman to the female child. There is no clear boundary between patriarchal rule and following father into his bed when so ordered.

No one should be surprised when the women-and-children dyad merges and blurs in sex as it does in the family, the economy, and the minds of some men. Sexual abuse of children will not disappear until power-inequity pornography disappears, until idealization of the big man and the little girl disappears, until rape is not a hair's breadth removed from the ideal of sexual seduction, and until men cease to believe themselves emasculated by taking no for an answer from a woman, or a child (Firestone, 1970; McConahay and McConahay, 1977; Rush, 1974; Steinem, 1977).

A parent's only hope is that the autonomous, self-respecting child will not tolerate victimization and will not accept degradation as her (or his) sexual obligation. We cannot truly guarantee our children protection from sexual abuse, but perhaps we can raise sons who disavow violence as a badge of manhood, and daughters whose bodies belong to themselves and not to any man.

We have given our children life; now we must give them nonsexist sexuality to enjoy it.

References

Alan Guttmacher Institute Report. *11 million teenagers*. New York: Planned Parenthood, 1979.

Barclay, A. M. Sex and personal development in the college years. In A. Arkoff (Ed.), *Psychology and personal growth*. Boston: Allyn and Bacon, 1975.

Bardwick, J. *The psychology of women*. New York: Harper and Row, 1971.

Belotti, E. G. *What are little girls made of?* New York: Schocken Books, 1976.

Boston Women's Health Book Collective. *Our bodies, ourselves.* New York: Simon and Schuster, 1973.

Brady, K. *Father's days.* New York: Seaview Books, 1979.

Brody, J. Personal health: Menstruation. *New York Times,* May 24, 1978, p. C10.

Brody, J. Teenagers' use of contraception trend by survey to be effective. *New York Times,* June 7, 1978, p. A18.

Calderone, M. S. Eroticism as a norm. *Family Coordinator,* October 1974, *23,* 337-341.

Calderone, M. S. *Nothing less than the truth will do.* Report to Girls' Clubs of America National Seminar, Racine, Wisconsin, June 1978, p. 30.

Cannon, K. L., and Long, R. Premarital sexual behavior in the sixties. *Journal of Marriage and the Family,* 1971, *33,* 36-49.

Church, J. *Understanding your child from birth to three.* New York: Random House, 1973.

Coplan, F. (Ed.). *Parents' yellow pages.* New York: Anchor Books, Doubleday, 1978.

Currier, R. L. Debunking the double think on juvenile sexuality. *Human Behavior,* 1977, *6,* 16.

Dalton, K. *The menstrual cycle.* New York: Pantheon Books, 1969.

Debrovner, C. Personal communication, November 1979.

DeFrancis, V. (Ed.). *Sexual abuse of children.* Denver: American Humane Association, 1967.

Dinnerstein, D. *The mermaid and the minotaur.* New York: Harper and Row, 1976.

Dodson, F. *How to father.* Los Angeles: Nash, 1974.

Douvan, I., and Adelson, J. *The adolescent experience.* New York: John Wiley and Sons, 1966.

Dwyer, J., and Mayer, J. Psychological effects of variations of physical appearance during adolescence. *Adolescence,* 1968-1969, *3,* 353-380.

Eichler, M. Power and sexual fear in primitive societies. *Journal of Marriage and the Family,* 1975, *37,* 922.

Elias, J., and Gebhard, P. Sexuality and sexual learning in childhood. *Phi Delta Kappan,* 1969, *50,* 401-406.

Ernster, V. L. American menstrual expressions. *Sex Roles,* 1975, *1,* 3-13.

Fass, J. S. *How to raise an emotionally healthy child.* New York: Pocket Books, 1969.

Faunce, P. S., and Phipps-Yonas, S. Women's liberation and human sexual relations. *International Journal of Women's Studies,* 1978, *1,* 83-85.

Firestone, S. *The dialectic of sex.* New York: William Morrow, 1970.

Fisher, S. *The female orgasm.* New York: Basic Books, 1971.

Fisher, S. *Understanding the female orgasm.* New York: Bantam Books, 1973.

Fisher, S., and Fisher, R. L. *What we really know about child rearing.* New York: Basic Books, 1976.

Flaste, R. Is it harmful for children to see parents in the nude? *Medical Aspects of Human Sexuality,* 1971, *5,* 35-41.

Flaste, R. Parental nudity: Bad for youngsters? *New York Times,* September 17, 1976, p. B6.

Fosburgh, L. The make-believe world of teenage maternity. *New York Times Mag-*

azine, August 7, 1977, pp. 29-34.

Frazier, A., and Lisonbee, L. Adolescent concerns with the physique. *School Review*, 1950, *58*, 397-405.

Gadpaille, W. J. Adolescent sexuality: A challenge to psychiatrists. *Journal of American Academy of Psychoanalysis*, 1975, *3*, 168. (a)

Gadpaille, W. J. *The cycles of sex*. New York: Charles Scribner's Sons, 1975. (b)

Gagnon, J. H. The creation of the sexual in early adolescence. In J. Kagan and R. Coles (Eds.), *Twelve to sixteen: Early adolescence*. New York: W. W. Norton, 1972.

Gagnon, J. H. The interaction of gender roles and sexual conduct. In H. Katchadourian (Ed.), *Human sexuality: A comparative and developmental perspective*. Berkeley: University of California Press, 1979.

Gagnon, J. H., and Simon, W. *Sexual conduct: The social sources of human sexuality*. Chicago: Aldine, 1973.

Galenson, E., and Roiphe, H. Some suggested revisions concerning early female sexual development. *Journal of American Psychoanalytic Association*, 1976, *24*, 29-58.

Gallatin, J. *Adolescence and individuality*. New York: Harper and Row, 1975.

Gartrell, N., and Mosbacher, D. Sex differences in the naming of children's genitalia. In progress, 1979. (Obtainable from Gartrell, Beth Israel Hospital, 330 Brookline Ave., Boston, Mass. 02215.)

Gomez, J. *A dictionary of symptoms*. New York: Bantam Books, 1972.

Gordon, S., and Dickman, I. R. *Sex education: The parents' role*. Pamphlet No. 549. New York: Public Affairs Committee, 1977.

Gordon, S., and Snyder, C. Tomorrow's family. *Journal of Current Social Issues*, 1978, *15*, 31-34.

Haeberle, E. J. *The sex atlas*. New York: Seabury Press, 1978.

Herman, J., and Hirshman, L. Father-daughter incest. *Signs*, 1977, *2*, 735-756.

Herndon, V. Some surprises about male nudity. *Ms.*, March 1978, p. 12.

Hildebrandt, K. A., and Fitzgerald, H. E. Adult's perceptions of infant sex and cuteness. *Sex Roles*, 1979, *5*, 471.

Hopkins, J. R. Sexual behavior in adolescence. *Journal of Social Issues*, 1977, *33*, 81.

Hymes, J. L. *How to tell your child about sex*. Pamphlet No. 149. New York: Public Affairs Committee, 1977.

Jaffe, F. S. *Teenage pregnancies: A need for education*. Report to Girls' Clubs of America National Seminar, Racine, Wisconsin, June 1978, p. 23.

Jerome, E. *A physician's view of the adolescent woman*. Report to Girls' Clubs of America National Seminar, Racine, Wisconsin, June 1978.

Katz, P. A. The development of female identity. *Sex Roles*, 1979, *5*, 168-169.

Kinsey, A. C., Pomeroy, W. B., and Martin, C. E. *Sexual behavior in the human male*. Philadelphia: W. B. Saunders, 1948.

Kinsey, A. C., Pomeroy, W. B., Martin, C. E., and Gebhard, P. H. *Sexual behavior in the human female*. Philadelphia: W. B. Saunders, 1953.

Kirkendall, L. A. Why boys lose respect. In I. Rubin and L. A. Kirkendall (Eds.), *Sex in the childhood years*. New York: Association Press, 1970.

Klemesrud, J. Parents encounter teen age sex. *New York Times*, June 6, 1978, p. C1.

Kline-Graber, G., and Graber, B. *Women's orgasm*. New York: Popular Library, 1976.

Landis, P. H. *Coming of age: Problems of teenagers*. Pamphlet No. 234. New York: Public Affairs Committee, 1973.

Larsen, V. L. Psychological study of colloquial menstrual expressions. *Northwest Medicine*, 1963, *62*, 877.

Latorre, R. A. Body parts satisfaction and sexual preferences. *Psychological Reports*, 1975, *36*, 430.

Lerner, H. E. And what do little girls have: Some thoughts on female sexuality. *Behold the woman*. Topeka, Kansas, September 1975, 5-6.

Lerner, H. E. Parental mislabeling of female genitals as a determinant of penis envy and learning inhibitions in women. *Journal of the American Psychoanalytic Association*, 1976, *24*, 269-283.

Levine, M. I., and Seligmann, J. H. *The parents' encyclopedia*. New York: Crowell, 1973.

LoPiccolo, J., and Heiman, J. Cultural values and the therapeutic definition of sexual function and dysfunction. *Journal of Social Issues*, 1977, *33*, 166-183.

Malamuth, N. M., Feshbach, S., and Yaffe, Y. Sexual arousal and aggression: Recent experiments and theoretical issues. *Journal of Social Issues*, 1977, *33*, 110-133.

Masters, W. H. and Johnson, V. E. *Human sexual response*. Boston: Little, Brown, 1966.

McConahay, S. A., and McConahay, J. B. Sexual permissiveness, sex role rigidity and violence across cultures. *Journal of Social Issues*, 1977, *33*, 134-143.

Mead, M. *Coming of age in Samoa*. New York: William Morrow, 1973.

Meuli, J. K. In brief. *NOW Times*, August 1972, p. 2.

Moms are still mum about sex. *Human Behavior*, 1979, *8*, 58.

Money, J., and Tucker, P. *Sexual signatures*. Boston: Little, Brown, 1975.

Money, K. E. Physical damage caused by sexual deprivation in young females. *International Journal of Women's Studies*, 1980, *3*, 431-437.

Murdock, G. *Social structure*. New York: Macmillan, 1960.

Mussen, P. H., and Jones, M. C. Self-conceptions, motivations, and interpersonal attitudes of late and early maturing boys. *Child Development*, 1958, *28*, 243-256. (a)

Mussen, P. H., and Jones, M. C. The behavior-inferred motivations of late and early maturing boys. *Child Development*, 1958, *29*, 61-67. (b)

Neill, A. S. *Summerhill: A radical approach to child rearing*. New York: Hart, 1960.

New York Times study asks earlier education about sex. *New York Times*, August 28, 1979, p. C11.

Nicholi, A. M., Jr. The adolescent. In A. M. Nicholi (Ed.), *Harvard guide to modern psychiatry*. Cambridge, Mass: Harvard University Press, 1978.

Paige, K. E. Sexual pollution: Reproductive sex taboos in American society. *Journal of Social Issues*, 1977, *33*, 144-163.

Pogrebin, L. C. Competing among women. *Ms.*, July 1972, p. 78.

Pomeroy, W. *Your child and sex*. New York: Delacorte Press, 1974.

Pomeroy, W., and Arnow, P. A conversation. *Resource Guide*. San Francisco: Multi-Media Resource Center, 1977.

Reinhold, R. Birth rate among girls 15-17. Rises in puzzling 10-year trend. *New York Times*, September 21, 1977, p. 1.

Roberts, E. J. et al. *Family life and sexual learning: A study of the role of parents in the sexual learning of children.* New York: Population Education, 1978.

Rook, K. S., and Hammen, C. L. A cognitive perspective on the experience of sexual arousal. *Journal of Social Issues*, 1977, *33*, 14.

Rosenbaum, M. B. The changing body image of the adolescent girl. In M. Sugar (Ed.), *Female adolescent development.* New York: Brunner/Mazel, 1979.

Rubin, L. *Worlds of pain: Life in the working class.* New York: Basic Books, 1976.

Rubin, T. I. How teenagers can survive. *Ladies Home Journal*, July 1978, p. 64.

Rush, F. The sexual abuse of children. In N. Connell and C. Wilson (Eds.), *Rape: The first sourcebook for women.* New York: NAL, 1974.

Rush, F. The Freudian cover-up. *Chrysalis*, 1977, *1*, 33ff.

Rush, F. *The best kept secret: Sexual abuse of children.* Englewood Cliffs, N.J.: Prentice-Hall, 1980.

Russell, D. E. H., and Griffin, S. On pornography. *Chrysalis*, 1977, *4*, 11-17.

Sackman-Reed, G. Who pays the price? *NOW Times*, September/October 1979, p. 1.

Safilios-Rothschild, C. *Women and social policy.* Englewood Cliffs, N.J.: Prentice-Hall, 1974.

Salk, L. *What every child wants his parents to know.* New York: McKay, 1972.

Sarnoff, S., and Sarnoff, I. *Sexual excitement, sexual peace.* New York: M. Evans, 1979.

Sears, R. R. Sex-typing, object choice, and child rearing. In H. A. Katchadourian (Ed.), *Human sexuality: A comparative and developmental perspective.* Berkeley: University of California Press, 1979.

Sears, R. R., Maccoby, E. E., and Levin, H. *Patterns of child rearing.* Evanston, Ill.: Row Peterson, 1957.

Selzer, J. G. *When children ask about sex.* Boston: Beacon Press, 1974.

Sherfey, M. J. *The nature and evolution of female sexuality.* New York: Random House, 1972.

Simon, W., and Gagnon, J. H. On psychosexual development. In D. Goslin (Ed.), *Handbook of socialization theory and research.* Chicago: Rand McNally, 1969.

Simon, W., and Gagnon, J. H. Psychosexual development. In J. Heiss (Ed.), *Family roles and interaction.* Chicago: Rand McNally, 1976.

Snow, L. F., and Johnson, S. M. Myths about menstruation: Victims of our own folklore. *International Journal of Women's Studies*, 1978, *1*, 64-72.

Spock, B. *Baby and child care.* New York: Pocket Books, 1976.

Stannard, U. The mask of beauty. In V. Gornick and B. K. Moran (Eds.), *Woman in sexist society.* New York: Basic Books, 1972.

Steinem, G. Child pornography. *Ms.*, August 1977, pp. 43-44.

Thomas, I. Daddy's little girls: Growing up with love and sex. *Village Voice*, October 17, 1977, pp. 27-28.

Thornburg, H. D. Educating the preadolescent about sex. *Family Coordinator*, 1974, *23*, 35-39.

Vaughter, R. M. Psychology. *Signs,* 1976, *2,* 131.

Vener, A. M., Stewart, C. S., and Hagar, D. L. The sexual behavior of adolescents in middle America. *Journal of Marriage and the Family,* 1972, *34,* 696-705.

Weber, E. Sexual abuse begins at home. *Ms.,* April 1977, pp. 64-65.

Weinberg, I. K. *Incest behavior.* New York: Citadel Press, 1955.

Weissberger, E. *Your young child and you.* New York: E. P. Dutton, 1979.

Weitz, S. *Sex roles: Biological, psychological and social foundations.* New York: Oxford University Press, 1977.

Wetzsteon, R. Woody Allen: Schlemiel as sex maniac. *Ms.,* November 1977, p. 140.

White, L. A sexual revolution? *Boston Herald-American,* December 17, 1978.

Yates, A. *Sex without shame: Encouraging the child's healthy sexual development.* New York: William Morrow, 1978.

Zacharias, L., Rand, W., and Wurtman, R. *Obstetrical and Gynecological Survey,* 1976, *31,* 4.

Appendix A

For very young children:

Gordon S. *Girls are girls and boys are boys: So what's the difference?* Charlottesville, Va.: Ed-U Press, 1979.

Sheffield, M., and Bewley, S. *Where do babies come from: A book for children and their parents.* New York: Alfred A. Knopf, 1973.

Waxman, S. *What is a girl? What is a boy?* San Francisco: Peace Press, 1976.

For school age children:

Aho, J. J., and Petras, J. W. *Learning about sex: A guide for children and their parents.* New York: Holt, Rinehart and Winston, 1978.

Comfort, A., and Comfort, J. *The facts of love.* New York: Crown, 1979.

Johnson, C. B., and Johnson, E. W. *Love and sex and growing up.* New York: Bantam Books, 1979.

Nilsson, L. *How was I born?* New York: Delacorte Press, 1975.

For adolescents:

Carlson, D. *Loving sex from both sexes.* New York: Franklin Watts, 1979.

Gordon, S. *You.* New York: Times Books, 1976.

Kelly, G. F. *Learning about sex.* Woodbury, N.Y.: Barrons, 1976.

Mayle, P. *Will I like it?* New York: Corwin Books, 1977.

Mintz, R., and Mintz, L. M. *Threshold: Straightforward answers to teenagers' questions about sex.* New York: Walker, 1978.

For parents:

Hass, A. *Teenage Sexuality.* New York: Macmillan, 1978.

Hymes, J. L. *How to tell your child about sex.* New York: Public Affairs Pamphlet no. 147, 1977.

Yates, A. *Sex without shame: Encouraging the child's healthy sexual development.* New York: William Morrow, 1978.

Reclaiming Our Bodies:
A Feminist Experience in Sex Education

Paula Brown Doress and Wendy Coppedge Sanford

We are two members of an 11-member group which has been meeting, writing, teaching, and strategizing around women's health issues for 12 years. We wrote the books *Our Bodies, Ourselves* (1979) and *Ourselves and Our Children* (1978), and recently some of us collaborated on *Changing Bodies, Changing Lives* (1980), a book for teens about sex and relationships. We meet weekly as a personal as well as a work group and are committed to trying for that important balance between working hard together and sharing from our personal lives. Our observations in this paper will reflect our professional experiences in sexuality workshops, interviews, and outreach which have let us hear from thousands of women. They will also reflect our personal experience in the close and trusting circle of the 11 of us in our group, as we listen, support each other, and strive for better understandings of our own sexuality.

Because we put "feminist" in the title of our paper, we want to give you our definition of feminism, which is so often distorted by the media. To us, feminism is an attitude held by women and men. A feminist takes women seriously as whole human beings with a right to full participation in all aspects of public life and full equality in private life. Our feminism does not simply seek to enter women into the world of men's institutions: we see tremendous potential for beneficial change in our social and political institutions as feminist women move into them, asking questions, in particular, about the use and abuse of power.

In writing this paper we considered what our group and the women's movement in general have to offer as preventive mental health measures for sexual problems. We want to address three themes: the crucial interconnections between the personal and political where sex is concerned, the movement toward a more inclusive definition of sexuality, and the power of shared information. We will also outline some of our group's encounters with the new right in the struggle over freedom of access to all kinds of sex education.

Warm up

Since we cannot work in small groups, which is how we best like to work, we would like to ask you to think silently for a moment, to go inside yourself and touch base with your own experience in the areas that we will be writing about. We have a few questions which will invite you to do this. Sometimes this is difficult at first, but it means that you will be more actively involved. If a certain question gets you off into thoughts and feelings, stay with it. These moments are for you, and there is nothing you have to "report back" on.

Think about your own sexual relationships, either past or present:

With whom in your life do you talk about sex? What is hardest to talk about? Is there something about sex, a problem or dissatisfaction or a doubt, which you have never mentioned to anyone? What would make it easier to bring up?

Think over how you feel about your body, some of the different places in you. In what ways do the media images you see of the human body affect how you experience yourself?

Are you sexually "normal" according to society's definition? How would your experience make you want to stretch that definition?

Do you worry about performance in sex? If so, what shape does this take for you?

In your sexual relationships, who initiates in lovemaking, and does this vary?

Do you ever do things in sex that you do not really want to do? Are there things you would like to try but have never suggested? Do you ever pretend that you like sex more than you do? Do you ever hold back from letting on how much you enjoy it? What would help with any of this?

Do you or your partner ever apologize for not wanting to make love? What seems to be going on there?

How do you feel about yourself when you are not in a sexual relationship? What have times of celibacy brought you in your life?

Picture a group of people in your life with whom you might like to talk about these issues in a relaxed way. Gather them together in your mind, see who they are, imagine how you might help each other.

Now take a minute to trace the themes in what you have been thinking. See which among them you would feel comfortable talking about with someone. Some will be private, but some will be talkable.

These are the kinds of issues that came up all the time for us in our women's group once we started to talk honestly about our sexuality. They have to do not with the facts of sex and sexual response, but with the context in which we are living our sexual relationships. They are personal issues, and political ones as well, for they point beyond us as individuals to factors in our society, to social attitudes and institutions and prescriptions which affect every one of us. Good sex education gives people a chance to raise these issues and to help each other with them.

The Personal Is Political

We have titled our paper "Reclaiming Our Bodies," a phrase which rings of possession, property, and politics. There are so many examples of men or male-dominated institutions laying claim to women's bodies: fathers, husbands, obstetricians, drug companies, hospitals, the advertising industry, legislators, and priests. The motive is sometimes profit, sometimes the need to control women, often both. As women begin to say no to this male ownership and control, we begin to experience our sexuality differently.

It is often in consciousness-raising groups that women first begin to make connections between our personal stories and the wider political scene. (A consciousness-raising group is composed of eight to ten women without professional leadership who are committed to talking honestly about their lives and to helping each other build solutions that are not just individual.) We begin to see that many of the things we suffer over and blame ourselves for in private turn out, once we speak up about them, to be experienced by many. We find that they are caused in large part by the social, political, and economic context in which we are living our lives.

Let us use this political or personal lens to look at sex. Often a woman will say, usually apologetically, "I just don't enjoy sex much, and my husband is getting more and more frustrated. There must be something wrong with me." To know what is going on, we have to look beyond her marriage bed, past whatever techniques they may or may not be using, past even the particulars of their relationship, to the social and political roots of their situation. We see the lack of sex education in the schools she and her husband attended, the absence of any legitimized setting in which sexual feelings and issues could have been discussed. We see sex role stereotypes that make her too shy to assert her need for pleasure. We see an institution-alized heterosexuality that has perhaps thrust them together without a knowledge of alternatives. We see social and economic inequalities: she earns, statistically, 59¢ for every dollar he earns, and the leaders in their society are almost exclusively men. As our first newsprint edition of *Our Bodies, Ourselves* declared in 1969, "There's no reason to expect the sense of inferiority and inadequacy to go away between the sheets!" This is still true. And she wonders whether there is something wrong with her!

In the public domain, sex is used to sell products. It becomes, like rape, an expression of hatred and domination. In the media it is interwoven with violence. When a man and woman go to bed together, no matter how much they love each other, these social and public meanings of sex creep in under the bedroom door to distort what they are doing. The media's efforts can convince them that her body is not good enough and that he should know all the moves. With violence toward women a daily reality, how can he express and she enjoy the full vigor of his passion? With sex so acutely depersonalized in public, can they re-own it in service of inti-macy with any real sense of trust? External cultural factors can and do poison our intimate relationships and severely damage the role sex plays in re-creation and bonding between people.

Sex role stereotypes, heterosexism, and the double standard require us to fit our sexual feelings into a prescribed mold. When the fit is not right, we are encouraged to blame ourselves. Professionally, we see the results of this cruel syndrome. As a group of professionals and lay people explor-ing the prevention of sexual problems, we need to open our eyes to the ways in which social institutions and attitudes reach into the bedroom. In our work as counselors and educators, we can no longer look merely to personal solutions or to improving technique. More and more often we will encourage people who have individual sexual problems to join with others in order to grow in personal understanding, to mobilize and work for change in ways that are impossible alone. We ourselves will inevi-tably become advocates for certain kinds of social change. We will see women's sexuality in particular as existing in the context of reproductive rights; that is, in order to be able to express her sexuality freely and with love, a woman must have full access to birth control information and abortion services and to good prenatal care, all at prices she can afford. We must draw our circle of concern more widely.

From Personal Experience to Political Vision

Linking the personal and the political also encourages us to look into our personal lives for images of how our society might be different. When we feel safe enough to talk honestly with others about our explorations in intimacy, we can let our personal experience point toward a new politics.

What elements are you exploring in your lives which may have relevance for the wider society? Take lovemaking, for example: sexual intimacy has for so long been a reenactment of the power relationships in society: more crudely, man on top and woman beneath. Today many couples are trying to move beyond this picture. They seek to meet as two equal human beings who love each other, to bring their sexual feelings to each other as offerings and not demands, to let feelings draw them together, to touch each other with respect. Women explore initiating and men receptivity. Then, in turn, men may reexplore aggressive modes and women their more passive fantasies, on a new basis of equality and consensus between them. Positions for making love are arrived at in concert or spontaneously; for heterosexual couples, penis-in-vagina thrusting becomes only one of the things they might do, not the prescribed culmination.

Mutuality is the word that comes to mind. In sex as in other areas, like shared income-earning and shared parenting, couples are exploring a love grounded in equality, not hierarchy: in common experience, not separate worlds. The kind of mutuality we are discovering—in many cases struggling to achieve—has a value we need to integrate into our society. We would do well to carry this vision of mutuality into our public as well as our private lives.

Another personal experience which extends beyond itself belongs perhaps more particularly to men: the admission of vulnerability. In men's discussion groups and in sexual relationships based on a growing mutuality, men have been discovering how boxed in they have been by their need to appear strong, invulnerable, and all-knowing. They are finding deep feeling and experience possible only after they unlock their vulnerabilities, express their softer sides. It is risky, of course, but that is inevitable. Women, too, are taking risks to discover their powerful, autonomous selves. As we break through the double standard and rigid gender stereotypes in our personal relationships, we begin to see the possibility of a public life, a national life, which is not posited on tough, macho, super self-reliant male aggressiveness juxtaposed with female passivity and martyrdom.

We end this section by quoting a writer (Anonymous, 1981) who focuses the political/personal lens on her changing sexual experience. The passage is from an article in *Second Wave*, a women's journal published yearly in Boston. The writer has recently become a lesbian, which puts her outside the direct experience of some of us here, yet she expresses thoughts and feelings we will all recognize. Her words are a good example of what we are calling a feminist experience in sex education.

My relationship to myself is different in loving a woman, this woman. Sex was where I noticed it first. With men I always felt guilty when I didn't want sex. Even with a man who wasn't particularly pushy for sex, I always knew he'd want it again sooner or later, and so I'd watch my urges, hoping they'd rise in time. Rarely did a man hold off from sex long enough for me to feel my own desires move me. I got freer about saying "No, not right now," or "Let's just hold each other," but there was always the edge of apprehension, the sense that I'd better enjoy this moratorium while it lasted.

Underlying all this was the assumption that my body somehow belonged to him, not me. I thought I owed my partner my sexuality and should muster it up for him when he wanted or needed it....Whether or not he thought I owed him my sexuality was irrelevant, because the assumption that I did was deep in the culture and deep in my own sense of myself....

With my lover now I feel more consistently erotic than I ever have with men....But I remember the first night I didn't feel like making love when I thought she probably did, and my sudden surprising attack of guilt and awkwardness. There was a lot on my mind that week, and my erotic energy had vanished somewhere. So I went to sleep on "my" side of the bed and slept poorly, as I often had with men after an evening of turning away from sex: would she "want it" in the morning, and would I "have it" to give? Before dawn I woke her up to talk about it, heart in my mouth; it was such an old and potent guilt. What became clear for us was that while she would have liked to make love, she didn't "have to have it." The absence of my erotic energy didn't feel like a rejection; what she wanted more was my honesty, the truth of my feelings, and this I had given her. "Sex is only one part of our relationship," she reminded me. What a relief! Only then did I see what a betrayal of myself it was ever to have apologized to anyone for not wanting to make love.

We have begun to see our sexual desire as a gift which comes to us, not a product which can be mustered up or manipulated at will. I think this marks an important shift in our relationship to our bodies and feelings. Owing our bodies to no one, our role is to be with the sexual feelings when they come, and to let them lead us into connection with each other. Freed of ownership and obligation, sexuality *is* a gift; the ebb and flow of it, respected as a life-rhythm, not only nourishes our loving but also fills us with energy for the work we want to do in the world.

Radical feminists suggest that sexuality as patriarchally defined has been used to colonize woman's body and psyche. As I admitted the guilt feelings, heard my lover's response, and let go of the sense of owing my sexuality to her, I experienced a major step in *de*colonization: I was re-owning my body. I believe this step may be easier between lesbians (and perhaps gay men), because the politics between us are less loaded in terms of history, social expectations, and the realities of power in a sexist patriarchal society. But it also happens between men and women lovers who struggle toward mutuality; that is, toward self-respecting and other-respecting love. Couples like these challenge the patriarchy as deeply as anyone does. Whenever people facilitate such a decolonization in each other, such a re-owning of self—especially if they are able to see the wider politics of it—I think it is a step towards a world in which ownership of others no longer operates as the central metaphor for human relations. (Anonymous, 1981, pp. 25-26)

Making Our Definitions of Sexuality More Inclusive

Our cultural images of sexual people tend to portray the able-bodied, the affluent, the heterosexual, and people within the limited age range of 20 to 45. Although every human being is sexual, the conventional sexual images in our culture narrow our ideas about who can be sexual and work to make substantial groups in the population feel that their sexual options are severely restricted. This narrow definition of so-called normal sexuality hurts both the people who do not fit it and in more subtle and equally destructive ways hurts all of us by making us repress in ourselves what does not fit. We are all aware of the distortions which occur in the media, but we, as sex educators, must be attentive not only to the words we use but to the graphics in our work, making sure that they are inclusive of a wide range of body types, ages, and forms of expressing sexuality.

The women's movement has expanded women's sexual options. Today, women have alternatives to the traditional life-style which include relationships with younger men, childfree marriage, living together without marriage, and relationships with women. Yet the inequalities between women and men persist and continue to limit the options that women have in all spheres of life, including the sexual.

Aging and Changes in Sexual Needs and Opportunities

Women over 40 are bombarded with messages that they must protect themselves against the fading of their sexual appeal, as if women's sexuality is a fragile flower that briefly blossoms, then fades away. Aging is differentially evaluated in women and men: Women are wrinkled, men are craggy; women are matronly, men are distinguished.

Part of the oppression experienced by middle-aged women today is the steadily decreasing age of the cultural prototypes of sexual women. The use of very young women and even children as sexual objects may be part of the backlash against the greater freedom and increased sexual options women have begun to enjoy. By portraying the ideal sexual female as a girl—childlike, pliable, and nonthreatening to the male ego—the mature woman is dismissed as overly demanding, scary, and therefore sexless. In this way, sexism and agism combine to invalidate older women's sexuality.

We must resist the pronatalist ideology that sex exists mainly in the service of reproduction. Such expressions as "over the hill" and "past her prime" equate women's sexuality with reproductive capacity. Yet, as Rosetta Reitz (1979) so clearly demonstrates in her groundbreaking work on menopause, many older women enjoy sex more. Here are some excerpts from a chapter called "Sex Is Better When You're Older":

Ellen, 51: Not worrying about getting pregnant—that did it for me, that turned everything around. The same sex is different, it's better....
Maggie, 49: Once I decided the rest of my life is for me, I was shocked how easy it became to get what I want. There's hardly a thing I can think of sexually that I want to experience that I can't. I'm amazed and wonder why it took me so long not to be afraid to ask....
Deborah, 56: When I was younger, I used to feel that eventually we'll get used to each other, which meant I let [a new partner] do what he wanted—but I don't anymore. The first encounter has got to count. I say "be gentle," at the start....If they don't oblige, there's nothing to get used to, that's it for me. (1979, pp. 151, 153, 155.)

Although women with advancing age gain in their capacity for sexual arousal and orgasm (Sherfey, 1972), men during this same period may worry about a decline in sexual interest. A man in his 50s told us:

We've had a good marriage with lots of good sex. Now we have all the kids out of the house and we travel a lot and have fun together. But I just don't want sex as often as Liz does and it's really hard to tell her that.

Some men, like this one, may be pretty clear that they are the ones who are changing. Others who feel they must live up to a performance standard of male sexuality may choose to blame their wives. For the older woman, the culturally induced fears of losing her sexual attractiveness may seem to be confirmed by her man's decreasing sexual interest.

While we want to recognize that everyone is sexual, we must also be aware that not everyone has the same sexual options or interest. As health professionals concerned with openness toward sexuality we may have gone so far in our efforts to combat the old notion of sex as dirty or bad or harmful that we have put in its place an ethos of sex as "healthy," a prescriptive notion that a healthy person must be sexually active. For those whose sexual opportunities are restricted or who simply do not care to have sex much, this view may prove almost as oppressive as the old restrictions. People may wonder, "What's wrong with me if I'm not sexually active?" It is important for people to hear from health professionals that being in a relationship is not the only thing that makes a person sexual.

Divorce and Relearning Skills

As we expand our notions of "normal" sexuality, we find ourselves going beyond the concept of a linear development of sexuality and sexual skills. With one in two marriages ending in divorce and one-sixth of these occurring among those over 45, many people find themselves back at square one in terms of sex. Many experience something like a second adolescence, having to relearn ways of initiating a sexual relationship or living with periods of celibacy. A divorced woman in her 40s told us:

One of the first social events for single people that I went to after getting separated was a brunch for single and divorced professional people. I couldn't get over the way people interacted with each other. Here were all these mature adults standing around looking like wallflowers waiting for someone to talk to them, especially the men. They looked terrified. Thrown back on my teenage resources, I picked out the best-looking man in the room and started talking to him. I felt as though I had passed some test.

A divorced man told us:

When my wife moved out I felt sexually and emotionally numb. I just had no interest in anyone because I was completely preoccupied with my own pain. Then I started seeing a woman I'd met, and my sexual feelings took me by surprise. One day for the first time in years and years, I spent a whole afternoon making love.

As we look at the sexual lives of divorced women and men, a feminist perspective helps us examine the political, economic, and social factors that may be influencing their choices. The father who does not have custody of his children may lose out on the familiar and homey side of his life, but he has more freedom to explore this second adolescence without the encumbrances of seeking babysitters, explaining every lover to the children (or the children to the lover). The woman who has custody of her children finds her chances to meet new people limited by the wish to protect the children from disruptions of their accustomed routine. Moreover, we must not underestimate the impact of economic constraints on the social life of single mothers. Although alimony has gone out of style, the income gap continues to grow. Large numbers of divorced fathers fail to meet their child support obligations. One woman told us:

It's hard to feel up to going out to meet someone when your clothes are all worn and out of style, all your pantyhose have runs in them, and you've barely scraped together the money for the next month's rent. It's hard to feel sexy when you can't afford to get your teeth fixed.

This woman may want to expand her experience of sexuality, but her circumstances are not giving her a chance. The women's movement with its emphasis on women supporting one another can be a tremendous source of strength and resilience for women in this situation.

The Disabled as Sexual Beings

One group beginning to move beyond limiting stereotypes of "normal" sexuality is the physically disabled. Although feminists discovered early how crucial it is to learn to affirm diversity—racial, ethnic, and class diversity were what we became aware of first—it has taken us years to open our new understandings of sexuality to the voices and experiences of disabled women. Ideally, a feminist sex education would affirm the sexual feelings and special concerns of disabled people, but the 1976 edition of *Our Bodies, Ourselves* contains very little of this. Ignorance of, prejudices toward, and awkwardness around physical disability run deep in all of us, based mainly on a vicious cycle of fear for ourselves and lack of contact with those who are physically different. (The lack of contact, of course, comes from enforced isolation of disabled people, which then leads to more fear and prejudice.)

In the May 1981 issue of *Off Our Backs,* a monthly women's news jour-

nal from Washington, D.C., disabled women have spoken up in a way
that invites each of us to change how we see them and how we see ourselves. Here are a few excerpts ("Women and Disability," 1981). From a
woman with muscular dystrophy:

In terms of sexual independence, I never saw my vulva, because my mother dressed
and bathed me and I couldn't get a mirror. Just remember that a disabled woman
may not be as aware of her body because of problems like this. She may have
little privacy so can't even get to masturbate alone. A disabled woman is apt to
be ashamed of her body anyway. People look at you, stare, avoid looking, so there
is a lot of inhibition to get rid of. (p.4)

The same woman goes on to talk about the isolation:

Some...are uncomfortable just being around a disabled woman, others are comfortable with being a friend, but can't consider a sexual relationship....People have
often believed that if you are with a [disabled person] you can catch "it". . . . We
are not allowed to be sexual beings. (p. 4)

An able-bodied woman whose lover is disabled speaks movingly about
what they have learned:

My lover has been disabled since she was a baby....Health care professionals have
handled her body again and again, without allowing her control over the process. So obviously it is difficult for her to let go of the control over her body and
to entrust her lover with this control. I need to honor her experience, and to know
that it is not my fault or my inadequacy as a lover, or hers. We have discovered
that honest and loving communication, with no blame or criticism, leads us to
finding...ways to experience sexual pleasure with each other. (p. 20)

She finished with an insight for all of us:

I find that I need to change my basic conceptualizations, beginning with the linking of "healthy" and "disabled" as opposites. It's oppressive, and not even true,
that a person who is disabled cannot be healthy. My lover is filled with light and
wisdom. (p. 20)

A male friend of ours who was disabled by polio at 15 has found where
the stereotypes do not fit (Zola, in press):

There is the absence of a certain spontaneity in my sexual courting. There's simply
no sexy, subtle, or even fast way for me to remove my braces and get undressed.
And though I've often fantasized about having someone disrobe me, I've never
been able in real life to do it very easily.

He goes on to say:

The women's movement with its emphasis on greater mutuality in sex has removed some of this burden....I'm also benefitting from women's lib since a lot more women seem to enjoy being on top and in many ways (given some of the residuals of my polio) that's easiest for me.

He is able to point out to all of us the limitations in our performance-oriented approach to sex:

Society has focused on sex as capacity and instrumentality. We have located far too much of our identity in our sexual organs....Where the chronically disabled are concerned, professionals search for compensatory techniques, devices, or symbols to reclaim the lost ability. [I suggest instead we look for] ways to reclaim the lost warmth, wholeness, and sense of being.

As we who are able-bodied listen to these women and this man, we are challenged to alter both how we respond to disabled persons and how we experience our own physical limitations. As a woman disabled from infancy by polio wrote, "Our society creates an ideal model of the physically perfect person unencumbered by weakness, loss or pain." Madison Avenue would have all of us find our bodies inadequate and buy expensive products to try to "improve" them. Hearing from disabled women and men as they seek ways to affirm and express their sexuality helps us find ways we could be less bullied by these cultural images of what an ideal body should look like, and of what ideal sex should be like. We are invited to focus less on capacity and technique and genitals, and more on loving. The courage of our disabled sisters and brothers helps us accept who we are and helps us let our sexual lives flow from that self-acceptance.

Including Homosexuality

Literally hundreds of lesbians and gay men have spoken up over the past decade to expand further our notions of what is "normal" sexuality. They challenge us to look at our homophobia (the irrational fear and hatred of homosexuals taught to nearly every child growing up in this country). They invite us to come to terms with our own sexual feelings for people of our same sex, to own and even enjoy those feelings whether or not we choose to act on them. They point to possibilities of mutuality and a freedom from power politics and role playing between lovers that many heterosexual couples would like to learn from. Most exciting, some homosexuals who are aware of the politics of their sexual preference urge us to look at our own heterosexual preference with new eyes.

Adrienne Rich (1980) puts this challenge to us in an important article called "Compulsory Heterosexuality and Lesbian Experience." Rich points to the many ways that heterosexual marriage has through the centuries been made the only possible choice for women: heterosexuality has been enforced by women's economic disadvantages, by the fear of rape, by child marriage, by the chastity belt, by erasure of lesbian existence in art and history. Rich gives the ugly facts:

Attacks on unmarried women have ranged from aspersion and mockery to deliberate gynocide, including the burning and torturing of millions of widows and spinsters during the witch persecutions of the fifteenth, sixteenth, and seventeenth centuries in Europe, and the practice of suttee of widows in India. (p. 635)

She suggests that it is important for all of us to question the assumption that most women are innately heterosexual:

To acknowledge that for women heterosexuality may not be a "preference" at all but something that has had to be imposed, managed, organized, propagandized, and maintained by force, is an immense step to take if you consider yourself freely and "innately" heterosexual. Yet the failure to examine heterosexuality as a [political] institution is like failing to admit that the economic system called capitalism or the caste system of racism is maintained by a variety of forces, including both physical violence and false consciousness. (p. 618)

Rich proposes that the "lie" of compulsory heterosexuality distorts love relationships between women and men. According to her, "The absence of choice remains the great unacknowledged reality" (p. 657). She leads us to ask what it would mean for women and men who love each other to see their coupling as possible but not inevitable, as choice and not institution. This would free up a kind of creativity in loving that would be scarey and risky but refreshing. Rich extends her promise and challenge to women, but in this final statement she could be speaking to men as well:

To take the step of questioning heterosexuality as a "preference" or "choice" for women—and to do the intellectual and emotional work that follows—will call for a special quality of courage in heterosexually identified feminists, but I think the rewards will be great: a freeing-up of thinking, the exploring of new paths, the shattering of another great silence, new clarity in personal relationships. (p. 648)

Some of the most creative thinking today about sexuality and relationships is coming from homosexual people and from the physically disabled. Living on the edge, they are led to question our long-held assumptions and expectations about what loving should look like. Letting ourselves be educated and enriched by their insights is one of the benefits of the feminist attempt to define sexuality more inclusively.

Information as Power

At age 26 I walked into a roomful of 50 women talking about sex. It was the early women's movement, and I was totally new to such a scene. When they started talking about masturbation, I was spellbound. I had never even heard the word spoken aloud. Going home after the meeting, my friend awkwardly ventured, "That's the first time I've heard masturbation...talked about....Yet I do it." I gulped. "So do I." The silence was broken, and neither of us would ever be quite the same. I had masturbated and felt guilty about it since I was a child. To hear women speaking so openly about it started me on a process of self-acceptance which took me, some years later, to my first experiences of masturbation without that rush of guilt and shame next to the pleasure. I was beginnning to accept myself as a sexual person. (Unpublished material).

We have something to learn from this early women's movement success story. Information is crucial, it is healing, it prevents distress. *How* we get information is important, too. This woman learned about masturbation in the context of a group of informed women speaking honestly from their own experiences. Learning such things so personally, in a way that no textbook alone could ever convey, makes the information accessible in a different way: it becomes a tool for use in one's life. Our appreciation for this learning process shaped how we wrote *Our Bodies, Ourselves*, always interweaving the facts with the voices of women talking about their lives.

The story also raises the important question of "What information are we dealing with, anyway?" Who decides what the "facts" are? With masturbation, a generation of doctors and parents passed on the "fact" that masturbation hurts you and ruins you for adult sexual functioning. Women's ovaries and clitorises were surgically removed in the 19th century in order to prevent this and other forms of "unruliness." With female orgasm, psychologists and gynecologists argued as "fact" that mature women had orgasms vaginally. What we discovered finally in our women's groups was that these facts did not fit. We began to help each other to trust our own experiences.

In this new light, research itself got redefined. Innovative and courageous women began to pioneer a new kind of research: Betty Dodson (1974) wrote *Liberating Masturbation*; Mary Jane Sherfey (1972), *The Nature and Evolution of Female Sexuality*; Shere Hite (1977), *The Hite Report*. Women in the women's self-help movement all over the country started with the women themselves—ourselves—looking, touching, tasting, listening, to build up a more accurate set of "facts" about women's sexual patterns and possibilities. As Shere Hite declared, "Researchers must stop telling women what they *should* feel sexually and start asking them what they *do* feel sexually" (p. 60).

This new kind of research revealed masturbation as a consistently satisfying act of self-pleasure and self-exploration, which deepens women's understanding of their own sexual responses and affirms their sexuality whether or not they are in a relationship with someone else. Intercourse, too, took on a new look. Shere Hite found that a full 70 percent of her 3,000 women respondents never experienced orgasm through intercourse alone, though many of these did experience orgasm quickly in masturbation. This led Hite to challenge the male experts' definition of satisfactory intercourse, with its emphasis on penile penetration. She questioned whether intercourse was ever meant to produce orgasm for women and cited the awkward language Masters and Johnson had to use in their attempt to reaffirm penile intercourse by showing that the clitoris gets enough stimulation through the tugging of the labia. She challenged the labels of frigid and dysfunctional used on women who do not experience orgasm that way. Feminist research on female orgasm has freed women from self-blame and opened us to a new sense of activity and entitlement in sex. Feminists are now demystifying older women's sexuality as well, through menopause self-help groups and pioneers like Rosetta Reitz.

Thus the very "facts" about sex are in flux, and necessarily so. Getting them out in an accessible way gives people the power to take charge of important parts of their lives, from the simple control of pregnancy to the more complex emotional growth brought by self-acceptance and self-pride in a part of our life that has for generations been considered shameful.

Teenagers and the Power of Shared Information
In working on the sexuality sections of the new book for teens, *Chang-*

ing Bodies, Changing Lives (Bell et al., 1980), I was reminded that teen-agers are prime targets for the worst kinds of misinformation about sex. Concerned parents will sometimes say, "My child isn't ready for the sex information in your book." But if that child is over 9 years old and has eyes and ears, chances are she or he is getting sex information all the time—from TV, disco lyrics, movies, jokes at school, porno magazines on the racks in local variety stores, and the ads which use sex to sell everything from cars and liquor to home insurance. These parents have to decide not "Will my child get a sex education?" but "What kind?" Those who try to counteract all this misinformation and attitude warping with silence are not helping their kids. Often they are the very ones who will find their teenage daughters pregnant—the daughters who say, "I thought I couldn't get pregnant if I didn't have my period yet...if I did it during my period...if we did it standing up."

We would probably all agree that kids need sex education early, that they need to know it is a safe topic to talk about at home. We would agree, too, that the facts alone are not enough, that kids need frequent chances to talk over the feelings and pressures in a safe and trusting atmosphere. We would also probably agree that it does not help to tell teenagers that *all* premarital sex is bad. Not only does prohibition not work in helping them set their limits, it even damages their ability to take responsibility for what they *do* do.

Let us look at how prohibition cuts down on responsibility. Despite being bombarded with sex by the media, most kids are given almost no clear, useful information about sex at home or in school or at church. Parents and teachers say they fear that if you tell teens about sex they will go out and "do it." Even parents who do not say don't often keep a silence around the topic which gives the same message. Yet here teenagers are with changing bodies, skyrocketing hormones, burgeoning sexual feelings, a growing capacity for real caring about another person, and abundant messages from the media that sex is cool, so *of course* many of them start exploring sex, no matter what their parents have said. We know that by age 19, 69 percent of all metropolitan area teens are sexually active (Kantner and Zelnik, 1978).

In talking about having intercourse, teens use images which express their overpowering feelings: feeling such a rush that you could not stop to think about birth control, so swept away that you could not help yourself or think about the consequences. Drugs and alcohol play into this scenario beautifully. People conclude that teens are too immature to think about the consequences of their sexual actions. Yet during these same years most teenagers are also working hard on their values. "What is a good friend?" they are asking. "Am I loyal to my friends? What causes do I believe in? How do I want to treat other people? Be treated by them?" By our massive, institutionalized disapproval of teen sexuality, combined with our shameless exploitation of sex in the media, we rob them of a chance to let their sexual actions be guided by the same kind of values that they are working on in other areas of their life. You cannot plan for something you are not supposed to be doing. You cannot ask yourself what your and the other person's true needs are when sexual impulses themselves are hidden in a cloud of guilt.

If sex education at home and in school can bring sexual feelings into the light of acceptance and self-acceptance, of honesty and humor, then teens' decisions about sex will at least have as fair a chance of being value centered as their decisions about how they treat their family and friends. Speaking openly about sex in this way will not totally eliminate the hurts or the unplanned pregnancies or the spread of sexually transmitted diseases (STDs) among teens, because these years will always be a time of experimentation and learning from mistakes. But it could reduce these greatly and have some psychological benefits as well.

It was with this aim in mind that we included a section in the teen book on making love making better. This is the part of the book we are always advised not to mention on TV or radio. Certain more liberal parents will say to themselves, "Okay, they're doing it, so we'd better give them the facts so they don't get into trouble." But even these would probably draw the line at increasing their kids' enjoyment of sex; many parents are uneasy even about their own sexual enjoyment. The bottom line is, then, that teens shouldn't be "doing it," that teen sex is an unavoidable evil to be dealt with but certainly not nurtured. This attitude communicates itself to the teenagers, and it backfires.

We chose to write in our book about getting privacy, learning how to talk with your partner about sex, getting used to being naked together, what to do if you do not have an orgasm and want to, how to cope with premature ejaculation. We included these as an act of respect for the teens as whole sexual beings and as an invitation to their self-respect. Once a young couple has decided to make love, they deserve to enjoy it. Part of that enjoyment comes from knowing you are protected against pregnancy.

Teenagers' enjoyment of sex is important in both the long and short term. Many of us know the distressing long-term consequences of early sex that we did not enjoy. We know the patterns of anxiety, defense, self-distrust, exploitation, guilt, self-protection, which reach years later into our loving relationships to distort our sexual relationships. We would like to help spare today's teenagers from some of that later suffering.

In the short term, being encouraged to consider their mutual enjoyment as something they can learn and plan for will help teenagers feel more self-respecting in sex and more respectful of it. Sex is not just something you fumble around with in the back of a car and then get your clothes together and pretend nothing happened. Something did happen, something that can be a source of energy, joy, pleasure, and human connection. Affirming this will help teenagers do all those things we so desperately hope they will do: use birth control, say no when they do not want to go any further, protect themselves against STDs. If you are encouraged to see your sexual relating as part of your whole self, you are more able to be responsible about it to yourself and to others.

For teenagers, then, as for all of us, information about sex is power— power to make choices, to take charge, to grow.

The Political Gets Personal: Keeping the New Right out of Our Bedrooms and Our Wombs

We are not the only ones who know that information is power. The right knows it, too. During the past several years we have seen an all-out attack on U.S. citizens' access to sex information and to the medical services which allow us to control our reproductive and sexual lives. If we learned in the early days of the women's movement that the personal is political, we are now dismayed to discover that the political has become personal in a way that threatens to turn the clock back on all our advances toward sexual equality and reproductive freedom.

We are seeing a massive effort by right-wing groups to enforce their rigid prescriptive views of sexuality on all of us, through legislation, court decisions, and/or a constitutional amendment. Here are some of the kinds of laws which have been proposed and even passed in some states:

Laws which would limit teenagers' access to information about birth control and sexually transmitted diseases;

Laws which would prohibit abortion or require consent of both parents or of a judge or of the spouse;

Laws which so define the beginning of life that abortion would be considered murder and certain forms of birth control would be outlawed;

Laws which would criminalize sexual intercourse between two consenting minors and would require a physician to report to a teenager's parents if she or he came in for birth control, or to report to the parents any reason to suspect sexual activity;

Laws which would infringe upon the civil rights of homosexuals and prohibit them from practicing certain professions;

Laws which would require mothers receiving welfare to submit to sterilization in order to receive their checks or to answer personal questions regarding where and with whom and when they had sex.

Listening to this list of proposed and incipient legislation, you can see again why we called our paper "Reclaiming Our Bodies." As one woman we know suggested, the right claims it is trying to get government off our backs, while it is actually working to insinuate government into our bedrooms and our wombs.

As counselors and as teachers and human service workers, we are going to see a lot of distress as these kinds of laws are enacted. As human beings who want to love and be loved freely in our own intimate relationships, we will face larger and larger obstacles.

This attack on sexual freedom goes hand in hand with an overall assault on women's new roles in the world of work. The so-called Moral Majority speaks openly about its goal of sending women back into the home. At the same time, the right wing's fiscal program cuts budgets for community services of many kinds. The sectors of the economy being cut back are those which offer some professional mobility for numbers of employed women. The despair of being out of work, out of money, and unable to use one's professional skills may propel many women back into traditional roles.

Each of us is affected on several levels by this monolithic backlash. We need a broad coalition of feminists, social service professionals, and clients. Many of us find ourselves in all three of these categories. We must respond to any attack on all of these levels. When a school system we teach in is threatened, we must respond as parents and as citizens and as teachers. When a community sex education program is threatened, we must respond not only as professionals about to lose our jobs, but as human beings who know the value of sexuality counseling to people's lives. As feminists we must be deeply concerned about attacks on particular sectors of the economy that employ large numbers of women or that primarily serve women and children.

The Moral Majority has mounted a well-financed campaign to force their particular view of religion and morality on the rest of us. Senators and members of Congress with long records of support for civil liberties and for human needs have been defeated by the single-issue campaigning of the right-to-life movement, so that today the configuration in Congress provides the numbers to pass a human life statute. The strength amassed by this movement comes from their grass-roots organizing which brings together an army of housewives frightened by social changes that seem to threaten their way of life. The strength and fanaticism of this well-organized minority now poses a threat to our work. We must respond quickly and effectively. We can no longer afford to think of sex education and counseling as occurring in a friendly climate or in a political vacuum.

Censorship is one of the right's primary weapons. The attacks on our reproductive freedoms are coupled with attacks on our rights to speak, to teach, to write. It is no coincidence that since the election of Ronald Reagan, banning efforts against public libraries have risen fivefold (*New York Times,* December 8, 1980, p. 1). As an ACLU regional counsel commented, "This is getting out of hand. Pretty soon we're going to have some very small libraries" (Cimons, 1981).

In our work as coauthors of *Our Bodies, Ourselves,* we have been directly affected by this movement toward censorship. We would like to share some of that history with you, because we have firsthand knowledge of it and we think it provides a way to track the gradual buildup of the strength of right-wing forces in this country.

Our Bodies, Ourselves has become a prime target of right-wing censorship activity. Paradoxically this began when, in 1976, the Young Adult Division of the American Library Association selected *Our Bodies, Ourselves* as one of their "best books for young adults." Since librarians around the country frequently use this list as a guide in selecting books, *Our Bodies, Ourselves* made its way into libraries in many small towns and semirural areas, where it attracted the notice of conservative groups such as the Eagle Forum and, more recently, the Moral Majority.

By 1977 we began to hear of banning attempts in small town high schools and libraries scattered through the Midwest, the South, and rural New England. Gradually a pattern emerged in that the Eagle Forum seemed to be involved in many of these banning campaigns which continued through 1978. The Eagle Forum even attacked the use of *Our Bodies, Ourselves* in a course for adult women given at a YWCA in Rockford, Illinois. They demanded that the course be dropped on the grounds that it was not consistent with Christian values and that another course, called "One Nation under God" be substituted.

The tactics employed by right-wing groups have ranged from quoting material out of context and making personal slurs against the authors to individual actions such as withdrawing books from libraries and refusing to return them. One parent argued that her local library should not be allowed to stock any material which she would not be willing to have in her own home! A minister demanded that his local library furnish him with the names of all persons who had withdrawn certain books in order to check the list for minors.

The 1980 campaign spearheaded by the Moral Majority has moved beyond the small towns of America to the big city dailies and the TV networks. Jerry Falwell targeted *Our Bodies, Ourselves* in a major fundraising letter, asking, "Do you want your children or the children of your loved ones reading this type of immoral trash? This is out and out humanistic garbage!" Falwell's instigation has stepped up the pace of banning efforts in local high schools and libraries. The Planned Parenthood Federation of America has informed us of numerous attempts to get the book out of their clinics and of a rash of phone calls to members of Congress requesting "obscenity hearings" to stop the purchase of *Our Bodies, Ourselves* with federal funds for agencies and clinics.

We have been heartened to hear of spontaneous defense groups arising in some communities. In Helena, Montana, an ad hoc coalition, Helena Citizens for Freedom of Expression, organized a defense in collaboration with the ACLU, which has been most helpful in many of these incidents. In Muskegon, Wisconsin, the local chapter of NOW defended attacks on *Our Bodies, Ourselves.* In Belfast, Maine, the school committee voted seven to three to keep *Our Bodies, Ourselves* in the school library despite a strong banning attempt by a local clergyman. These expressions of support signal the presence of a largely untapped core of progressives who will struggle with us for the preservation of choice and freedom in all our lives. We urge you to seek out such pockets of support in the communities where you work.

As a collective, our response to these attacks has been to step up our efforts to get information out to the people who need it. We are actively fundraising to be able to do this better; if you have any ideas, please let us know. To those resisting local attempts to ban *Our Bodies, Ourselves*, we have put together a packet of letters of endorsement from professionals who use our book in their work with adolescents and young adults, along with a list of localities that we know about where other banning attempts have taken place and news clippings of these episodes. You can order these materials from us.

As the campaign against *Our Bodies, Ourselves* escalates, we have been considering a more direct response to the Moral Majority. We welcome your ideas and support.

The new right is a grass-roots movement. It musters mailing lists, volunteers, and phone chains which reach literally millions of people. These are the ones our legislators are hearing from. Many of us in the prochoice, prosex education movement have lost the feel of this kind of grass-roots work. After the Supreme Court abortion decision in 1973, we hoped we would never need to do it again. But we do.

We feel saddened that we must take the time in which we could be learning from one another, advancing our knowledge of how to help ourselves and others, in order to sound the alarm and devise a strategy to fight back. But if we were to pinpoint the one thing we could do that would have the greatest effect in preventing sexual problems and promoting sexual responsibility in the next generation, it would be just this: to devise a strategy to defeat the Moral Majority and to prevent them from imposing their ideology on our communities and our nation. We must thoughtfully and energetically confront these reckless attacks on our freedom to provide sex information and resources. If we fail to do this, the risk is great that we may never meet as a conference of sex educators and family planners again.

References

Anonymous. Notes from just over the edge: A new lesbian speaks out. *Second Wave*, Summer 1981, *6*, 20-26.

Bell, R. et al. *Changing bodies, changing lives: A book for teens on sex and relationships.* New York: Random House, 1980.

Boston Women's Health Book Collective. *Our bodies, ourselves: A book by and for women* (Rev. ed.). New York: Simon and Schuster, 1979.

Boston Women's Health Book Collective. *Ourselves and our children: A book by and for parents.* New York: Random House, 1978.

Cimons, M. Feminist health book comes under Moral Majority's fire. *Los Angeles Times*, March 20, 1981.

Dodson, B. *Liberating masturbation: A meditation on self-love.* New York: Bodysex Designs, 1974. (Available from Bodysex Designs, P.O. Box 1933, New York, N.Y. 10001; $4.00.)

Hite, S. *The Hite report.* New York: MacMillan, 1976.

Kantner, J., and Zelnik, M. Contraceptive patterns and premarital pregnancy among women aged 15-19 in 1976. *Family Planning Perspectives*, May-June 1978, *10*, 135-142.

Reitz, R. *Menopause: A positive approach* (Rev. ed.). Radnor, Pa.: Chilton Books, 1977; New York: Penguin Books, 1979.

Rich, A. Compulsory heterosexuality and lesbian experience. *Signs*, Summer 1980, *5*, 631-660.

Sherfey, M. J. *The nature and evolution of female sexuality.* New York: Vintage Books, Random House, 1972.

Women and disability. *Off Our Backs*, May 1981, p. 11.

Zola, I. *Missing pieces: Chronicle of living with a disability.* Philadelphia: Temple University Press, in press.

Appendix A

Recommended Reading

Barbach, L., and Levine, L. *Shared intimacies: Women's sexual experiences.* Garden City, N.Y.: Anchor Books, Doubleday, 1980.

Boston Women's Health Book Collective, and ISIS. *International women and health resource guide.* Boston: Boston Women's Health Book Collective, 1980. (Available from Boston Women's Health Book Collective, P. O. Box 192, W. Somerville, Mass. 02144-0192; $5.00 [surface mail], $8.00 [air mail].

Corea, G. *The hidden malpractice: How American medicine mistreats women.* New York: Harcourt Brace Jovanovich, 1978.

Ehrenreich, B., and English, D. *Witches, midwives, and nurses: A history of women healers.* Old Westbury, N.Y.: Feminist Press, 1972.

Ehrenreich, B., and English, D. *For her own good: 150 years of the experts' advice to women.* New York: Anchor Books, Doubleday, 1978.

Gordon, L. *Woman's body, woman's right: A social history of birth control in America.* New York: Penguin Books, 1977.

Hite, S. *Hite report on male sexuality.* New York: Alfred A. Knopf, 1981.

Oakley, A. *Women confined: Towards a sociology of childbirth.* New York: Schocken Books, 1980.

Scully, D. *Men who control women's health: The miseducation of obstetrician-gynecologists.* Boston: Houghton Mifflin, 1980.

Seaman, B. *The doctors' case against the pill* (Rev. ed.). New York: Doubleday, 1980.

Zilbergeld, B. *Male sexuality.* New York: Bantam Books, 1978.

Appendix B

Following our presentation at the conference, an ad hoc meeting was called to discuss a response to the Moral Majority and other right-wing groups. The following resolution was developed for use with our professional constituencies and was passed by acclamation at the meeting of the whole conference the following morning.

As a group of 200 women and men who are mental health professionals, health educators, and teachers, we stand committed to continued work for free access to the information, sex education and medical and mental health services which enable all persons to express their sexuality in whatever nonexploitative ways they choose. We affirm our right to teach, to write, to speak, to learn from one another and to encourage people to grow.

We deplore the goals and tactics of a vocal right-wing minority to impose their narrow, prescriptive views of religion and sexuality on all the citizens of our country. We find the policies of this movement to be anti-life in the most profound ways.

We affirm parenthood by choice.	We oppose enforced parenthood, which has been proven to result in a dramatic rise in child abuse.
We affirm a full range of birth control choices	We oppose the prohibition of certain crucial methods of birth control like the low estrogen pill and the IUD.
We affirm the need for adequate food, shelter, health education, and social services for everyone.	We oppose cutbacks in critical human services.
We affirm a woman's freedom to choose abortion when necessary.	We oppose criminal penalties for women who have abortions. When legal abortion is not available, women seek illegal abortions, and many die.
We affirm our commitment to a society which nourishes and protects our diversity.	We oppose a rise in sexism, racism, anti-semitism and homophobia.
We affirm our inherent right to liberty in our personal and family life.	We oppose invasion of the most private aspects of personal and family life.

We pledge ourselves as individuals and professionals to a renewed grass-roots effort to mobilize the *real* majority of responsible citizens who believe in democracy and freedom as best expressed in the Constitution of the United States of America.

Religious Dimensions of Sexual Health

James B. Nelson

Religion is a terribly ambiguous human enterprise, and it ought never to be confused with God. Religion is the patterning of human responses to what is *perceived* to be the divine, responses that take shape in doctrine, moral instruction, patterns of worship, styles of piety or spirituality, and religious institutional life. The power of religion for good is that the divine life does indeed break through these human forms in ways that fulfill persons, create life-giving human relationships, and transform social structures. But the power of religion for evil is just as great. The religious enterprise, that most dangerous of human enterprises, is always tempted to claim ultimate authority and sanction for its humanly constructed doctrines and precepts. Nowhere is all of this ambiguity more apparent than in sexual matters.

While I write here as a Christian, I believe that these observations will have considerable applicability to Judaism as well. Somewhere in the first few centuries of the Christian church, the patristic era, there arose two lists: the seven deadly sins and the seven virtues. As I attempted to formulate my observations about the religious dimensions of sexual health, two things occurred. First, I could not talk about the positive elements without talking about the ways in which Western religion has contributed mightily to sexual disease. Second, I discovered that my points fell, quite miraculously, into two groups of seven. Although these make no attempt to reflect the early Christian lists, I submit seven deadly sins which Western religion has contributed to sexual disease, countered by seven virtues (or positive resources) which the Judeo-Christian tradition offers to sexual health.

All of this is predicated upon certain assumptions about sexual health. The definition offered by the World Health Organization (WHO) (1975) is useful: "Sexual health is the integration of the somatic, emotional, intellectual, and social aspects of sexual being, in ways that are positively enriching and that enhance personality, communication and love" (p. 6). That is a remarkable definition, not only because it affirms the multidimensional and relational aspects of sexual health, but also because it is (to the best of my knowledge) the first time any major health organization has used the concept of love in a health policy statement. Not incidentally, the WHO definition reflects the best in the Judeo-Christian tradition concerning sexuality and leaves out the worst! Now to the sins and virtues.

The first two deadly sins—spiritualistic dualism and sexist dualism—are the most basic, fundamental sins, and they are counterparts of each other (Ruether, 1975). Yet, for the moment they can be viewed separately. Any dualism is the radical breaking apart of two elements which belong together; it is seeing the two dimensions of life coexisting in uneasy truce or open conflict.

Spiritualistic dualism, the first deadly sin, was quite foreign to the Jewish Old Testament heritage. However, through the impact of the Greco-Roman culture and its Hellenist philosophy, it found its way into early Christian life and thought. The spirit was viewed as eternal and pure, while the physical body was seen as temporal, material, corruptible, and corrupting. Whatever salvation meant, it somehow involved escape from the distractions and temptations of bodily life into the realm of the spirit. Although, as we shall see in a moment, this spiritualistic dualism ran counter to the most basic insights of both Jewish and Christian traditions, it had an enormous impact, particularly upon Christian life, which is still with us.

Such dualism has multiple results. The body is viewed with suspicion, and its sexual feelings must be denied in favor of the higher life. A ladderlike image of true spirituality emerges, with celibacy reserved for the higher rungs. The alienated body produces a mind detached from the depth of feelings. Dichotomized thinking emerges from the mind-body dissociation; we become resistant to ambiguity, seeking simple and single reasons for understanding things. Both the body and its sexuality are depersonalized; the body is seen as a physical object to be possessed, controlled, and used by the self. Such are the wages of this deadly sin, spiritualistic dualism.

But what of the positive resources? Israel of the Old Testament knew nothing of this body-spirit split. It regarded the person as all of one piece. With a strong doctrine of the goodness of all of creation, Israel could not denigrate the body and its pleasures. They were gifts of God.

And what of Christianity? In spite of the fact that Hellenistic dualism made dramatic inroads, Christianity nevertheless remains a religion of incarnation. In its central affirmation, Christianity claims that the most decisive experience of God comes to us not principally in doctrine, not in philosophic abstraction, not in mystical otherworldly experiences, but *in flesh*. Even if ancient heresies (Gnostic and Docetic) still cast suspicion upon the goodness of material, bodily life and still question the full humanity of Jesus of Nazareth, the mainstream of Christianity has attempted to say that the most decisive, memorable, revelatory meeting place of God with humankind is in the meeting of flesh with flesh. And that has something to do with our sexuality.

So, the good news, the virtue (as opposed to this first sin) is this: the fully physical, sweating, lubricating, ejaculating, urinating, defecating bodies that we are are the vehicles of the divine experience. God continues to be most decisively experienced in the fleshly, embodied touching of human lives. The Word still becomes flesh and dwells among us, full of grace and truth.

Word becoming flesh: this is the mystery of communication and communion. The secret of our sexuality is our need to reach out to embrace others physically, emotionally, spiritually. The good news of a Jewish creation-affirming faith and a Christian incarnationalist faith is that our body-selves with all of their rich sexuality are God's way of inviting us into authentic humanness, through our need to reach out and embrace. Our sexuality is the divine plot to tease us into becoming "body-words of love." Our sexuality is both the physiological and the psychological grounding of our capacity to love. It is that basic. We who take these core religious affirmations seriously are bidden to celebrate the body as a means of grace. That is good news from religion for sexual health.

The second deadly sin is sexist or patriarchal dualism. It is the twin of spiritualistic dualism in some basic ways. For centuries men have assigned to themselves the primary characteristics of spirit and mind, and have labeled women as body and emotion, hence inferior and needing to be subdued by the higher powers.

If spiritualistic dualism was foreign to the Hebraic Old Testament culture, sexist or patriarchal dualism was not. Women were second-class citizens in the community of faith and much of the time looked upon as male property. The patriarchal culture continued its influence into the Christian era and is still pervasive. The essence of sexist dualism is the systematic and systemic subordination of women by men in institutional life and in interpersonal relations.

That this is a deadly sin in regard to the health of women hardly needs elaboration. That it is a deadly sin for males, also, is true. Unquestionably, women have borne the brunt of the manifold forms of injustice. For both women and men, the sexist estrangement takes its toll in patterns of dominance and submission. Women compete with women for male acceptance, which they have been taught is essential for their self-worth. Men find emotional intimacy and tenderness with other men to be threatening to the masculine, heterosexual image. Spouses find it difficult to speak honestly with each other about their sexual needs and anxieties, and performance fears invade their sexual love making.

What is the good news, the virtue that Western religion might contribute here? The Apostle Paul expresses it: "There is neither Jew nor Greek, there is neither slave nor free, there is neither male nor female, for you are all one" (Galatians 3:28).

The internalization of this reality makes possible the growth of our androgyny. (I realize that "androgyny" is an ambiguous term, inasmuch as it trades upon the very sexual stereotypes which it attempts to overcome. Nevertheless, it is a useful interim word, reminding us that societal sterotypes do not define our authentic being.) None of us is intended to be either rational or emotional, either assertive or receptive, either cognitive or intuitive, either strong or vulnerable, either initiating or responding, but all of these. A core religious affirmation is the *oneness* of human being and human becoming. Actually, we do not have to become androgynous, for each of us essentially is. We only need to be allowed to be actually what we are essentially, and the religious affirmation is important here (Singer, 1976, p. 333).

Moreover, the Judeo-Christian understandings of God are crucial to our own self-understandings. Stereotypically, masculine language and images have shaped that perception: God is "He" and "Him." Masculine titles have predominated: God is King, Lord, Master, Father. But, one of the best kept secrets in the Bible (particularly the Old Testament) is the abundance of feminine images for God. God is there likened to a woman in childbirth, bringing forth new creation; God is there as a nursing mother drawing humanity to her full breasts; God is there as a seamstress clothing her children with garments in the wilderness (Russell, 1973, pp. 97ff).

If this kind of religious imagery is internalized and experienced, it can lead to a more androgynous experience of the self. It might lead, also, to a more androgynous spirituality. A masculinized imagery and spirituality has emphasized God as structure, judgment, law, order, intellect, and logic. A feminist imagery would lead to the experience of God as nature more than society, as mystical oneness more than cognitive analysis, as flow and change more than structure, as immanence more than transcendence. Both dimensions are needed for sexual health, for each of us is created with androgynous capacities destined to be realized in unique ways.

The third sin is homophobia. The word was coined a few years ago to denote an irrational fear of homosexuality (Weinburg, 1973, Chap. 1). It has been, tragically enough, part of the Judeo-Christian legacy. Nevertheless, the antihomosexual bias simply cannot be justified by careful biblical interpretation (Boswell, 1980, Chap. 4; Nelson, 1978, Chap. 8). The Bible does not actually deal with homosexuality as such. This understanding of a psychosexual orientation toward those of one's own sex is distinctly modern. Furthermore, when the Bible deals with homosexual acts (as distinguished from orientation), it deals with them in the context of lust, idolatry, rape, and with the notion of leaving, giving up, or turning away from one's natural orientation. Thus, heterosexual orientation is presupposed. There is no biblical guidance on the matter of same-sex expression for those so oriented, within a context of mutual respect and love.

If the biblical legacy does not explain our persistent homophobia, misogyny (male distrust, fear—even hatred—of women) does. Patriarchal control idealizes a disembodied, detached rationality and enforces compulsory heterosexuality for both men and women. The only respectable alternative to heterosexuality is either celibacy or asexuality. Harrison (1981) writes:

More than anything else we now need a clearer historical appreciation for the ways in which this long-standing and deeply rooted antipathy toward women in the Western Christian tradition interfaced and interacted with anti-body and anti-sensual attitudes. The fact is that the stigma of homosexuality in this society incorporates and encompasses all of the power dynamics of misogyny. Until we recognize this fact, we will not even begin to grasp why homophobia is such an intense and 'nutty' madness among us. (p. 8)

The antihomosexual attitudes of the dominantly Christian West thus cannot be explained simply by historical influences. As Boswell's (1980) careful study has pointed out, misogyny is a more consistent trend in Christian history than is homophobia. The connection, however, is quite clear. In male homosexual activity there is the stigma that some men must be passive, act like females, that is, like "failed males."

If both Jewish and Christian cultures have been dominantly homophobic, there are, nevertheless, positive resources for sexual health within these traditions. First, there is biblical affirmation of same-sex loving relationships. This material is usually overlooked by the antihomosexual proof texters, but it is there. For example, the close emotional bonding of David and Jonathan, of Ruth and Naomi, of Jesus and the beloved disciple are celebrated by the biblical writers. These are not, I assume, accounts of genital expression, but that is not the point. The point is that careful biblical scholarship simply cannot sustain the sweeping condemnation of all deep same-sex feeling which often has been asserted in the name of the Bible.

Another religious resource follows upon the recognition that the Bible does not deal with the issue of same-sex genital expression in the context of mutual respect and love. That resource is the affirmation that the morality of homosexual genital acts must be judged by the same fundamental criterion as the morality of heterosexual genital acts. To this theme I will return later.

In terms of the psychodynamics of homophobia, there is a more basic religious resource still. It is the message of God's radical affirmation of each and every person. In both Old and New Testaments this is called grace. It is the spontaneous, unmerited acceptance of the self by God. Here is the foundation for a sense of personal security in the self.

One of the strong dynamics of homophobia seems to be insecurity about one's own sexual identity and, hence, the tendency to condemn in another what is feared in the self. For the one, however, who has discovered a basic sense of inner worth through the divine acceptance, there is less need for fear. As a male I need not fear "the woman" within. As one predominantly heterosexual, I need not fear the homosexual feelings within. Nor need I be envious of the apparently greater sexuality of gays and lesbians (for our stereotypes constantly draw our attention to what they do in bed).

A common dynamic of what the religious tradition calls "sin" is thus false security. It is a false security rooted in an inner insecurity which then attempts to punish those who seem to threaten the self. That the security-creating divine acceptance, grace, can undercut this destructive dynamic is good news, indeed.

The fourth deadly sin which contributes to sexual disease is guilt over self-love. Christian theology has not had a good record in dealing positively with self-love. The dominant interpretation has seen self-love equivalent to self-centeredness, hence incompatible with the religious life. Self-love has been interpreted as acquisitive, individualistic, concerned with the self's private satisfactions, and prone to use others as tools for one's own desires. Thus, a sharp disjunction has been drawn between *agape* (selfless, self-giving love perceived in God and held normative for the faithful) and *eros* (human desire for fulfillment). Although, to be sure, a more positive appreciation of self-love has been present in certain elements of the tradition, the negative evaluation has been dominant.

When a suspicion about self-love combines with a suspicion of the body and of sexual feelings, there is a sure formula for sexual disease. The self-hate which emerges is usually of an indirect sort, but it *is* a rejection of one's actual self. Alongside this is often an idealized image of the self, but, since this is unattainable, hurt pride and self-hate emerge together.

In sexual expression, such self-rejection (or rejection of self-love) finds guilt in spontaneous sexual pleasure. Masturbation is an obvious arena of guilt, simply because giving oneself sexual pleasure is understood as sheer self-centeredness. But there is also a "works-righteousness" syndrome which becomes performance anxiety in sexual relations with the partner. In performing I always split myself into two people—one doing the performing, the other watching both the performance and the audience response. Such self-conscious splitting, watching, and judging further nurture my anxiety and undermine my capacity to commune with the other.

If guilt over self-love is a deadly sin, the good news from the religious heritage is that love is indivisible and nonquantifiable. Jesus said, "Love your neighbor *as* yourself," not "instead of yourself." It is not true that the more love we save for ourselves the less we have for others. Authentic self-love is not narcissism nor is it a grasping selfishness. Rather, it is that self-acceptance which comes through the affirmation of one's own graciously given worth and (in spite of all our distortions and flaws) our creaturely fineness.

Self-love is not only basic to personal fulfillment, but also to the capacity for authentic sexual intimacy with the partner. If I cannot say yes to myself, I cannot offer myself fully to another. I can surrender to the other, but I will have lost the gift I was asked to bring. True sexual intimacy depends upon a solid sense of identity in each of the partners. The entanglements in which identity is confused and diminished become symbiotic relationships in which one person becomes an extension of the other.

Sexual intimacy is love's communion, not unification. Sexual intimacy, then, rests in some large measure upon each partner's sense of personal worth. Without this we easily elevate the other into the center of our lives, hoping that the other's affirmation of us will assure us of our own reality. But this is too large a burden for the partner, for then the beloved has become idolatrized and confused with the divine.

Genuine self-love, furthermore, personalizes the body. When we can love ourselves as body-selves, we are aware of bodily tensions and their causes. There is more spontaneity of the body-self, for when we find the security not to demean ourselves we need not deaden any aspects of ourselves or dissipate our energies in useless rituals. Self-acceptance brings with it the profound sense that I am the body which I live, the sense that I have a real self with which to relate to others. I do not desire to absorb or be absorbed by another. I am a unique self interested in communication and communion, not in conquest and dependency. And that points to sexual health.

The fifth deadly sin is a legalistic sexual ethics. Legalism is the attempt to apply precise rules or laws to actions regardless of the unique features of the context. Legalism is the assumption that an objective standard can be applied in the same way to whole classes of actions without regard to the meanings those actions have to persons.

Many adherents of both Jewish and Christian faiths in our society have fallen into more legalism about sexual morality than virtually any other arena of human behavior. If one looks at such issues as masturbation, homosexual expression, and, in fact, virtually any form of genital expression outside heterosexual marriage, it is easy to find the legalistic posture in Orthodox and Conservative Judaism, in the official natural law stance of Roman Catholicism, and in a variety of conservative Protestant groups.

Adding to the confusion of this ethical scene is that some of the stringent sex rules of traditional orthodox religion have been based, at least in some significant measure, upon erroneous biological assumptions. Jews and early Christians alike made the biologically inaccurate and patriarchal assumption that the male semen was the carrier of life, the woman furnishing only the ground into which the seed was planted. Furthermore, it was frequently assumed that in any one male the total amount of semen was limited. Add to these assumptions the quite understandable concern of these early religious peoples for reproduction and the survival of the tribe in a threatening environment, and it is not difficult to understand why any deliberately nonprocreative male sex act was anathema.

The virtue which speaks to this deadly sin of legalism is love. Our sexuality is intended to be a language of love. Our sexuality is God's way of calling us into communion with others through our need to reach out, to touch, and to embrace—emotionally, intellectually, physically. It is God's beckoning us into the communion of love.

Since we have been created with the will to communion, the positive moral claim upon us is to become what we essentially are: lovers—in the richest, most inclusive sense of that word. The negative side of this, sin, is not basically a matter of breaking moral codes or disobeying laws (though it may involve that). More fundamentally, it is the failure to become what we are. It is the alienation which inhibits fulfillment and communion. It is the failure of love.

The values which emerge from love are several, and they become those criteria by which specific sexual acts might be measured in a nonlegalistic manner (Kosnick, Carroll, Cunningham, Modras, and Schulte, 1977, pp. 92-95). These values apply equally, I believe, to both heterosexual and homosexual expression. First, love is self-liberating. In a sexual act it expresses one's own authentic selfhood and yearns for further growth. Moreover, such love is other enriching; it has a genuine concern for the well-being and growth of the partner. Also, sexual love is honest; it expresses as candidly and truthfully as possible the meaning of the relationship which actually exists between the partners. Further, it is faithful; love expresses the uniqueness of the relationship, yet without crippling possessiveness. In addition, sexual love is socially responsible, aware of, and concerned for the larger community to which the lovers belong. It is life serving; the power of renewed life is shared by the partners. Finally, true sexual love is joyous, exuberant in its appreciation of love's mystery and life's gift.

An ethics centered in this kind of love will not guarantee freedom from mistakes in the sexual life, but it will serve the sexual health of persons crippled by legalism. It will serve their human becoming and their maturation as lovers after the image of the Cosmic Lover by whom they were created.

The sixth deadly sin of which our religious traditions are often guilty is a sexless image of spirituality. This has been more a bane of Christianity than of Judaism, for the church far more than the synagogue has been influenced by the Hellenistic, Neoplatonic split between spirit and body. Consequently, in the early Christian era a ladder image of spirituality emerged. True virtue was associated with movement upward, away from the earth.

Bodily mortification and celibacy were elevated as particularly honorable. Even among married Christians, those who abstained completely from sex were deemed more virtuous than those who had intercourse with the intent to procreate. And those who made love in order to express affection and because they enjoyed it were least meritorious of all.

The good news, however, is that a sensuous, body-embracing, sexual spirituality is more authentic to both Jewish and Christian heritages. A clue is found in an Old Testament book, the Song of Songs. Here is a biblical love poem celebrating the joys of erotic love between a woman and a man. Although much of Christian interpretation over the centuries allegorized this poem into a symbol of "the purely spiritual" relation of the soul and God, devoid of any carnal reality, it is, in fact, a sexual story. The setting is an erotic garden. The lovers delight not only in each other's embodiedness, but also in the sensuous delights surrounding them: flowers, fruits, trees, fountains. Here there is no body-spirit split. Here there is no sexist dualism, no hint of patriarchy, no dominance or submission. The woman is fully the equal of the man. She works, takes initiatives in their meetings, and has an identity of her own apart from her lover (Nelson, 1981, pp. 90-91).

It is true, there is another garden story in our religious heritages, the Garden of Eden. Here the sexual dualisms have become apparent. There is shame in nakedness. Childbirth and daily work alike are cursed by pain, and the woman is derivative from the man. While the erotic garden of the Song of Songs represents a creation-centered spirituality, the Garden of Eden in Genesis represents a sin-and-redemption-centered spirituality. While the latter type has clearly dominated the notions of Western Christian spirituality, it is not the only (or perhaps even the most authentic) type.

We are beginning to realize that repressed sexuality "keeps the gods at bay" and that repressed human development does not bode well for the human-divine relationship. We are beginning to see that the bodily dimensions of feeling and emotion, longing and desire, are not foreign to but rather essential to a healthy spirituality. Such a spirituality will help men and women "discover that their flesh and its desires are not inherently evil, but are sharings in the passionate longings of God...to relate to creation, sharings in God's own lust for life. Spirituality must show forth that God who is shamelessly, even scandalously, in love with earth" (Deschene, 1981, p. 33).

The seventh deadly sin of our religious traditions has been the privatization of sexuality. Here, my pun is intended. Sexuality has been located essentially in "the privates," and hence our understandings of its dynamics have been restricted to the domain of private, interpersonal morality. But such a genitalization of sexuality in itself is a mark of sexual sin and alienation. For our sexuality is far more than genitals; it is our way of being in the world as female or male persons, our capacity for sensuousness, our self-understanding as body-selves, that deep inner drive toward communication and communion with the earthiness of earth and earth's Creator-Spirit. As such, our sexuality pervades the whole of life, including all of our social and institutional relationships.

To the extent that we can transcend a narrowed privatization in our understanding of sexuality, we can also comprehend the fact that an enormous range of social justice issues are at stake. Some are more obvious than others: justice for women, gays, and lesbians; commercialized sex; sexual abuse of women and minors; abortion; population control; the sexual rights of the aged, the handicapped, and the institutionalized. Moreover, a wholistic view of sexuality can help us all see more clearly and respond more effectively to those sexual dimensions present in social issues which appear to have little to do with our subject.

White racism in American society is one such issue. Historically, the schizophrenic attitudes of white males toward women ("there are two kinds—the good ones and the bad ones") were organized along racial lines. The white woman was elevated as the symbol of purity, and the black woman ("the other kind") was used for economic and sexual purposes. Then white male guilt was projected onto black males, who were fantasized as dark sexual beasts never to be trusted around white women. Further, the insecurity of many white people with their own flesh (for the respectable notion of religious virtue does not seem to accommodate many body feelings) frequently led to a "dirty body" image of those whose skin is so obviously different. These sexual dynamics, unfortunately, are still virulently alive in white racism.

Social violence is another issue with important sexual dimensions. The fact that violent crime in this society is overwhelmingly a male phenomenon is no accident. Nor is it an accident that men are directors of an insane global arms race ("my rocket is bigger than your rocket"). The machismo cult of competitiveness, toughness, superiority, potency, and homophobia is terrifyingly present. We are also beginning to learn about the interconnection between the deprivation of body pleasure and tendencies toward physical violence.

The list could be extended. The links between a Western white culture's inability to live in ecological harmony with the earth and our proneness toward self-body dissociation may be significant. The connections between a pervasive consumer mentality and our sexual alienation might also need more understanding.

Religion, then, is an ambiguous human enterprise. There are at least seven deadly sins, and perhaps even more, which certain elements in the Judeo-Christian heritage have contributed to our sexual disease. But speaking from faith's perspective, I am even more convinced of the positive resources of this religious tradition for sexual health. For, God the Cosmic Lover has a passionate love for this earthy creation and has made our sexuality a fundamental dimension of our own passion for wholeness, health, and love. This God somehow keeps breaking into our ambiguous religious ways with fresh resources for our healing.

References

Boswell, J. *Christianity, social tolerance, and homosexuality.* Chicago: University of Chicago Press, 1980.

Deschene, J. M. Sexuality: Festival of the spirit. *Studies in Formative Spirituality*, 1981, *2* , 25-38.

Harrison, B. W. Misogyny and homophobia: The unexplored connections. *Integrity Forum*, 1981, 7, 7-13.

Kosnick, A., Carroll, W., Cunningham, A., Modras, R., and Schulte, J. *Human sexuality: New directions in American Catholic thought.* New York: Paulist Press, 1977.

Nelson, J. B. *Embodiment: An approach to sexuality and Christian theology.* Minneapolis: Augsburg, 1978.

Nelson, J. B. Between two gardens: Reflections on spirituality and sexuality. *Studies in Formative Spirituality*, 1981, *2*, 87-97.

Ruether, R. R. *New woman, new earth.* New York: Seabury Press, 1975.

Russell, L. *Human liberation in a feminist perspective.* Philadelphia: Westminster Press, 1973.

Singer, J. *Androgyny: Toward a new theory of sexuality.* Garden City, N.Y.: Anchor Books, Doubleday, 1976.

Weinberg, G. *Society and the healthy homosexual.* Garden City, N.Y.: Anchor Books, Doubleday, 1973.

World Health Organization. *Education and treatment in human sexuality: The training of health professionals.* Geneva: World Health Organization, 1975.

Overcoming Self-Hate through Education:

Achieving Self-Love among Gay People

Brian R. McNaught

When the American Psychiatric Association's board of directors voted unanimously in December 1973 to remove homosexuality from its *Diagnostic and Statistical Manual of Psychiatric Disorders*, it did not "cure" the nation's 22 million gay men and women overnight.

When Ford and Beach demonstrated in 1951 that homosexual behavior is evidenced in every species of mammal, gay people did not suddenly think of their sexual activity as "natural."

When the Catholic Theological Society of America's Committee on Sexuality insisted (Kosnick, Carroll, Cunningham, Modras, and Schulte, 1971) that scriptural passages traditionally used to condemn homosexuality had been taken out of context and misinterpreted, gay men and women did not suddenly feel loved and accepted by God.

Despite all of the advances in the last 60 years in our understanding of human sexual response; despite the studies and subsequent statements by social scientists which underscore the appropriateness of homosexual behavior for some persons; despite evidence of an increased tolerance of gay people in many segments of society, including some quarters of the Catholic Church, I believe self-hate continues to be the biggest hurdle for many gay people. Ignorance, I believe, is the creator of this hurdle and therefore the enemy of gay men and women and of all those persons who are dedicated to serving the needs of gay people, such as counselors, clergy, therapists, educators, and social workers.

Despite all the public emphasis on civil rights, I suggest that the greatest goal of gay men and women today is to love and to be loved maturely. In conquering self-hate through education, the gay person begins the important process of growth toward love of self and of others, and learns to overcome the obstacles which currently discourage meaningful relationships.

These conclusions are drawn from the observations of personal experiences and through written and verbal communication with a large cross-section of gay men and women throughout the United States and Canada. The communication with the gay people resulted from articles I have written, speeches I have given, or media interviews with me on the subject of homosexuality, conducted since 1974.

Seven years ago, on a nondescript Saturday morning, I grabbed a bottle of paint thinner and drank it. At the time, I seemingly had everything for which to live. I was 26 years old, attractive and intelligent. I was an award-winning columnist on the staff of a Catholic newspaper, a frequent host of a church-sponsored television talk show, and a popular speaker at parish functions. My family celebrated my presence, even when I was accompanied by my handsome and articulate lover, a minister.

My goal in life was to be God's best friend, or a "saint" as we would say in the Catholic Church. I desperately wanted to be loved and associated love with approval. The approval of others, I reasoned, was the only sign we had that it was appropriate to like yourself. In my attempt to experience self-love, I eagerly sought the approval of everyone I encountered, from aunts and uncles to grocery store clerks. If I could make them smile, I must be a person worthy of love, I insisted. I was good at getting smiles, but they were never enough. People who find their worth in the approval of others, I learned, have an insatiable appetite.

Of particular concern to me was the approval of my church, the institution around which nearly all our family social life revolved; the institution which had educated me for 16 years and nurtured in me the idea I was special. Considered a "prince of a boy" by the nuns in grade school, the brothers in high school, the Catholic readers of my weekly column, I was polite, creative, sensitive, and likeable. Nevertheless, I lacked an important sense of self-worth.

I am convinced that my lack of self-esteem resulted from my lifelong awareness of homosexual feelings. To be sexual at all in an Irish Catholic environment in the 1950s was discouraged. Sex was an inappropriate topic for discussion. Because no one ever spoke of homosexuality (boys loving boys and girls loving girls) except in the crudest jokes, I kept my feelings a secret from the time I developed my first crush on a male lifeguard at age 9 and dreamed at night about sleeping with Tarzan.

Like every gay person with whom I have talked, I did not think of myself as a "queer" when I was a youngster; at least I would not accept the term as an accurate description of my feelings. Queers were "sissies" and I was no sissy; I excelled in a variety of sports. Queer boys were supposed to hate girls and at the same time want to be a girl. I liked being a boy and had lots of girl friends. "But if I'm not a queer, what am I?" I wondered.

The myths surrounding homosexuality were presented as truths when I was in grade school and, in many places in this country, they continue to be. Children with a homosexual orientation grow up thinking there is something "queer" about their feelings; something sick and immoral; something which when revealed will eliminate the love and respect of their parents, siblings, and friends.

By the time I entered high school, I figured out that my feelings for other men—my attraction to the male aura—made me a homosexual. Still, I did not see the contradiction between liking the bodies of other boys and eventually getting married. Like millions of other gay people through-out history, I reasoned that I must be the exception.

I do not remember reading anything in popular literature about homo-sexuality. There was no available book or copy of the *Saturday Evening Post* to which I could turn. Outside the office of the guidance counselor there was a rack of pamphlets on a variety of subjects like drinking, dat-ing, and drugs but nothing on homosexuality; nothing that could answer my questions.

"If you come into my office and tell me that you've screwed a chick, I'll talk to you," declared the guidance counselor in a talk to my all-male senior class, "But if you tell me you're queer, I'll kick you out of the office." Until he made that announcement, I had seriously considered telling the counselor my long-held secret. He frightened me into maintaining silence, which I was as good at as I was in securing his approval of me in other areas. When I graduated, the guidance counselor was one of the faculty members who voted unanimously to honor me with the Christian Lead-ership Award.

The process of learning to hate myself was well underway. I knew, for instance, that I would never win the high school award if I revealed my sexual feelings. Even though I felt I was a good person, insofar as I kept the Ten Commandments, discouraged "impure thoughts," and enthusiastically performed various "acts of charity," I began to believe that homosexuals, as a group, were bad people and that I shared somehow in that sin.

I lived two lives—a public one which drew positive attention and a private one which was tormented with fear and anxiety. When I drank the paint thinner, I did so to escape the contradiction between my public and private self. I feared losing the affirmation of others and at the same time could no longer bear lying about my sexual orientation. As far as I was concerned, I was going home to God to whom I would explain myself and from whom I would seek an answer to my pain. How could a father who loved his child allow him or her to be a homosexual?

As I had my stomach pumped, I decided that my secret was literally killing me and that if I cared to live, I had to learn to be myself, accept myself, and love myself regardless of the consequences. It was while sitting on the table in the emergency room of the Catholic hospital that I decided never again to live my life based on other people's expectations. Shortly thereafter, I broke up my relationship because it was beyond repair; I started reading about homosexuality and I joined an organization of gay Catholics called Dignity. After attending a conference on Christian ministry to the homosexual, I wrote a column for the Catholic newspaper on the beauty of gay love. I formed a chapter of Dignity in the city and told the editor and each of the staff people about my homosexuality.

Within a month of opening my new inner-city apartment as a center for gay people, I agreed to be interviewed in a daily newspaper. The next working day, my column was dropped from the Catholic newspaper. In the following weeks, I began legal proceedings against the Church, organized pickets of the newspaper, and began speaking publicly about homosexuality. Three weeks after my column was dropped, I undertook a hunger strike in protest of the sins of the Church against gay people. The fast ended after 24 days when the bishops of Detroit wrote me a letter in which they pledged to work to educate the clergy about homosexuality. The following day I was fired from the remainder of my responsibilities at the newspaper.

In the process of this public ordeal, I alienated my family, most of my readers, and my television viewers. All of the signs of my sainthood, my acceptance, were stripped away. I lost my job, my friendships with many gay and nongay people, the approval of my Church, and my high school Christian Leadership Award (for a period of time). Yet, for the first time in 26 years, I felt authentic, adult, and worthy of admiration and love.

Today, I am in a relationship with another man which is honest, open, sensitive, and supportive. I have many friends who love and support me as a whole person. While I may lack many of life's traditional signs of success, like write-ups in the alumni newsletter and a healthy salary for my work, I have never contemplated suicide again, and I feel fully alive.

My understanding of my homosexuality today is that it is a natural variation; that the genital expression of same-sex feelings ought to be responsible; that gay people are beloved children of God and, like heterosexuals, are called to reach our full potential. My position on the Catholic Church's official teaching is that they are in error when they suggest homosexuality is an "abomination," and that they will one day change their stand.

For me, the process of emerging from an image to a reality, from a secret to a song, from self-hate to self-love is ongoing. Frequently there are temptations to be inauthentic, to return to the closet, or to an image for the sake of approval. The tools I use to continue that growth process remain the same. The most important step I took was educating myself to the truths about homosexuality, truths which tore down the myths of the past and helped me rebuild a positive self-image.

"Modern man's aspirations include not only liberation from *exterior* pressures which prevent his fulfillment as a member of a certain social class, country or society," wrote third world theologian Gustavo Gutiérrez. "He seeks likewise an *interior* liberation, in an individual and intimate dimension; he seeks liberation not only on a social plane but also on a psychological [one]" (1973, p. 30). Gutiérrez argues that our understanding of God must flow not from academic learning but from our experience of everyday oppression and our struggle for liberation. On the other hand, he suggests that those involved in the liberation of others must be concerned not with just their civil rights but also with their self-esteem.

In *The Art of Loving*, Erich Fromm (1967) insists that self-love (interior liberation) requires *knowledge, care, respect,* and *responsibility*. Other observers have used different names for the same concepts, but each insists that the individual must *know* himself or herself in order to feel self-esteem.

Being gay does not make a person an expert on homosexuality. Unfortunately, I feel that many, if not most, of the gay people I have encountered know little of the current data on homosexuality, data which I would suggest liberate a gay person to experience self-love. Many gay people do not know of the findings of Alfred Kinsey or the studies of Evelyn Hooker. They are unaware of the vote by the American Psychiatric Association.

Ten years ago, I made statements such as "I would never sleep with a man I liked" because of my negative attitudes toward my homosexuality. Today, I hear similar comments on a frequent basis.

"My mother caused me to be homosexual," insisted one medical student at a symposium.

"Do you think we are going to hell?" inquired a gay Franciscan priest.

The negative self-image frequently manifests itself in alcohol and drug abuse, irresponsible contact with sexual partners by individuals who know they have a venereal disease and, certainly the most tragic, the physical abuse of one homosexual by another. Humphreys and Miller (1980) found evidence to suggest that homosexual victims of violent crimes are most often those most fearful of being identified as gay. For this reason, gay men and women who seek my help receive homework reading assignments. There are a variety of worthwhile books on the market which I can enthusiastically recommend.

Young people who are confused by their sexual feelings are encouraged to read *A Way of Love, A Way of Life* by Frances Hanckel and John Cunningham (1979). I also encourage teachers of high school and college students to show the filmstrip *The Hidden Minority: Homosexuality in Our Society* (Guidance Associates, 1979).

As general resource books I suggest Tripp's (1975) *The Homosexual Matrix*; *Society and the Healthy Homosexual* by George Weinberg (1972); *Loving Someone Gay* and *Living Gay* by Don Clark (1977, 1979); and *Positively Gay*, edited by Robert Leighton and Betty Berzon (1979).

Women who are interested in reading more about the lesbian experience are encouraged to read *Our Right to Love: A Lesbian Resource Guide*, edited by Ginny Vida (1978); *The Joy of Lesbian Sex* by Emily Sisley and Bertha Harris (1977); and Rita Mae Brown's (1973) *Rubyfruit Jungle*.

Materials recommended for men include *The Joy of Gay Sex* by Charles Silverstein and Edmund White (1977); *Men Loving Men* by Mitch Walker (1977); *The Best Little Boy in the World* by John Reid (1976); and *The Front Runner* by Patricia Nell Warren (1974).

Religion, I have found, is a critical area for many gay people. Too many educators and therapists who are not interested in religion overlook the tremendous influence a religious background can have upon an individual's sense of self-worth. Today, especially, with the so-called Moral Majority and other reactionary groups using the Bible as a weapon in their war against gay civil rights, it is important that gay people and their families have accurate information about the Scriptures and their approach to homosexuality.

Most of the books I recommend are by Catholics but, because of their treatment of both the Old and New Testament, I feel they are helpful to persons of both Christian and Jewish backgrounds. By far, the most important book on the subject is *Christianity, Social Tolerance and Homosexuality* by John Boswell (1980). Also quite helpful are *The Church and the Homosexual* by John McNeill, S.J. (1976); *Embodiment* by James Nelson (1978); and *Human Sexuality: New Directions in American Catholic Thought*, a study commissioned by the Catholic Theological Society of America (Kosnick et al., 1977).

Another critical area of concern for gay people which often influences their ability to love themselves is the response of their families to homosexuality. My parents had many questions, which I attempted to answer, but they seemed to be especially helped by reading books by "impartial" observers whom they could trust. Of particular help at the time was Laura Hobson's (1976) book, *Consenting Adult*. Since then, Betty Fairchild and Nancy Hayward (1979) have written *Now That You Know: What Every Parent Should Know about Homosexuality*, a book which has been successful in moving many parents from a position of fear to one of understanding.

It is not uncommon to hear skepticism from a gay person who has read his or her first book on homosexuality. The opinions of one author who affirms homosexuality are welcomed but distrusted by readers who have spent 18, 30, or 50 years learning to approach their sexuality negatively. However, learning positive new things about one's sexual orientation is not unlike eating peanuts: it is not easy to stop. The people with whom I have worked generally ask for a more extensive book list, with fiction, poetry, history, and biographies included.

A second step which I took and which I recommend to people seeking to build positive self-images is associating with other gay people. I met my minister lover in a bar to which I vowed I would never return once I had "roped" him into a relationship. I viewed the people in the bar as the pathetic "queers" who had been described to me throughout my life and with whom I could not relate. Had I attempted to talk with them, I would have made new friends and therefore probably would not have felt so trapped in my relationship. However, I saw my lover as "not like those others," and I did my best to keep us both away from their influence.

When I broke up my relationship, I soon began meeting a variety of gay people. Some of them I liked very much and some of them I did not, but I came to a growing awareness that "gay" is an adjective and not a noun; that I was a gay man who was part of a community. I met other gay Catholics and gay atheists. I talked with gay Republicans, Democrats, and also gay anarchists. I listened to people defend monogamy and defend open relationships. In this process I felt liberated to choose my own path, to say "I am doing this because it is 'Brian's way' and not because it is the 'gay way.' "

The knowledge which I accumulated by reading enabled me to feel more secure when I encountered other gay people and nongay people. It enabled me to begin taking *responsibility* for my life, to see the need to *care* for my uniqueness, and to *respect* myself. The gay men and women I encourage to join local gay organizations, attend religious services for gay people, and participate in gay social functions return with similar stories. Some people begin dressing in clothing they prefer as opposed to the clothing they wore because they thought it was "gay." Those who find the gay bars to be compromising situations or places in which they are prone to drink too much begin to avoid them and feel better about themselves for doing so. Other people report that while they used to use terms like "queen," "faggot," "fruit," and "fairy" to describe themselves and their friends, they no longer see these terms as humorous or appropriate.

In order to find the gay organizations, the gay religious services, or the social functions sponsored by the community, I suggest that people purchase a copy of the *Gayellow Pages*. This national directory lists all the organizations, publications, and services for gay people in each city in the United States and Canada. It is an invaluable resource for gay men and women and for professionals seeking to meet their needs.

Although I would avoid at all costs "pushing" someone out of the closet, I do believe that "coming out" is an important part of the self-affirmation process. Individuals who are constantly forced to lie to parents, peers, and fellow workers about their social life are denying the joy and beauty of their same-sex feelings and undermining the positive attitudes they might have developed through private reading. While some persons find leading a double life a small price to pay for a successful career or similar goal, most persons with whom I have talked seem unwilling to play the games. Those persons who have "come out of the closet"—who have affirmed their sexual orientation to themselves and to significant others—frequently pay an initial price of rejection by some people, but at the same time they report a unique sense of self-determination, worth, and honesty.

In addition to coming out, I believe participating in your own liberation is important to the notion of care, respect, and responsibility. For many years, I had worked with other disadvantaged minorities in their struggles for civil rights. I did so as a white, presumed-to-be-heterosexual male. As such, my privileged status was maintained, and I was limited in my ability to feel the sense of growth experienced by those more intimately involved. When I lost my column, and then my job, however, I had to begin fighting for my own rights and, in so doing, experienced the same pride which I had seen in the faces of the black people, the Hispanics, and the women with whom I had marched.

There are two national gay organizations which I encourage gay people and their supporters to join. The first is the Gay Rights National Lobby (GRNL), located at 930 F Street, N.W., Washington, D.C., 20004. GRNL is the organization which lobbies Congress to pass legislation favorable to the civil rights of gay people. The National Gay Task Force (NGTF), located at 80 Fifth Ave., New York, N.Y., 10011, is the organization which monitors the media's presentation of homosexuality, works to educate the general public, solicits nondiscrimination clauses from major corporations, and acts as a liaison with the White House and others on issues of concern to the gay community. Persons interested in working for changes in their respective churches are also encouraged to join the gay caucuses which exist in nearly every denomination. Their names and addresses are available in *Gayellow Pages*.

From my discussions with various gay men and women, I suggest that the primary concern today for gay people is being enabled to love and be loved maturely. I have read that one-third of the population (gay and straight) wants a long-lasting relationship with another person, one-third says they want one but are unable to maintain a committed relationship, and one-third has no interest in being involved with the expectations and demands of a one-on-one marriage.

Perhaps because of my reputation as a gay man who supports relationships, the majority of the people with whom I have talked want to be in a committed relationship and dream of it lasting the rest of their lives. Although the men tend to be more flexible than the women on the subject of genital exclusivity, members of both genders talk enthusiastically about having one special person whom they would love and by whom they would be loved. The two questions most frequently asked are: "How do I meet a potential mate?" and "How do I maintain the relationship when there are no role models and no support systems?"

Professionals who would like to assist gay people in this process need to remember that most gay people have been denied the important period of dating and have missed the many lessons such a period teaches. Because most gay people were confused and closeted in high school and college, they generally faked the dating ritual and frequently selected a safe companion for the sake of appearances. When an individual comes out at age 21, he or she has probably never had the experience of kissing, holding the hand of, or even dancing with a person of his or her choosing. The male or female walking into their first gay bar has never had the intimate opportunity to learn that the most sexually attractive person does not necessarily possess the best personality, that race, religion, sense of humor, intelligence, and economic background frequently influence whether or not one person will be compatible with another. Furthermore, many gay people do not have a sexual experience with another homosexual until they have come out of the closet. When they do finally emerge into a gay social scene, they frequently conduct themselves like children in a candy shop, or, as I did, rush into a relationship merely for the sake of affirmation and security. Both the gay person and the professional should be aware that individuals who have only recently come out of the closet will need a period of time for social and sexual adjustment; to expect otherwise is to invite disappointment and more negative self-images.

Because of social attitudes toward homosexuals, the number of healthy social settings available to gay people are limited, though they have increased tremendously since 1969, the birth year of the modern Gay Pride Movement. Gay bars continue to be the most popular meeting places but are not always conducive atmospheres for getting to know another person. In fact, some gay people complain they have never had an intelligent conversation in a gay bar, due in no small part to the loud music, dim lighting, and sexually tense aura of most gay bars.

Gay newspapers (also listed in *Gayellow Pages*) generally record weekly or monthly social activities, such as picnics, sporting events, parties, and so forth, which are designed to meet the needs of the community. They also list organizations such as the gay mountain climbing group, the lesbian mothers' group, and the gay college athletes' association. These different organizations enable gay people to come into contact with people of similar interests. Each year, new social and professional groups are formed, offering that many more opportunities for gay people to find someone with whom they might establish a relationship.

Maintaining a relationship in a society which discourages permanence is difficult enough for heterosexuals, but for gay people who generally receive no support for their efforts from family, employers, the church, or the state, the task can seem impossible. They are forced to make choices. With whom should they spend the holiday—unsuspecting parents or a lover? With whom do they attend office social functions—lover or friend? How do they make sacred their commitment, when their church discourages their union? How do they share a home when some communities will not sell to two unrelated persons of the same gender and many apartment owners prohibit rentals to the same? Is it any wonder that many gay people find it difficult to maintain a committed relationship?

On the other hand, because there are no preconceived notions or role models for gay relationships, they are free to grow into their own unique shapes. Gay couples most successful at maintaining a committed relationship discourage roles and insist on open, honest communication. With increasing frequency, gay couples and liberated heterosexual couples are seeing that their relationships are virtually the same. They share the same goals, many of the same problems and frustrations, and the same joys.

Successful gay relationships are those in which the individuals are sensitive to each other's needs, share tasks equally, leave space for growth, and encourage each other's creativity. If sexual activity is to be engaged in outside of the relationship, it is done with mutual consent.

In this paper I have concerned myself mainly with encouraging gay people to love themselves by eliminating negative self-images through education. My approach has been to destroy the myths of the past through the reading of current literature and contact with other gay people and to encourage in the gay person respect, care, and responsibility. A person who has learned to love himself or herself is able to love another person maturely.

But what about our efforts in behalf of those boys and girls who are aware of homosexual feelings but have not yet had those feelings polluted by ever present myths? While it is important that we meet the needs of yesterday's and today's victims of hatred, fear, and ignorance, it is essential that we not merely try to repair their wounds, but also get about the business of primary prevention.

144   Brian R. McNaught

Young people need to learn at an early age that it is OK to be different from the majority; they need to know that there is no such thing as an unnatural thought. From their school texts, the attitudes of their teachers, sex education courses, television programs, magazine and newspaper articles, popular songs and church sermons, youngsters need to learn that it is all right to be homosexual. Although some parents seem concerned that presenting homosexuality in a positive light will encourage their children to become homosexual, no study supports such fears. On the contrary, healthy, broad-based sex education tends to create healthy, confident people, regardless of their sexual inclinations. Sexually mature people are not intimidated by the sexuality of others.

Educators and others with access to the public need to include "gay people" in sentences where appropriate, have books and other resources available for interested persons, and discourage the telling of antigay jokes. Persons interested in helping homosexual men and women develop positive attitudes toward sexuality and self should diligently watchdog the media, praising the networks and commercial sponsors when the gay subject matter is handled well and criticizing them when it is not, or when there is no attention given to gay people. Letters to the editor in local and national publications which comment on a gay news event or feature are another means of raising public consciousness, eliminating ignorance, and guaranteeing that more people will grow up with a healthy attitude toward themselves and others.

Finally, I applaud the courage of heterosexual men and women who publicly support the healthiness of homosexuality and who champion gay civil rights at the risk of being identified and scourged as homosexual. Although whites can march with blacks, and men can march with women without losing their "privileged status," nothing separates the heterosexual from the homosexual in the front page photo of a gay pride march.

In the same breath, I suggest that professionals, such as my high school guidance counselor, who ought to be comfortable with gay men and women but are not, should examine other career options.

References

Boswell, J. *Christianity, social tolerance and homosexuality*. Chicago: University of Chicago Press, 1980.
Brown, R. M. *Rubyfruit jungle*. New York: Daughters, 1973.
Clark, D. *Loving someone gay*. New York: Signet, 1977.

Clark, D. *Living gay*. Millbrae, Calif.: Celestial Arts, 1979.

Fairchild, B., and Hayward, N. *Now that you know: What every parent should know about homosexuality*. New York: Harcourt Brace Jovanovich, 1979.

Ford, C. S., and Beach, S. A. *Patterns of sexual behavior*. New York: Harper and Bros., 1951.

Fromm, E. *The art of loving*. New York: Bantam Books, 1967.

Gayellow Pages. (Obtainable from Renaissance House, Box 292, Village Station, New York, N.Y. 10014. Published annually.)

Guidance Associates. *The hidden minority: Homosexuality in our society*. White Plains, N.Y.: Guidance Associates, 1979.

Gutiérrez, G. In Sr. C. Inda and J. Eagleson (Eds. and trans.), *A theology of liberation*. Mary Knoll, N.Y.: Orbis, 1973.

Hanckel, F., and Cunningham, J. *A way of love, a way of life*. New York: Lothrop, 1979.

Hobson, L. *Consenting adult*. New York: Warner Books, 1976.

Humphreys, L., and Miller, B. Lifestyles and violence: Homosexual victims of assault and murder. *Qualitative Sociology*, 1980, *3*, 169-185.

Kosnick, A., Carroll, W., Cunningham, A., Modras, R., and Schulte, J. *Human sexuality: New directions in American Catholic thought*. New York: Paulist Press, 1971.

Leighton, R., and Berzon, B. (Eds.). *Positively gay*. Millbrae, Calif.: Celestial Arts, 1979.

McNeill, J., S.J. *The church and the homosexual*. Mission, Kans.: Sheed, Andrews and McMeel, 1976.

Nelson, J. *Embodiment*. Minneapolis: Augsburg, 1978.

Reid, J. *The best little boy in the world*. New York: Ballantine, 1976.

Silverstein, C., and White, E. *The joy of gay sex*. New York: Crown, 1977.

Sisley, E., and Harris, B. *The joy of lesbian sex*. New York: Crown, 1977.

Tripp, C. A. *The homosexual matrix*. New York: McGraw-Hill, 1975.

Vida, G. (Ed.). *Our right to love: A lesbian resource guide*. Englewood Cliffs, N.J.: Prentice-Hall, 1978.

Walker, M. *Men loving men*. San Francisco: Gay Sunshine Press, 1977.

Warren, P. N. *The front runner*. New York: William Morrow, 1974.

Weinberg, G. *Society and the healthy homosexual*. New York: St. Martin's Press, 1972.

Defining Responsible Sexuality

Carol Cassell

Beneath the beguiling question "What is responsible sexuality?" may lie the anxiety and bewilderment that accompany most people's feelings about sex. "What is responsible?" becomes a synonym for "What is normal?" and "What is moral?" Responses are then translated into morality and couched as value judgments of right and wrong, what one "should" do.

Whether or not one perceives a form of sexual behavior as moral or responsible is closely aligned to one's own idiosyncratic perspective of the world. The flow and direction of culture influence the prevalent social values that teach us how and when to channel our sex drives and the physiological tensions that accompany them. We are taught (and carefully so) what to feel and do sexually, when and with whom to do it. "The way we handle our sexual desires and feelings may seem to be innate, instinctive, and natural, but no one is born knowing how to behave sexually. Beginning in infancy, we learn about sexuality from the world around us, from parents, friends, relatives, religious leaders, communication media. Most of this learning has been acquired unconsciously, without our ever realizing that we are being taught" (Strong, Wilson, Clarke, and Johns, 1978, p. 2).

Thus, arriving at a definition of responsible sexuality is no easy task. A definition could be confined to factual and analytical data about the structure and function of sexual organs, sexually transmitted diseases, and health care. Or it could describe how sex is acted out in our society: the norms and mores governing our sex roles and relationships. A definition could be molded from the notion that what is responsible is what most people believe is responsible. But definitions that are based on the beliefs and behavior of the majority of the people may not be "right" in the moral or ethical sense. Katchadourian and Lunde (1975) wrote: "There are standards, to which we all refer at some time or other, that go beyond the consensus and reflect belief in certain principles or moral guidelines, whether the specific issue is sexual behavior, business practices, or war" (pp. 527-528).

To arrive at a definition of responsible sexuality is not to describe a simple set of terms, but rather to describe a kind of reasoning that culminates in a personally held belief in moral or ethical principles about sexual attitudes or behavior or both.

In this paper I examine the issues involved in the resolution of defining sexual behavior that is responsible. I also discuss the need to deal with both personal and professional responsibility in the issues involved in education about sexuality.

Societal Facts and Changes

A difference in interpretation of what is responsible behavior is one consequence of the generation gap between today's young people, their parents, and their grandparents. Social changes during the last decade have been vast. Although most of the facts are familiar, they bear repetition when sexual values and morals come under review: the young mature at an earlier age than they did a decade ago—puberty takes place at an increasingly younger age; the American family is in a state of transition—the age of marriage is later and divorce rates are escalating; more and more children are raised in a single-parent family setting; a majority of mothers are now working outside the home for either economic or psychological reasons.

Beginning in the 1960s, some segments of our society began to discover new ways for couples to relate to each other in response to these complex social changes. They experimented with new family structures and compositions. They wanted couples and families to be formed out of caring, loving, free relationships, not bound by law and religious customs which kept people together regardless of ill feelings and their possible consequences. Although the Moral Majority extremists insist that the women's movement is destroying the family, this movement has arisen partially in response to the failures, destructiveness, and inadequacies of the nuclear family in our complex environment of technological and population change (Lee, 1979).

For example, there is a greater percentage of young women who have had sex, yet the average age of marriage has risen. In the past, people in Western cultures generally married right after puberty. For them the proscriptions against premarital sex were not that significant. But today the period of 8 to 10 years between puberty and marriage continues to be extended. Entering marriage today—"Till death us do part"—is a longer commitment (on the average) than it used to be. Couples live longer after children have gone and have more leisure time. In the early 1900s, between marriage at 18 and death at around 50, approximately 30 years elapsed. Today's marriage, beginning at age 22 to 24 on the average, might easily last 25 years longer than it did in the early 1900s, as the average age of death is around 70 (Stackhouse, 1980).

Paul Glick (cited in Gordon, Scales, and Everly, 1979), a noted demographer, has reported that cohabitation is the fastest growing life-style among young people in the United States. Although his figure does not include those under 18, it could indicate future choices of today's teenagers. Furthermore, Glick estimates that the 1960s saw an increase in couples who were cohabitating that was 23 percent greater than the number of young adults living with a spouse. With increasing opportunities for intercourse and without the necessity of marriage in order to live with someone, "premarital sex" as an indicator of respectability may be as outdated as the dinosaur. Zelnick and Kantner's studies of teenage sexual activity show a marked increase in the percentage of young people engaging in sexual intercourse (chapter in Gordon et al., 1979). Concurrently, there is a wider acceptability of sexual activity among high school and college students. It is now commonplace to feel intercourse is acceptable as long as it is voluntary and provided there is affection between partners.

In a society in which marriage contracts are now subject to renegotiation or termination, in which families may relocate far from each other geographically, it is difficult to know which values are "normal," and which to pass on to young people to teach them the responsible way to behave about sex. For example, today's intercourse may not lead to pregnancy, and premarital sex does not automatically ruin a woman's chances for a successful marriage. Masturbation is no longer viewed as necessarily harmful to mental and physical health.

One important variable in any discussion about sexuality and, particularly, responsible sexuality, is the fact that perspectives are closely related to emotional and religious experiences and personal idiosyncrasies and are influenced by one's historical context. Quite often the significant variables of age, race, religion, and social status are forgotten or clouded over when a statement is made about responsible sexuality. One's perception of what is responsible sexuality is closely aligned to the situation one grows up in and to who one is. It is important for education efforts to focus on how to encourage responsible decisions within any relationship, regardless of marital status and/or the level of intimacy between partners (Gordon et al., 1979).

The Dimensions of Defining Responsible Sexuality

Any person interested in the field of human sexual behavior soon recognizes the extreme difficulty of trying to define precisely what is and what is not responsible sexual behavior. There is no consensus about what is or what is not responsible sexual behavior; even the terminology is inconsistent. For example, throughout the current literature the term "sexually active" is used to describe young women (much more often than young men) who are nonvirgins. Yet when you look into the literature, there is great variance in precisely what sexually active means. In some studies it refers to anyone who has had sexual intercourse. In other studies it refers to someone who is currently having sexual intercourse. If you had sexual intercourse at age 14 and have not had intercourse for 5 years, are you sexually active? Or does sexually active imply intercourse within the last week, month, or year?

Other definitions include activities such as masturbation, petting, and oral-genital sex, which are viewed by some as perversions. Yet, masturbation is recommended by some as a responsible way to deal with sexual feelings. Although the "missionary" coital position is not widely practiced anywhere except in a few Western countries, whether it is moral or not is often discussed. Therefore, any valid discussion of what is responsible sex must consider cultural expectations.

Adding to the confusion over terms relative to responsibility is the task of defining "normal" behavior. An arbitrary determination of which types of sexual behavior are considered normal or appropriate might deal with the traditional double standard of morality for men and women: girls must be virgins until marriage, whereas boys are allowed, even expected, to have many premarital experiences. Gordon et al. (1979) stated:

Normal sexuality is voluntary, genuinely pleasurable, and inclined to enhance the personalities of the people involved. Abnormal or immature sexuality tends to be involuntary. People engage in it not because they want to but because they can't help it. Immature sexuality is generally exploitative, rarely enjoyable, and often degrading. Responsible sexuality, by contrast, is characterized by respect for oneself and by genuine caring for another human being. (p. 28)

There is also difficulty in defining responsible sexuality because what would have been identified as responsible sexuality in the late 19th and early 20th century would hardly be considered responsible by today's standards. For middle-class and working women during those Victorian times, one sexual misstep (i.e., having sexual intercourse) could result in sexual and social ostracism. At the same time, male sexual involvement with prostitutes or servants was tolerated, if not officially acknowledged, because no respectable man would trifle with a respectable woman. Legitimate sexual behavior was restricted to the marriage bed, where procreation rather than pleasure was the goal. Although most Victorians did not live by these norms of respectability, this ideology of sexual control and repression came to be reflected in our laws and social institutions (Roberts, 1980). Contrast this with today when responsibility is often translated as avoiding unwanted pregnancy and not spreading V.D.

Using traditional values to determine what constitutes responsible sexuality is not a valid solution. When one explores what exactly are traditional values, one finds a great deal of confusion and misunderstanding (Verheyden-Hillard, 1978). The first question to be asked is: whose traditional values? For someone age 18, the values of the early 1900s are hardly those considered traditional; instead, he or she may look to the 1950s for traditional values (thus the current preppie rage). On what period of time are traditional values based? Exactly what and whose traditions? Quite often traditional values reflect the double standard of women as "good girls" and men as "playboys." But, these traditions are offensive to a great number of people and are being dismissed as invalid.

Responsibility is a word that is almost always referred to as "a difficult one to define" (Stackhouse, 1980). Apparently it is much easier to define irresponsible sexuality than responsible sexuality. Irresponsible sexuality may be defined as having sexual intercourse exploitatively, coercively, or compulsively; not using contraceptives; spreading venereal disease; or committing sex crimes such as rape or child molestation (Gordon et al., 1979).

However, responsibility has been defined. Stackhouse (1980) says:

Responsibility is one's responsibility for oneself and for or to others...it involves caring for one's whole self and other persons in their totality. It involves being liable, answerable, and accountable for one's actions. It is being sensitive, responsible to the core of oneself and others...caring for others as much as one cares for oneself. (p. 9)

Responsibility is also defined as accepting any individual preferences. This is stated as: "the right [of each young adult] to decide sexual morality for themselves, free from patronizing or condescending attitudes on the part of adults and free from conformist pressure from friends" (Gordon et al., 1979, p. 257).

Responsibility has been described as part of one's rights. Kirkendall (cited in McCary, 1978) prepared a bill of sexual rights and responsibilities that has been endorsed by approximately 38 other authorities in the field of sex education. He felt this statement was needed because sexuality has been denied its proper place as a part of human rights for too long. Since a discussion of each of his points would be lengthy, the rights and responsibilities are simply listed:

The boundaries of human sexuality need to be expanded.

Developing a sense of equity between sexes is an essential feature of a sensible morality.

Repressive taboos should be replaced by a more balanced and objective view of sexuality based on a sensitive awareness of human behavior and needs.

Each person has both an obligation and a right to be fully informed about the various civic and community aspects of human sexuality.

Potential parents have both the right and the responsibility to plan the number and time of birth of their children, taking into account both social needs and their own desires.

Sexual morality should come from a sense of caring and respect for others; it cannot be legislated.

Physical pleasure has worth as a moral value.

Individuals are able to respond positively and affirmatively to sexuality throughout life; this fact must be acknowledged and accepted.

In all sexual encounters, commitment to humane and humanistic values should be present.

A Personal Definition

Although all of this is helpful, before we define for others what responsible sexuality implies, we have to wrestle with our own personal definitions. For example, how do you personally feel about homosexuality? How do you feel about teenage pregnancy? The Egual Rights Amendment? If a 15-year-old cannot raise a child, should she bear one? Should a 15-year-old who is a father be responsible for raising his child? Do you describe responsible sexuality as not bringing unwanted children into the world? Do you feel that men are equally responsible for conception, contraception, and childrearing? Do you feel responsible adults can fulfill their roles in guiding young people if they do not discuss the pleasures as well as the consequences of sexual intercourse with them? How do you personally feel about masturbation? How do you feel about abortion? How do you define promiscuity?

It is impossible to be in a field where we help other people understand their own human sexuality and talk about responsible sexual decision making without having defined our own personal credo.

The Professional Role in Education about Sexuality

After we have developed a personal set of beliefs about sexuality and sexual behavior, our professional role can be considered. If we want young people to take responsibility for their sexual behavior, they must have access to information and an understanding of how sexuality fits into their own lives.

One course of action is to advocate and provide sex education even though the search for a direct, causal relationship between the current forms of sex education and responsible sexuality is probably illusory. One reason for this can be found in the "theoretical and educational neglect of some of the most important variables that influence the way knowledge is acquired and the manner in which sexual behavior is expressed" (Gordon et al., 1979, p. 177). However, a person's sex education and his or her responsible sexual behavior may depend upon the type of relationship in which the behavior occurs, the person's level of literacy, and the extent to which sexual partners communicate. Without knowing these variables it is difficult to look for specific effects of education upon responsible behavior. Sommerville (cited in Gordon et al., 1979) mentioned a key qualification to studies of the effects of sex education: the need to realize that sex education remains a sensitive, political issue in many communities, and that any evaluation of programs should take into account how well communities are "able to withstand the organized attacks on family life and sex education" (p. 166).

Unfortunately, it has become almost a trend for professional sex educators to state that sex education is not only vague but does not promote responsible sexuality. Recent years have seen a recycling of an opposition to sex education. Inadvertently, many professionals have added fuel to the controversy by claiming (on the basis of scanty research) that sex education may not have significant effects upon individual behavior, making such remarks as: "Without real analysis the differences for contraceptive behavior between those who have taken a sex education course and those who have not is insignificant." Their conclusions are misleading because, "notably absent in these reports are such critical factors as whether the course was interesting or boring, whether the teacher was adequately trained, whether the course gave a comprehensive, semester-long treatment or single hurried lecture, whether 'communication,' 'responsibility,' 'sexual attractiveness,' 'love' and other concepts were discussed or whether only 'the facts were presented'" (Gordon et al., 1979, p. 257).

Most often, professionals find themselves in endless debates about the normalness or the appropriateness or the morality of different sexual behaviors such as abortion, masturbation, premarital sex, and homosexuality. It is a useless and endless debate because it is not a debate of facts but of one's own personal views. McCary (1978) noted that "some people arbitrarily evaluate certain sexual behavior—their own, of course—as the only normal sexual behavior, and will go to great lengths to impose their views on others. Anyone who fails to comply with these arbitrary standards is considered an anti-Christ, pervert or sexual inferior" (p. 11). It is from these roots that antisex education sentiments grow.

Thus, a primary responsibility for the professional is to make other individuals aware that the sex education debate is primarily based on individual views of the world and on whether or not education is valued and trusted or feared. In other words, we need to view it as a "battle for freedom to learn" based on differences in values and philosophy, rather than as a moral debate on responsible sexuality.

Rubin (cited in McCary, 1978), analyzed the debate by showing the two opposing points of view on providing sex education for young people. He found that a delineation of "liberal or open" attitudes or "conservative or closed" attitudes toward sex education is related to basic attitudes about learning and education. The closed attitudes:

hold that sex education is primarily a function of the home and oppose all but the most limited kind of reproductive education in the school;

conceive of sex education as a negative process needed to inhibit any sexual behavior prior to marriage and as a means of cutting down on venereal disease, illegitimacy, and teenage sex;

insist that sex education consists of an indoctrination of fixed moral codes of conduct;

prefer an atmosphere of conformity rather than open questioning and critical evaluation.

In other words, it is really our responsibility to bring out the fact that stands for or against school sex education depend upon very different points of view. Compare the closed concept of sex education with what might be called the more open point of view of people who:

see sex education in broad terms of self-understanding and interpersonal relationships rather than as a unit in reproduction;

conceive of sex education as a positive process aimed at developing individual sexuality to its fullest potential;

accept an atmosphere conducive to open-minded questioning;

see sex education as a genuine educational process that provides insight and information to enable the individual to make intelligent and responsible choices among competing alternatives of sexual behavior and value systems.

McCary (1978) noted that there is a danger that unconscious religious or cultural biases will filter into school sex education programs. For example, courses in public schools are likely to reflect the most conservative ethical values of the community as interpreted by the teacher or the school administration. Otherwise it is feared the programs may be criticized or condemned as being immoral:

Many people accept the theory that frank sex education is fine, as long as it reflects a high moral religious theme. But these people have difficulty with the idea that responsible sexuality can be discussed without reference to marriage, love, God, and religious beliefs. Without these elements, sexual behavior somehow becomes irresponsible and/or filthy or immoral in their minds. An interesting debate can be staged on the appropriateness of public school teachers, counselors and administrators advocating sexual behavior only if it is consistent with a particular religious point of view. (Bruess and Greenberg, 1981, p. 13)

All the evidence suggests that ignorance and misunderstanding of human sexuality are still widespread in our society, and the situation continues to be self-perpetuating.

We must get the message across that, in the absence of family, community, and school support, today's children and adolescents are often left alone to make sense of the confusing and contradictory messages about sexuality that bombard them from all directions.

Young people are accused of being irresponsible about their sexual behavior because many adults are painfully unclear about what they truly believe to be acceptable or responsible sexual behavior. This has resulted in confusion and uncertainty about the place of sex education in schools and in communities. A major role for professionals is to dispel the fear, anxiety, and misinformation that permeate most of these attitudes.

The responsibility of a public advocacy role then is to legitimize sexuality and to discuss publicly its effect on the quality of life throughout the whole community. We must reassure the general public that "sexuality is not an immutable, predetermined entity that proceeds uncontrollably along some predestined course, but is a malleable set of behaviors, fantasies, beliefs and attitudes that can be changed and shaped by learning, choice and action" (Roberts, 1980, p. 3).

If somewhere in this paper you have been looking for a definitive definition of responsible sexuality, you are about to be disappointed. The only definitive statement is: there is not one definition—defining responsible sexuality is an extremely personal activity. We need to see the issue as one of a multitude of differences between people over sexual values, attitudes, and behavior.

It is our responsibility to increase public awareness about the need to guide sexual learning more effectively and more positively by providing more adequate opportunities for young people and adults to learn about sexuality and to understand sex roles, relationships, and behavior. We can begin by examining the assumptions made about sexuality through the institutional policies and practices that make up the fabric of our society.

References

Bruess, C. E., and Greenberg, J. S. *Sex education: Theory and practice*. Belmont, Calif.: Wadsworth, 1981.

Gordon, S., Scales, P., and Everly, K. *The sexual adolescent*. North Scituate, Mass.: Duxbury Press, 1979.

Katchadourian, H. A., and Lunde, D. T. *Fundamentals of human sexuality* (2nd ed.). New York: Holt, Rinehart and Winston, 1975.

Lee, M. How will our daughters grow? In R. Crow and G. McCarthy (Eds.), *Teenage women in the juvenile system: Changing values.* Tucson, Ariz.: New Directions for Young Women, 1979.

McCary, J. L. *McCary's human sexuality.* New York: D. Van Nostrand, 1978.

Roberts, E. J. Dimensions of sexual learning in childhood. In E. J. Roberts (Ed.), *Childhood sexual learning: The unwritten curriculum.* Cambridge, Mass.: Ballinger, 1980.

Stackhouse, B. *Teenage pregnancy: A challenge to do right by each other.* New York: United Church Board for Homeland Ministries, 1980.

Strong, B., Wilson, S., Clarke, L. M., and Johns, T. *Human sexuality: Essentials.* St. Paul, Minn.: West, 1978.

Verheyden-Hillard, M. E. Counseling: Potential superbomb against sexism. In *Today's girls: Tomorrow's women.* Report to Girls' Clubs of America National Seminar, Racine, Wisconsin, June 1978.

On the Sources of Sexual Change

John H. Gagnon

There is probably general agreement among most persons in this society that sexuality is different nowadays from what it was in the past. Although we agree on this, however, we do not usually consider whether all or only some aspects of sexuality have changed, how much difference there is between past and present, and, indeed, what the actual date might be in the past which serves as our baseline moment. Without a minimum specification of these issues it is impossible to understand the social and psychological processes through which various aspects of sexuality may have changed (if indeed they have). It is only after having considered such problems that we can tentatively approach the relation between programs of preventive mental health and sexuality, and how one might influence the other. An understanding of how contemporary sexual practices have emerged from the past may provide some clues about the leverage points for programs of change. It may also limit optimism about how much individual programs can accomplish, not only whether they may produce change, but, more importantly, whether they can produce positive changes.

Sexuality: Change and Continuity

There does exist, with reference to some aspects of sexuality, information from a variety of sources that can give us some rough sense of what some of the directions of change have been since the 1930s and 1940s when minimally adequate sexual bookkeeping for this society began. A few examples should suffice.

There is a substantial body of evidence to support the theory that since the data reported in the Kinsey studies on white and largely youthful college-educated people (Kinsey, Pomeroy, and Martin, 1948; Kinsey, Pomeroy, Martin, and Gebhard, 1953), the incidence of premarital inter-

Partial support for this research was provided by a grant from the John and Markle Foundation and The Bio-Medical Research Support grant, the State University of New York, Stony Brook.

course among young women has increased and that intercourse now occurs with more partners and starts at an earlier age for some segments of the population (for a summary of these changes see Chilman, 1979). For college student populations we can roughly date the beginning of the behavioral aspects of these changes back to the early to middle 1960s. The first target cohort to examine would thus seem to be those born around 1945 and after, those at the beginning of the baby boom. Further increases in these measures of premarital sexuality have occurred since the mid-1960s, and various recent contextual social effects (e.g., the influence of larger numbers of sexually experienced peers, the availability of birth control) also need to be studied. Two correlates of these changes include increased rates of premarital pregnancy and premarital cohabitation (Chilman, 1980; Gagnon and Greenblat, 1978).

It is proper to note that these well-documented changes in premarital heterosexuality of young women have produced considerable ideological conflict. The sexual property value of women and the control of reproductivity remain social concerns, and rises in these rates have usually been read as indicators of individual and collective moral collapse. This struggle for control over the sexuality of young women has largely obscured changes in the premarital heterosexuality of young men. Thus the fact that young men, at least since the 1940s, are less likely to have their first coital experience with prostitutes, that the frequency of such intercourse has declined, and that there is some evidence that young men are acquiring similar patterns of premarital intercourse (both behaviorally and psychologically) to young women has excited little concern (Miller and Simon, 1974). None of these patterns of change is as yet well understood, although some links in the process have been clarified. For instance, the relation between the decision to begin coitus and the availability of birth control appears to be zero.

In another domain of sexuality there is evidence from many sources (the mass media, a few scientific studies, the existence of activist social movements, and the character of daily life, at least in some cities) that gay men and lesbians have a different relation to the dominant heterosexual style in the society than 20 years ago. One can locate changes over time among gay men and lesbians in the experience of self-identification, in forms of community participation, in the nature of emotional, intellectual, and political commitments (for a review of the recent literature, see Gagnon, 1981). Most critically, the definition of homosexuality and heterosexuality as polar opposites—the fact that our everyday conception of the one is predicated on the absence of the other—is in a preliminary state of collapse. The erosion of a boundary between homosexuality and heterosexuality means that the differences and similarities between both forms of conduct may be readdressed in order to construct a new form of social reality.

Certain aspects of sexuality have become more present in the landscape of everyday life. The availability of visual sexual stimuli, both chosen and unchosen, increased steadily between the mid-1950s and the late 1960s and exploded during the 1970s. There are probably few urban places without at least one X-rated bookstore or X-rated movie theater. Television, subscription or free, programs or advertising, brings into the home that which was not even on respectable newsstands after World War II. The ubiquity of the change, the current sense of its routineness even by those who oppose it, makes the past not only dim and far away, but in some palpable way, false. Did any of us really grow up in a world where the female nude was invisible; where nudist magazines were sold in brown wrappers from under the counter in special bookstores; in which the corset ads in the Sears Roebuck catalogue were the acme of sensuality; in which women could be viewed as having no interest in visual sexual stimuli because there was something different about their brains (Kinsey et al., 1953)?

We tend to be fascinated by (and hence unquestioning of) the evidence presented in support of these changes; neither those who welcome sexual change nor those who abominate it deny its ubiquity. The media abet our narrow focus because they both foment our interest in change (novelty is news) and satisfy it in an instant. Yet there are a substantial number of domains of sexual life in which the evidence for change is not very substantial.

An examination of all of the reliable and even marginally reliable studies of marital intercourse suggests that rates, no matter how measured, have remained remarkably stable over the last four decades (Gagnon, Greenblat, and Roberts, 1978; Greenblat, 1982). Both the average number of times per month for the aggregate and the rate for various age groups in the population are exceptionally stable. There has been some drift upward that can be attributed to improved contraception and reduced time in childbearing, but no substantial shifts (Trussell and Westoff, 1981). Despite the legitimacy of marital sex, the proliferation of prosex marriage manuals, the availability of sex therapy, and the opportunity for derivative sexual arousal from the more titillating TV shows, rates of marital coitus have changed very little. There is no evidence that this is because it has reached some biological maximum in the population.

What little data we have on masturbation suggest that the incidences and frequencies observed by Kinsey remain much the same today (Atwood, Gagnon, and Simon, 1982; Kinsey et al., 1953). Not only does this continuity stretch back to the 1950s, but to the 1920s among middle-class populations. The differences that Kinsey observed between women and men still seem to obtain. No study suggests major increases in female masturbation with regard to incidence or to frequency.

As we are forced to take account of stability it becomes more difficult to evade the fact that we do not have good explanations of why change has taken place. Furthermore, it raises issues about what the connections are between those aspects of sexual conduct that we have always assumed to have something to do with each other. If there is a substantial increase in the incidence and perhaps even the frequency of premarital sex, why has marital sex even among younger populations stayed the same? If the world is more erotic in its everyday character, why has the masturbation rate stayed the same?

A number of extremely serious theoretical and practical questions emerge from these apparent contradictions. Is it possible that the domain of sexual acts is not a singular and well-connected set of activities which mutually influence each other and which have a common set of causes? Is it possible that though sexual acts all seem to involve the genitals, they are not all the same in their social or psychological meanings or origins? My colleague William Simon and I have already raised some questions about the degree to which events that are identified as sexual early in the lifespan are consequential for what is labeled and even experienced as sexual later in life. Thus there is doubt whether genital touching among infants is related to adult masturbation—the activity is not experienced similarly nor is its presence or absence causative of adult conduct (Simon and Gagnon, 1968). An expanded version of this argument would suggest that various domains of adult sexual conduct may have little to do with each other (e.g., masturbation may not influence premarital coitus), even though adults experience the conduct as part of the same general area of living. Our problem is that we do not have a good theory of the origins and maintenance of what we call sexual conduct, and this in itself constrains our ability to talk about sexual change or nonchange. A second problem is that we tend to look inward into the sexual or the parasexual in order to find causal origins rather than to expand our vision to include a wide range of institutions and processes that are formative of and supportive of the sexual domains that exist today. Too often we have been obsessed by sexual theory rather than developing discipline-based theories of sexuality with their roots outside of sexology.

Parents' and Children's Sexual Learning

Perhaps one way to begin is to examine some recent research on the role that various institutions have played in transmitting and sustaining sexual learning. During the late 1970s the Project on Human Sexual Development at Harvard University developed a research action program dealing with the family, the community, and television in their roles as sex educators. The conception of sexuality we used was a wide one—the concern was not only with the erotic and reproductive elements, but with those that were implicated in gender role, affectional styles, the role of body, expectations about personal life-styles, as well as questions of moral responsibility. Since all of these are present in the ultimate doing of sexual things, even if only as tacit knowledge, we were concerned with how they were formed, how they were changed or maintained, and in what institutional and personal contexts (see Polanyi, 1968, for a discussion of tacit knowledge). Although in the project we dealt with only a few contexts in detail, we attempted to keep in mind each of the others as we tried to account for stability and change in sexual conduct.

Part of this research project focused on the role of the family in informing young children about sexuality. Because this study was formulated early in the research, the focus was more narrow and limited than it would have been if it had been done last instead of first. The largest body of information we gathered was on the information-giving roles of parents of 3- to 11-year-old children about sex and reproduction. The data was gathered from a probability sample-survey in which 1,482 mothers and fathers were interviewed, a sample that included both currently intact couples as well as single parents from one large metropolitan area in the Midwest. The children were not interviewed, although both the mother and father were in about three-quarters of the cases.

The findings of the survey about the amount and character of information transmitted by parents to these children would be uniformly depressing to those who want parents to be primary sex educators (Gagnon and Roberts, 1981). The tension between parents and professional sex educators about sex education is probably not as profound as in the past when the former were viewed by the latter as the potential enemies of their children's future sex lives; however, the very low baseline of effort recorded by the study might still drive the professional back to the schools even if only on the basis of cost effectiveness. Although parents wanted to be helpful to their children, they felt unprepared and uneasy. They reported not knowing what to say as well as not knowing how to say it. Perhaps most apparent was their fear that sex information had the potential to provoke sexual conduct. That is, they felt that the information that they gave to their children, particularly as the latter approached puberty, was likely to be converted into overt conduct. When forced to give information, they did so using the single inoculation method: "Tell them once and you won't have to do it again."

The most telling findings were the answers to the questions about the relation between intercourse and pregnancy. When parents were asked when children should be told about the fact that the fetus grows inside the mother, they commonly gave an early age even though there was evidence that many of them had not yet given such information to their children who were over this age. When asked when children should be told about intercourse and its connection with pregnancy, this was always at some much later age. Those with 5-year-olds said at 10; those with 10-year-olds, 13 or 14. These findings are correlative with those that indicate that parents have not spoken to their 10- and 11- year-olds about events such as masturbation and menstruation. Furthermore, parents report traditional responses to the sex education needs and the potential sexual lives of boys and girls. Girls need to know about menstruation, boys do not; masturbation when it is approved is more appropriate for boys than girls.

It is evident from this sample that these practices are not much improved when we contrast parents by whether they are well or poorly educated, by whether they are single or married, by whether they are sexist or nonsexist in attitude or in the division of household labor. Of course, there are some differences, but what is striking are similarities between all parents in the volume of information they provide and in the ways it is provided. A gross but not inaccurate summary is that mothers rather than fathers tend to provide information to both male and female children. Such information provision tends to be infrequent, is more about reproduction than eroticism, declines with the age of the child, and is more often initiated by the child than by the parent.

Part of the dilemma that parents face is that there is little evidence from their own experience that giving sexual information to their children is going to do much good, whereas they believe that they do have evidence that it might do harm. In the trade-off between providing information about intercourse, and the possibility that it might reduce sexual dysfunction in the child's future marriage, and the possibility of preventing a premarital pregnancy by information restriction or negative injunction, parents choose the latter. These fears may be the best case that can be made for the many parents who do not give their children information about sexuality. Also in this group, however, is a substantial number of parents who are morally opposed to sexual expression of any kind other than marital intercourse for their children. They believe that all nonmarital sexuality is wrong; even if there were evidence that sex information and sexual conduct (e.g., masturbation) improved mental health, they would still argue against it. It is true that there are parents who currently provide reproductive and sex information for their children in forms thought to be useful and an unknown number who could be persuaded to do so if they were properly approached, persuaded, and trained—but at the moment they are a minority.

The issue here, however, is not whether parents if offered new programs would join up; it is the similarity of these findings to what we would have found 30 years ago in terms of parental participation in the sexual education of their children. Our study was conducted in the late 1970s and included a number of youthful parents, that is, parents who were born after 1955 and who were reared in the 1960s. The lack of differences between this study and the past, and between the younger and older parents does not suggest basic changes in parental attitude toward sexuality. This is not to say that other important changes may not have occurred in the other domains which we viewed as important to sexuality: changes in gender role, training, and expectations; changes in the way parents teach children about their bodies; changes in the ways in which emotions are expressed and constrained; changes in the ways in which parents approach the questions of moral responsibility. However, a review of the literature that exists suggests that these domains of parenting have not changed a great deal either. Perhaps the one change has been the larger number of children who have been reared in nonnuclear households for at least part of the youthful period. Thus familiarity with parental divorce, single parenting, parental dating, remarriage, and stepparenting is more common and therefore might influence the range of life-style options thought appropriate. At the same time it is possible that some may acquire a preference for more traditional styles as a result of living unconventional childhoods.

Parents may indeed influence the sexual lives of their children, but evidence for how and to what degree remains obscure. What we do know is that the processes are commonly indirect and rarely take place through the provision of reproductive and erotic knowledge. The absence of teaching may be consequential, but only inasmuch as it creates an informational vacancy in which other agents can take up residence. In addition it is clear that the family institution is probably not the major force behind changes in the sexual lives of young people. Furthermore to the degree that the family remains a desexualized institution between parents and children, it may also remain so in the relation between husband and wife. The fears of the sexual that seem to pervade parent-child relations may also characterize familial sexual relations in general. Whatever evidence there is suggests that husbands and wives do not communicate about sexuality and that their sexual lives are governed more by silence than speech (Greenblat, 1982). An understanding of the reasons why men and women do not communicate about sexuality, a failure of communication that may be leading to low rates of marital sexuality, may also lead us to some fruitful ideas about why they do not talk about sexuality with their children.

Absence of input about eroticism by parents may well be one reason that peers tend to dominate the social context in which young people learn about erotic sexuality. However, parents are not only important for what they fail to do but for the ways in which they reinforce traditional gender role values. By training their male and female children differently they set up the conditions for a division between young men and women in adolescence that allows separate peer worlds to emerge. In these two separate and unequal worlds boys learn about genital sexuality and masturbation while girls learn about love and the importance of boys. Parental absence allows peers to control erotic learning and practice; parental presence reinforces traditional gender role stereotypes (Gagnon and Simon, 1973). As parents have grown less powerful in the lives of their adolescent children, peers have grown more important. What may be learned from this is that when parents' views are heavily reinforced, as in the case of gender roles, parents retain their significance; when they are both absent and resisted, as in the case of erotic learning, other forces take control.

The Significance of Television

In contrast to the constancy of parents, the media in a number of forms have substantially changed their sexual content over the last 40 years. The media, however, should be considered as a complex and often contradictory set of sources, rather than as a single set of mutually reinforcing influences. The media focus on elements of sexual conduct that differ according to age. There are advice books for children, for adults for children, for adults, sexuality textbooks for college students, prime-time television (documentaries, advertisements, and news, as well as entertainment), and the cinema (with ratings from PG to X) all of which present differing versions of the world of sexuality to different audiences.

Perhaps what is most apparent are the ways in which the media have become the major repository for values and attitudes about sexuality which were once embedded in the community and the family. The argument here is not that parents or communities in the past were especially active in providing information, but that they were the primary arenas of sexual opportunity and sexual constraint. As the society has grown more urban and even urban villagers have drifted into suburban sprawls, the mechanisms for informing (if not constraining) the young and the old about sexuality have moved into the hands of those who are in control of the media. In addition, these media systems have been central in creating a national set of sexual images, values, and knowledge, which is available everywhere and instantaneously. The regionalism of the United States, which in some cases lasted until the late 1960s, allowed various locales to preserve local values and styles long after they had disappeared in the urban centers. The contemporary capacity of single-issue groups to mobilize national constituencies via the media is an ironic result of the techniques and skills of a national media network that welds together geographically diverse minorities into one national constituency.

The critical single institution that has influenced national life is, of course, network television; the television set is the closest thing to a new family member since radio. The problem with television, however, is the complex ways in which it shapes sexual conduct. If we respond to it in terms of our traditional model—that a single sexual stimulus automatically provokes a significant behavioral sexual response, a theory which was the basis for the 1940s' and 1950s' reactions to what was then called pornography—our focus on television will be on unacceptable language, explicitly sexual situations (or the preliminaries to them), unacceptable life-styles or roles (a homosexual character, a sexually active woman, an illegitimate child), or the exposure of parts of the body in what is viewed as a provocative manner. Although prime-time TV is now somewhat sexier than it was in the past, particularly as the soap operas move from the afternoon to prime time, it is not clear that such programs have a serious effect on overt conduct.

Perhaps this is true because the sexual materials are systematically placed in programmatic contexts that are nearly entirely traditional, at least in terms of the covert sexual traditions in the society. If we examine those other components of sexual life (the significance of gender roles, attitudes toward the body, the expression of the emotions), there is little evidence on television that any but the most acceptable values are reinforced. And it is *reinforce* that must be the operative word—television works, as do all genre literatures, by the constant repetition of formulaic routines. Even the best of routine television operates symbolically in this same fashion. Such programs depend on stereotyping and the avoidance of surprise, unlike works which fall outside of the popular or genre traditions. At the core then, television reinforces sex role stereotypes about men and women, age stereotypes about adults and children, attractiveness stereotypes about men and women, and stereotypes about the expression of emotion.

The erotic content of television is minuscule and focuses largely on patterns of heterosexual activity among the attractive, and the punishment—drawn out, of course—of those who violate various sexual taboos. Such programs are similar to romance comic books or pulp novels or mass audience best-sellers in their cultural consequences. Whatever erotic excitement exists is kept within tight bounds by the contexts of presentation. J. R. Ewing has the same value for the watching audience as do Billy Martin or other figures of moral notoriety in the society. They are the equivalent of Mardi Gras or carnival culture, time out from the real world.

What is real about contemporary television is its mixture of consumption desires and sexuality. This is, of course, not original to television, but little of substance is. Television offers the goods and services of upper-middle-class life as the backdrop to nearly all of its stories. It is these goods that are the most powerful motivators for the audience; it is their presence as the potential rewards of conformity which is overwhelming. As advertisements, as the backdrops to shows, as the things given away on the game shows, it is the goods that are the fundamental message of television. It is not known what the effects are on sexual values of this confluence of largely conformist values presented in the context of material rewards. There is some evidence that, for heavy viewers at least, there is a consolidation of traditional values—that TV plays a major role in reality creation (Gerbner, Kross, Morgan, and Signorielli, 1981). It may be that those forms of sexuality which appear to provide access to consumption goals may be those most reinforced. Since sexuality directed toward mutual pleasure and intimacy offers very little as a pathway to getting such goods, it might be expected that very little will change in this direction as a result of prime-time television.

Television has taken on a more distinctly sexual air in the last 5 years. That is, television has been able to treat certain taboo topics as part of the subject matter of its prime-time fare and in some cases treat these topics sympathetically from a liberal standard. As a result, adultery, prostitution, child molestation, homosexuality, and other topics have become, if "tastefully" treated, part of the routine fare of evening viewing. There are more breasts, more wiggling buttocks, more bikinis, and the standard continuation of vaudeville humor. The consequences of this recent surge are presently unknown, but one can speculate that the effects will be collectively modest, though there will be some portions of the audience who will be particularly affected by a single show and its material.

The Social Science Media

There is another media system that exists sometimes parallel to and sometimes interacting with television, which in some cases offers materials for programs or justification for them. This is the reasonably voluminous flow of materials which has issued from the social and behavioral sciences over the last 40 years with reference to sexuality. These materials have served as the basis for and the grist for the social science journalist and the journalist social scientist. The sociologist Robert Park once spoke of sociology as super journalism and the margin between scientific social science and popular social science has eroded. Thus surveys are now conducted by magazines, some of them meeting many of the technical rules of sampling, and first publication of these materials is scheduled as part of the magazine's fare. In most cases the studies are close to worthless and in other cases harmful because they falsify the world; however, the need of the media machinery for new social facts to place between the advertisements is nearly endless (Gagnon and Greenblat, 1978).

New sexual facts are prime candidates for inclusion in such media reports and commentary. What is important about them is that they often offer alternative forms of sexual conduct both in terms of what persons do and why they might do them. The result of this mass of sexual information and theory from the social sciences has been to conventionalize increasingly what were previously forms of sexual deviance (Gagnon, 1977). One need only examine the sexuality textbooks meant for college students or the books for parents and children to recognize the themes that emphasize the tolerance of difference and include that which was once considered different within the orbit of the usual. A number of strategies have been adopted to reduce previously noted differences. The first has been to point out that what was formerly valued and formerly disvalued have much in common (the Shylock strategy): do not gay men and lesbians hold jobs, care for their parents, love their children, pay their taxes, share leisure pursuits in the same manner as the dominant heterosexual class? The second has been the claims of common origin: is not prostitution simply just another way of making money, is it not merely just another occupation such as being a doctor, a lawyer, or a nurse? Even motivational histories can look the same: the young woman who has premarital sex for love, belonging, and fulfilment has the same emotional needs as the young woman who joins the 4H Club. There is a systematic erosion of what were clear-cut differences between the virtuous and the corrupt: masturbation and surrogates in sex therapy are now the necessary adjuncts of sexual health in many clinics around the country (LoPiccolo and Heiman, 1977).

These alternative visions of the sexual (which take their force from the relativism of modern science) do not have immediate effects on sexual conduct. What they may do is to make the population far more tolerant; they give to the formerly deviant explanations and evidence for their moral worth, and in some cases they influence the police functions of the society. They change the contexts for sexual conduct and alter how various forms of sexual conduct are evaluated. Perhaps in the long run, they may have consequences for another generation's sexuality, but their short-term effects are limited.

The Complexity of Sexual Change

What is suggested by these arguments is the complexity of the processes of sexual learning and the competition that exists among the messages sent and the agents of communication. Not only do we have to concern ourselves with communicators and messages, but we also have to attend to the fact that individuals change over the life-span. We cannot even limit our interests to the narrowly sexual since there is unimpeachable evidence that factors close to the sexual (e.g., beliefs about the body or gender role learning) and factors that are far more distant (e.g., consumption desires) have consequences for our sexual lives. Finally, we must confront the fact that various components of sexual conduct are the result of quite different causal configurations. The gender differences historically found in masturbation may remain relatively unchanged during adolescence because they are linked to traditional peer group learning opportunities—premarital intercourse may take on a more similar pattern among young men and women as a result of the role of sex in the formation of intimate heterosocial relations before marriage. What may affect one aspect of sexuality may not affect another.

As important for issues of preventing psychopathology is an understanding of the sociopolitical forces which define one form of behavior as sickness and another as health. One of the major transformations of the last 30 years has been the steady change of labels for many forms of sexual conduct from sin to sickness, from deviance to unconventionality. Because these changes have taken place so rapidly, fervent supporters of each point of view can be found not only in the marketplace of ideas, but also in the legislatures and the police stations. The political processes by which various aspects of sexuality have had their moral and legal labels changed are part of the context of acquiring and maintaining sexual mores.

How psychopathology can be prevented depends on what is considered to be psychopathology. In the case of sexual conduct one of the fundamental changes may well be the increasing independence of various forms of conduct from the label psychopathology—hence they may no longer need to be prevented. Perhaps this is the final irony—that the ways in which conduct comes to be defined as psychopathology is part of the problem of changing sexual conduct.

References

Atwood, J. D., Gagnon, J. H., and Simon, W. *Masturbation in adolescence and young adulthood*. Mimeo, 1982, 40 pp.

Chilman, C. S. *Adolescent sexuality in a changing society*. Washington, D.C.: DHEW Publication (NIH) 79-1426, 1979.

Chilman, C. S. (Ed.). *Adolescent pregnancy and childrearing*. Washington, D.C.: DHEW Publication (NIH) 81-2077, 1980.

Gagnon, J. H. *Human sexualities*. Glenview, Ill.: Scott, Foresman, 1977.

Gagnon, J. H. Books from the gay male and lesbian bookshelf. *American Journal of Orthopsychiatry*, 1981, *51*, 560-568.

Gagnon, J. H., and Greenblat, C. S. *Life designs*. Glenview, Ill.: Scott, Foresman, 1978.

Gagnon, J. H., Greenblat, C. S., and Roberts, E. J. *Stability and change in rates of marital intercourse*. Paper presented at the annual meetings of the International Academy of Sex Research, Toronto, 1978.

Gagnon, J. H., and Roberts, E. J. Parents' messages to pre-adolescent children about sexuality. In J. M. Samson (Ed.), *Childhood and sexuality*. Montreal: Editions Etudes Vivants, 1981.

Gagnon, J. H., and Simon, W. *Sexual conduct*. Chicago: Aldine, 1973.

Gerbner, G., Kross, L., Morgan, M., and Signorielli, N. The mainstreaming of America: Violence profile No. 11. *Journal of Communication*, Winter 1981, 10-29.

Greenblat, C. S. *Accounting for marital intercourse*. Paper presented at the annual meeting of the American Sociological Association, San Francisco, 1982.

Kinsey, A. C., Pomeroy, W. B., and Martin, C. E. *Sexual behavior in the human male*. Philadelphia: W. B. Saunders, 1948.

Kinsey, A. C., Pomeroy, W. B., Martin, C. E., and Gebhard, P. H. *Sexual behavior in the human female*. Philadelphia: W. B. Saunders, 1953.

LoPiccolo, J., and Heiman, J. Cultural values and the therapeutic definition of sexual function and dysfunction. *Journal of Social Issues*, 1977, *33*, 166-183.

Miller, P. Y., and Simon, W. Adolescent sexual behavior: Context and change. *Social Problems*, 1974, *22*, 58-76.

Polanyi, M. *Personal knowledge*. Chicago: University of Chicago Press, 1968.

Simon, W., and Gagnon, J. H. On psychosexual development. In D. G. Goslin (Ed.), *The handbook of socialization theory and research*. Chicago: Rand McNally, 1968.

Trussell, J., and Westoff, C. F. Contraceptive practice and trends in coital frequency. *Family Planning Perspectives*, 1981, *12*, 246-249.

Sex Research in Preventive Psychiatry

Paul H. Gebhard

In keeping with our general history of medicine in which the emphasis has been on intervention after, rather than before, the onset of a problem, there has been too little attention paid to the prevention of specific sexual dysfunction. Most of our sex education has been so diluted and nonspecific that its preventive role is minimal. Our health service professionals have been so busy with the treatment of life-threatening disorders that they have given little attention to the prevention of sexual problems. Even psychiatry and psychology have necessarily focused on the acute presenting symptoms rather than on preventive programs. This unfortunate imbalance could be quickly corrected if we were to adopt the old Chinese tradition of paying one's doctor to keep one healthy and suspending payment during illness. However, I doubt that the American Medical Association would embrace such a policy. The best we can do is to encourage all preventive medicine programs and hope that some of them will extend into the field of sexuality. To facilitate such extension we must give our health service professionals better education and training in sexuality; however, the immediate prospects for doing so are dim.

Prior to the 1960s there were virtually no sex education programs in medical schools, but thanks to the efforts of Dr. Harold Lief and the general liberality of the late 1960s and early 1970s the majority of medical schools developed such programs. These were ordinarily elective, not required. Now the tide has turned and the medical schools are abandoning their sex education programs.

There are several reasons for this. First, the expansion of medical knowledge has been so great that there is scarcely time to teach what is considered essential; thus no time remains for sex education or other subjects deemed somewhat peripheral or of lesser importance. Second, external funding for medical sex education has become increasingly difficult to obtain. Third, a substantial number of the sex education programs were of poor quality. A typical example would consist of a number of lectures, usually not covering even one semester, given by volunteer colleagues with limited expertise in sexology. These people often lectured on topics which they covered in their routine courses at other times. The program would literally be fleshed out with some films of people in sexual activity, there would be the inevitable professorial jokes designed to reduce tension, and there would be occasional exhortations to be objective and tolerant. Although such a program is better than nothing, it can scarcely compete with courses on the latest developments in medicine. I would like to see some well-designed programs lasting at least a full semester made compulsory for students specializing in psychiatry, gynecology, and urology, but I fear this hope will not be realized for years.

Before considering preventive action we must repeat the question Dr. Richard Green, a psychiatrist at the State University of New York, Stony Brook, asked: what do we wish to prevent? In attempting to answer this, we are immediately faced with the fact that society defines what is desirable or undesirable, and the health service professionals, being products of the society in which they live, tend to translate these socially determined value judgments into diagnosis and treatment. All societies establish norms of sexual attitudes and behavior; some are publicly proclaimed as laws, and others, which do not necessarily conform to public norms, are held privately by the majority of individuals. Any attitude or behavior which departs markedly from these public or private norms is at once given a pejorative label and negative value. It is viewed as queer, kinky, deviant, perverse, abnormal, or pathological. Through this process of definition, societies create many of their sexual disorders and problems. Indeed, Freud once said that neurosis was the price of civilization.

Although we realize that the individuals must to a large extent adapt to society, we must not abandon scientific objectivity and unquestioningly allow society to determine our concepts, our counseling, and our therapies. It is at this point that sex research plays a vital role, for it is only through objective research that we can better understand how attitudes and behaviors develop and at what points in the development intervention can be most effective, and that we can ascertain the long-term consequences of various attitudes and behaviors on individuals and society as a whole. Armed with such necessary factual knowledge we can then formulate courses of action, preventive or therapeutic, within the bounds of social practicality. These bounds vary according to geographic location and time. What constitutes realistic counseling in San Francisco could be completely impractical in a small town in Iowa, and, as we all know, sexual norms have changed drastically in recent decades and may continue to do so.

Nevertheless, there are certain sexual behaviors which the majority of the public and health service professionals would agree should be prevented or halted. First of these are sexual acts forced upon unwilling persons, rape and sexual harassment being prime examples. Second is the exploitation of those particularly vulnerable such as children, the mentally incompetent, and persons who are incarcerated. Third are sexual acts done in public which offend and distress the majority of those who behold them, and thus infringe their rights. Fourth, and last, are sexual acts between consenting adults or by lone individuals which result in serious physical damage; sadomasochists must stop short of mayhem.

These four axiomatic statements are, of course, fraught with definitional problems. There are degrees of unwillingness, and we can scarcely try to prevent seduction, the art of transmuting unwillingness into willingness. Exploitation is also hard to define. Since we do not plan to prevent sex among peers, how much of an age discrepancy must exist before one person can be said to be exploiting someone younger? Another vexing question: in protecting the mentally incompetent are we denying them all sociosexual activity, something which we regard as normal and desirable? Turning to the matter of preventing public offense, we must realize that what is or is not thought offensive varies enormously according to social class, locale, and age. With respect to voluntary physical damage, I think society has the right to prevent people from maiming themselves to a degree which would result in their being incapable of supporting themselves and their dependents, thus adding to the welfare burden. However, we cannot logically prevent people from enjoying potentially dangerous sexual acts while we continue to permit equally dangerous sports.

Many other sexual attitudes and behaviors cannot be so simply and pragmatically defined, but are largely matters of ethics, social philosophy, and taste. For example, we can clearly attempt to prevent pedophilia because it often exploits children, infringes parental rights, and exposes the pedophile to serious punishment, but what do we do about pedophilia's mirror-image: gerontophilia? Do we want to prevent people from being attracted sexually to persons many years their senior? I personally hope not! Many other rhetorical questions can be asked: do we want to prevent transsexualism, fetishism, homosexuality, voyeurism, consensual sadomasochism, and group activity? We might add to this list an even greater sexual deviance: protracted virginity.

In attempting to answer these questions we must consider three variables: the consequences of the attitude or behavior for the individual, the consequences for other persons, and the degree of individual freedom from social control.

Taking first the consequences for the individual, we must think in terms of physical health, the amount of conflict with society, and emotional well-being. Few consensual sexual activities are physically harmful in and of themselves; sadomasochism often is, but to a limited degree. Excessive copulation may result in pelvic congestion and genital soreness. Anal penetration encourages hemorrhoids or, in extreme cases, fecal incontinence. Most sociosexual activity involves some degree of physical risk ranging from venereal disease to the common cold, and contacts involving the anus carry the possibility of hepatitis. Copulation in early adolescence with multiple partners increases the chance of later cervical neoplasms. However, physical risk or harm is usually so improbable, preventable, or inconsequential in ordinary sociosexual activity that it is not an important factor in determining the desirability of a specific activity.

However, the amount of conflict with society is an important factor since a person's sexual life, or what is assumed to be sexual life, often has a direct impact upon employment and social relationships. Many corporations insist their upper echelon officers be married and free from public scandal. The federal government can bar foreigners from entering this country or from being naturalized purely on the basis of their sexual lives. Security clearance, a requisite for various positions, always takes into account sexual history. While politicians generally have an unspoken agreement not to attack one another on sexual grounds, sexual scandal has spoiled many a career. The result of this emphasis on conformity is that those who deviate from it must frequently eschew high status positions and work at levels below their competence.

The emotional well-being of the individual is importantly influenced by his or her sexual life, and this is true not only of persons within the statistically normal range, but for those who deviate from it. The main disadvantage of deviance is that it adds to the inescapable commonplace problems of sex we all share: the problems of finding a partner of similar inclination and of concealment. The more bizarre one's sexual desires, the fewer potential partners exist and the more necessary it is to conceal one's activities from relatives, employers, and neighbors. This produces a higher degree of frustration, stress, and anxiety.

Having discussed the consequences of deviant sexual behavior for the individual, we may now consider the consequences for others. These range from the positive, as when two people discover they share the same atypical interest, to the extreme negative, as when a spouse and children discover unsuspected deviance. The possible complexities of the effect of deviance upon personal relationships cannot be fully explored here.

We also need to consider the matter of individual freedom versus social control. As the world becomes more densely populated and urbanized, greater social interaction results and brings with it the need for greater social control. Since human rights and obligations exist only in our minds and not as external realities, it is up to us to determine the balance between freedom and control. The majority of sex researchers, therapists, and legal scholars believe that what consenting adults do sexually in private should not be subject to legal control, and over a score of states have accepted this viewpoint in their legal codes. However, just because something is not illegal does not make it desirable. It is not illegal to be neurotic, yet we all feel neurosis should be prevented or cured. Therefore, if we believe something is undesirable for the individual and/or others, we have the obligation to try to prevent it regardless of its legal status.

The list of undesirable sexual attitudes or activities is so large that we must exercise selectivity; there is little point in expending much effort to prevent something which is extremely rare. I think we can agree that necrophilia is undesirable because it upsets the relatives of the deceased and contributes little or nothing to the psychological well-being of the necrophile, but it is not worthwhile to design a program specifically to prevent necrophilia. Here again, sex research is needed to determine what is truly rare as opposed to what is merely hidden: everyone thought transsexualism was very rare until the availability of the operation brought thousands of transsexuals out of their closets. Another form of selectivity must be exercised—that of not confusing solutions with problems. Too often today, with the unthinking crusade of the Moral Majority and similar groups, attacks are made upon abortion, whereas in fact the attack should be upon unwanted pregnancies; additionally, attempts are made to suppress divorce rather than to ameliorate marital conflict.

The crux of the matter is determining who decides what should be prevented. The public expresses various and conflicting sentiments; the law does not always reflect majority opinion and covers only a portion of sexuality; and there is not always consensus among the health service professionals. In terms of prevention, public mores are probably the strongest for they mold us from birth onward, but in a complex polymorphic society such as ours the mores are contradictory and are becoming weaker. In the final analysis it is the health service professionals, particularly physicians, who decide. Although they take public opinion and the law into consideration, the final decisions are theirs. In formulating the last edition of the *Diagnostic and Statistical Manual*, which lists all the pathologies and disorders, the psychiatrists did not conduct a public referendum, nor did they consult the American Law Institute; they alone decided what sexual items merited therapy and prevention. These decisions, I must add, were far from unanimous. The omission of homosexuality as a disorder per se caused great commotion and finally one variety of homosexuality was added to the list of psychosexual dysfunctions. This variety was labeled "egodystonic homosexuality," which in plain language means being upset because one is homosexual. Now I have no objection to such persons receiving psychotherapy, but I wonder about "egodystonic adultery," "egodystonic masturbation," and all the other sexual things concerning which one can be upset? To have singled out homosexuality was, in my opinion, a sop thrown to the conservatives.

Having mentioned earlier the generally accepted need to prevent sexual acts forced upon the unwilling, the need to prevent exploitation of the particularly vulnerable, and the need to prevent public offense, I should face some of the rhetorical questions I asked previously. It is easy to deal with the psychosexual dysfunctions—these are unwanted by almost everyone. I use the qualifying word *almost* because I can imagine someone who has chosen to abstain from sex welcoming a lack of sexual interest and response; however, no one else wants trouble achieving sexual response and orgasm. Therefore, we can agree that we need to prevent the dysfunctions such as inhibited desire, inhibited orgasm, vaginismus, dyspareunia, and so forth. I think that we would also agree that it is desirable to prevent gender identity disorders, for doubts or dissatisfaction about one's gender are distressing. The problem lies with homosexuality and the paraphilias, each of which merits separate discussion.

A substantial number of homosexuals report that from their earliest recollections onward they have consistently been more attracted to members of their own gender, though they have no negative feelings about the opposite sex. My opinion, for what it is worth, is that this sort of homosexuality is almost impossible to prevent and that attempts to do so are a waste of time and possibly counterproductive. Indeed, I suspect it may involve a genetic or endocrinological predisposition. Also, there does not seem to be much point in preventing occasional or temporary homosexual activity, some of which may be the only sociosexual option open to the involuntarily incarcerated. There are only two homosexualities which we should prevent. One is a homosexuality which seems to spring from disgust toward and hatred of the opposite sex rather than from an affection for the same gender. This strikes me as an emotional pathology with homosexuality as merely a consequence, and the patholoy merits prevention. The second homosexuality is one which seems to stem from a mixture of laziness and cupidity and which seems largely confined to males. It occurs when a primarily homosexual young male discovers he can live an easy life as a kept boy or prostitute and as a result neglects his education, never develops a skill or profession to enable him to become self-supporting, and never manages a satisfactory durable sexual relationship with either men or women. This is really a character defect with homosexuality as a symptom; it should be, if possible, prevented.

Turning now to the paraphilias, exhibition and peeping should be prevented not so much because they are offensive to the target person, but because they are usually true compulsions over which the afflicted individual has little control, and which cause him distress and ultimately arrest. Voyeurism, excluding peeping, blends so inextricably with a normal interest in seeing nudity and sexual activity that no need exists for preventive measures. Even in its extreme form it represents no more than a somewhat expensive retreat from reality into a fantasy world of "pornutopia," an eccentricity falling under the protection of the civil liberty of the individual.

Zoophilia is certainly not regarded as the epitome of mental health and social adjustment, but as long as the animal is not in pain or injured there seems no reason to make its prevention part of a program. The laws governing cruelty to animals should suffice. Anyway, most zoophilia is not some bizarre madness, but merely the utilizing of an animal as a masturbatory device.

Fetishism and transvestism are problematic: in their milder forms they may be regarded as simply ornamental enhancements of sexuality and need not be prevented. In their extreme forms they often make it difficult to achieve or maintain a satisfactory sociosexual relationship and hence should be prevented. How one can predict what fetishistic or transvestitic tendency will become extreme I do not know, but neither do I see any rationale for supressing black lace lingerie or high heels.

Sadomasochism presents a more acute problem because it is linked with the social problem of violence in general. Although I know of sadomasochists who confine their activity to other consenting sadomasochists and who inflict no physical injury which will not heal within a week or so, I feel that sadomasochism should be discouraged. Sex in our culture suffers from enough problems without having it linked with violence, and I cannot set aside the visceral feeling that the fusion of pleasure and pain—normally opposite ends of a spectrum—is somehow biologically and socially deviant. Moreover, an unrestrained growth in sadomasochism would probably encourage some truly pathological individuals to escalate their activity to undesirable or even homicidal levels. Last, sadomasochists have difficulty finding suitable partners, and some of the specialized forms of sadomasochism almost guarantee either a lonely life or a dependence on prostitutes.

Assuming that health service professionals can come to some agreement as to what sexual things should be prevented, how can prevention be accomplished? The initial problem is access to the public. People ordinarily do not seek help unless motivated by discomfort or fear. In such cases it is often too late for prevention: the disorder is already there. The best that can be done is to alleviate the presenting problem and in the meantime investigate what other potential sexual troubles might be staved off. This is locking the stable after one horse has been stolen.

Prevention is necessarily impeded by the fact that the counselor, educator, or therapist has little or no control over the current or future sexual partners of the person they are trying to influence. We cannot protect people from all the slings and arrows of outrageous fortune. The best that can be done is to provide useful knowledge and insights particularly regarding those areas in which problems appear likely to occur, to strengthen a person's feeling of competence, and to increase toleration for the imperfections of humanity, society, and self. In this way we can arm people against future psychosexual problems. This combination of education, therapy, and maturation is difficult to effect in a short time. We must not, therefore, rely wholly upon the few minutes or hours with those whom we wish to influence in our clinics, offices, or classrooms; we must make increasing use of the mass media. It is likely that the articles on sex in magazines such as *Cosmopolitan* and *Redbook* have prevented more female psychosexual dysfunctions than the direct efforts of health service professionals. Even if the content of the articles is superficial or if they advocate unattainable utopian ideals, just the repeated reading and thinking about sexual adjustment lowers inhibitions, reduces embarrassment, and makes sex seem a birthright to be enjoyed. Therefore, in addition to clinical practice or standard educative work, we should attempt to reach the public via print, lectures, and television.

Having thus discussed virtually everything except sex research, how do I tie it in with what I have been saying? The answer is obvious: sex research is absolutely necessary in order to provide the factual data upon which we can base our value judgments, predictions, therapies, and educative efforts. Without sex research we would have to depend upon religious dogma and vague clinical impressions in determining what to prevent and how to do so. This nasty combination has not worked well during the past few thousand years, and it is high time it was discarded in favor of objective empirical sex research. I will close by quoting Robert Kolodny (1978), who stated, "Preventative programs of all varieties must be based on the availability of secure research data describing the causes, incidence, and natural history of the particular disorder in question" (p. 195).

References

Kolodny, R. Ethical issues in the prevention of sexual problems. In C. B. Qualls, J. P. Wincze, and D. H. Barlow (Eds.), *Prevention of sexual disorders*. New York: Plenum Press, 1978.

PART II

The Damaging Consequences of Sexism

Introductory Notes

When we attempt to identify the diagnostic parameters of mental illness, we commonly consider the presence of delusions—false beliefs about the world—as signs of pathology. Another diagnostic criterion is "dangerousness"; the person considered to be dangerous to self and others is often regarded as emotionally disordered. By these and other criteria sexism should qualify as a pathognomonic sign. The belief that all members of a sex (or a class or a race) are inferior (or superior) is delusional and clearly dangerous to the maligned group. But diagnosticians are members of the culture and often share widespread cultural delusions, making them unable or unwilling to see faults that they themselves share.

Conference participants and speakers made frequent observations about the damaging effects of sex role stereotypes on sexual relations. Those not fully aware of this problem were soon made aware of its dimensions. Sexism is so pervasive, so much a part of the culture, that all efforts at primary prevention must begin with it as a critical cause of sexual disorders and as a chief impediment to healthy, mature, and equalitarian sexual relations. The papers in this section focus on some specific consequences of sexism, though it is clear that most writers included in this volume consider the problem to be relevant.

Harold Leitenberg raises an interesting question, one that warrants serious consideration by students of contemporary sexuality. He suggests that transsexuality is the epitome of the expression of sexism in our society. Leitenberg argues that a transsexual's denial of his or her biological sex is based upon a perception of mutually exclusive sex roles for males and females. Using case studies and autobiographical reports he shows how transsexuals illustrate with great clarity the cultural prejudices about maleness and femaleness, and he traces the development of these gender identity disorders from sexual stereotypes and homophobic attitudes in the culture. He further suggests that the social acceptance of transsexual surgery reflects and reinforces sexism and homophobia. In his review of the literature Leitenberg deals with the early development of transsexual individuals and provides some intriguing evidence that these beliefs (that one is really a girl in a boy's body or a boy in a girl's body) are often defenses against perceptions of "failed" masculinity and femininity as well as defenses against unacceptable homosexual impulses. His paper makes a thoughtful contribution to the development of our understanding of the deep and pervasive effects of sexism on our culture.

Edward Donnerstein examines the research literature on pornography and considers the effects of pornography on aggression toward women. He concludes that one must differentiate between the forms of pornography. It is important to distinguish between erotic material and sexual material with aggressive themes, particularly themes of eroticized aggression against women. All too often literature, art, and popular periodicals may present erotic and sexually explicit material that gets classed as pornography. Several of the authors in this volume actually suggest the strong possibility of widespread benefits from erotic as distinguished from pornographic material. Often sex education materials, for example, may include explicit depictions of human nudity and of sexual activity that may be offensive to the Puritan ethic. But such material may be useful and valuable.

On a more immediately pragmatic level Gene Abel suggests that recognizing the antecedents to rape provides us with a means of prevention. Instead of waiting for a rape to happen and then treating both the rapist and the victim, we must prevent rape from occurring. Since 35 percent of rapists will rape again, rapists in prison should have appropriate intervention aimed at eliminating their aggressive urges. However, our legal system makes even this difficult since if the rapist conceals these urges and other offenses he may have committed, he is more likely to receive both a shorter sentence and a speedier parole. Professionals who work with rapists and other sexual offenders suffer from high burn-out and a lack of appreciation from society. Many rapes are not reported and even when the rapist is charged, the probability of his being convicted is low (13 percent). Abel suggests a number of ways to combat these problems.

In a society that prefers to treat and to punish rather than to prevent, it is particularly important to make the public aware that rape is not an innate behavior (there are no born rapists) but a "behavior that follows logically from a variety of antecedents." One wishes that Abel's paper could be made required reading for a number of people, including high school counselors, youth workers, juvenile court officials, and prison officials; in fact, all those who, being able to recognize these behaviors antecedent to rape, might be in a position to intervene to prevent rape.

Gertrude Williams reviews the present knowledge about child abuse in general and the sexual abuse of children in particular. That unwanted pregnancy or unplanned pregnancy is correlated with general child abuse seems only logical, but as teenage pregnancies increase each year, so do the number of young mothers who keep their babies, constituting a group at high risk for child abuse. The Pro-Lifers fight abortion but once the children are born, take no responsibility. Why do people who clearly cannot cope want children so desperately? How do we stop this cycle of pregnancy and abuse? Williams provides a number of possible answers.

Williams perceives a strong relationship between sexist attitudes and child oppression. She also sees the entrenched patriarchy of our society as responsible for widespread sexual pathology. One form of sexual pathology which a patriarchal society spawns is, of course, father-daughter incest, and this Williams analyzes in great detail. Initially we pretended that it did not exist. Male psychiatrists and physicians followed Freud's lead in labeling women who claimed incestuous relationships with fathers or uncles as hysterics. Even when the fact of incest is acknowledged, the blame is shifted to the victims: mothers are frigid; daughters ask for it. Clearly Williams regards ideological change as essential for any meaningful prevention efforts. She is fiercely critical of the overemphasis on treatment, and of our neglect and denial of the social origins of these problems.

Transsexuality:
The Epitome of Sexism and Homosexual Denial

Harold Leitenberg

Imagine the following:

Since early childhood this 30-year-old biological black male has felt he was white. He believes there are certain behavioral and psychological differences between blacks and whites and that he acts and thinks like a white person rather than a black one. This individual feels inwardly and insists to the world he is a white person trapped in a black body. He is convinced he can only be happy if he is operated on to make his body look like that of a white person. Assume this is medically possible, through a combination of surgical and hormonal treatment. Should the physician provide this treatment? What are the social implications if this is done? What does this individual's request imply about his attitude toward black and white people in our society?

Transsexuals are biologically normal males and females who question their gender identity and wish it changed. Thus, a male-to-female transsexual is a person who repudiates his male body and his male identity. He thinks of himself as a female. A female-to-male transsexual is a person who rejects her female body and female identity. She thinks of herself as male. This "gender dysphoria" has usually been longstanding, having its origins in early childhood. As adults, transsexuals often seek hormonal and surgical treatment—so-called sex change or sexual reassignment—so they can live more easily as members of the opposite sex.

A close examination of the transsexual phenomenon is fascinating and important not because of the numbers of people involved but because of the clinical and social dilemmas it poses. Because the transsexual rejects in the most extreme fashion possible one sex role in favor of another, it could be argued that transsexuality is the purest expression of individual

I wish to thank Peggy Brozicevik, Tim Rushford, and Leslie Slavin for their assistance in collecting and analyzing these data.

sexism possible. As far as they themselves are concerned, one type of sexual identity is detested and another is idealized. Albee in a recent paper (1981) defined sexism as "ascribing superiority or inferiority, unsupported by any evidence in traits, abilities, social value, or personal worth to males or females as a group" (p.20). He goes on to state that "sexism, like other forms of prejudice can validly be regarded as a species of delusion—false beliefs rooted in emotional and personal needs" (p.20). I believe transsexuality fits within this framework.

A strong case can also be made that transsexuality provides a relatively unusual example of how treatment to ease an individual's suffering may be in direct contradiction to the aims of prevention. One argument I will make in this paper is that by acceding to the desperate request of the transsexual to have his or her body altered, the broader goal of preventing sexual identity disorders from arising in the first place may be undermined. A related thesis, one that Janice Raymond in her recent book *The Transsexual Empire* (1979) enunciated most clearly, is that transsexuality is largely based on a corrosive foundation of sexual stereotypes.

Gender identity is a nebulous concept, often couched in vague terms, especially when the context of transsexuality arises. Most transsexuals report that as far back as they can remember they always believed they were of the opposite sex (Green, 1974). These reports may or may not be accurate. But even if they are, what could make a person believe, despite all the physical evidence to the contrary, that he or she is really of the opposite sex? What does it really mean when a male, for example, who does *not* deny the reality of his genitalia and reproductive system, says he always felt he was a female rather than a male. Although researchers, and most of the rest of us, make a distinction between basic gender identity grounded on biological criteria (I am a male or I am a female) and gender role behavior (so-called masculine and feminine behavior), it could be argued that people who suffer from gender identity confusion do so just because they fail to make this distinction. Gender identity and sex role stereotypes essentially become one and the same, both being defined in terms of social and psychological criteria. The adult male-to-female transsexual will usually relate that as a child he preferred "female" toys; he did not like rough-and-tumble games; he preferred to play with girls rather than boys; he preferred frilly clothes, and so on. In other words, for whatever reasons, he liked doing what he erroneously thought only girls are supposed to do, and he did not like doing what he thought all boys are supposed to do. It is not a far step for a developing child with these characteristics and with these rigid definitions of appropriate masculine and feminine behavior to then conclude that inside he must be a girl and that his outward bodily appearance is some cruel mistake. The apparent logic is: I act like a female; I want to be treated like a female; ergo I am a female. This becomes a passionate conviction. The male body is repugnant because it does not reflect the image the male-to-female transsexual has of himself. Thus the frequently heard phrase: I am a female trapped in a male's body, or in the case of a female-to-male transsexual, "I am a male trapped in a female's body." But is this conviction really anything more than a delusional rationalization of an extreme preference for one sex role over another?

Furthermore, if transsexuals have homosexual urges (and they usually do) these are denied as being truly homosexual because the male-to-female transsexual wants to be loved not as a male by another male but as a female by a male. Similarly the female-to-male transsexual wants to be loved as a male, not as another female. But once again, is this really anything more than another rationalization, a denial of homosexual feelings?

The transsexuals' anguish is sincere; their desperation to have their bodies transformed is unquestionable. Herein lies the agonizing dilemma. By being tolerant, by being compassionate, by helping the transsexual achieve selfdetermination via surgery and hormonal treatment, are not the medical and mental health professions, however inadvertently, at the same time endorsing the sexual stereotypes and homophobic attitudes which underlie the development of gender identity disorders? Social acceptance of transsexual surgery seems contradictory to social change efforts designed to eradicate false barriers between male and female behavior and to break down arbitrary, rigid distinctions between so-called masculinity and femininity. If these dichotomies were eliminated, and if homosexuality were not condemned by society, is it not possible that transsexuality and requests for genital surgery would also disappear? By assisting the transsexual, are we not in effect reinforcing sexism and homophobia?

Before going further with these arguments, it would help to provide some background information about transsexuality.

Characteristics of Transsexuality, Transvestism and Homosexuality

Table 1 attempts to draw some rough distinctions between transsexuality, transvestism, and homosexuality. Using the example of the male-to-female

TABLE 1

Characteristics of Male-to-Female Transsexuals,
Transvestites and Male Homosexuals

	Gender Identity	Cross-Dressing Frequency	Sexual Partner	Fetishistic Component to Cross-Dressing	Desire for Sex Change Surgery
Transvestite	Male	Occasional	Female	Sometimes Present	No
Transsexual	Female	Permanent	Male	Seldom Present	Yes
Homosexual	Male	Occasional	Male	Seldom Present	No

transsexual, the major distinction is that only the transsexual wants to permanently assume a female body appearance.

The most salient feature of transvestism is cross-dressing, that is, wearing clothes customarily worn by females. There are supposedly two types of male transvestites. One is the man who has a fetish for wearing certain female garments on an intermittent basis. Touching and putting on these clothes is associated with sexual excitement. The second type of transvestite is the man who occasionally dresses entirely in stereotypic women's clothing and uses makeup, wigs, and so forth, to transform his appearance so that he can pass as a female. Sexual excitement while dressed as a woman may be absent (Benjamin, 1966; Brierly, 1979; Feinbloom, 1976). This sort of transvestite instead reports that wearing female clothes is satisfying and relaxing without any overt sexual stimulation. In both types of transvestites, however, there is no gender identity confusion. The transvestite feels he is primarily male and he has a heterosexual orientation. In everyday life he feels himself a male; the only difference is that he believes he has a female side, usually some stereotypic conception he has of a female, which occasionally needs to be expressed. Even while dressed as a woman, however, he enjoys knowing he has a penis, though he may feel he is a differenct personality at the time. Both in fantasy and in reality, he is only interested in sexual activity with females, and there is no evidence of any heterosexual inadequacy or dysfunction.

By contrast, the male-to-female transsexual considers himself to be a

By contrast, the male-to-female transsexual considers himself to be a female trapped in a man's body. He is said to be suffering from gender dysphoria. He wishes to be converted into a permanent anatomic female via sex reassignment surgery. He is repulsed by his male genitalia and wants to be rid of his penis. Whereas the transvestite usually feels content in the male role, the transsexual does not. Regardless of male or female apparel, the male-to-female transsexual always feels like a woman, whatever that means to him. He is interested in sexual relations with males, but he thinks of himself as a female, not as another male engaged in homosexual activity. Unlike homosexuals, he prefers having another male attracted to his female rather than his male characteristics.

A small percentage of male homosexuals also obtains pleasure from cross-dressing and impersonating females. The homosexual "queen" dressed in "drag," however, is different from both the transvestite and the transsexual. In contrast to the transvestite, the homosexual queen is interested in sex with other males, not with females. The homosexual queen also cross-dresses differently from the transvestite. The male in drag wears exaggerated and garish female clothing as a sexual come-on to other males, whereas the transvestite is *not* trying to attract the attention of other males; instead, he dresses in a sedate and unobtrusive fashion hoping to fool other people into thinking he is a woman. The homosexual in drag also bears little resemblance to the transsexual. The homosexual male sees himself as male and wants to stay that way. The reverse is true of the transsexual.

Transvestism appears to be unique to males; however, this is not the case for transsexuality or homosexuality. Stoller (1968) argues that female transvestites do not exist in our culture. Women, of course, often wear "men's" clothing, but they are not striving to pass as males when they do so. Our society permits a much greater range of fashion to women than men. No one looks askance at a female in slacks, but the same cannot be said of males who put on dresses. Perhaps if the same latitude in style of clothing were available to males, there would also be no such thing as male transvestism. In any case, as Stoller points out, even those women who dress all the time as men are not transvestites, because they are not wearing these garments in order to be sexually aroused. They may be female transsexuals, but as in the case of males, transvestism and transsexualism are not the same. A female transvestite, if she existed, would not want surgery to remove her breasts and alter her genitalia. On the other hand, a female transsexual would seek such surgery because she does not want

men's clothing also fails to meet the various criteria of a true transvestite
or transsexual. The homosexual female who dresses in male clothing does
not question that she is properly assigned as a female as does the transsexual;
nor is she sexually excited by wearing male apparel, or interested in passing undetected as a male, or in having sexual relations with men as would
be the case for the hypothetical female transvestite.

For purposes of exposition, clear-cut separations between categories are
drawn in Table 1; in reality they may sometimes be blurred. For example, in some males it could be argued that transsexuality is simply a more
extreme version of either transvestism or homosexuality rather than a
qualitatively distinct phenomenon. Such a notion, however, would be
vehemently denied by transsexuals.

Incidence and Prevalence

Studies done in Sweden, the United State, England, and Canada suggest that approximately one out of 35,000 males over age 15, and one out
of 100,000 females over age 15 are transsexuals (Hoenig and Kenna, 1974;
Walinder, 1968).

If one examines people who have requested sex reassignment surgery,
or samples of patient case loads, the proportion of males to females is
typically 3 to 1. Why should there be so many more males than females
who seek sex reassignment surgery? A number of explanations have been
suggested. One of these is that greater publicity of famous male-to-female
transsexuals (Christine Jorgensen, Jan Morris, and Renee Richards were
males prior to conversions) has encouraged more male-to-female transsexuals
to come forward. Another is that surgery for males is more advanced than
for females; it is much easier to construct a functional vagina for a male
than a functional penis for a female. As a result, sex change surgery is more
available for male than for female transsexuals. These explanations assume
that there are actually an equal number of male-to-female and female-to-
male transsexuals but that circumstances have caused more males to be
counted because more males than females come to sex change clinics.
Another set of explanations, however, suggests that different social (sexist)
forces have led to a real difference in the incidence of male-to-female and
female-to-male transsexuals.

Society censors males for deviating from the stereotypic male role more
than it does females. In children, "tomboys" are somewhat acceptable, but

than it does females. In children, "tomboys" are somewhat acceptable, but "sissies" are not. As adults, women have much more latitude in their attire. Society is also more tolerant of a woman who acts somewhat masculinely and aggressively than it is of a man who acts somewhat femininely and passively. Why does not society as readily or as intensely condemn the female who dresses and acts like a male? Perhaps the answer is because it places a higher value on stereotypic masculine characteristics than on female characteristics, on males than on females. In any case, if society is indeed more hostile to males than to females who deviate from stereotypic sex role norms, then one can hypothesize much more anxiety being engendered in male than in female transsexuals. One way to escape this censure and reduce anxiety is to have a sex change operation. Such an operation may legitimize behavioral deviance. Also, no one would know that the person they are talking to who looks and supposedly acts like a female is really a male. Without such knowledge there would be no threat of ridicule and condemnation.

There is also a much greater stigma attached to male homosexuality than to female homosexuality. Many males who request sex reassignment surgery can be considered "homophobics" (Morgan, 1978). They are repulsed by homosexuality and vehemently deny any such predilection. One seldom hears of homosexual panic in females, but this is not an uncommon phenomenon in males. Thus there may be more male transsexuals than female transsexuals because males justifiably have greater fears of being considered a homosexual than do females. (The question of homosexual denial will be considered in more detail in a later section of this paper.)

Why Transsexuals Seek Surgery and Why It Is Provided

Transsexuals admittedly suffer a great deal in our society. Their childhoods are usually a time of conflict with parents and peers because they fail to conform adequately in their behavior to culturally defined norms of masculinity and femininity. The pressure of social rejection is enormous. Sex change surgery is a way to escape from this pressure and is considered an opportunity to live more freely the way they wish without attendant anxiety of being discovered.

The professional, who in good conscience is interested in trying to relieve the distress of transsexuals, seems at first glance to be faced with only two choices: change their bodies to conform to their identities, or change their seemed impossible. Psychotherapy had not been successful in altering the fixed idea transsexuals had that they belonged to the opposite sex. To the extent possible, male-to-female transsexuals wanted to live as completely as possible as females (and vice versa for female-to-male transsexuals). Psychotherapy could not convert the male-to-female transsexual into a "more masculine person" or a "less feminine person." Because of this failure of psychotherapy, surgery, now that it was available, seemed the only humane alternative. Reports were extant of miserably unhappy transsexuals who engaged in self-mutilation, who attempted and sometimes succeeeded in suicide. Their life histories were tragic; their distress and desperation were only too real. As a result members of the medical community felt a responsibility to help them in the only way they knew how: hormonal and surgical treatment.

Modern History of Transsexual Surgery

Sex reassignment surgery and transsexuality have recently received considerable popular attention and seeming social and medical acceptance. However, the modern history of transsexuality and sex change surgery is actually quite short and volatile. Although autobiographical accounts and instances of sporadic surgery were reported earlier in Germany, Casablanca, and Switzerland, the first big splash of publicity in the United States occurred in 1952-1953, when Christine Jorgensen (formerly George Jorgensen) went to Denmark and had a sex change operation. In the 1950s and 1960s acceptance of transsexuality continued to grow (Benjamin, 1966). But the stamp of ultimate legitimacy in the United States did not occur until 1966 when a gender identity clinic was established at the Johns Hopkins Medical Center, and for the first time sex reassignment surgery was made available in this country. In the first 2½ years of the clinic's existence, more than 1,500 people requested sex reassignment surgery. Since Johns Hopkins, a number of other highly reputable university-affiliated hospitals have offered such surgery. From the mid-60s to the present, numerous professional conferences and publications have been devoted to transsexuality (e.g., Green, 1974; Green and Money, 1969; Stoller, 1968, 1975). In addition, sensational cases were well publicized on TV talk shows and in magazines and newspapers, including, most notably, Jan Morris, a well-known English reporter and author, and Renee Richards, who joined the female professional tennis circuit following sex conversion from a male to female.

Approximately 3,000 to 4,000 sex change operations for transsexuals have been carried out in the United States since 1966. However, like many other forms of surgery which were once faddish and are no longer so, such as tonsillectomy and hysterectomy, there is reason to wonder if the roller coaster for sex reassignment surgery has reached its peak and is about to descend. In 1979, Johns Hopkins announced that its clinic was being closed, and sex reassignment surgery would no longer be offered. Other hospitals may or may not follow suit. The explanation for this shift in professional practice is not simple: it may have to do with practicality (no surgeons available in a particular setting) and economics (it costs too much; insurance carriers may refuse reimbursement); or it may have to do with more important questions of social values, ethics, and effectiveness.

Presurgery Evaluation

A request for sex reassignment surgery is not a sufficient criterion for transsexuality. Many people who request such surgery are not considered true transsexuals. Some are transvestites; some are clearly homosexuals who cannot accept homosexuality; some are psychotic; and some are inadequate personalities who have not been able to establish any satisfactory social or physical relationships and believe that sex change surgery will magically resolve their difficulties.

Whether or not a reliable diagnosis of transsexuality is ever possible on initial referral is questionable. As a result, a trial period of 1 to 2 years' duration is usually imposed before genital surgery is seriously considered. During this period, the candidate for surgery has an oportunity to prove he or she can live continuously as a member of the opposite sex. For the male-to-female transsexual a course of hormonal therapy may be started, presurgical counseling on the limitations of surgery will be provided, the motivation for seeking surgery can be fully explored, electrolysis treatment to remove facial hair can be undertaken, speech therapy can be provided to alter the voice in a more feminine direction, and other difficulties in mannerisms, physical characteristics, family and social adjustment can be addressed. For a female-to-male transsexual the preoperative trial is similar, with the exception of electrolysis.

Hormonal Treatment and Sex Reassignment Surgery

Surgery, of course, does not really change a biological male into a biological female or vice versa. Raymond (1979) quotes George Burou, a Casablancan physician, who has operated on over 700 American men: "I transform male genitals into genitals that have a female aspect. All the rest is in the patient's mind" (p.10). Hormonal treatment and sex change surgery does not alter chromosomal make up or reproductive capacity. Following surgery a male-to-female transsexual cannot ovulate and become pregnant, and a female-to-male transsexual cannot produce sperm or ejaculate. Hormonal treatment and sex change surgery can, however, dramatically alter external genitalia and physical appearance.

Description

Since men have more facial hair than women, a male considering sex reassignment will embark on a slow and costly process of depilation via electrolysis. Second, he will be placed on a regimen of estrogen therapy. This will have the following effects: (a) his body shape will be altered somewhat in that fatty tissue will be redistributed to the hips; (b) some slight breast development will gradually take place, but often transsexuals are not satisfied by the extent of such development and request silicone or other forms of breast implantation; (c) body hair will be gradually reduced; (d) testosterone output will decline, and the capacity to have erections may disappear after some time (there may also be some irreversible testicular atrophy); (e) skin texture may become softer and more feminine; (f) muscular strength will diminish. After surgery the transsexual will have to continue with hormonal treatment indefinitely. (Although this remains a disputed topic, there is some suggestion in the medical literature that long term maintenance on exogenous estrogens may increase the likelihood of breast cancer.)

The third step in the male-to-female conversion process is genital surgery. This has three components: (a) testicular castration; (b) penile amputation and shortening and redirection of the urethra; (c) construction of a vaginal channel, vaginal lining, labia majora and minora. Scrotal and penile tissue are used to fashion the vagina and since these tissues contain erogenous sensory nerve endings, sexual stimulation and orgasm are possible, though this seems to vary widely. Although the reconstructed vagina has no natural lubrication, artificial lubricants are available for purchase in any pharmacy.

A major source of postsurgical complication, however, is that the walls of the artificial vagina often narrow even if repeated dilation is provided. This may result in requests for further surgery. Requests for surgery may also not end with vaginal construction. Aside from further surgery to correct complications, some male-to-female transsexuals seek additional cosmetic surgery for nose, Adam's apple, eye shape, and so on, to try to achieve their idealized body image of a woman.

The female-to-male transsexual who wants to be reconstructed into a male also receives hormonal treatment prior to surgery. Administration of androgen will have the following effects: (a) facial and body hair will grow (acne may be an unwanted side effect); (b) menstruation will be eliminated; (c) the voice will lower slightly; (d) muscles will grow somewhat and shoulders widen; (e) clitoral size will increase somewhat, but it will not extend to penile size; (f) there may be a miniscule decrease in breast size; (g) hips will be narrowed. As with male transsexuals, hormonal treatment has to be maintained indefinitely.

The most frequent surgical operation for female-to-male transsexuals is a bilateral mastectomy. Hysterectomies are also common. However, surgical procedures for penile (and testicular) construction are still in an experimental stage. Furthermore, even if a penis is constructed in a cosmetically satisfactory manner, it is not capable of erection without some additional prosthetic device. Since there is also no sexual sensitivity in the constructed penis, the clitoris is usually maintained to provide sensory sexual stimulation.

Social Problems Following Surgery

Surgery is not the end of the transsexual's ordeal. There may be legal, family, and job complications. Some countries will permit a change in birth certificate and other sources of identification, others will not. Employment discrimination against transsexuals is not legally proscribed. According to a ruling of the U.S. District Court in California, Title 7 of the Civil Rights Act of 1964, which prohibits sexual discrimination, does not apply to a transsexual. An employer is permitted to discharge a transsexual or not hire a transsexual simply on the grounds of transsexuality. No other excuse is apparently needed. Postsurgical counseling may be necessary not only because of these legal and employment problems. The transsexual may need further practical training in mannerisms, speech pattern, dress, and so on, in order to learn to act in closer conformity to the cultural expectations for their new sexual identity.

Outcome

Hormonal treatment and sex change surgery do not guarantee future happiness for the transsexual. Initial reports, however, were generally quite favorable. Understandably the transsexual now had less to fear about detection. They also felt more at peace with themselves since a greater degree of correspondence had been achieved between their bodily appearance and their preferred identity.

Pauly in 1968 was able to find published reports on the outcome of sex reassignment surgery for 121 male-to-female transsexuals. After a mean 5-year follow-up, 63.5 percent were considered to have made satisfactory adjustments, 29 percent had unknown outcomes, and only 7.5 percent were unsatisfactory. Money (1971) reported a 4-year follow-up of 17 male and 7 female patients. All the males and 6 of the females felt positive about their surgery. One female was dissatisfied because of failed phalloplasty. On more objective measures, 9 original males and 3 original females were found to have improved their employment status, and 7 original males and 3 original females married for the first time. Randall (1969) reported the outcome for 29 male-to-female and 6 female-to-male transsexuals. The majority shifted in a positive direction: 21 were rated in the "excellent" and "good" categories after surgery, whereas only 4 could be so categorized before surgery. Four male-to-female transsexuals were much worse, and 2 of these committed suicide. Hastings and Markland (1978) report on the postsurgical adjustment of 25 male-to-female transsexuals who underwent surgery at the University of Minnesota Medical School Hospital. Although there were 2 psychotic episodes and 4 serious suicide attempts postsurgery, no patient expressed regret about his sex transformation surgery.

Unfortunately, these are not rigorous outcome studies. Measures are not sufficiently objective, and, more important, no long-term follow-up was made of transsexual patients who underwent surgery as compared to transsexual patients who did not. Although some clinical investigators such as Stoller (1975, p.254) cautioned prudence, pointing out this was not a "minor, benign surgical procedure, but rather one with significant surgical risks, with frequent post-operative complications," and that "any other new

TABLE 2

*Comparison of Original Operated, Operated During Follow-up,
and Operated Patients*[a]

Status	Number of Patients	Sex M F	Race W B Other	Average Age	Socio-economic Level	Average Number Gender Identity Clinic Consultations (%) Before Follow-up	During Follow-up	Where Operated (%) Johns Hopkins	Other	Surgical Complications %	number per patient
Operated[a]	15	73 27	66 27 7	30.1	3.9	5.8	1.2	67	33	53	1.8
Unoperated, subsequently operated	14	93 7	100 0 0	30.9	4.2	2.4	2.9	36	64	29	1.3
Unoperated, not subsequently operated	21	76 24	90 10 0	26.7	3.5	2.0	1.2	–	–	–	–

SOURCE: From "Sex Reassignment: Follow-up" by J. K. Meyer and D. J. Reter, *Archives of General Psychiatry*, 1979, *36*, 1010-1015. Copyright 1979 by American Medical Association. Reprinted by permission.
[a]Patients with full genital reassignment or surgical removal of reproductive organs.

and potentially dangerous surgical procedure would have been better tested," it was not until 1979 that the first and only comparison study of operated and unoperated transsexuals was reported (Meyer and Reter, 1979). The initial sample of unoperated transsexuals consisted of people who had been accepted as candidates for surgery at Johns Hopkins, but had yet to embark on the 2-year presurgery trial period. Some of these patients subsequently received surgery during the follow-up period. Thus three groups were actually compared: operated (15 patients), initially unoperated but subsequently operated (14 patients); unoperated, not subsequently operated (21 patients). Table 2 summarizes the demographic and surgical data presented by Meyer and Reter for the three groups. All patients had an extensive interview at follow-up sessions, and adjustment scores on legal, economic, marital or cohabitational, and psychiatric variables were obtained. Although there was a positive shift in adjustment, *there was no significant difference between the operated and unoperated* transsexuals on any of these measures. Both unoperated and operated transsexuals improved over time, but the operated group failed to demonstrate any superiority on objective measures of behavioral and social adjustment. Meyer and Reter (1979) concluded as follows: "Sex reassignment surgery confers no objective advantage in terms of social rehabilitation, although it remains subjectively satisfying to those who have rigorously pursued a trial period and who have undergone it" (p.1015). This may not be the final verdict on sex reassignment surgery; but the essentially negative results, and the fact that the study was performed at Johns Hopkins, the institution associated with introducing sex reassignment surgery to the United States, may have a chilling effect on the prevailing positive attitude toward such surgery.

Cross-gender Identity Disturbance in Children

Can future adult transsexuals be detected during early childhood? If so, then their cross-gender identity problems might be more easily changed at that point in development, thus preventing subsequent transsexuality. If only it were so simple!

Studies of atypical sexual identity in children have focused almost exclusively on boys (Green, 1974). One reason is that divergence from stereotypic feminine behavior in young girls is not usually considered objectionable or a cause for alarm. Few parents will bring their daughters in to clinicians so that they can be cured of their masculine behavior. Second, many girls are tomboys, yet few later become female transsexuals.

The situation is somewhat different for boys, albeit unjustifiably so. "Sissy," unlike "tomboy," is a pejorative term. Boys who have toy preferences traditionally associated with girls, cross-dress, prefer to play with girls, and have an aversion to rough-and-tumble play and sports, are subject to considerable ridicule, humiliation, abuse, and rejection by peers, parents, and teachers. In addition, adult male transsexuals characteristically report effeminate behavior in boyhood. However, this does not mean that all boys who exhibit such behavior will grow up to be male transsexuals. Only a few prospective studies have been carried out, and their results indicate that only a small minority of extremely feminine boys are destined to be transsexuals. Zuger (1966) found out of 6 such boys, 3 were later homosexually oriented but only 1 showed signs of possible transsexuality. Lebovitz (1972) found that of 16 subjects who had exhibited extreme feminine behavior as young boys, 3 became transsexual, 2 homosexual, and 1 was a transvestite. Green (1974) reports that in a sample of 5 very feminine boys, 3 were later clearly homosexual, 1 probably homosexual, and 1 probably bisexual. Thus out of a total of 27 very feminine boys who were followed to adulthood, only 3 definitely developed into transsexuals; the rest were either heterosexual or homosexual.

The following is a description of a 5-year-old boy said to be suffering from a gender identity disorder. This is taken from one of the first treatment studies conducted in this area (Rekers and Lovaas, 1974).

[Kraig] continually displayed pronounced feminine mannerisms, gestures, and gait, as well as exaggerated feminine inflection and feminine content of speech. He had a remarkable ability to mimic all the subtle feminine behaviors of an adult woman. At the same time, he seemed void of masculine behaviors, being both unable and unwilling to play the "rough-and-tumble" games of boys his age in his immediate neighborhood. He regularly avoided playing with his brother, he declined to defend himself among peers, and he was very fearful of getting hurt. On the other hand, he preferred to play with girls, and one neighborhood girl in particular; even when playing house with the girls, he invariably insisted on playing the part of the "mother" and assigned the part of "father" to one of the girls. For a child his age, Kraig had an overly dependent relationship with his mother; he demanded her attention almost continuously. He appeared to be very skillful at manipulating her to satisfy his feminine interests (e.g., he would offer to "help mommy" by carrying her purse when she had other packages to carry). He seemed almost compulsive or "rigid" in the extent to which he insisted on being a girl and in his refusal of all contact with masculine-like activities. From casual observation, normal 5-year-old girls show much more flexibility than Kraig did in choosing between sex-typed behaviors. (p.174)

Green (1974), who has done the most research in this field, believes that the origins of extreme "feminine" characteristics in boys is multi-faceted. He suggests these children are not all the same and that they did not necessarily arrive at their feminine behavior via the same route. In his book *Sexual Identity and Conflict in Children and Adults*, he lists at least 12 factors which may be involved:

Parental indifference to feminine behavior in a boy during his early years.

Parental encouragement of feminine behavior during his early years.

Repeated cross-dressing of a young boy by a female.

Maternal overprotection and inhibition of "boyish" or rough-and-tumble play.

Excessive maternal attention and physical contact resulting in a lack of separation and individuation of a boy from his mother.

Physical beauty of a boy that influences adults to treat him in a feminine manner.

Absence of an older male as an identity model during a boy's first years.

The father finds that his son has little interest in sports and father-son activities and experiences rejection. A degree of father-son alienation ensues. The frustration of the father is transmitted to the son, who becoming aware of his father's demands and annoyance, retreats further toward the accepting reactions of his mother.

Lack of male playmates during a boy's first years of socialization.

Maternal dominance of a family in which the father is relatively powerless.

Early socialization to feminine activity and companionship poses an obstacle to same-sex peer integration. Because of his feminine interests, he is teased, resulting in further alienation from his male group.

Defense against castration fears.

A series of recent papers provides sufficient evidence to conclude that the stereotyped feminine role behaviors of young boys can be modified via systematic behavioral retraining, provision of appropriate male role models, and alteration of parental reinforcement contingencies (e.g., Green, Newman, and Stoller, 1972; Rekers and Lovaas, 1974; Rekers, Lovaas, and Low, 1974; Rekers and Varni, 1977a, 1977b; Willis, Yates, Rosen, and Low, 1977; Rekers, Yates, Willis, Rosen, and Taubman, 1976).

One ostensible purpose for trying to alter the behavior of these children is to prevent adult disorders. The question is, what disorders? We have already noted that only a small minority grow up to be adult transsexuals. Many more grow up to be homosexuals. Should therapists intervene during childhood to prevent someone from developing an adult homosexual orientation?

Moreover, there is reason to believe that interventions designed to alter the feminine behavior of boys are supporting sex role stereotyping (Nordyke, Baer, Etzel, and LeBlanc, 1977; Winkler, 1977; Wolfe, 1979). For example, examine the treatment plan designed by Rekers and Lovaas (1974) for Kraig, the boy previously described. In the clinic, the mother was taught to reinforce Kraig for playing with "masculine" toys and not for playing with "feminine" toys. Included in the list of masculine toys were: a plastic toy submachine gun; a highway road scraper; a plastic car; a plastic tugboat; three miniature plastic soldiers; a set of five small plastic airplanes; and a plastic dump truck. The feminine toys included: a baby doll; a doll crib;

a doll bath, two purses, one child-size and one doll-size, a set of toy plastic tea dishes, and a wicker doll buggy.

Other behavioral targets for which the child was rewarded or punished at home included mannerisms and whom he played with. For example, he was punished for playing with girls. As Nordyke et al. (1977) point out, the treatment description and the way the results are presented imply that boys should only play with aggressive toys and never with nurturant toys, and they should never play with girls or dolls. Nordyke et al. (1977) conclude their critique of the Rekers and Lovaas (1974) study as follows:

> There are alternative procedures that the experimenters could have used to avoid sex-role typing. The behaviors listed as justification for treatment were quite numerous and included: slovenly and seductive eyes, a high screechy voice, a "swishy" walk, feminine gait, feminine content of speech, feminine inflection, feminine mannerisms, mimicking the subtle feminine behaviors of an adult woman, avoidance of his brother, avoidance of rough-and-tumble games, fear of getting hurt, lack of self-defense, lack of ability to throw or catch a ball, excessive crying, feminine clothing, oppositional behavior, and the worry of the parents. However, the behaviors chosen for modification were toy choice, playing with girls, feminine gestures, and feminine role-playing. Without dealing with these potential problematic behaviors, the child's repertoire could have alternatively been expanded to include some "traditional masculine" behaviors considered appropriate for all children, female or male. These might have included self-defense, cooperation, independence, and even throwing and catching a ball; all skills the boy lacked. Additionally, a better outcome might have been extracted through modifying behaviors that are considered inappropriate for either males or females, i.e., the boy's extreme fears, excessive crying, avoidance of his brother, or avoidance of certain types of play activities. If such behaviors were so extreme that they would be inappropriate for either females or males, they could have been treated in a manner appropriate for both females and males. (p. 556)

Another stated reason, and perhaps the major justification, for changing the behavior of boys like Kraig, is to alleviate ridicule and other forms of social rejection which will undoubtedly come their way. However, who should be modified? The people who heap the scorn on the child with atypical behavior or the child who exhibits the atypical behavior? As Nordyke et al. (1977) insightfully note, a pacifist or a feminist or homosexual or any person who engages in behavior offensive to the views of the social majority will suffer societal rejection. Should these people's behavior be modified so they will not experience this stress? Wherein lies the problem? In the atypical individual or in society's intolerance?

There is still another reason to suggest that some of these interventions with young children may be misguided. They seem to be predicated on changing one sex role sterotype for another: switching exaggerated feminine behaviors by reinforcing exaggerated masculine behaviors. Yet Bem (1975) has found that boys as well as girls who strongly identify with sex-typed masculine or feminine roles are less well adjusted than those who are more flexible, more androgynous.

Green (1974) provides a reasoned summary of the position of both sides of this dispute:

> Opponents of treatment aver that intervention will stamp out esthetic, sensitive qualities in the child and crudely press him into the stereotyped mold demanded by the sexist society. Proponents of treatment disagree. When consulted by the family of a boy whose atypical behavior causes him current hardship and portends increased distress, our goal is to reduce that social hardship. The aim is not to suppress sensitivity and compassion, not to promote a thirst for aggression and violence. Rather, it is to impart a greater balance where a radically skewed development has precluded a comfortable range of social integration. We believe that by so doing, the child may suffer less immediate distress and may subsequently have available to him a wider range of social and sexual options. (p. 245)

This is a controversial topic (Wolfe, 1979), and it will probably remain unsolved until a comparison is made of the long-term adjustment of treated and untreated cross-gender-oriented boys.

Sexual Stereotypes as the Root Cause of Transsexuality: What Is the Evidence?

First it should be noted that *no* chromosomal abnormality, anatomic abnormality, or prenatal or postnatal hormonal abnormality has ever been demonstrated to be present in the vast majority of transsexuals. There is simply no good evidence to support an organic basis for transsexuality. This not to deny the possibility that hormonal factors during fetal development may predispose an individual toward certain role behaviors which are traditionally associated with one sex rather than the other, for example, aggression for males. But even if very few sex differences are partially influenced by brain-hormone links prior to birth, this would not provide evidence in support of a solely endocrinological explanation of transsexuality. Social forces after birth always interact with biological factors during development to determine any complex human behavior, and this truism certainly applies to transsexuality as well. Furthermore, aside from the fact that hypothesized hormonal imbalances have not been confirmed in the transsexual population, the literature is quite clear that the vast range of role behaviors are not biologically fixed. In addition, it is not at all clear that the actual behaviors of transsexuals differ that substantially from many other members of their sex. Most males with so-called feminine behavioral traits do not become transsexuals. Similarly, most females with so-called masculine traits do not become transsexuals. What seems to distinguish transsexuals is their distorted belief systems about the meaning of atypical gender role behavior, not their behavior per se.

Sex stereotyping and sex bias seem to lie at the core of transsexuality. The way transsexuals speak about themselves (as well as the way some professionals who work with transsexuals speak about them) reflects these stereotypes. Their words reveal that they believe females act one way and males another way with very little overlap between the two. The dichotomies drawn are unrealistic, rigid, and prejudiced as well in that more often than not they imply superiority for one role over another. The evidence is in their remarks, and the only way to document this is through quotations. Although selected biographical statements are not the sort of evidence an objective science of human behavior usually aspires to, in this area at this time, they are all that are available. In addition, as you will see, these statements are so blatantly sex-biased that I think the possible criticism of their being taken out of context can be readily dismissed. I start with two statements from Dr. Harry Benjamin (1966), sometimes known as the father of transsexuality both because he introduced the term to our language and because of his pioneering work on behalf of legitimizing hormonal and surgical treatment of transsexuals.

In the course of this evaluation, no evidence of serious mental illness has been found. The patient is not psychotic, and I do not believe she ever will be. Her *character* structure is essentially that of a woman, and she has adjusted very well to the feminine role....

Finally, but highly important, how do you know you can make a living as a woman? Have you ever worked as a woman before? I assume that so far, you have only held a man's job and have drawn a man's salary. Now you may have to learn something entirely new. Could you do that? Could you get along with smaller earnings? (pp. 45, 109; italics added)

The assumptions behind these statements clearly reflect sexist attitudes.

The following are two interchanges between physicians and transsexual patients contained in Richard Green's landmark book *Sexual Identity Conflict in Children and Adults* (1974). The first is particularly noteworthy because the male has changed his mind about seeking transsexual surgery after becoming sexually attracted to a woman.

Dr.: When you were here the first time you said you didn't feel like a man. You enjoyed doing women's things, housework, sewing, and cooking and so on.
Patient: I still like to cook.
Dr.: That's what I said the first time. A lot of men like to cook.
Patient: That's right. So what's the big deal? There is no big deal. I like to cook. I'll probably always like to cook.
Dr.: A month ago you felt that was an indication of femininity.
Patient: Right, Right. I was narrow-minded. I had one way of thinking. (p. 89)

The second is an interchange between a physician and a female-to-male transsexual.

Dr.: You say you've never spoken to anyone about this before?
Patient: No.
Dr.: How have you managed to keep it to yourself so long?
Patient: Partly it's something you don't go around talking about, and also some people are kind of narrow-minded about it. I don't consider myself homosexual. I think that's one thing people would think of automatically. I just feel like the opposite sex.
Dr.: To what extent?
Patient: Everything I do I feel very unnatural. Wearing women's clothing. Things I do, usually sport, outdoors, swimming. I don't know how to explain it. There are a lot of little things. I have wanted to be a boy ever since I can remember, but there are no logical reasons for what I feel inside.
Dr.: When you were a kid you felt like this?
Patient: Yes. Part of the time it used to be if you were a boy you could do more things. It was just sort of the way I felt. I used to like playing football. I didn't like being a girl and doing things girls do, and lately, it's gotten more so. I feel very awkward being dressed up and going places as a girl.
Dr.: To what extent is your family aware of your feelings?
Patient: They knew it very much. They always considered me a tomboy. My mother used to always try to get me to play with dolls and everything, and I wouldn't do it. I played cowboys and Indians with the boys, climbed trees and rode horses, went hunting and fishing with my brothers. I was always out wrestling

with the boys. I wasn't doing what she thought I should be doing, but she kind of got used to it, I guess. I never really did change much. (p. 130)

This patient still believes that divergence from stereotypic roles is terribly unusual, and acceptable only if she were a male.

The next two quotations are from male-to-female transsexuals. They clearly reveal distorted stereotypes of what it means to be a woman or a man.

Self-reliance, a certain aggressiveness, and dominance are expected of a man. This is against my nature. It is not expected of a woman. Therefore, as a woman, I feel at ease, more secure and my true self. (Benjamin, 1966, p. 43)

Women are more emotional and sensitive; men are more cold and insensitive. (Raymond, 1979, p. 78)

Jan Morris is a famous English male-to-female transsexual, who, in 1974, wrote an eloquent autobiograhy about her experiences entitled *Conundrum*. Prior to going through hormonal and surgical treatment at age 46 she was known as James Morris. Both as James Morris and since as Jan Morris he or she is the author of many well-received books on travel and history. What is always brought out in introductions to her history is that Jan Morris was also the father of 5 children, served for 4 years in the 9th Lancers Brigade, was a journalist for the *Manchester Guardian* and the London *Times* for many years and, while a journalist, climbed a good part of Mount Everest as the reporter assigned to the first British expedition to climb this mountain successfully—all testimoney to "masculine" attributes. Yet, even during these "manly" exploits she always felt female and detested being a male. Why?

Despite the protestations Jan Morris makes against the way society downgrades women, her autobiography is replete with conventional stereotypes of both women and men. The views she has of women are intended to be positive, though I doubt many feminists would agree.

A virginal ideal was fostered in me by my years at Christ Church, a sense of sacrament and fragility and this I came slowly to identify as femaleness . . . .

The noblest aspects of the liturgy aspired to what I conceived as the female principle. Our very vestments (pink, white, and scarlet) seemed intended to deny our manhood and the most beautiful of all the characters of the Christian story, I thought, far more perfect and mysterious than Christ himself, was the Virgin Mary whose presence drifted so strongly and eloquently through the gospels, an enigma herself . . . .

My own notion of the female principle was one of gentleness as against force, forgiveness rather than punishment, give more than take, helping more than leading....

I am one whose ideals of womanhood had been molded by military patterns, and who liked a man to be in charge of things....

It was a superbly successful expedition [reference is to the ascent of Mt. Everest]—nobody killed, nobody disgraced—and looking back upon it now I see its cohesion as a specifically male accomplishment. Again constancy was the key. Men more than women respond to the team spirit, and this partly because, if they are of an age, of a kind, and in a similar condition they work together far more like a mechanism. Elations and despondencies are not so likely to distract them....

For myself, I suppose I instinctively associated those deceits with the male condition, since then even more than now the world of affairs was dominated by men. It was like stepping from cheap theater into reality, to pass from the ludicrous goings-on of minister's office or ambassador's study into the private house beyond where women were doing real things, like bringing up children, painting pictures, or writing home....

Venice was always feminine to me, and I saw her perhaps as a kind of ossification of the female principle—a stone equivalent, in her grace, serenity and sparkle, of all that I would like to be....

But I wanted none of it. It was repugnant to me. I thought of public success itself, I suppose, as part of maleness, and I deliberately turned my back on it, as I set my face against manhood. I resigned from my last job, withdrew from the chances of public life, and took to writing books, or traveling on my own behalf. I was cultivating impotence....

Then I had felt lean and muscular; now I felt above all deliciously *clean*. The protuberances I had grown increasingly to detest had been scoured from me....

Psychologically I am distinctly less forceful. It is not merely the loss of androgens that has made me more retiring, more ready to be led, more passive; the removal of the organs themselves has contributed for there was to the presence of the penis something positive, thrusting, and muscular. My body then was made to push and initiate, it is made now to yield and accept, and the outside change has had its inner consequences....

But let me analyze myself, on an ordinary morning in Bath, where I go to write my books. Let me see what everyday inessential sensations I conceive as specifically female. First I feel small and neat, I am not small in fact, at 5'9" and 133 lbs., and not terribly neat either, but femininity conspires to make me feel so. My blouse and skirt are light, bright, crisp. My shoes make my feet look more delicate than they are, besides giving me, perhaps more than any other pieces of clothing a suggestion of vulnerability that I rather like. My red and white bangles give me a racy feel, my bag matches my shoes and makes me feel well organized. I do not like make-up much, but what there is on my face is enlivening, fun, like a fresh lick of paint on a front door. When I walk out into the street I feel consciously ready for the world's appraisal in a way that I never felt as a man. (pp. 11-18, 75-108, 157-174)

Stereotypes about appropriate masculine and feminine behavior also carry over into expectations regarding how people will react to males as compared to females. For example, a male-to-female transsexual may wish to assume a female gender identity in order to get other males to react to them in a different manner. For instance, it is assumed that most men act more "coldly and insensitively" to other men than to women. A male-to-female transsexual may expect that other men will show more warmth and affection to him if he assumes a female identity. Concurrent acceptance of a subservient role does not seem to be that much of a negative price to pay—at least in the minds of male-to-female transsexuals. Even Jan Morris, who is clearly a high achiever in either guise, seems to express a bemused acceptance of second-class status.

If the condescension of men could be infuriating, the courtesies were very welcome. If it was annoying to be thought incapable of buying a second-class return to Liverpool, it was quite nice to have it done for one anyway. I did not particularly want to be good at reversing cars, and did not in the least mind being patronized by illiterate garage men, if it meant they were going to give me some extra trading stamps . . . .

We are told that the social gap between the sexes is narrowing, but I can only report that having, in the second half of the twentieth century, experienced life in both roles, there seems to me no aspect of existence, no moment of the day, no contact, no arrangement, no response which is not different for men and for women. The very tone of voice in which I am now addressed, the very posture of the person next in the queue, the very feel in the air when I entered a room or sat at a restaurant table, constantly emphasized my change of status . . . .

My lawyer in an unguarded moment one morning, even called me "my child;" and so addressed every day of my life as an inferior, involuntarily month by month I accepted the condition. I discovered that even now men prefer women to be less informed, less able, less talkative, and certainly less self-centered than they themselves; so I generally obliged them . . . .

My view of life shifted too. I was even more emotional now. I cried very easily, and was ludicrously susceptible to sadness or flattery. Finding myself rather less interested in great affairs (which are placed in a new perspective, I do assure you by a change of sex), I acquired a new concern for small cues. My scale of vision seemed to contract, and I looked less for the grand sweep than for the telling detail . . . .

I want to add to them a frank enjoyment, which I think most honest women will admit to, of the small courtesies men now pay me, the standing up or the opening of doors, which really do give one a cherished or protected feeling . . . . The past is receding more than usually quickly and I am losing the last comparisons: the male stride, the male assurance, the problems and perquisites of malehood, the constancy and the strength, the independence, the supremacy . . . . On a physical plane I have myself achieved, as far as is humanly possible, the identity I craved. Distilled from those sacramental fancies of my childhood has come the conviction that the nearest humanity approaches to perfection is in the persons of good women—and especially perhaps in the persons of kind, intelligent, and healthy women of a certain age, no longer shackled by the mechanisms of sex but creative still in other kinds, aware still in their love and sensuality, graceful in experience, past ambition but never beyond aspiration. In all countries, among all races, on the whole these are the people I most admire; and it is into their ranks, I flatter myself, if only in the rear file, if only on the flank, that I have now admitted myself. (pp. 163-179, 192-193)

From her autobiography it seems as if Jan Morris aspired to be a woman primarily because she developed an idealized image of a female during childhood. She was on a quest for a spiritually higher level of being which she believed could only be reached through transformation to a woman. This is in interesting contrast to the autobiograpy of Chirstine Jorgensen (1967) where the motivation was apparently less to approach a new status than to escape an old one. Christine Jorgensen thought of herself as a failed male and sought relief in the female role.

There were other ways in which I didn't measure up to the acceptable standards of budding young male . . . .
Around the age of seventeen, I recall that I was even more keenly aware that I was different from other boys. Once I overheard one of them say, "George is such a strange guy." At other times, they didn't have to say it; I could read the thought in their attitudes . . . .
I've tried for more than twenty years to conform to the traditions of society. I've tried to fit myself into a world that's divided into men and women . . . to live and feel like a man, but I've been a total failure at it. I've only succeeded in living the life of a near recluse, completely unable to adjust. (p. 14, 21, 65)

Most transsexuals seem to be expressing a dual motivation: repugnance and hatred for the gender identity they wish to discard and romantic glorification of the gender identity toward which they are striving. It is not always clear which tends to be the more powerful force. However, if reference is made exclusively to anatomy, then it is relatively obvious that disgust with their original body is stronger, largely because it is the main impediment to acceptance of their "true self." After all, transsexuals recognize that following surgery their new body is still imperfect. Thus, in regard to anatomy alone, escape from the original form seems to be the more powerful motivation. Once again a quote from Jan Morris (1975) illustrates the point.

I loathed not merely the notion of my maleness and the evidence of my manhood. I resented my very connection with the male sex and hated to be thought, even by my dearest friends, a member of it. (p. 98)

Another reason for believing that escape tends to be the more powerful motivating force has to do with the finding that there are more male-to-female transsexuals. If males are the preferred sex in our society, why should there be more male-to-female transsexuals rather than the reverse? One possible reason is that there is less leeway in the male role, and thus males may more readily feel a sense of failure because of social rejection. Hence, escape into a new sexual identity may be the only way they can see to escape this censure.

A second question which can be asked is which came first, the conviction that one is really a member of the opposite sex or the sexual stereotypes and gender biases—harshly negative toward original identity and overly idealized toward the sought after identity? As yet there is no empirical evidence on which to base an answer to this sort of cause and effect question. Transsexuals would, of course, argue that the conviction came first, but these are obviously biased recollections. More likely the influences are bidirectional rather than unidirectional. The passionate *idée fixé* of a transsexual about his or her true gender identity colors views about masculinity and femininity at the same time that these views reinforce the obsessive conviction about being caged in the wrong body. If the transsexual and society as a whole were more tolerant of androgynous behavior, would there be any identity confusion or anguish?

Denial of Homosexuality: Another Motivating Force of Transsexuality

Despite the denials of most transsexuals, their autobiographical statements suggest that homosexual feelings and fear of social censure for homosexuality play an important part in the etiology of transsexuality. Just as many transsexuals cannot accept in themselves atypical gender role behaviors, presumably both because of social condemnation and prejudice on their own part, they also cannot accept in themselves the notion that they have homosexual desires and preferences. Morgan (1978) estimates that at least 30 percent of males who seek sex reassignment surgery are "homophobic." I suspect the number is higher. Once again the words of transsexuals speak for themselves.

Dr.: When did you become aware of sexual feelings toward men?

Patient: When I was in the Cub Scouts. I was about nine, and I just knew I was different then, 'cause I got a crush on one of the boys.

Dr.: What did you think that meant?

Patient: I don't know. I just knew I liked him. I'd follow him all over the place.

Dr.: Lots of boys that age have buddies.

Patient: Oh, no. It wasn't good buddies.

Dr.: How was it different?

Patient: He was very good looking. I liked to be with him. I thought of him, I think now, as a little girl thinks of little boys. I know when my youngest aunt married this fellow I was very attracted to him, and I used to have these day-dreams—he was going to run off with me. You know, the knight on the white horse.

Dr.: Did you think that there was something wrong with your having these thoughts?

Patient: You know, the first time that it dawned on me that I was abnormal—it was really weird—it was my sophomore year in high school. I could remember the exact day because I was in class, and just being seated the first day of school. Right next to me there was this kid standing there, and he was just the type I'm drawn to, very blond, very, very rugged, and I took a look at him and my whole heart seemed to go right in my throat. I felt like I must have blushed because I felt very warm and tingly. Every time he would look at me, it seemed, I'd just melt. And after school I went out to the beach. It was cold and foggy, and I sat there on the sand and these were the exact words I said to myself, "I started today. I've started something different. I don't know what it is, but I can't go back."

Dr.: Did you feel that you were homosexual?

Patient: Not homosexual. I felt that I was drawn to me. I could never think of myself as a man. I just couldn't (Green, 1974, pp. 49-50)

Another example from Green (1974):

Patient: For a while I thought the homosexual life would be the answer, and it wasn't.

Dr.: Why wasn't it?

Patient: I found it revolting. To me the idea of two men in bed with each other is sickening. While a man and woman together is perfectly natural.

Dr.: How does that differ from the relationship you are in now?

Patient: I am a woman. I have a problem—a growth—but I'm a woman. I am in no way like a male.

Dr.: Except that you have a penis and testes, and you don't have a uterus, and you don't have ovaries.

Patient: Yes.

Dr.: So, anatomically—

Patient: Anatomically, I am female, with those things stuck on.

Dr.: But there are homosexual couples, for example, in which one does all the domestic chores and in effect functions as a wife, while the other member of the team goes out as the breadwinner and carries on the male role, socially, economically, and sexually. I am not sure I understand the difference you are making between that kind of a gay marriage and the kind of relationship you have with your husband.

Patient: Well, I've met gay couples and their way of life, and they don't act like husband and wife. Their idea of marriage—many of them play around outside of the marriage.

Dr.: Heterosexual couples do too.

Patient: That's true.

Dr.: In what other ways don't you feel that gay couples have a real marriage?

Patient: Well, in the eyes of God, for one thing. God didn't create a man for men. He created a woman for man. The male homosexuals have sex with each other, they are both men and they think of themselves as male. When I had relations with men before I met my husband, I never thought of myself as a male, and I didn't want them to touch me down there. (p. 51)

Yet another example:

Dr.: Did you really think about having a sex change at eight?

Patient: I thought about it. I used to go, "Oh, gee, I wish I was a girl instead of a boy." I thought I'd be a lot better off. And then when I was about eleven I thought more about it.

Dr.: Why?

Patient: I just didn't have no feelings for girls. I didn't really like 'em. You know,

I liked 'em to hang around, and talk to, and stuff like that. But as far as having sex with them, I don't think I could . . . . I want female hormones.

Dr.:What would hormones do for you?

Patient: Well, first, they'd kill all this ugly hair. Kill the hair roots and make peach fuzz grow back. And then they'd start filling out my calves and thighs.

Dr.: Why would you like that?

Patient: I guess so I'd look more like a woman.

Dr.: What if someone were to say to you, now at seventeen, "Ok, you can have a sex change operation"?

Patient: I would take it.

Dr.: Why?

Patient: Because I think I'd be more happier that way, because right now I know people talk about me.

Dr.: What do they say?

Patient: Oh, they go, oh, I'm a big old queer and "Oh, you faggot." And then they do, "You should have been a girl."

Dr.: So if you had the surgery what would you do?

Patient: Well, I wouldn't have to—to be ashamed of myself, try to hide that I am a homosexual. Because I wouldn't be no more, right?

Dr.: What would you be?

Patient: I'd be a woman, I guess. (Green, 1974, p. 63)

Jan Morris's autobiography (1975) also contains similar revealing segments.

I hope I will not be thought narcissist if I claim that I was rather an attractive boy, not beautiful perhaps, but healthy and slim. Inevitably, the English school system being what it is, I was the object of advances, and thus my inner convictions were thrown into an altogether new relief. It seemed perfectly natural to me to play the girl's role in these transient and generally light-hearted romances, and in the platonic aspects I greatly enjoyed then. It was fun to be pursued, gratifying to be admired, and useful to have protectors in the sixth form. I enjoyed being kissed on the back stairs, and was distinctly flattered when the best-looking senior boy in the house made elaborate arrangements to meet me in the holidays.

When it came, nevertheless, to more elemental pursuits of pederasty, then I found myself not exactly repelled, but embarrassed. Aesthetically it seemed wrong to me. Nothing fitted. Our bodies did not cleave, and moreover I felt that, though promiscuity in flirtation was harmlessly entertaining, the intimacy of the body with mere acquaintances was inelegant . . . . It was a very far cry from Virgin Birth. It was also worrying for me, though my body often yearned to give, to yield, to open itself the machine was wrong. It was made for another function, and I felt myself to be wrongly equipped . . . .

You are wondering how I now saw men and women. Clearly, I would say, for the first time. I had no inhibitions, no half-conscious restraints. Nor was I atrophied now, for I felt the sexual urges cheerfully revived. Looking back at my old persona, I sadly recognized my own frustrated desires, plain at last, but irretrievably wasted. I saw how deeply I had pined for the arms and the love of a man. I saw how proud and brave a wife I would like to have been, how passionate a mother, how forlornly my poor self had yearned to be released into its full sexuality—that flowering which, *faute de mieux*, I had so often redirected into words, or patriotism, or love of place. The shutters were removed at last, no longer clamped down, like those clanking steel blinds of the Cairo shopkeepers, to keep the unwanted at bay during the long siesta. I was walking along Jermyn Street one day when I saw, for the first time in twenty years, a member of the Everest team of 1953. My goodness, I said to myself, what an extraordinarily handsome man. I knew he had been handsome all along, but I had allowed myself to like him only for his gentle manners, and it was only now that I permitted myself the indulgence of thinking him desirable. (pp. 24, 172-173)

Similar evidence of homosexual repulsion is contained in Christine Jorgensen's autobiography (1967):

I received a letter from Tom telling me he had joined the Navy and, after his boot training, would be sent to the South Pacific. Reading that letter, I remember being overwhelmed by the revelation that, despite earlier denials, I was in love with him....here was something—a forbidden emotion—of which I had to feel ashamed, and it was abhorrent to me....

During the months in service, I had seen a few practicing homosexuals, those whom the other men called 'queer'. I couldn't condemn them, but I also knew that I certainly couldn't become like them. It was a thing deeply alien to my religious attitudes and the highly magnified and immature moralistic views that I entertained at the time. Furthermore I had seen enough to know that homosexuality brought with it a social segregation and ostracism that I couldn't add to my own deep feeling of not belonging....

Even now I can remember that I was appalled and disgusted at his behavior, and I may even have known a moment of fear—a fear of homosexual contact that was based on the hidden belief that I, too, deviated from what was termed "normal." (pp. 25, 33, 45)

The above examples of homosexual denial are all from male-to-female transsexuals. The next two are from female-to-male transsexuals:

Dr.: What about in your early teens? Did you have any kind of fantasies about kissing or hugging?

Patient: Yes, the physical, the kissing. But that was more in dreams. I would be kissing another female, the female that I had a crush on.

Dr.: When were you first aware of adult-type sexual feelings? Genital types of feelings?

Patient: Very late. I would say when I was a teenager, around sixteen or seventeen.

Dr.: What do you daydream now?

Patient: That I will be a male kissing another female I was attracted to.

Dr.: How would your life be changed now if you were to be living as a man?

Patient: I would be dating, for one thing.

Dr.: You would be dating? Why not now? It wouldn't be the first time in history that two women have dated.

Patient: I would have a homosexual hang-up. I don't know. I don't think I would feel right in doing this. And I think that would also be true of the other person. In other words, society frowns upon this, and I don't want to seem different. I also think that if I wanted to have a lasting relationship with someone, I wouldn't want to start it now. I would prefer to have the operation and then start.

Dr.: Will you explain that to me further, your being able to do something you can't do now because of breasts, and no facial hair?

Patient: I don't think I could do it. I just couldn't do it. Not now.

Dr.: Why would you be able to do it if your breasts weren't there?

Patient: Because the desire, wanting to do it, is there. But I just have too much of a hang-up this way, a psychological hang-up! (Green, 1974, p. 107)

Yet again.

Patient: I can remember as I got a little older always looking at women, always wanting a woman.

Dr.: Now you're talking about what age?

Patient: Fifteen and sixteen, but I was so busy in sports that I didn't let myself until I was about eighteen years old, because, like I say, I was brought up very religiously, and it scared me. I didn't know why I felt like this. Why didn't I feel like other girls?

Dr.: Do you consider yourself homosexual?

Patient: Well, I must be. I'm a woman and I love women, and yet I cannot call myself one, because I don't feel like one. I feel like a man, and I feel like my loving a woman is perfectly normal. (Green, 1974, p. 110)

Assuming these excerpts are reasonably representative, one is left with the question of why these individuals can accept their transsexual desires but not their homosexual desires. Furthermore, if they could accept their homosexual impulses, would the motivation for transsexual surgery be substantially reduced?

In purely statistical terms, transsexuality is by far a more socially deviant response pattern than homosexuality. Could it nevertheless be that transsexuality carries with it less of a moral and social stigma than homosexuality, not only in the minds of transsexuals but for society as well?

I recently conducted a questionnaire study to try to get a preliminary answer to this question. The purpose was to compare attitudes toward transsexuality and homosexuality in a heterosexual population. College students (106 males and 212 females) enrolled in an introductory psychology course were administered two questionnaires. Each contained an identical set of questions, one addressed to transsexuality and the other to homosexuality. The order was counterbalanced, so that half the students answered the questions concerning transsexuality first, and the other half answered the questions concerning homosexuality first. Two questions were specifically directed at general attitudes toward transsexuality and homosexuality; the others concerned issues of legal rights and job discrimination. I will only report the results from the attitude section here.

Each year from 1972 through 1978 the National Opinion Research Center, as part of its general social surveys, has obtained responses to three questions about premarital, extramarital, and homosexual relations respectively (Glenn and Weaver, 1979). In the present study we repeated their question about homosexuality, namely:

What is your opinion of sexual relations between two adults of the same sex: (check only one)

(a) always wrong

(b) almost always wrong

(c) wrong only sometimes

(d) not wrong at all

(e) don't know

Similarly, phrasing for the transsexuality questionnaire was: "What is your opinion of transsexuals who want to have their sex changed?" with the same five response choices provided as in the question about homosexuality.

Unfortunately there was a significant order effect: Attitudes expressed

TABLE 3

Percentage of Respondents Who Said Transsexuality or
Homosexuality Is "Always Wrong"

	Transsexuality	Homosexuality
Female Respondents (n = 209)	17.8%	29.6%
Male Respondents (n = 103)	26.2%	31.1%

toward transsexuality were more negative when the transsexual questionnaire was filled out after than when it was filled out before the homosexual questionnaire. (This did not show up in the reverse direction, i.e., attitudes toward homosexuality were not tempered as a result of first responding to questions dealing with transsexuality). Thus, a less contaminated
picture of the separate attitudes toward transsexuality and homosexuality
can best be obtained by examining the results on the first questionnaire
the subjects answered. The percentage endorsing the "always wrong"
response choice for transsexuality and homosexuality respectively is indicated in Table 3 for males and females separately.

As can be seen in this table, more male and female students felt that
homosexuality was "always wrong" than felt transsexuality was "always
wrong." The female students especially were less negative in their opinion of transsexuality than in their opinion of homosexuality. A chi-square
analysis showed that these differences were statistically significantly
(transsexuality versus homosexuality: $X^2 = 4.28$, $p < .05$).

The second question we asked in the attitude domain was: "Should a
homosexual be allowed to adopt a child?" This was asked in regard to
both a male homosexual and a female homosexual. The phrasing for the
transsexual questionnaire was again nearly identical: "Should a transsexual
who has had sex-reassignment surgery be allowed to adopt a child?" This
was answered separately for a male transsexual converted to look like an
anatomic female and a female transsexual converted to look like an anatomic male. The response choices were a simple yes or no.

Because there was no difference depending on whether the question had
to do with male or female homosexuals or transsexuals, the results for both
were combined. Table 4 reveals that more people were of the opinion that

TABLE 4

Percentage of Respondents in Favor of Transsexuals or Homosexuals Being Allowed to Adopt a Child

	Transsexuals	Homosexuals
Female Respondents (n = 209)	51.0%	37.0%
Male Respondents (n = 103)	38.6%	31.9%

transsexuals should be permitted to adopt a child than were of the opinion that homosexuals should be allowed to adopt a child ($X^2 = 4.64$, $p < .05$). Once again, this difference in favor of transsexuals was more striking in female than male respondents.

Granted, first- and second-year college undergraduates enrolled in an introductory psychology course in a New England state university are not representative of the general population. However, though the exact percentages endorsing the "always wrong" response choices would undoubtedly be higher in the general population (i.e., the percentage who felt that homosexuality was "always wrong" in the National Opinion Research Center surveys consistently hovered around the 70-75 percent mark), there is no reason to believe that the direction or even the magnitude of the differences obtained in the present study between expressed attitudes toward transsexuals and homosexuals would be altered in a more representative sample. In any case, for the time being, these results are the only data which exist that compare attitudes toward transsexuality and homosexuality. They clearly suggest that, for whatever reasons, transsexuality is less of an affront or less threatening to conventional morality than is homosexuality. Perhaps transsexuality implies a greater biological imperative and thus evokes less condemnation and less guilt than homosexuality, or perhaps transsexuality is relatively more acceptable because it is not associated as much with sexual behavior per se, an arena in which many individuals' sense of morality is seemingly more easily tapped than is the case for larger social and political concerns. For example, to be accused of being a "sexual pervert" has quite a different onus than to be accused of being sexist. Another possibility is that transsexuality just does not have the same past history of religious condemnation and persecution as does homosexuality—particularly male homosexuality.

In summary, then, I think it fair to conclude that the transsexuals' disavowal of homosexuality in themselves, their insistence that their sexual desires for a member of the same sex should not be construed as homosexual because they are really a person of the opposite sex, may simply reflect society's greater moral tolerance for transsexuality than for homosexuality.

Alternatives to Sex Reassignment Surgery

Hormonal treatment and sex reassignment surgery were originally made available to transsexuals not only because they passionately demanded it, but also because no one could see any alternative. There was considerable pessimism about the effectiveness of any alternative intervention. Traditional psychotherapy had not succeeded in persuading transsexuals to accept their biological identity, and only two choices were ever posed: alter the conviction to fit the body or alter the body to fit the conviction.

In fact, there are other choices. Recent research indicates that the transsexual conviction is not always lifelong or ineradicable. Using a variety of behavioral therapy techniques, Barlow, Reynolds and Agras (1973) and Barlow, Abel, and Blanchard (1979) reported successful outcomes in three male-to-female transsexuals. The therapeutic procedure involved rather painstaking and detailed training in how to sit, stand, walk, and talk in a more masculine manner. It also involved other social skills training and modification of sexual fantasies and arousal patterns. One male-to-female transsexual assumed a completely heterosexual orientation (which has been maintained over a 6½-year follow-up), and the other two retained their homosexual preference but no longer engaged in stereotypic feminine behaviors or believed they had a female identity. Barlow, Abel, and Blanchard (1977) also recently reported the case of a classic long-standing transsexual who was near to having surgery when he was "exorcised" of his mistaken gender identity by a faith healer in 2 hours. Obviously, these are only a very small number of cases. They are striking, however, because they counter the strong belief that such changes in gender identity could never be obtained in adult transsexuals.

Because the feminist movement and the gay liberation movement were in their infancy in the 1950s and the early 1960s, another alternative, namely, fighting sex role stereotyping and homosexual intolerance, has to this date never been systematically explored in a transsexual population. Rather than providing transsexual surgery or attempting to train male-to-female transsexuals to engage in more masculine motor, social, and sexual behaviors (and vice versa for a female-to-male transsexual), perhaps consciousness raising and support groups would enable them to accept androgyny and homosexuality and learn to cope more effectively with social rejection and anxiety.

Conclusion

If trends in our society toward greater role equality between the sexes continue and if leeway in traditional masculine and feminine role behavior is encouraged, people who formerly would be transsexuals may be able to achieve their goals of living and acting the way they want to without having to disguise and disfigure their bodies to avoid social condemnation. Similarly, if there were less moral condemnation of homosexuality, transsexuals might be less apt to try to escape this stigma by claiming to be members of the opposite gender and thus not truly interested in sexual activity with same-sex partners. Therefore, why not concentrate our efforts where they would do the most good, both for society as a whole as well as for transsexuals? These statements are, of course, laden with values and speculations: that it would be better for society to strive for flexible rather than rigid gender lines; that currently transsexual surgery is in effect a stamp of approval for extreme sex typing and antithetical to promotion of varied gender roles for either sex; that if the latter were accomplished, there would probably be no need for sex reassignement surgery in the future.

However, even now, in the seeming midst of a changing zeitgeist, surgeons could reasonably argue that changing cultural values is all well and good but not easily achieved. In the meantime the clinical and social dilemma remains. Hormonal treatment and surgery can provide relief for a transsexual's psychological pain even if it is admitted that at the same time it probably does indirectly reinforce cultural stereotypes of masculinity and femininity and nonacceptance of homosexuality—which are, in turn, the original sources of such pain. In talking about larger social goals, are we losing sight of the individual's anguish? The following quote from Jan Morris (1975) illustrates the quandary.

If I were trapped in that cage again nothing would keep me from my goal, however fearful its prospect, however hopeless the odds. I would search the earth for surgeons .... I would take a knife and do it myself without fear, without qualms, without a second thought. (p. 188)

In other words should some people be left to suffer in the vague hope that this might help in the effort to eradicate hypothetical sexist and homophobic causes of transsexualism? Understandably, this conflict is cause for considerable debate. I hope this paper has been a constructive addition to such debate.

References

Albee, G. W. The prevention of sexism. *Professional Psychology*, 1981, *12*, 20-28.

Barlow, D. H., Abel, G. G., and Blanchard, E. B. Gender identity change in a transsexual: An exorcism. *Archives of Sexual Behavior*, 1977, *6*, 387-395.

Barlow, D. H., Abel, G. G., and Blanchard, E. B. Gender identity change in transsexuals. *Archives of General Psychiatry*, 1979, *36*, 1001-1007.

Barlow, D. H., Reynolds, E. J., and Agras, W. S. Gender identity change in a transsexual. *Archives of General Psychiatry*, 1973, *28*, 569-579.

Bem, S. L. Sex-role adaptability: One consequence of psychological androgyny. *Journal of Personality and Social Psychology*, 1975, *31*, 634-643.

Benjamin, H. *The transsexual phenomenon*. New York: Julian Press, 1966.

Brierly, H. *Transvestism: A handbook with case studies for psychologists, psychiatrists, and counsellors*. Oxford: Pergamon Press, 1979.

Feinbloom, D. H. *Transvestites and transsexuals: Mixed views*. New York: Delacorte Press, 1976.

Glenn, N. D., and Weaver, C. N. Attitudes toward premarital, extramarital, and homosexual relations in the U.S. in the 1970s. *Journal of Sex Research*, 1979, *15*, 108-118.

Green, R. *Sexual identity conflict in children and adults*. Baltimore: Penguin Books, 1974.

Green, R. and Money, J. (Eds.). *Transsexualism and sex reassignment*. Baltimore: Johns Hopkins University Press, 1969.

Green, R., Newman, L., and Stoller, R. Treatment of boyhood "transsexualism." *Archives of General Psychiatry*, 1972, *26*, 213-217.

Hastings, D., and Markland, C. Post-surgical adjustment of twenty-five transsexuals (male-to-female) in the University of Minnesota study. *Archives of Sexual Behavior*, 1978, *7*, 327-336.

Hoenig, J., and Kenna, J. C. The prevalence of transsexualism in England and Wales. *British Journal of Psychiatry*, 1974, *124*, 181-190.

Jorgensen, C. A. *A personal autobiography*. New York: Bantam Books, 1967.

Lebovitz, P. J. Feminine behavior in boys: Aspects of its outcome. *American Journal of Psychiatry*, 1972, *128*, 1283-1289.

Meyer, J. K., and Reter, D. J. Sex reassignment: Follow-up. *Archives of General Psychiatry*, 1979, *36*, 1010-1015.

Money, J. Prefatory remarks on outcome of sex reassignment in 24 cases of transsexualism. *Archives of Sexual Behavior*, 1971, *1*, 163-166.

Morgan, A. J. Psychotherapy for transsexual candidates screened out of surgery. *Archives of Sexual Behavior*, 1978, 7, 273-283.

Morris, J. *Conundrum*. New York: Signet, 1975.

Nordyke, N. S., Baer, D. M., Etzel, B. C., and LeBlanc, J. M. Implications of the stereotyping and modification of sex role. *Journal of Applied Behavior Analysis*, 1977, *10*, 553-557.

Pauly, I. B. The current status of the change of sex operation. *Journal of Nervous and Mental Diseases*, 1968, *147*, 460-471.

Randall, J. Preoperative and postoperative status of male and female transsexuals. In R. Green and J. Money (Eds.), *Transsexualism and sex reassignment*. Baltimore: Johns Hopkins University Press, 1969.

Raymond, J. G. *The transsexual empire: The making of the she-male*. Boston: Beacon Press, 1979.

Rekers, G. A., and Lovaas, O. I. Behavioral treatment of deviant sex-role behaviors in a male child. *Journal of Applied Behavior Analysis*, 1974, 7, 173-190.

Rekers, G. A., and Lovaas, O. I., and Low, B. P. The behavioral treatment of a "transsexual" preadolescent boy. *Journal of Abnormal Child Psychology*, 1974, *2*, 99-116.

Rekers, G. A., and Varni, J. W. Self regulation of gender role behaviors: A case study. *Journal of Behavior Therapy and Experimental Psychiatry*, 1977, *8*, 427-432. (a)

Rekers, G. A., and Varni, J. W. Self-monitoring and self-reinforcement processes in a pre-transsexual boy. *Behavior Research and Therapy*, 1977, *15*, 177-180. (b)

Rekers, G. A., Willis, T. J., Yates, C. E., Rosen, A. C., and Low, B. P. Assessment of childhood gender behavior change. *Journal of Child Psychology and Psychiatry*, 1977, *18*, 53-65.

Rekers, G. A., Yates, C. E., Willis, T. J., Rosen, A. C., and Taubman, M. Childhood gender identity change: Operant control over sex-typed play and mannerisms. *Journal of Behavior Therapy and Experimental Psychiatry*, 1976, 7, 51-57.

Stoller, R. J. *Sex and gender: The development of masculinity and femininity* (Vol. 1). New York: Jason Aronson, 1968.

Stoller, R. J. *Sex and gender: The transsexual experiment* (Vol. 2). New York: Jason Aronson, 1975.

Walinder, J. Transsexualism: Definition, prevalence, and sex distribution. *Acta Psychiatrica Scandinavica*, 1968, Supplement 203, 255-258.

Winkler, R. C. What types of sex-role behavior should behavior modifiers promote? *Journal of Applied Behavior Analyses*, 1977, *10*, 549-552.

Wolfe, B. E. Behavioral treatment of childhood gender disorders: A conceptual and empirical critique. *Behavior Modification*, 1979, *3*, 550-575.

Zuger, B. Effeminate behavior present in boys from early childhood. *Journal of Pediatrics*, 1966, *69*, 1098-1107.

Aggressive Pornography: Can It Influence Aggression toward Women?

Edward I. Donnerstein

The purpose of this paper is to examine in some detail recent research on the effects of aggressive pornography and subsequent aggression toward women. The research to be reviewed is quite recent and, as we will see, presents a somewhat different picture of the effects of pornography. At the outset, however, it is important to note that the types of effects that are found are not so much a function of pornography, but rather of aggressive images of women in the media. A close examination of the research will indicate that nonaggressive erotic or pornographic images have really no measurable effect on aggression toward women. These results are important to keep in mind. It is obvious that pornography takes many forms, and it is *only* the aggressive forms that seem to produce the type of negative effects which will be discussed below. The present chapter is divided into a number of sections that are intended to give an overview of the topic of pornography and aggression. The first section will provide a brief summary of the effects of pornography and aggression in general. The second section will examine what effect nonaggressive pornography has on violence toward women, while the third section will introduce the role of aggressive pornography. We will then examine the role of the victim in aggressive behavior toward women. Finally, we will look at the effects of nonerotic aggressive images.

Erotica and Aggression

In recent years, there has been increasing concern about rape and other forms of aggression toward women. Although there have been many explanations offered for the increase in violence toward women, the role of the media, and in particular pornography, has been considered as one important contributor (e.g., Brownmiller, 1975; Burt, 1980; Donnerstein, 1980b). Although the 1971 report of the Commission on Obscenity and

Pornography concluded that there was no direct relationship between exposure to pornography and subsequent aggression, particularly sexual crimes, recent criticisms of these findings (e.g., Berkowitz, 1971; Cline, 1974; Dienstbier, 1977; Wills, 1977) have led a number of investigators to reexamine the issue. For the most part this research has indicated that under certain conditions exposure to specific types of erotic materials can increase subsequent aggressive behavior (e.g., Baron and Bell, 1977; Donnerstein, in press; Donnerstein, Donnerstein, and Evans, 1975; Malamuth, Feshbach, and Jaffe, 1977; Meyer, 1972; Zillmann, 1971, 1979). The brief review which follows is an overview of these recent findings.

Aggression-Enhancing Effects of Erotic Exposure

A number of studies in which subjects have been angered, and later exposed to some form of erotic stimulation, have revealed increased aggressive behavior (e.g., Zillmann, 1971; Zillmann, Hoyt, and Day, 1974). Such findings have come to be interpreted in terms of a general arousal model stating that under conditions where aggression is a dominant response, any source of emotional arousal will tend to increase aggressive behavior (i.e., Bandura, 1973). Thus, in accordance with this model, aggressive behavior in subjects who have previously been angered has been shown to be increased by exposure to arousing sources such as aggressive or erotic films (Zillmann, 1971), physical exercise (Zillmann, 1979), and noise (Donnerstein and Wilson, 1976). It would seem, then, that because of their arousing properties erotic stimuli can have aggression-facilitating effects under certain conditions. Although there has been research which has indicated that erotic stimuli might increase aggression without anger arousal (e.g., Malamuth et al., 1977), the majority of the evidence to date would suggest that prior anger arousal is an important condition for a facilitative effect of erotic exposure.

Aggression-Inhibiting Effects of Erotic Exposure

A second group of studies (e.g., Baron, 1977; Baron and Bell, 1973; Frodi, 1977) have shown, however, that exposure to erotic stimuli can actually reduce subsequent aggression. A number of explanations have been suggested for this effect: erotic stimuli are somehow incompatible in their emotional state with aggression (Baron, 1974; Zillmann and Sapolsky, 1977); the level of anger arousal is inappropriate for an aggressive response (Frodi, 1977); or erotic exposure shifts attention away from previous anger instigation (Donnerstein et al., 1975). Whatever the explanation, however, there is sound evidence to suggest that under certain conditions erotic stimuli can reduce subsequent aggressive behavior.

A Reconciliation of the Research

Although at first glance such results seem somewhat contradictory, recent studies by Donnerstein et al. (1975) and Baron and Bell (1977) seem to have resolved this controversy temporarily. It is now believed that as erotic stimuli become more arousing they give rise to increases in aggressive behavior. At a low level of arousal, however, such stimuli act to distract a subject's attention from previous anger (Donnerstein et al., 1975) or act as an incompatible response with aggression (Baron and Bell, 1977), thus reducing subsequent aggressive behavior. The evidence for this curvilinear relationship between sexual arousal and aggression seems fairly well established (i.e., Baron and Bell, 1977; Donnerstein et al., 1975). In fact, Baron has shown that this type of relationship also occurs when females are exposed to mild and highly erotic stimuli (Baron, 1977).

Erotica and Aggression toward Women

Although the current theorizing on the relationship between erotic stimuli and aggression seems fairly conclusive, it is interesting to note that all of the above-mentioned studies were concerned with same sex, primarily male-to-male, aggression. Yet, the social implications of this research would be more applicable had an examination been done of male aggression toward females. For, as noted by the Presidential Commission on Obscenity and Pornography (1971):

It is often asserted that a distinguishing characteristic of sexually explicit materials is the degrading and demeaning portrayal of the role and the status of the human female. It has been argued that erotic materials describe the female as a mere sexual object to be exploited and manipulated sexually. (p. 201)

In those studies which have examined the effects of erotica on aggression toward females, the general conclusion has been that no differential sex effects occur. Thus, in one series of studies, Mosher (1971) found no increase in "sex-calloused" attitudes or exploitive sexual behavior toward females, nor any increase in aggressive verbal remarks. More recent research by Jaffe, Malamuth, Feingold, and Feshbach (1974) and Baron and Bell (1973) has also indicated that erotic exposure by males does not differentially affect aggression toward males or females. One problem with these studies, however, was that anger instigation and high arousal from film exposure were not systematically investigated. These two variables had been shown in earlier research to be important contributors to the facilitating effect of erotica on aggression in general. Recently, Donnerstein and his colleagues (Donnerstein, 1980b; Donnerstein and Barrett, 1978; Donnerstein and Hallam, 1978) studied the effects of these two variables on aggression toward females. The results of these studies indicated that when aggressive restraints are lowered in male subjects, exposure to highly arousing erotic films can increase aggression toward women in previously angered males. Without these lowered restraints, however, there was no evidence that exposure to erotic stimuli affects aggressive behaviors toward women. It seemed important, then, for additional research to examine other factors which might act to reduce aggressive restraints, given that this factor plays an important role in mediating the relationship of erotica and aggression toward women (e.g., Malamuth et al., 1977).

The Role of Aggressive Erotica

Although early research examined factors external to film content as a means of influencing aggressive restraints (e.g., delayed aggression), there is evidence to suggest that aspects of the film itself could play a crucial role. For example, there is ample documentation to suggest that the observation of aggressive films reduces restraints against subsequent aggressive behavior (e.g., Geen, 1976). Until recently research on the effects of erotica and aggression toward women has employed films that did not contain any aggressive content. Beyond the reduction in aggressive restraints, there are a number of other reasons why aggressive erotica should be examined as a potential mediator in the relationship of erotica and aggression toward women. First, there is now a substantial amount of evidence to suggest that aggressive erotica have been on the increase in the past few years (e.g., Eysenck and Nias, 1978; Malamuth and Spinner, 1980; Malamuth and Check, in press-a). Second, theoretical work by Berkowitz and his colleagues (e.g., Berkowitz, 1974) suggests that aggressive erotica have an effect on aggression, particularly toward women. Specifically, this work has shown that one important determinant of whether an aggressive response is made is the presence of aggressive cues. Not only objects but individuals can take on aggressive cue value if they have been associated with observed violence. Thus viewing aggressive erotica might facilitate

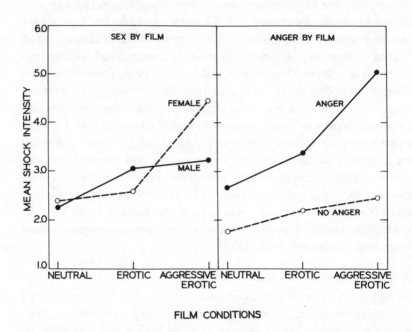

Figure 1. Mean shock intensity as a function of sex of target and content of films, and of anger of subject and content of films.

subsequent aggression toward a woman because repeated association of females with the victim of observed violence increases the aggression-eliciting stimulus properties of a female. Finally, there is now increasing evidence that certain types of aggressive erotica can have undesirable attitudinal and other behavioral effects. For example, it has been shown that exposure to aggressive erotica by males can result in (1) self-generated rape fantasies (Malamuth, in press); (2) an increase in sexual arousal (Malamuth, Heim, and Feshbach, 1980); (3) a lessened sensitivity to rape (Malamuth and Check, in press-b); and (4) an increased acceptance of rape myths and interpersonal violence toward women (Malamuth and Check, in press-a) as well as the self-reported possibility of raping (Malamuth, Haber, and Feshbach, 1980).

Based upon the information noted above, Donnerstein (1980a) sought to determine the effects of aggressive erotica on actual aggressive behavior toward women. Male subjects in this study were angered or treated in a neutral manner by a male or female confederate and then given the opportunity to view one of three films. Two of the films were selected for their sexually arousing content, but they differed in aggressive content. The results of this study, which are shown in Figure 1, showed that exposure to an aggressive erotic film increased aggressive behavior to a level higher than was found for an erotic film. These findings were most noticeable in subjects who had previously been angered. With respect to the sex of the aggressive target, when angered subjects were paired with males the aggressive erotic film produced no more aggression than the erotic version. Those subjects paired with females, however, *only* displayed an increase in aggression after viewing the aggressive film. In fact, this increase occurred even if subjects were not angered. Given that both films were equally arousing, why would aggression be increased toward the females only after exposure to the aggressive erotic film? One explanation is that the females' association with the victim in the film made them stimuli which could elicit aggressive responses (e.g., Berkowitz, 1974). The combination of anger arousal and film arousal heightened this response and led to the highest level of aggression toward females. But, even under nonangered conditions aggression was increased. This was not the case for subjects paired with males. It would seem, then, that the females' association with the *victim* in the film was an important contributor to the aggression directed toward them.

Reactions of the Victim in the Film

The role of the victim in aggressive erotica is important in the relationship of such stimuli to attitudes and behaviors toward women. A common theme in pornography is that women find pleasure from sexual aggression (e.g., Brownmiller, 1975; Gager and Schurr, 1976). In the work of Malamuth and his colleagues which was discussed above, the increased sexual arousal and negative attitudes toward rape were found in aggressive depictions that showed this type of reaction on the part of the film's victim. These effects do not occur when the film's victim is seen to continuously abhor the assault. Furthermore, the self-reported likelihood of raping was highly correlated with the perception that the women in the aggressive erotic stimuli found the assault pleasurable and with a general belief that women derive pleasure from being raped (Malamuth and Check, in press-b). In the Donnerstein (1980a) study, which found that aggressive erotica increased violent behavior toward a woman, films were not chosen with victim reactions as a factor. The type of film employed, however, was a standard aggressive erotic film which was later judged to show no negative reactions on the part of the female victim. It would seem reasonable to assume that the viewing of an aggressive erotic film which presents a positive reaction from the female victim should not only act to reduce inhibitions, but would in many ways act to reinforce any aggressive tendencies generated from the film and prior anger instigation.

What would be the effect of films which display the victim as not enjoying the situation, but instead finding it both painful and abhorrent? From the work of Malamuth and others (Abel, Barlow, Blanchard, and Guild, 1977; Malamuth and Check, in press-b), we know that such depictions do not increase sexual arousal. However, there is a good possibility that they may actually increase aggressive behavior. In the human aggression literature, victim pain cues have been shown to have two types of effects. For individuals who are not angered, victim pain cues tend to *reduce* aggression (e.g., Baron, 1977). For angered individuals, however, the effect seems to be just the opposite. There is evidence indicating that when individuals are highly provoked victim pain cues actually *increase* aggression (e.g., Baron, 1977). While the findings for nonangered subjects are discussed in terms of the empathetic feelings aroused by the signs of pain (Baron, 1977), the findings with angered individuals are seen in terms of the reinforcing aspects of the victim's pain (e.g., Berkowitz, 1974; Swart and Berkowitz, 1976).

When we deal with aggressive erotica, however, we are discussing a condition in which pain and discomfort are vicarious. The subject's instigator is not harmed, nor does the subject himself cause the harm. Would this factor tend to make a difference? In reviewing the media violence literature, Goranson (1970) argues that observed pain cues could increase aggressive inhibitions by sensitizing individuals to the harm they themselves might inflict. Hartmann (1969) found, however, that the observation of pain cues by angered subjects increased subsequent aggression. Hartmann argued that anger instigation raises the threshold for empathy. He further noted that increased arousal would have the same effect. This would obviously suggest that exposure to a highly arousing aggressive erotic film with

TABLE 1

Mean Self-Report and Physiological Changes to Various Film Conditions
Experiment 1

| | Film Condition | | | |
| | | | Aggressive | Aggressive |
Ratings of Film	Neutral	Nonaggressive	Erotic	Erotic
Interesting	1.6a	3.4b	3.3b	3.2b
Sexually Arousing	1.1a	3.7b	3.7b	3.9b
Aggressive	1.4a	1.4a	3.5b	4.8c
Sexual Content	1.4a	6.0b	5.9b	5.6b
Ratings of Victim				
Suffering		1.7a	2.7b	4.8c
Enjoyment		6.3a	5.1b	2.6c
Responsible		5.6a	4.1b	2.9c
Mean Blood Pressure	-0.9a	+6.1b	+8.5b	+5.5b

NOTE. Means with different subscripts differ from each other at the .05 level by Duncan's procedure. Film ratings are on a 7-point scale.

a negative ending should increase aggression in angered individuals. Bandura (1973) has also speculated on the effects of observed pain cues. First, he noted that a victim's suffering is more likely to reduce aggression when the pain is produced by the individual him- or herself than when it is observed. Second, an increase in arousal increases the conditioning of pain cues as a reinforcer. Finally, pain cues can acquire reinforcement value if they are repeatedly associated with sexual gratification. This reasoning would also suggest that a negative/aggressive erotic film should increase aggression in previously angered males. Two recent experiments by Donnerstein and Berkowitz (in press) were designed to examine these issues.

In this first study we were interested in how reactions on the part of the film's victim would affect aggression toward male and female targets. Male subjects were first angered by a male or female confederate and then given the opportunity to observe one of four films. Three of the films were highly erotic in nature but differed in their aggressive content. The first was a standard nonaggressive erotic film. The other two erotic films were aggressive in nature, but differed in terms of outcome. One version was designed to have a positive ending while the other version depicted a negative outcome. The final film was neutral with respect to aggression and erotica. Since it was possible that any increase in aggression found

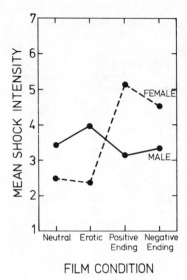

Figure 2. Mean shock intensity as a function of sex of target and ending of film.

for the aggressive erotic films could be explained by increases in physiological arousal (e.g., Zillmann, 1971), all the erotic films were chosen to be equal in arousal level.

After having viewed the films all subjects were asked to rate them on a number of scales. These ratings are presented in Table 1. As can be seen, the negative/aggressive erotic film was seen as more aggressive than the positive version. This is interesting in light of the fact that the actual aggressive content was the same in both films. In addition the victim in the negative film was seen as suffering more and enjoying herself less than her positive counterpart. Furthermore, the woman in the positive/aggressive erotic film was seen as being more responsible for what had happened. The physiological data indicated that all the erotic films were more arousing than the neutral film, though they did not differ from each other. The aggression data are presented in Figure 2. As can be seen, none of the films affected aggression toward a male target. However, both the positive and negative aggressive erotic films increased aggression toward the female. This level of aggression was higher than the male target conditions except for the erotic film.

These results suggest that aggressive erotica does increase aggression against women. Although both types of films increased aggression equally, we could suggest that the effects were obtained differently. For the positive/aggressive erotic film we could conclude that in addition to the aggressive cue value in the film, the positive ending allowed any aggressive inhibitions to be reduced. In a sense, the ending suggested that aggression was permissible in this situation. Malamuth and Donnerstein (in press) have shown that when male subjects are angered by a female and exposed to aggressive erotic pictures, aggression will be increased when subjects are given disinhibitory cues (e.g., it is OK to behave aggressively). It is highly likely that this process was operating in the present study.

For subjects exposed to the negative film version we could assume that the vicarious pain cues served as a reinforcement for subsequent aggression. Given prior anger instigation and the highly arousing nature of the film, this reinforcement explanation would support past research findings (e.g., Bandura, 1973; Hartmann, 1969). If the observation of pain cues acts as a reinforcement for angered individuals, then one might suggest that for nonangered subjects the negative/aggressive erotic film would have just the opposite effect. Previous research does indicate that signs of suffering in one's victim do reduce aggressive behavior (e.g., Baron, 1977). The effects for observed violence are not that clear cut. Hartmann (1969) found that for one measure of aggression (shock intensity) nonangered male subjects increased their levels of aggression after observing an aggressive film with pain cues. On another measure of aggression (intensity x duration), however, no increase in aggression was observed. It has been suggested that when inhibitions are high, observed suffering in a victim will *not* increase aggression in nonangered individuals. If this is the case, then it could reasonably be predicted that for nonangered male subjects, exposure to a negative/aggressive erotic film will not increase aggression toward a female. The second study by Donnerstein and Berkowitz (in press) sought to examine this possibility.

Male subjects in this experiment were first angered or treated in a neutral manner by a female confederate. Following this manipulation subjects were exposed to one of the four films employed in the first study. After making ratings of the films all subjects were given an opportunity ostensibly to administer shocks to the female confederate. As in previous studies psychological reactions were monitored at various points in the experiment.

Table 2 presents the film ratings for subjects from this second study. As can be seen they were identical to those in the first study, with the negative version being seen as more aggressive, the woman suffering more,

TABLE 2

Mean Self-Report and Physiological Changes to Various Film Conditions
Experiment 2

| | | Film Condition | | |
| | | | Aggressive | Aggressive |
Ratings of Film	Neutral	Nonaggressive	Erotic	Erotic
Interesting	1.6a	3.8b	3.8b	3.2b
Sexually Arousing	1.6a	4.7b	3.7c	3.7c
Aggressive	1.2a	1.8a	4.3b	6.2c
Sexual Content	1.3a	6.4b	5.9bc	5.5c
Ratings of Victim				
Suffering	(no anger)	1.7a	3.0b	5.7c
Enjoyment	(anger)	5.6ac	5.9ac	1.6b
		6.5a	4.9c	3.2d
Responsible		5.6a	4.3b	2.3c
Mean Blood Pressure	-0.5a	+8.3b	+10.7b	+8.9b

NOTE. Means with different subscripts differ from each other at the .05 level by Duncan's procedure. Film ratings are on a 7-point scale.

enjoying less, and being less responsible than her positive aggression counterpart. Physiological data also indicated that the three erotic films were seen as more arousing than the neutral presentation though not differing from each other. Figure 3 presents the results for the aggression data: for nonangered subjects only the positive/aggressive erotic film increased aggression toward the female victim. There was a slight tendency ($p < .10$) for the negative film to increase aggression beyond the neutral presentation. For angered subjects, however, both the negative and positive versions increased aggression, as in the findings in the first study.

The results of this study further support the idea that observed victim suffering can act as a reinforcement for aggression toward women. Although angered subjects exposed to the negative/aggressive erotic film showed an increase in aggression, this was not the case for those male subjects who were treated in a neutral manner by the confederate. The slight tendency for the negative film to increase aggression beyond the neutral version is interesting. It is possible that the arousing nature and the aggressive meaning of the film raised the threshold for empathy reactions on the part of subjects. The finding that aggression could be increased in nonangered subjects by exposure to the positive film further supports the finding of the earlier study by Donnerstein (1980b), which found that an aggressive

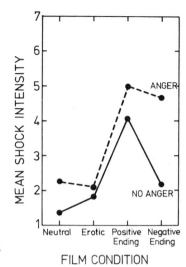

Figure 3. Mean shock intensity as a function of anger of subject and ending of film.

erotic film was capable of increasing aggression toward a female by nonangered males. These findings would suggest that the aggressive responses elicited by the film were heightened by the arousal in the film itself. In addition, the disinhibitory cues present in the film (e.g., aggression is OK) acted to reduce any aggressive inhibitions on the part of the male subjects.

The Role of Nonerotic Aggressive Images of Women

The research so far has concerned itself with aggressive erotica. However, there are many nonerotic aggressive images of women which have recently appeared in films and on TV (e.g., Malamuth and Donnerstein, in press). There is some recent evidence to suggest that even nonerotic aggressive images can produce effects similar to those of aggressive erotica. For example, Malamuth and Check (in press-a) have shown that exposure to commercial films such as *The Getaway* and *Swept Away* which contain aggression toward women can increase the acceptance of myths about rape on the part of male subjects. In order to examine more systematically the effects which nonerotic aggressive material would have on actual aggressive behavior, we conducted another study in this present series.

In this study male subjects were first angered by a male or female confederate. They were then exposed to one of four films. The first was a

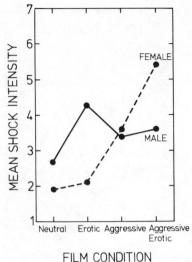

Figure 4. Mean shock intensity as a function of sex of target and content of film.

nonaggressive erotic film identical to that employed in earlier studies. The second was an aggressive erotic film, the same as that used in the study above. The third film was a nonerotic aggressive presentation in which a woman at gun-point is supposedly taunted by a man. She is tied up, slapped around, and generally aggressed against. There was no nudity or even simulated sexual activity. It was chosen to be as close in content, except for aggression, as the rape film but without sexual behavior. The final film was a neutral presentation. Self-reported data from subjects indicated that the aggressive film was seen as being less sexual than the two erotic films (which did not differ from each other). In addition, the aggressive film and the aggressive erotic film were also seen as equally aggressive. Physiological data also showed that the erotic and aggressive erotic film were equal in arousal level but higher than the neutral and aggressive film. This study, then, would seem to be a reasonable test of the contributions of arousal, erotic, and aggressive content on subsequent aggression toward women.

The results of this study are presented in Figure 4. When subjects were angered by a male, only the erotic film increased aggression. This finding is quite similar to past research in this series. For those subjects who were angered by a female the aggressive erotic film produced the highest level of aggression, higher in fact, than any male target condition. The nonerotic aggressive film, however, also increased the level of subsequent aggression, although differing from the aggressive erotic presentation.

This study seems to indicate that film arousal is not a necessary component in facilitating aggression toward women. The more crucial factor seems to be the aggressive cue value of the female target, which is established through the target's association with observed violence. This does not mean that arousal is not important. As we have seen in this and in the preceding studies, the aggressive responses elicited by the aggressive erotic film were heightened by the arousal from previous anger instigation and from the film itself. The fact that no increase in aggression was observed for male targets after exposure to the aggressive film and the aggressive erotic film further supports the idea that the films need to have some "aggressive meaning" to the individual.

Summary of Studies

These studies point to a number of important factors in the relationship of aggressive erotica and violence toward women. First, they point to the importance of the female's association with observed violence as a critical component in the facilitation of aggression toward women. As we have seen, aggression toward male targets is not affected by exposure to aggressive erotica in which a female is the victim. Furthermore, while anger instigation does tend to heighten the level of aggression, facilitated aggression can occur in the absence of prior instigation. These findings suggest that even nonsexual images of aggression toward women can act to increase the likelihood of subsequent aggressive behavior toward female victims.

Second, these studies point to the role of the victim's reaction in the film as a crucial factor in how male subjects behave toward a female. As we noted earlier, a common theme in pornography is that women enjoy aggression. The following, from authors in the sexual assault area, highlight this theme:

First, sexual sadism is presented as a source of sexual pleasure for women. The male fantasy insists that beatings, rape, humiliation, and pain turn women on. (Barry, 1979, p. 177)

The pattern rarely changes in the porno culture . . . . after a few preliminary skirmishes, women invite or demand further violation, begging male masters to rape them into more submission, torture, and violence. In this fantasy land, females wallow in physical abuse and degradation. It is a pattern of horror which we have seen in our examination of sex cases translated again and again into actual assaults. (Gager and Schurr, 1976, p. 244)

The data from two studies presented in this paper suggest that positive victim reactions (those which are most common in pornography) can act to justify aggression and also to reduce general inhibitions against aggression (Malamuth and Donnerstein, in press). Negative reactions, on the other hand, seem to reinforce aggression in angered individuals and also raise the threshold for empathy reactions, which should occur when suffering is observed.

Victim reactions also tended to affect responses other than aggression. In both studies it was found that subjects exposed to the positive/aggressive erotic film found the film less aggressive and the victim more responsible than those subjects who were exposed to the negative version. The finding for perceived aggression seems to support those of other researchers (e.g., Malamuth and Check, in press-b), who have found that exposure to certain sexual violence reduces the sensitivity to rape. The results for responsibility also have important implications. At least in this study a positive reaction on the part of the rape victim, independent of the events which have occurred previously, makes the victim more responsible for her actions. This shifting of responsibility to the victim might be one factor which accounts for the increasingly callous attitudes toward rape and for the self-reported willingness to commit rape observed in subjects who have been exposed to aggressive erotica (e.g., Malamuth and Check, in press-b). This shift of responsibility might also affect judicial decisions in rape cases. It would seem important, then, for future research to examine more closely the reasons and implications for this apparent change in attribution.

Finally, this series of studies adds support to other research that seems to indicate that exposure to aggressive erotica effects a general pattern of behavior and attitudes that have the capacity to stimulate various negative reactions to women. As we have seen, male subjects exposed to various forms of aggressive erotica become sexually aroused, more accepting of rape myths and of interpersonal violence toward women, and report a greater likelihood of committing a rape. These attitudinal and intentional changes have also been correlated with actual aggression and a desire to hurt a woman (Malamuth and Donnerstein, in press). From the present research we can see that there is a direct causal relationship between exposure to aggressive erotica and violence toward women.

References

Abel, G. G., Barlow, D. H., Blanchard, E., and Guild, D. The components of rapists' sexual arousal. *Archives of General Psychiatry*, 1977, *34*, 395-403.

Bandura, A. *Aggression: A social learning analysis*. Englewood Cliffs, N.J.: Prentice-Hall, 1973.

Baron, R. A. Aggression as a function of victim's pain cues, level of prior anger arousal, and exposure to an aggressive model. *Journal of Personality and Social Psychology*, 1974, *29*, 117-124.

Baron, R. A. *Human aggression*. New York: Plenum Press, 1977.

Baron, R. A., and Bell, P. A. Effects of heightened sexual arousal on physical aggression. *Proceedings of the 81st Annual Convention of the American Psychological Association*, 1973, *8*, 171-172.

Baron, R. A., and Bell, P. A. Sexual arousal and aggression by males: Effects of type of erotic stimuli and prior provocation. *Journal of Personality and Social Psychology*, 1977, *35*, 79-87.

Barry, K. *Female sex slavery*. Englewood Cliffs, N.J.: Prentice-Hall, 1979.

Berkowitz, L. Sex and violence: We can't have it both ways. *Psychology Today*, May 1971, pp. 14-23.

Berkowitz, L. Some determinants of impulsive aggression: The role of mediated associations with reinforcements for aggression. *Psychological Review*, 1974, *81*, 165-176.

Brownmiller, S. *Against our will: Men, women and rape*. New York: Simon and Schuster, 1975.

Burt, M. R. Cultural myths and supports for rape. *Journal of Personality and Social Psychology*, 1980, *38*, 217-230.

Cline, V. B. Another view: Pornography effects, the state of the art. In V. B. Cline (Ed.), *Where do you draw the line?* Provo, Utah: Brigham Young University Press, 1974.

Dienstbier, R. A. Sex and violence: Can research have it both ways? *Journal of Communication*, 1977, *27*, 176-188.

Donnerstein, E. Aggressive erotica and violence against women. *Journal of Personality and Social Psychology*, 1980, *39*, 269-277. (a)

Donnerstein, E. Pornography and violence against women. *Annals of the New York Academy of Sciences*, 1980, *347*, 277-288. (b)

Donnerstein, E. Erotica and human aggression. In R. G. Geen and E. Donnerstein (Eds.), *Aggression: Theoretical and empirical reviews*. New York: Academic Press, in press.

Donnerstein, E., and Barrett, G. Effects of erotic stimuli on male aggression toward females. *Journal of Personality and Social Psychology*, 1978, *36*, 180-188.

Donnerstein, E., and Berkowitz, L. Victim reactions in aggressive erotic films as a factor in violence against women. *Journal of Personality and Social Psychology*, in press.

Donnerstein, E., Donnerstein, M., and Evans, R. Erotic stimuli and aggression: Facilitation or inhibition. *Journal of Personality and Social Psychology*, 1975, *32*, 237-244.

Donnerstein, E., and Hallam, J. Facilitating effects of erotica on aggression against women. *Journal of Personality and Social Psychology*, 1978, *36*, 1270-1277.

Donnerstein, E., and Wilson, D. W. Effects of noise and perceived control on ongoing and subsequent aggressive behavior. *Journal of Personality and Social Psychology*, 1976, *34*, 774-781.

Eysenck, H. J., and Nias, H. *Sex, violence, and the media*. London: Spector, 1978.

Frodi, A. Sexual arousal, situational restrictiveness, and aggressive behavior. *Journal of Research in Personality*, 1977, *11*, 48-58.

Gager, H., and Schurr, C. *Sexual assault: Confronting rape in America*. New York: Grosset and Dunlap, 1976.

Geen, R. G. Observing violence in the mass media: Implications of basic research. In R. G. Geen and E. O'Neil (Eds.), *Perspectives on aggression*. New York: Academic Press, 1976.

Goranson, R. E. Media violence and aggressive behavior. In L. Berkowitz (Ed.), *Advances in experimental social psychology* (Vol. 5). New York: Academic Press, 1970.

Hartmann, D. P. Influence of symbolically modeled instrumental aggression and pain cues on aggressive behavior. *Journal of Personality and Social Psychology*, 1969, *11*, 280-288.

Jaffe, Y., Malamuth, N. M., Feingold, J., and Feshbach, S. Sexual arousal and behavioral aggression. *Journal of Personality and Social Psychology*, 1974, *30*, 759-764.

Malamuth, N. M. Rape fantasies as a function of exposure to violent-sexual stimuli. *Archives of Sexual Behavior*, in press.

Malamuth, N. M., and Check, J. The effects of mass media exposure on acceptance of violence against women: A field experiment. *Journal of Research in Personality*, in press. (a)

Malamuth, N. M. and Check, J. Penile tumescence and perceptual responses to rape as a function of victim's perceived reactions. *Journal of Applied Social Psychology*, in press. (b)

Malamuth, N. M., and Donnerstein, E. The effects of aggressive erotic stimuli. In L. Berkowitz (Ed.), *Advances in experimental social psychology* (Vol. 15). New York: Academic Press, in press.

Malamuth, N. M., Feshbach, S., and Jaffe, Y. Sexual arousal and aggression: Recent experiments and theoretical issues. *Journal of Social Issues*, 1977, *33*, 110-133.

Malamuth, N. M., Haber, S., and Feshbach, S. Testing hypotheses regarding rape: Exposure to sexual violence, sex differences, and the "normality" of rape. *Journal of Research in Personality*, 1980, *14*, 121-137.

Malamuth, N. M., Heim, M., and Feshbach, S. The sexual responsiveness of college students to rape depictions: Inhibitory and disinhibitory effects. *Journal of Personality and Social Psychology*, 1980, *38*, 399-408.

Malamuth, N. M., and Spinner, B. A longitudinal content analysis of sexual violence in the best-selling erotica magazines. *Journal of Sex Research*, 1980, *16*, 226-237.

Meyer, T. P. The effects of sexually arousing and violent films on aggressive behavior. *Journal of Sex Research*, 1972, *8*, 324-333.

Mosher, D. L. Pornographic films, male verbal aggression against women, and guilt. In *Technical Report of the Commission on Obscenity and Pornography* (Vol. 8). Washington, D.C.: Government Printing Office, 1971.

Report of the U.S. commission on obscenity and pornography. Washington, D.C.: U.S. Government Printing Office, 1971.

Swart, C., and Berkowitz, L. Effects of a stimulus associated with a victim's pain on later aggression. *Journal of Personality and Social Psychology*, 1976, *33*, 623-631.

Wills, G. Measuring the impact of erotica. *Psychology Today*, November 1977, pp. 30-34.

Zillmann, D. Excitation transfer in communication-mediated aggressive behavior. *Journal of Experimental Social Psychology*, 1971, *7*, 419-434.

Zillmann, D. *Hostility and aggression*. Hillsdale, N.J.: Lawrence Erlbaum, 1979.

Zillmann, D., Hoyt, J. L., and Day, K. D. Strength and duration of the effects of aggressive, violent, and erotic communications on subsequent aggressive behavior. *Communication Research*, 1974, *1*, 286-306.

Zillmann, D., and Sapolsky, B. S. What mediates the effect of mild erotica on annoyance and hostile behavior in males? *Journal of Personality and Social Psychology*, 1977, *35*, 587-596.

Preventing Men from Becoming Rapists

Gene G. Abel

Rape, though it appears to be a chaotic act, an irrational act perpetrated for no apparent reason, can be understood. If we interview the men who rape and systematically investigate the antecendents to their violent crime, we discover consistent patterns that precede the act. Knowing the antecedents, we can change the pattern that leads to rape and can break that pattern before the actual rape. Although scientific studies have revealed these crucial patterns, our ability to intervene at an early developmental point is obstructed.

First, investigation of rapists' behavior prior to rape has been previously invalidated because investigators did not deal with the rapists' desires to keep their thoughts and activities secret for fear of prosecution. Useful investigation requires a methodology that allows rapists to reveal, without fear of incriminating themselves, what drives them to rape. This has been accomplished by research limited to rapists who are outside the legal system and who as out-patient volunteers have been given confidentiality.

Even when a rapist's confidentiality is fully protected, many rapists still will not or cannot reveal the truth. Their motives, drives, and ability to control their compulsive urges remain secret. To overcome this obstacle, a new system of evaluation was incorporated into the research methodology: Direct psychophysiologic assessment of the rapist's sexual arousal pattern. This new system allows objective assessment of rapists by quantifying the rapist's arousal to violent and nonviolent sexual themes.

This quantification in the laboratory allows experimental studies of fac-

The study was supported in part by grant MH-33678 awarded to the author by the Center for the Studies of Crime and Delinquency. Support for the statistical analysis portion was provided by Mental Health Clinical Research grant MH 30906-03 from the National Institute for Mental Health.

The author wishes to thank Jerry Cunningham-Rathner, Nora Harlow, and Edna G. Johnson for their assistance in preparation of this manuscript.

tors that may contribute to rape. These assessment methods have considerable face validity; these studies are of men who have actually raped and, before treatment, had a high likelihood of raping again; men who were assured absolute confidentiality; men whose self-reports were confirmed by psychophysiologic assessment (Abel, Barlow, Blanchard, and Guild, 1977; Abel, Blanchard, Barlow, and Mavissakalian, 1975; Abel, Blanchard, and Becker, 1978; Abel, Blanchard, Becker, and Djenderedjian, 1978; Barbaree, Marshall, and Lanthier, 1979).

Studies of rapists who have been assured of confidentiality and whose self-reports were confirmed by laboratory measurement of their sexual arousal, have given us valuable information about the antecedents to rape. The antecedents include: compulsive use of rape fantasies for sexual arousal; rapelike behavior; displaced anger toward women; and distorted cognitions about rape.

Before one examines the antecedent patterns to rape, one should have a clear definition of rape and an understanding of the two distinct types of rapists.

Defining Rape

There can be considerable variation in how rape is defined. At one extreme, some only consider an act to be rape when the perpetrator has physically penetrated an orifice of the victim with his penis and the victim's resistance has been so vigorous that she has been physically injured during the act. At the other extreme, some consider any form of verbal or physical intrusion upon the physical and /or emotional space of another as rape. For the purposes of this chapter, we will consider rape as a hands-on intrusion by the rapist of the victim, with the rapist having an explicit goal of attempting to commit a sexual act against the victim's will.

The relationship between the rapist and his victim is another complex dimension of rape. Some rapes occur between strangers; other rapes involve closer relationships between perpetrator and victim, such as acquaintance rapes, date rapes, spouse rapes, and incest. Since those who rape the greatest number of victims choose victims whom they barely know or do not know, this chapter will emphasize the prevention of rapes between strangers.

Categorizing Rapists

Men who rape victims unknown to them can be divided into two types. The first type, the antisocial, has a history replete with antisocial activities. He does not report having ongoing thoughts of rape or urges to commit rape. He is self-centered and hedonistic. His social and work relationships are poor, and beginning at an early age, he carries out a variety of antisocial activities such as robbery, assault, and larceny. When he does rape, which is infrequently, he rapes during the course of another crime. His victim and his decision to rape are unplanned. Because so few rapes are committed by the antisocial rapist, our focus will be on the second type, the psychological rapist.

The psychological rapist has repeated urges to rape. He has frequently had these urges since his mid-teens, when he begins to masturbate to fantasies of rape. His urges gradually become stronger, and he attempts to resist acting on them, realizing that rape is morally wrong. As he continues to use fantasies of rape during masturbation or orgasm, his arousal and urges to rape become progressively more powerful. As thoughts of rape become stronger, his other sexual thoughts gradually become weaker and may even disappear (Abel and Blanchard, 1976). Eventually the psychological rapist begins to act on his rape urges. His commission of rape is frequently followed by considerable anxiety, guilt, depression, and diminution of his rape urges. These emotional responses, however, are generally short-lived; his urges to rape once again reappear, and the rape cycle repeats itself.

The psychological rapist, unlike the antisocial rapist, may commit from 2 to 100 rapes. The act of forcing himself on a victim becomes more and more erotic, so that eventually, given the choice between sex with a partner by mutual consent and forcing himself on that same partner, he would prefer to use force (Abel et al., 1975). The characteristics of the psychological rapist's sex offenses are similar to those of exhibitionists, child molesters, and other paraphiliacs. Each of these sex offenders has recurrent urges to commit the sex crime; their control breaks down; they commit the crime; they feel temporary guilt and anxiety immediately afterwards; their urges temporarily diminish, only to recur, and the process repeats itself.

Although we can identify four distinct antecedents to rape, preventing men from becoming rapists requires recognition of these precursors and the ability to actually intervene at an early stage in this developmental pattern. Implementing this intervention is inhibited on all sides: by the professionals who are in contact with rapists, by the legal system that attempts to control the rapist, by the society's acceptance of the pre-rape behavior, and by the rapist himself. Not only must we identify the steps to the primary prevention of rape, but we must also be aware of the techniques that can be used to overcome the obstacles that stand in the way of primary prevention.

Arousal Patterns That Are Antecendent to Rape

Studies of the psychological rapist indicate that he has had fantasies of rape and violence long before becoming a rapist. Since the fantasies of rape always precede the actual act of rape, it would be quite possible to evaluate those men who compulsively use rape fantasies and treat those men who have the greatest probability of becoming rapists. Unfortunately, a number of obstacles prevent us from reaching these men.

First, our culture views the control of an individual's sexual urges as simply a problem of willpower. If a man finds himself with recurrent urges to rape, he usually assumes that he must control these fantasies himself, by relying on his strength of character. This belief gains credence because the consequences from the breakdown of one's willpower are usually incidental: if you eat more cake than you probably should have, if you watch television excessively, no one is significantly hurt. Losing control over urges to rape is quite another thing. Men need to understand that as the consequences of loss of control increase, so does the need for consultation and assistance in order to ensure that control is maintained and victimization is prevented. In order to cope with violent thoughts, a client needs a treatment program that combines a comprehensive assessment and a systematic treatment intervention in multiple areas (Abel, Blanchard, and Becker, 1978).

Second, not only does the general population lack an understanding of the relevance of rape thoughts and attraction to sexual violence, but professional helping agents likewise share much of the public's naiveté. Practitioners have not been taught how to question their clients about their proclivitis for sexual violence. They ignore the reality that rapes occur at a rate of 20-40 per 100,000 individuals at risk, and that someone must be committing these rapes. We justify not asking clients about their sexual fantasies and urges for sexual assault by rationalizing that the potential rapist is of a low socioeconomic group, of low moral character, and certainly not like any of the people we evaluate. However, rapists come from all economic, ethnic, educational, and religious backgrounds. The practitioner needs to relinquish some of his or her stereotypes of rapists and ask clients about this issue. To ensure that practitioners feel comfortable about asking such questions, professional education should include role-playing interview skills in the area of sexual violence. We should not expect practitioners to begin to ask about sexual violence until they have learned how to pose such questions appropriately. A practitioner must know how to ask questions about sexual aggression in a way that allows the client to answer truthfully and thereby gain access to treatment.

Third, most individuals view their sexual lives as a taboo topic, something that they should not discuss with others. When the individual's sexual urges are more deviant than the general population's, when he has obsessive fantasies of raping a woman or a child, he becomes even more reluctant to reveal such thoughts. The rapist usually concludes that if he does not think or talk about his rape fantasies, they will go away in some magical way. This misbelief probably evolves because of the manner in which deviant fantasies develop (Abel and Blanchard, 1975). During genital arousal, our fantasies become associated with the enjoyment from intercourse, masturbation, and orgasm. For the rapist, the use of rape fantasies during masturbation and orgasm has been associated with progressively greater arousal to rape stimuli. Since rape thoughts have become more powerful because he has thought of rape, not thinking of rape should logically reduce arousal.

Studies where paraphiliacs were satiated with their deviant fantasies (Abel, Becker, and Skinner, in press, Marshall and Barbaree, 1978; Marshall and Lippens, 1977), however, suggest just the opposite. Externalizing these fantasies to the point of satiation destroys their erotic punch and allows the rapist to gain control over his aggressive fantasies. We therefore need to break through the taboo of talking about sexual topics, including the urge to rape, so that treatment agents can openly discuss with such individuals the existence of the problem and what men with urges to rape need to do to prevent themselves from acting on their urges.

Fourth, the legal system's method of dealing with the rapist appears to propagate the maintenance of rape thoughts and urges. The rapist is told in prison that anything he communicates to others will become part of his official record. The rapist learns that if he talks about his rape(s), its characteristics, and his persistent urges to rape, these comments will appear in his record. When this record reveals that he still has desires to rape, there is a high likelihood that the rapist's sentence will be prolonged and that he will be passed over for parole, and further investigation may result in his being charged with additional sexual assaults. The rapist subsequently stops talking about his rapes and instead attempts to convince prison personnel that though he had these thoughts at one time, the trauma of arrest and incarceration has destroyed them and he is now repentant and no longer at risk. Since he is no longer at risk, no treatment is in order in prison. He is released, his urges to rape accelerated and the circle is completed when he begins to rape again.

To disrupt this dangerous cycle, a system of confidentiality for rapists and those working with them needs to be developed both inside and outside of prison settings, so that potential rapists can describe their rape-related activities without fear of repercussion. With such confidentiality safeguards, the sexual aggressive could more easily describe his treatment needs, and helping professionals, armed with this information, could develop appropriate treatment programs to eliminate these urges. To continue to block this avenue of assistance to the rapist places him in a untenable position. We need more treatment methods that prevent rape, not methods that conceal the potentiality for the crime.

A final factor that prevents treatment from reaching those men with urges to rape is that most people believe that the majority of rapists are caught and imprisoned. In reality, most men who rape are still on the streets. Interviews with rape victims indicate that anywhere from 2 to 10 rapes occur for each 1 reported to the police. Since the most common "treatment" for rapists is arrest, and arrest is only possible if rapes are reported, the current system has little applicability to the majority of rape cases. Even when arrest does occur, only 13 percent of those charged with rape are actually found guilty and incarcerated (Csida and Csida, 1974). Should conviction and incarceration occur, recidivism rates 5 years after release indicate that at least 35 percent of rapists have recommitted their crime (Frisbie and Dondis, 1965).

The evidence is quite clear that our present legal approach is not effective, and additional methods are needed to combat rape. The difficult task will be to point out that while the fear of incarceration is a somewhat effective deterrent, it is not sufficient to prevent sexual violence. Treatment methods that can prevent men from acting on their urges to rape for the

TABLE 1
Rapists' Additional Paraphilias

Diagnosis	Percentage with Diagnosis
Heterosexual pedophilia	24.1
Exhibitionism (adult female targets)	18.5
Voyeurism	16.7
Heterosexual incest	9.3
Sadism	9.3
Homosexual pedophilia	5.6
Exhibitionism (young female targets)	3.7
Other	12.8

first time as well as preventing known rapists from repeating this violent crime exist and must be added to the limited impact of incarceration.

Behavioral and Emotional Antecedents to Rape

Rape prevention can be more effective if greater attention is paid to the types of behaviors that frequently precede the rape. In our studies of rapists, 49 percent were found to have histories of other types of paraphilias, generally preceding the rape behavior. When 34 rapists were questioned, they reported a total of 54 paraphilias, for an average of 1.6 other paraphilias per rapist. Table 1 demonstrates that the most common additional diagnoses were heterosexual pedophilia, exhibitionism, voyeurism, heterosexual incest, and sadism. This is not to imply that all men with various paraphilias will develop into rapists, but it does suggest that when a client is identified as having one of the paraphilias frequently associated with rape, the client should be questioned thoroughly about possible urges to rape. Unfortunately, many practitioners fail to do this.

Rapists may not have other paraphilias but often carry out aggressive acts short of rape. Henry, for example, was evaluated after being charged with two rapes. His history reveals that for 3 years prior to his rapes, he had been assaulting women in parking lots. He would follow women as they went to their cars, and while they were rearranging their packages and reaching for their keys, he would grab their genital areas and then run away. This behavior persisted for over a year, eventually occurred in his high school, and led to his expulsion. Ignored, his grabbing of women persisted and eventually he followed women into office buildings and escalated his sexual behavior to rape. What is impressive about Henry's case is that his family and school officials did not respond to his early grabbing behavior, even though this behavior duplicated four of the aggressive aspects of rape: hands on victim, aggressive attacks, unconsenting victim, and repetition. His behavior differed in only one aspect: his immediate escape from his victim once she had been touched. In Henry's case those around him ignored a form of sexual aggression that was identical in most respects to rape. Everyone appeared to be waiting for Henry's problem to get serious, but his grabbing behavior was serious. When we wait until rape actually occurs, it is too late: too late in this case because two innocent victims had already suffered severe trauma, and too late for Henry because once he had been arrested for rape, the likelihood of his receiving treatment was extremely remote. Treatment offered in prison is usually identical to the treatment given those who steal cars, evade income tax, or rob. However, those who display the behavioral antecedents of rape need a specific treatment for that specific sexual behavior, and by the time the client is arrested for rape, he no longer has access to appropriate treatment.

In addition to behavioral antecedents, emotional conflicts frequently precede rape. A common emotional antecedent is anger: the potential rapist becomes angry with a woman, but is unable to express that anger directly to her; instead, he inappropriately expresses that anger to an innocent woman by raping her.

Jim, at age 22, married Mildred, 14 years his senior. Jim had been raised in a mining town, where he had developed a variety of stereotypic attitudes about the importance of men being in charge and making all decisions. While dating in high school he had always determined the where, when, and what of dating. When unable to control the dating situation he would have outbursts of anger and "slap his girlfriends around" until they complied with his demands.

Following his marriage, he found that Mildred was equally domineering. Her behavior made him feel she was intruding into his life: She demanded that he be home at specific times and did not allow him to go hunting with his friends. Conflicts arose early in their marriage and he was increasingly displeased with Mildred. When his family heard that he was no longer able to do what he wanted, they supported his increasing confrontations with Mildred. Fights ensued and Jim left home and drove to a motel to live temporarily. That night, on returning from a bar, he stopped to help a woman whose automobile had broken down. While pretending that he was driving her to the closest gas station, he stopped the car, tied her up, gagged and blindfolded her, and sadistically raped her. In Jim's case, there was a direct relationship between his inability to assert himself with Mildred, the development of angry feelings toward her, and the subsequent rape of an innocent victim.

Recent experimental studies in the laboratory have confirmed a direct relationship between anger and increased sexual arousal toward rape themes. Marshall (1981) measured normal subjects' arousal to rape stimuli before and after subjects were confronted by a hostile, angry female (who was actually a rsearcher feigning anger toward the subjects). Following this brief confrontation, subjects showed definite increases in their sexual arousal to descriptions of rape.

If the inappropriate expression of anger by males is so closely linked to less inhibition toward violence toward women, training in the appropriate expression of anger may serve as a preventative measure against rape. This training could take the form of assertiveness training, a relatively common clinical intervention used to teach others how to ask appropriately for behavioral change in others, and how to express various positive and negative feelings.

Cognitive Distortions Antecedent to Rape

When interviewing rapists, one is struck by the cognitive distortions men display about the rapes they have committed, their victim's responses, and the interaction that preceded the rape.

Steven was interviewed in jail following his first arrest for rape, but he reported at least 21 other occasions that the interviewer would have called rape. Typically, Steven would begin by talking to women in bars. He was convinced that any woman in a bar had gone there specifically to meet a man to have sex with. He would next ask her to go for a ride with him in his car. He believed that any woman who agreed to go with him was also agreeing to have intercourse with him, irrespective of what she said to him later on.

In a secluded area he would then attempt to have intercourse with the woman and if she resisted, he would tear her clothes off and slap her repeatedly. All of his victims initially resisted these physical attacks but eventually stopped resisting for fear of injury. When they stopped fighting, however, he failed to interpret this as fear. He interpreted their lack of extreme resistance as another way of saying yes, they wanted to have sex with him. Steven's criterion for rape was that if he attempted to have sex with a woman and she unceasingly fought him while he escalated his violent attack, only then would he classify his act as rape. If she fought until he injured her or she was terrified of being injured, he mistakenly categorized this as normal courtship behavior that is typical of most women. Steven, like many other rapists, believed that a large percentage of women wanted to be "roughed up" during sex, so that they could justify having intercourse with a man without feeling guilty later.

These cognitive distortions are psychologically helpful to the rapist. By accepting these distorted beliefs, he justifies his rape behavior: his acts are not rape; they are normal courtship behaviors. The potential rape victim, however, is in a no-win situation. If she is in the bar, he sees her as an appropriate target to attack. If she resists, it is permissable to "slap her around" since she needs to be convinced to have sex so she will not feel guilty afterwards. Irrespective of what the victim does, the rapist can justify his behavior; therefore there is no reason for him to become upset or feel guilty afterwards since it really was not rape.

Even more startling is that many of the rapist's cognitive beliefs about rape are shared to some degree by over 50 percent of the general population (Burt, 1980; Malamuth, Haber, and Feshbach, 1980). If half the population believes that roughing up women is acceptable and possibly even sexually stimulating to many women, if 50 percent believe that only women "who are asking for it" get raped, if 50 percent believe that it is physically impossible for a healthy woman to be raped against her will, then the world is a dangerous place for most women.

A number of steps must be taken to prevent the development of cognitive distortions that support rape behavior. First, potential rapists and potential rape victims must learn that actual rapes are not like their usual fantasies of rape. Rape is not the rough seduction of an ambivalent woman who becomes overwhelmed by her biological response to a penis in her vagina or mouth and ultimately orgasms from the experience. Only a minute number of women have ever reported that they would be aroused by being raped, and when this small group was questioned in detail (Malamuth et al., 1980), they reported that the rape they were thinking of was one in which they were in complete control, a rape they could terminate at any time. However, real rapes are just the opposite: rape victims feel a complete loss of control. Victims report no sense of being able to stop the assault, but instead believe they are at the mercy of the rapist. Potential rapists (generally young men, 15 to 25 years old) must be taught to view rape as it actually is: a violent, life-threatening attack by a male, who beats up the victim, penetrates her orifices with his penis, and irrationally demands that she report being sexually turned on.

Second, the systems that support these cognitive distortions must be dismantled. The most obvious of these are the media that support the image of man as the aggressor, woman as victim of that aggression, and rape as a seduction game that ends with orgasms for the rapist and the victim. Not only do such depictions provide models for males to become aggressive with women, but they also teach women that it is acceptable and expected that women should be victims of men's aggression. These cognitive distortions must be debunked. What we need to see are examples of mutual caring and respect between men and women in all types of interaction, sexual or nonsexual.

Third, the potential rapists (men) must be helped to understand that it is their attitudes toward women as sexual objects and property that allow them to ignore similar attitudes in other males, who act on them and become rapists. It is because our fellow man acts on his cognitive distortions that our wives, sisters, and daughters are raped. If any man doubts the prevalence of such beliefs, he might try walking 10 feet behind his wife, sister, or daughter down any major street in any city in the United States and observe the men nearby.

Finally, males must become involved in the struggle to eliminate rape. As long as men see rape as a problem outside of themselves, committed by strangers for reasons totally unrelated to themselves, men will not be motivated to change the male attitude that leads to rape. In actuality men must realize that their own whistles and leers on the street are part of the cognitive distortions which become magnified in the minds of other men who eventually rape.

Providing Incentives for Those Working with Sex Offenders

A chronic problem in providing mental health care has been to motivate helping agents to work with aggressive client populations. For a variety of reasons, mental health providers have preferred to treat the "walking well," while the more difficult problems of working with the developmentally delayed, the drug and alcohol addict, and the violent offender are avoided. Of special relevance to those working with potential rapists is how working with such clients is viewed by the friends, relatives, and peers of the therapist. The general public assumes that individuals working with rapists must be doing so for some sick reason. Paradoxically, in our society where violence, and especially sexual violence, is becoming increasingly more common, these attitudes persist toward professionals attempting to reduce these same aggressive acts.

Greater incentives need to be provided for those treating the violent individual. A possible solution might be to enlarge the catchment area concept from mental health to include the reduction of sexual violence in a defined area. In this fashion, reducing overall violence in that area becomes the responsibility of a particular treatment agency. Under these circumstances, the agency responsible for reducing the incidence of sexual violence and the agency's funding base would be tied to its effectiveness at reducing sexual violence.

Finally, one cannot ignore the very personal impact of working day in and day out with rapists and potential rapists. The recounting and exploring of the details of such violent fantasies and atrocious acts in effect serve to surround the therapist in an emotional world of violence on top of violence. If the work force to prevent sexual violence is to be effective with its difficult task, we must be aware of the high burn-out of personnel, and we must provide staff training and staff development that can maintain that work force.

In summary, we must keep in mind that rape is not an innate behavior but a behavior that follows logically from a variety of antecedents. If we learn to recognize these antecedents, primary prevention can occur. Men who have compulsive psychological urges to rape can be distinguished from the general population and be taught to eliminate their urges to rape *before* they actually rape.

Currently this society's efforts to deal with rape occur almost exclusively *after* a woman has been victimized. No one wants rape victims. Effective primary prevention prevents two tragedies: men as rapists; women as rape victims.

250 Gene G. Abel

References

Abel, G. G., Barlow, D. H., Blanchard, E. B., and Guild, D. The components of rapists' sexual arousal. *Archives of General Psychiatry*, 1977, *34*, 895-903.

Abel, G. G., Becker, J. V., and Skinner, L. J. Treatment of the violent sex offender. In L. Roth (Ed.), *Clinical treatment and management of the violent person*. Washington, D.C.: Crime and Delinquency Issues, United States Department of Health and Human Services, in press.

Abel, G. G., and Blanchard, E. B. The measurement and generation of sexual arousal. In M. Hersen, R. M. Eisler, and P. M. Miller (Eds.), *Progress in behavior modification* (Vol. 2). New York: Academic Press, 1976.

Abel, G. G., Blanchard, E. B., Barlow, D. H., and Mavissakalian, M. Identifying specific erotic cues in sexual deviation by audio-taped descriptions. *Journal of Applied Behavior Analysis*, 1975, *8*, 247-260.

Abel, G. G., Blanchard, E. B., and Becker, J. V. An integrated treatment program for rapists. In R. Rada (Ed.), *Clinical aspects of the rapist*. New York: Grune and Stratton, 1978.

Abel, G. G., Blanchard, E. B., Becker, J. V., and Djenderedjian, A. Differentiating sexual aggressives with penile measures. *Criminal Justice and Behavior*, 1978, *5*, 315-332.

Barbaree, H. E., Marshall, W. L., and Lanthier, R. D. Deviant sexual arousal in rapists. *Behavior Research and Therapy*, 1979, *17*, 252-259.

Burt, M. R. Cultural myths and supports for rape. *Journal of Personality and Social Psychology*, 1980, *38*, 217-230.

Csida, J. B., and Csida, J. *Rape: How to avoid it and what to do about it if you can't*. Chatsworth, Calif.: Books for Better Living, 1974.

Frisbie, L. V., and Dondis, E. H. *Recidivism among treated sex offenders*. California Mental Health Research Monograph No. 5, 1965.

Malamuth, N. M., Haber, S., and Feshbach, S. Testing hypothesis regarding rape: Exposure to sexual violence, sex differences, and the "normality" of rapists. *Journal of Research in Personality*, 1980, *14*, 121-137.

Marshall, W. L. *The evaluation of sexual aggressives*. Paper presented at the third annual Conference on the Evaluation and Treatment of Sexual Aggressives, San Luis Obispo, California, 1981.

Marshall, W. L., and Barbaree, H. E. The reduction of deviant arousal: Satiation treatment for sexual aggressors. *Criminal Justice and Behavior*, 1978, *5*, 294-303.

Marshall, W. L., and Lippens, K. The clinical value of boredom: A procedure for reducing inappropriate sexual interests. *Journal of Nervous and Mental Diseases*, 1977, *165*, 283-287.

Responsible Sexuality and the Primary Prevention of Child Abuse

Gertrude J. Rubin Williams

There is a Jewish legend about the fools of Chelm, a community of
smug simpletons who lacked insight into their incredible stupidity.
They lived at the top of a steep mountain from which they had to
traverse a narrow, winding path to reach the market at the foot
of the mountain. In the course of their frequent journeys, droves of
Chelmsians were killed or maimed as they dropped from the narrow
path into the valley below. After decades of ignoring the carnage, the
surviving fools of Chelm took action to control the problem. They
built a hospital at the bottom of the valley to treat those unfortunates
who dropped off the mountain.

Descendants of the fools of Chelm are now attempting to bring child abuse
under control.

In his call for the prevention of sexism, Albee (1981) observes that "no
mass disorder . . . afflicting humankind has ever been brought under control by attempts to treat afflicted individuals." This observation is applicable to the mass disorder of child abuse, which treatment is failing to
control. Child abuse will be eradicated only by the prevention of sexism,
pronatalism, the sexual exploitation of children, and other irresponsible
sexual ideologies and practices, to which professionals themselves have often
contributed.

Futility of a Treatment Approach

The Child Abuse Prevention and Treatment Act of 1974 refers to prevention as a major goal, yet it has received insignificant attention in child
abuse programs. The overriding emphasis on the treatment of child abuse
to the virtual exclusion of prevention mirrors the American health care

model which deals almost exclusively with the treatment of illness, rather than with the maintenance and enhancement of health. Social agencies struggling vainly to meet the unremitting demands for emergency and long-term treatment of abuse families are too depleted to develop the imaginative programs and well-coordinated service delivery systems required for the primary prevention of child abuse (Fraser, 1979).

There are less obvious reasons for the overemphasis on treatment and the avoidance of primary prevention. The prevention of child abuse lacks concreteness, drama, and sensationalism, whereas treatment evokes the graphic images, righteousness, and rescue fantasies that inspire public support. Of paramount importance is the reality that if child abuse is ever to be prevented, radical transformations must occur in social ideologies, practices, and programs. Few professionals or politicians have been willing to sacrifice the good press, public approval, or government grants they receive for touting treatment and to risk the controversy related to exposing and working to annihilate the roots of child abuse.

Many critics contend that primary prevention is an overly idealistic, unaffordable fantasy and that we are entitled to rest on the laurels of the manifold programs across the nation treating child abuse. But is the treatment of child abuse effective? The answer, tragically, is a resounding no. The limited focus on treatment has opened a Pandora's box of travail devoid of the hope assured in the myth.

Helfer (1978) states that "every year 1½-2 percent of our children are reported as suspected victims of child abuse. While social agencies are working to help this year's 2 percent, they are still trying to figure out what to do with last year's 2 percent and are pleading with legislators for more money to deal with next year's 2 percent. The problems of abuse and neglect accumulate at the rate of 1½-2 percent each year." Nevertheless, child protection agencies continue on the treatment treadmill despite the impossibility of meeting these ever-increasing demands. Kempe (1979) describes child protection workers as "the only public servants willing to constantly stretch their case loads to meet demands ... because they are not a militant profession with defined duties" (p.x). These workers are expected to help abuse families with their manifold problems, despite inadequate training in carrying out tasks that would tax even expertly trained professionals; many workers have only an undergraduate degree. Despite recommendations by national child welfare groups of no more than 20 child abuse families per worker, case loads are often twice that amount.

In light of these dismal realities, it is not surprising that the field is characterized by low job satisfaction, burnout, and large turnover. Few abuse families see the same worker throughout the treatment process. Compounding these crushing problems, the treatment focus of child protection agencies does not necessarily assure that abuse families will even receive treatment. According to the U.S. Department of Health, Education and Welfare (1975), "Of the three components of the community-team program—identification and diagnosis, treatment, and education—treatment tends to be most notably lacking. It is not uncommon for a community to develop extensive identification and diagnostic resources and then find itself ill-equipped to help identified families" (p. 65). In many agencies that do provide treatment, treatment is often equated with medical care, casework, or psychotherapy, rather than with the wide range of services required for such multiproblem families (Cohn and Miller, 1977).

In line with the dubious philosophy of keeping abused children with their parents except as a last resort, treatment programs are directed to the abusive parents, not to the children they abused. Indeed, only adult members are receiving treatment services in 85 percent of the nationwide federally funded child abuse programs (Cohn and Miller, 1977). The treatment focus on abusive parents has been based on the 'trickle down' theory . . . the credo of protective services for one hundred years" (Kempe, 1979, p. xi). Help for the parents is unquestioningly assumed to trickle down to the abused child, who receives little or no treatment. The only study found on the effects of treating parents on child variables is that of Taitz (1980), in England, who reported that, of 38 abused infants whose families had received casework during a 5-year period, only 12 were classified as satisfactory in mental development, speech attainment, and growth outcome.

Recidivism in Treated Abusive Parents

Recidivism of abuse is a crucial measure of the effects of treatment on parents and, indirectly, on children. Early investigators (Friedman, 1972; Skinner and Castle, 1969) of recidivism reported ranges from 20 to 60 percent. Even higher recidivism rates are found in recent, more methodologically sophisticated research. In a follow-up study of 328 abuse families who had received services, Herrenkohl, Herrenkohl, Egolf, and Seech (1979) found 66.8 percent of verified incidents of parental reabuse compared to 25.4 percent officially reported incidents. Depending on the number of types, targets, and perpetrators of abuse in a family, recidivism ranged from 45 to 85 percent. Even after cases had been closed, presumably because abuse was no longer believed to be present, recidivism was found in 18.5 percent of the cases, 25 percent of which had received over 3 years of treatment. These grim findings were corroborated in England by Butterfield, Jackson, and Nangle (1979) in a 2½-year follow-up of extensive services to abusive parents. They reported that 46 of 69 children remained at risk, were reabused, or had a sibling who was abused.

Perhaps the most significant study of the effects of treatment is Cohn's (1979) evaluation of 11 federally funded demonstration projects on the treatment of child abuse. She found that a combination of highly skilled professional counseling and lay services was more effective than professional individual or group treatment alone in alleviating problems that trigger abuse. Recidivism remained high in all treatment groups, however, ranging from 47 to 62 percent of treated abusive parents. Regardless of treatment modality, recidivism of severe abuse occurred in 56 percent of cases considered serious at intake. Thirty percent of the entire sample of parents reabused the child during the course of treatment. Inasmuch as these measures of recidivism excluded mild physical abuse and neglect and emotional abuse and neglect, the findings are an underestimation of the recidivism likely to have been found had a broader definition of child abuse been used. It can also be assumed that recidivism rates are even higher in abuse families in treatment programs that do not have the benefits of services, consultation, funding, and other resources offered in the demonstration projects.

Irresponsible Sexuality and Child Abuse

Research evidence is demonstrating that current treatment programs cannot stem the ever burgeoning tide of child abuse, which will continue indefinitely unless the focus is changed to primary prevention. It is true that the causes of child abuse are complex, multiple, and interrelated, but there is little doubt about the major contributors to the problem. These include poverty, the oppression of children or reverse ageism, manifested in socially sanctioned corporal punishment, and irresponsible sexuality, manifested in inadequate provision for and utilization of contraception, abortion, and sex education, and in sexism and pronatalism (Gil, 1970; Light,

1973; Williams, 1976, 1980). This paper focuses on three kinds of irresponsible sexuality that are related to child abuse: unwanted pregnancy, irrationally wanted pregnancy, and father-daughter incest in childhood.

Unwanted Pregnancy and Child Abuse

The paucity of attention paid to contraceptive and abortion services, and sex education and counseling in the prevention of child abuse is especially remarkable because the circumstances of the conception and the attitudes toward pregnancy have been linked to child abuse in numerous investigations. Steele and Pollack (1968) state that "an infant born as the result of a premaritally conceived pregnancy or who comes as an accident too soon after the birth of a previous child, may be quite unwelcome to the parents and start life under a cloud of being unwanted and unsatisfying to the parents. Such infants may be perceived as public reminders of sexual transgression or as extra, unwanted burdens rather than need-satisfying objects" (pp. 128-129). Wasserman (1967) notes that a child conceived out of wedlock often becomes a "hostility sponge" for an unwanted marriage, reminds the mother of the man who deserted her during pregnancy, or is beaten by the mother and step-father who perceive the unwanted child as a public reminder of sexual transgression.

Numerous investigators (Bishop, 1971; Gaddis, Monaghan, Muir, and Jones, 1979; Gil, 1970; Green, 1976; MacCarthy, 1977; Prescott, 1976; Scott, 1980; Spinetta and Rigler, 1972) report significant relationships between child abuse and unwanted pregnancy, pregnancy occurring shortly after the birth of a previous child, and/or being a member of a large family with four or more children. Oates, Davis, Ryan, and Stewart (1979) in England, and West and West (1979) in Australia, found a significantly higher frequency of unplanned, unwanted, and illegitimate pregnancies among abusive parents compared to control samples. Ferguson, Fleming, and O'Neil (1972) report higher rates of child abuse and neglect among illegitimate children and in larger families in New Zealand.

Adolescent childbearing, two-thirds of which is unplanned (Green and Pottzeiger, 1977), is associated with a multitude of variables related to child abuse (Friedrich and Boriskin, 1976; Lynch and Roberts, 1977). These variables include a high risk of complications during the adolescent's pregnancy, labor, and delivery, and of prematurity, low birth weight, mental retardation, cerebral palsy, and epilepsy among infants of adolescent mothers.

Resnick (1970) reviewed the world literature since 1751 on the murder of the newborn and found that the vast majority of parents attributed the murder simply to not wanting the infant. Passivity was a prominent characteristic of these young women who planned neither the pregnancy nor the murder. However, "When reality is thrust upon them by the infant's first cry, they respond by permanently silencing the intruder" (p. 1416). Resnick contrasts the passivity of neonaticidal women with those who seek abortions; the latter recognize the reality of the unwanted pregnancy early and cope actively with the problem. So if abortion is murder, when shall the murder take place? *In utero* or at birth?

In these times of right-wing fanaticism, a statement made in 1969 by Dr. Lester Breslow, then the president of the American Public Health Association, is especially relevant:

Can anyone estimate how much physical harm is a byproduct of rigid abortion laws? The unwanted child, resulting from contraceptive failure or failure to abort, may be born only to be victimized by hostile parents.... Not only are battered children sometimes killed and often disabled but they are usually psychologically distorted. An enlightened policy on abortion would prevent much of this waste and callous infliction of pain.

Irrationally Wanted Pregnancy and Child Abuse

Although unwanted pregnancy is linked to child abuse, contraceptive and sex education and counseling, which should be mandatory components of all child abuse programs, are absent from most of them. Many abusive parents whose children have been removed from them keep bearing more children whom they abuse. Some abusive parents are ignorant of or indifferent to contraception and abortion. Others purposely bear more children to prove to themselves and society that they are good parents. For example, one pair of abusive parents, from whom four children had been removed, planned their current pregnancy because, as they put it, "We just love children to death." This sentiment is almost literally true. Two of the children they battered are brain damaged and one is nearly blind. All five have psychological problems. The agency permitted them to keep their fifth child, an infant who is already showing developmental delays. These abusive parents are eagerly awaiting the birth of their sixth "wanted" child.

Thus, though not wanting the pregnancy is a parental attitude related to child abuse, wanting the pregnancy is insufficient to prevent abuse.

Indeed, extreme yearning for a child may increase the probability of abuse. Lenoski (1974) describes a group of mothers who intensely wanted the child they subsequently abused. They were more likely than a nonabusive control group to name the child after a parent or to have worn maternity clothes earlier.

Martin and Beezley (1974) explain the seemingly contradictory findings of abusive parents who wanted the pregnancy, or adoptive parents who abuse their wanted adoptive children, as an extension of the findings of Steele and Pollack (1968), namely, that abusive parents typically expect the child to meet their own intense emotional needs. The parents lash out at the child, who is irrationally viewed as withholding love. Steele and Pollack also refer to a "splitting" in abusive parents between love for the child and a sense of righteousness about beating a disobedient, unrewarding child. These two contradictory systems, walled off from each other yet coexisting, are manifested in the abuse of children who were also wanted by their parents.

Walsh (1977) describes a group of abusive adolescent mothers who viewed pregnancy and motherhood as ways of defining their identity and social role and of providing the security absent during their own childhoods. When the baby they wanted so intensely failed to meet their irrational expectations, the adolescent mother expressed her frustration and rage by abusing the child.

The relationship between child abuse and wanting a child intensely is reported by Helfer (1975). He describes a group of abusive young women who refused contraception and abortion because of their strong desire to become pregnant, and with whom "family planning and birth control measures must be pursued even though frequently resisted" (p. 29). He recommends special counseling for such women, because referral to a family planning agency is ineffective.

These women had experienced the "world of abnormal rearing" (WAR), a pattern of abusive, rejecting, emotionally damaging relationships with their own parents. Their motivations for the pregnancy were "to free themselves from their unhappy home, prove to their parents and themselves they could indeed be good parents, provide them with someone to keep them company, or [they expect] the baby to role reverse and begin to parent the parents" (p. 34). The infants, incapable of granting these irrational wishes, became the target of their mothers' frustration.

The relationship between child abuse and wanting a child highlights the crucial importance of competent counseling for women with unplanned pregnancies. These distraught women are often exposed to a brand of "counseling" by antichoice proponents that can only be described as incompetent and unethical. Are these women helped to make informed, reflective, personally valid decisions at these significant points in their lives? This is the general goal of quality counseling services, including reputable abortion centers which do not try to dictate the pregnant client's choice. Yet fanatical antichoice advocates, under the guise of counseling, use brainwashing techniques on conflict-ridden clients such as dogmatically preaching that abortion is "killing the preborn child," displaying fetuses in bottles, reinforcing unfounded fears of sterility and death as outcomes of abortions, and other scare tactics.

If such propagandizing occurred with other clients, professional associations and the public would raise vociferous objections. Indeed, action, in the form of charges of violation of ethical standards, expulsion from professional associations, and malpractice suits, needs to be taken against counselors who use such tactics. The fact that abortion is a sensitive social issue does not alter the essential guideline of client-counselor relationships: *the counseling relationship should not be exploited for propagandistic purposes by the counselor, who is committed to fostering an emotional atmosphere conducive to the free choice of the client.*

Inasmuch as few women with problem pregnancies place their children for adoption, agencies which exhort distraught clients to carry the child to term are inadvertently contributing to child abuse. The irresponsible naiveté of antichoice proponents is manifested in their insistence on the ease with which their clients "discover" through "counseling" that they really want the child. They overlook the reality that wanting a child in no way rules out abuse of wanted children after they are born, especially if wanting the child is based on irrational motivation.

The children of these mothers are at especially high risk for abuse. Not only was the pregnancy unwanted, but the circumstances of the birth were likely to have been tumultuous. The mothers are often young, poor, uneducated, under stress, and unlikely to have received adequate prenatal care, variables that significantly increase the risk of child abuse, especially in combination. Their children are in further jeopardy because they are likely to possess medical problems that also predispose them to abuse, such as prematurity, low birth weight, and a variety of other vulnerabilities.

Valid questions regarding follow-through by agencies demand clear answers, for the postpartum period is an opportunity to put reverence-for-life preachings into practice. Do these agencies support the lives of the mother and fetus they rescue from abortion? Do they educate her for responsible sexuality by contraceptive education? Do they educate her for responsible parenthood so that the born child will, in fact, be able "to laugh and love," as their bumper stickers righteously proclaim? On the contrary, once the preborn becomes the *newborn*, their interest in the new mother and her child disappears and is redirected to further fetus rescuing. By obstructing abortion rights on clinical and public policy levels, counselors and agencies are perpetuating child abuse.

Findings that some women abuse the child they wanted also highlight the influence of sexism and pronatalism in the perpetuation of child abuse. If child abuse is ever to be eradicated, attitudes toward women's roles, child-bearing, and the definition of the family must be transformed. The abysmal failure of these women in a role they had sought with joyful expectations poignantly depicts the destructiveness of sexist and pronatalist upbringing. No doubt, these women learned to accept unquestioningly the major tenets of these destructive ideologies: sex role stereotyping and the views that anatomy is destiny, that the only fulfilling life-style for women is motherhood, and that a woman becomes validated as a person only when she bears a child. Despite their harsh backgrounds, these women need not have become child abusers. Had the culture offered these abusive mothers a range of choices in addition to motherhood, they might have become contributors to the community rather than a drain on its resources.

Clear social sanctions for the tenets of the women's movement and the National Alliance for Optional Parenthood would significantly contribute to the primary prevention of child abuse. These tenets include the view that anatomy is not destiny for either women or men, that the family should be redefined as families, a pluralistic institution with a wide variety of life-styles, and that child-free marriage and singlehood merit social sanctions equal to marriage and parenthood. Sexist and pronatalist ideologies continue to be promoted, not only in textbooks and advertising, but in some sex education courses. For example, few family life education courses give equal time to nonparenting life-styles. Some are preparing youth for the 1940s by perpetuating the myth that children define a family. Indeed, the substitution of courses on life-styles for courses on traditional family life would contribute to the primary prevention of child abuse. By being presented with a varied range of equally sanctioned, fulfilling life-styles, youths who learn that they lack generative motivation for childbearing or that they possess the negative attitudes toward childrearing associated with abuse could opt for a child-free life-style. Other youths who opt for parenthood on the basis of informed choice, rather than social pressure, are more likely to raise children nonviolently.

Father-Daughter Incest in Childhood

Sexism is also a major contributor to father-daughter incest, a form of child abuse which will be eliminated only by radical changes in power relations between females and males and between children and adults. Over 90 percent of child victims of sexual abuse by adult relatives are female, and the vast majority of abusers are male even when the child victim is male (Herman, 1981). The pattern of intergenerational incest parallels that of other sex crimes in that most assailants are males and most victims are females. The transcendence of parents' rights over those of their children also contributes to victimization. For example, "Fathers confronted with detection . . . often express surprise that incest is punishable by law and frequently insist that they have done nothing wrong. Some fathers believe sexual access to be one of their parental rights" (Hennepin County Attorney's Office, no date). Their dual status as females and as children intensifies the powerlessness of female victims of father-daughter incest. Therefore, it is understandable that the women's movement and child advocacy lobbies have promoted public recognition of this form of incest as a social problem.

The average age when incest is initiated is between 6 and 11 years (Browning and Boatman, 1977; Maisch, 1972), but infants and younger children are also sexually abused by their fathers. The abuse usually consists of fondling the genitals, masturbation, exhibition, and oral-genital contact. Some mental health professionals and judges erroneously minimize the harmful impact of incest on children because sexual intercourse is not ordinarily involved. The sexual abuse is likely to occur over many years beginning with the oldest daughter and to continue serially with the younger daughters (Cavallin, 1966).

In many cases, incest is not only a family affair but a sociocultural manifestation, in caricature form, of traditional sex role stereotypes played out in a patriarchal family scenario (Cormier, Kennedy, and Sangowicz, 1962; de Young, in press; Herman, 1981; Herman and Hirschman, 1977; Sgroi,

1979; Weinberg, 1955). The father, a "good family man," is also a tyrant; one arch-chauvinistic father even constructed a throne for himself (Summit and Kryso, 1978). The mother is passive, compliant, and extremely dependent on her husband for emotional and financial security. She is sometimes further trapped in the traditional female role by chronic illness or repeated childbearing. The oldest daughter, who is especially vulnerable to sexual abuse by her father, has strong, unmet affectional needs and models the submissiveness of her mother. She is expected to play the role of "little mother" and assume responsibility for housework and child care. This role reversal is an adaptive response to a dysfunctional family environment and is also present in many battered children. This precocity combined with the little girl's affect-hunger and poignancy may be viewed by the authoritarian father as sexual seductiveness.

The old saw that the male offers love to get sex and that the female gives sex to get love is applicable in these cases, for the father's power and the daughter's submissiveness, needfulness, and admiration of him constitute a major dynamic in the relationship. As Geiser (1979) explains: "The best summary of what went on in a father's mind when he turned to his daughter for sex was given by one father in response to his daughter's question, 'Why did you do it to me?' The father's answer: 'You were available and you were vulnerable' " (p. 52). The relationship is sustained by the father's intimidation of his daughter by threats that exposure of the incestuous secret will break up the family, punishment of both of them, and loss of financial security. Fear of loss of familial, emotional, and financial security may also contribute to the mother's denial of the incestuous relationship.

Sexism characterizes not only father-daughter incest per se but also the way in which incest is viewed. As in rape, wife battering, and other crimes against females, the response to incest has been to exonerate the criminal and blame the victim, a response that dates back to the Bible. In Chapter 19 of the Book of Genesis, Lot's wife was turned into a pillar of salt, a symbol of her emotional unavailability. Lot's daughters got him drunk and seduced him, thus justifying his participation in the incest. Some professionals are perpetuating this timeworn bias in incriminating the incest victim in the same way they incriminated the rape victim, namely, by depicting her as seductive and thus provocative or compliant. The wife, too, is viewed as blameworthy. Her coldness and rejection are presumed to explain her husband's incest with their daughter, but the basis of the wife's emotional unavailability because of his tyranny or her entrapment in a psychologically numbing sex role is rarely addressed. The injured party in the family is not the daughter but the father, an innocent victim of his wife's, his daughter's—and sometimes, his mother's—personality flaws. He is thus exempted from responsibility for the sexual abuse of his daughter who, like the rape victim, is viewed as "asking for it."

What are these children actually asking for? According to several investigators, they are asking for affection, attention, and caring. Peters (1976) concluded that the fathers were in a state of reduced ego control when they mistakenly interpreted their daughters' emotional needfulness as seductiveness. He urges professionals not to indict these children for their affection-seeking behavior, for it was the adult who initiated the specifically sexual behavior. Meiselman (1978) refers to adultomorphic misperception, the ascription of adult sexual motives to the child. After psychologically evaluating children at the National Center for the Prevention and Treatment of Child Abuse, Johnston (1979) contended, "It is difficult to understand the characterization of the child as the initiator or seductress since the child is frequently involved in sexual activity which she does not understand, to which she has not given informed consent and which is characteristic of a psychosexual stage beyond her developmental level" (p. 943).

The image of the carnal girl child has been depicted in *Lolita, Pretty Baby,* and *Taxi Driver,* as well as in child pornography and other expressions of adult sexual impulses and fantasies. These adult experiences are attributed to the child by projective identification, a complex psychological defense used by battering parents in the following way: "I am bad; the baby is bad just like me " (Steele and Pollack, 1968). From the standpoint of the abusive parent, the projected "badness" of the baby elicits and justifies the battering. From the standpoint of the incestuous father, the projected, adultomorphized sexual wishes of the child elicit and justify the sexual abuse.

The process of projective identification is expressed in myth, legend, and literature. The archetype of the female as temptress has been symbolized by Eve, Lorelei, and scores of other femmes fatales who tempt hapless males to perform evil or destructive acts. Poets and novelists have depicted the female child as "demon nymphette" (Rush, 1980), *Lolita* being the most notorious. In *annie died the other day,* the poet e.e. cummings (1961) sings of Annie, driven mad by her father's sexual abuse, but a child of exquisite sexuality, an incomparable "lay." Projective identification reaches the zenith in Dostoyevsky's *Crime and Punishment* (1886 /1962) as the child molester, Svidrigailov, dreams of an adultomorphized, carnal, 5-year-old girl:

There was something shameless and provocative in the quiet childlike face; it was depravity, it was the face of a harlot . . . . Now both eyes opened wide. They laughed . . . . There was something infinitely hideous and shocking in that laugh, in those eyes . . . . "What, at five years old," muttered Svidrigailov in genuine horror. "What does it mean?" And now she turned to him, her little face aglow, holding out her arms. (p. 537)

Cormier, Kennedy and Sangowicz (1962) state that incestuous fathers claimed that their daughters had provoked the sexual contacts, whereas the daughters claimed to have been coerced by their fathers. Gebhard, Gagnon, Pomeroy, and Christenson (1965) report that the matter of coercion was sidestepped in their interviews with convicted incest offenders because "the authoritarian position of the father makes the differentiation between threat, duress, acquiescence, and willingness almost impossible" (p. 207). Studies of court records by Gligor (1966) and Maisch (1972) indicate that daughters had shown seductive behavior in a small minority of cases, 12 percent and 6 percent respectively. McGaghy (1968) refers to incest offenders' projection of responsibility onto the child victims as one of the techniques of deviance disavowal used to preserve a normal, healthy self-image.

But what if the little girl was seductive or failed to resist the sexual advances of her father? Does this render incest harmless? The seductiveness and failure to resist of rape victims have often been used to discount the effects of rape, which, nevertheless, have been found to be serious and long term. The same is true of incest. Recent research is demonstrating an array of psychologically damaging effects of father-daughter incest which include interpersonal, marital, sexual, and identity problems, revulsion at being touched, school problems, antisocial behavior, and suicidal attempts (Anderson, 1979; Densen-Gerber, 1979; Finklehor, 1979; Geiser, 1979; Herjanic and Bryan, 1980; Johnston, 1979; Jorné, 1979; Kempe, 1978; Peters, 1976; Rush, 1980).

Seventy-five percent of a sample of adolescent female prostitutes in Minnesota had been victims of incest (Weber, 1977). Meiselman (1978) found that psychotherapy patients with a history of incest had more social, psychological, and sexual problems than those without a history of incest.

The majority of women who volunteered to discuss their childhood incest experiences reported marked to severe effects on a number of indices of psychological and social functioning (Courtois and Watts, 1980). Herman and Hirschman (1977) described a syndrome in women who experienced incest in childhood. This included difficulty in forming intimate relationships, low self-esteem, and a predisposition to becoming repeatedly victimized. In many cases, symptoms may not be present during childhood but may occur in adulthood when the victims become overwhelmed by greater emotional and sexual demands (Peters, 1976).

An early study of adult-child sex relations by Bender and Blau (1937) is often cited as evidence for the negligible effects of incest. Their sample of a total of 16 cases included only 4 cases of incest, 2 of them involving father-daughter incest, hardly a basis for scientific generalization. Furthermore, their conclusions were based on the remaining sample of 12 children who had been sexually molested by *strangers*. Other investigators took these conclusions out of context and erroneously applied them to child victims of incest. Even on the basis of their four incest cases, Bender and Blau concluded that incest was harmful. They state:

Anxiety states with bewilderment concerning social relations occur especially in children who are seduced by parents. Such incest experiences undoubtedly distort the proper development of their attitudes toward members of the family, and subsequently, of society in general. (p. 516)

Apparently sexist and child-oppressive attitudes clouded the objectivity of some professionals to such an extent that they distorted evidence actually supportive of the harmful effects of father-daughter incest on the child into support of its negligible effects.

Despite the findings of psychological damage to victims of intergenerational incest, a few liberal professionals and parents are promoting the practice as beneficial to children (Yudkin, 1981). This irresponsible view further perpetuates the sexual victimization of children. In the past and in some current households, wife battering has also been viewed as beneficial to family harmony or even to the wife, as this old adage illustrates: "A wife, a spaniel, and a walnut tree/ The more they're beaten, the better they be." Some abusive parents and extremist educators even tout severe corporal punishment as beneficial to children, in the face of the evidence of serious damage to them. In the opinion of author C. S. Lewis, the most oppressive tyranny is that exercised for the benefit of its victims.

Some women have survived the effects of intergenerational incest, just as some have survived the effects of other forms of child abuse. Indeed, some victims may learn to transform these and a variety of childhood traumas into exceptional personality invulnerabilities during adulthood. Nevertheless, no rational individual would use these outcomes as a basis for recommending childhood trauma as a means of strengthening personality in adulthood.

The consequences of sexual initiation of children by parents and other adults in our society differ from those in primitive cultures. The direct motor expression of sexual initiation is supported by the entire ethos and rituals in primitive cultures, whereas it is dysfunctional in ours. In modern technological societies, the intergenerational incest taboo is essential to protect children from sexual exploitation by adults. There can be no informed consent in sexual relationships between adults and children in our society. Here, children are victims of reverse ageism. Our laws and mores offer them minuscule protection against violent coercion and no protection against emotional coercion. The passivity of incest victims is not surprising. In our society, when a child is sexually exploited by an adult, "The entire world of adult authority bears down to confuse and confound the hapless victim" (Brownmiller, 1976, p. 300). Female children are the most vulnerable of all groups, for they are the victims of double oppression: sexism as well as reverse ageism.

The indirect transmission of sexual knowledge to youths by their elders through the mediation of language and conceptualization is the appropriate mode in our society. The modern equivalent of sexual initiation is sex education, not sexual exploitation.

Throughout history and into the present, crimes against the female have been rationalized by incriminating her and absolving the criminal. Father-daughter incest adds a new dimension of oppression in that the female child is blamed and the male adult exonerated. The extent to which child protection was sacrificed in the interests of father protection is incisively illustrated in Freud's intensely conflicted attempts to grapple with the problem of father-daughter incest.

In 1895, Breuer and Freud published *Studies on Hysteria* (1895/1955) in which they first put forward the thesis that hysterical symptoms in women result from childhood sexual trauma. This explanation was at odds with the prevailing genetic explanation of psychological problems, and with the Victorian zeitgeist. A letter from Freud to his confidant, Fliess, the same year the article was published demonstrates the intensity of Breuer's ambivalence to the explanation which he himself had coauthored:

Not long ago Breuer made a big speech about me at the Doktorenkollegium, in which he announced his conversion to belief in the sexual aetiology [of the neuroses]. When I took him on one side to thank him for it, he destroyed my pleasure by saying: "All the same I don't believe it." (p. xxvi)

In *The Aetiology of Hysteria* (1896/1955), Freud repeated the thesis that "at the bottom of every case of hysteria there are one or more occurrences of premature sexual experience which belong to the earliest years of childhood" (p. 203). About that time, Freud appears to have been swamped with evidence of incest. As he wrote in confidence to Fliess about one of his female analysands:

Then it came out that when she was between the ages of eight and twelve her allegedly otherwise admirable and high-principled father used regularly to take her to his bed and practice external ejaculation (making wet) with her. Even at the time she felt anxiety. A six-year old sister to whom she talked about it later admitted that she had had the same experiences with her father. A cousin told her that at the age of fifteen she had had to resist the advances of her grandfather. Naturally she did not find it incredible when I told her that similar and worse things must have happened to her in infancy. (Freud, 1887-1902/1954, p. 196)

In an unpublished letter to Fliess, dated Feburary 11, 1897 (Jones, 1961), Freud wrote that he had "inferred from the existence of some hysterical features in his brother and several sisters that even his father had been incriminated" (p. 211). In another letter, dated May 31, 1897, he confided: "I do not want to do any more work. I have laid even dreams aside. Not long ago I dreamt that I was feeling over-affectionately towards Mathilde [his daughter].... The dream of course fulfills my wish to pin down a father as the originator of neurosis and put an end to my persistent doubts" (Freud, 1887-1902/1954, p. 206).

Despite his patients' reports and his own personal experience of incestuous longing, Freud ended his doubts by disavowing the role of the sexually abusing father in the etiology of psychoneurosis in women. Instead, he explained psychoneurosis in terms of daughters' fantasies of incest rather than its actual occurrence. He corrected his "error" in a 1924 footnote to *The Aetiology of Hysteria* (1896/1955):

This section is dominated by an error which I have since repeatedly acknowledged and corrected. At that time I was not yet able to distinguish between my patients' phantasies about their childhood years and their real recollections. As a result I attributed to the aetiological factor of seduction a significance and universality which it does not possess. (p. 168)

Freud's conflict about accepting the existence of father-daughter incest in the childhoods of neurotic women is indicated by his confession, that in two cases reported in *Studies on Hysteria* (Breuer and Freud, 1895/1955) he had suppressed the fact that the female patients had been sexually molested by their fathers (Freud, 1924/1955, Vol. 1, pp. 134, 170. See also Vol. 3, p. 164). Ironically, the footnote that was included to correct his error in accepting incest as actual, rather than fantasied, ends with the statement: "Nevertheless, we need not reject everything written in the text above. Seduction retains a certain aetiological importance, and even today I think some of these psychological comments are to the point" (Vol. 3, p. 168).

In 1933, Freud again referred to his earlier theory of the sexually abusive father, this time unequivocally rejecting it. He stated, "Almost all my women patients told me that they had been seduced by their fathers. I was driven to recognize in the end that these reports were untrue and so came to understand that the hysterical symptoms are derived from phantasies and not from real occurrences" (Freud, 1933/1966, p. 584).

In the later development of psychoanalytic theory, the basis for the now-presumed fantasy of incest was assigned to the little girl's wish for a penis. Even if she had been sexually abused by her father in childhood, it was penis envy, not sexual abuse, that was the problem. Providing she attained a surrogate penis in the form of a husband and baby, especially a male baby, she would overcome her guilt and anxiety about her incestuous desires for her father and would develop normally. According to Freud's disciple, Abraham (1954), even if a little girl is sexually abused by an adult, she "yields to the trauma" and "already has a disposition to neurosis or psychosis in later life" (pp. 53, 62). Such theorizing led many psychotherapists to discount reports of sexual abuse of children by adults or to blame the victim in the allegedly rare event that harmful effects followed the abuse.

Courtois and Watts (1980) found that women in their sample who had sought psychotherapy reported having gone to several therapists before they found one who believed them. Although the finding requires further exploration, it is noteworthy that those who received psychotherapy for the incest suffered significantly more severe psychological effects than those who did not. Peters (1976) states:

It is my thesis . . . that both cultural and personal factors combined to cause everyone, including Freud himself at times, to welcome the idea that reports of childhood sexual victimization could be regarded as fantasies. This position relieved the guilt of adults....

Psychiatrists have in the past erred in the direction of ascribing to childhood fantasy real cases of sexual assault upon children. Experience in the rape victim clinics . . . and with patients in private psychoanalytic practice seem to indicate that reports of sexual assaults upon children are ignored or discounted at the expense of the psychologic well-being of the child victim. (pp. 401, 420)

The prejudices of many psychotherapists have contributed to the perpetuation of sexual abuse of the child by their denial of the victimization, by blaming the victim, and by overidentification with the adult male aggressor. They have added insult and more injury to the injury of father-daughter incest by probing the victim's role in allegedly eliciting the abuse, rather than helping her cope with it, protecting her from reabuse, and empathizing with her confusion, terror, rage, powerlessness, degradation, and despair. Like the rape victim, she is accused of lying, fantasizing the sexual victimization, or bringing it on herself because of her seductiveness, passivity, or failure to struggle. In *Sanctions for Evil* (Sanford and Comstock, 1971), Opton describes the psychosocial processes that permit individuals to tolerate the most inhumane acts. One such psychological mechanism, "It never happened and besides they deserved it," applies to the inhumane act of father-daughter incest.

Toward Responsible Sexuality and the Primary Prevention of Child Abuse

How can child abuse be prevented? By changing entrenched, worn-out solutions to the problem. Child abuse is but the tip of the iceberg. The glacier from which that iceberg formed consists of manifold expressions of irresponsible sexuality and the sanctioning of sexist, pronatalist, child-oppressive ideologies. The child abuse industry, with its overemphasis on treatment, creates the illusion that the glacier of social pathology undergirding child abuse does not exist and that treatment is all that is required to control the problem. This illusory optimism does not change the forecast that child abuse will continue indefinitely unless professionals and the public actively support sexually enlightened, egalitarian, child-advocating ideologies and programs directed toward primary prevention.

References

Abraham, K. The experiencing of sexual trauma as a form of sexual activity. In K. Abraham (Ed.), *Selected papers on psychoanalysis*. New York: Basic Books, 1954.

Albee, G. W. The prevention of sexism. *Professional Psychology*, 1981, *12*, 20-27.

Anderson, D. Touching: When is it caring and nurturing or when is it exploitative and damaging? *Child Abuse and Neglect*, 1979, *3*, 793-794.

Bender, L., and Blau, A. The reactions of children to sexual relations with adults. *American Journal of Orthopsychiatry*, 1937, *7*, 500-518.

Bishop, F. I. Children at risk. *Medical Journal of Australia*, 1971, *1*, 623.

Breslow, L. Unpublished paper presented at the first national Conference on Abortion Laws. Chicago, Illinois, 1969.

Breuer, J., and Freud, S. [Studies on hysteria.] In J. Strachey (Ed. and trans.), *The complete works of Sigmund Freud* (Vol. 2). London: Hogarth Press, 1955. (Originally published, 1895.)

Browning, D., and Boatman, B. Incest: Children at risk. *American Journal of Psychiatry*, 1977, *134*, 69-72.

Brownmiller, S. *Against our will: Men, women and rape*. New York: Bantam Books, 1976.

Butterfield, A. M., Jackson, A. D. M., and Nangle, D. Child abuse: A two year follow-up. *Child Abuse and Neglect*, 1979, *3*, 985-989.

Cavallin, H. Incestuous fathers: A clinical report. *American Journal of Psychiatry*, 1966, *122*, 1132-1138.

Cohn, A. H. Essential elements of successful child abuse and neglect treatment. *Child Abuse and Neglect*, 1979, *3*, 491-496.

Cohn, A. H., and Miller, M. K. Evaluating new modes of treatment for child abusers and neglectors: The experience of federally funded demonstration projects in the USA. *Child Abuse and Neglect*, 1977, *1*, 453-458.

Cormier, B., Kennedy, M., and Sangowicz, J. Psychodynamics of father-daughter incest. *Canadian Psychiatric Association Journal*, 1962, *7*, 203-215.

Courtois, C. A., and Watts, D. *Women who experienced childhood incest: Research findings and therapeutic strategies*. Paper presented at the annual meeting of the American Psychological Association, Montreal, Canada, 1980.

Densen-Gerber, J. Sexual and commercial exploitation of children: Legislative responses and treatment challenges. *Child Abuse and Neglect*, 1979, *3*, 61-66.

De Young, M. Promises, threats and lies: Keeping incest secret. *Journal of Humanics*, in press.

Dostoyevsky, F. *Crime and punishment*. New York: Laurel Press, 1962. (Originally published, 1886.)

Ferguson, D. M., Fleming, J., and O'Neil, D. P. *Child abuse in New Zealand*. Wellington, New Zealand: Department of Social Welfare, 1972.

Finkelhor, D. *Sexually victimized children*. New York: Macmillan, 1979.

Fraser, B. Child abuse in America: A de facto legislative system. *Child Abuse and Neglect*, 1979, *3*, 35-43.

Freud, S. [*The origins of psycho-analysis, letters to Wilhelm Fliess, drafts and notes: 1887-1902.*] (M. Bonaparte, A. Freud, and E. Kris, eds., and E. Mosbacher and J. Strachey, trans.). New York: Basic Books, 1954.

Freud, S. The aetiology of hysteria. In J. Strachey (Ed. and trans.), *Standard edition of the complete psychological works of Sigmund Freud* (Vol. 3). London: Hogarth Press and the Institute of Psychoanalysis, 1955. (Originally published, 1896.)

Freud, S. *The standard edition of the complete psychological works of Sigmund Freud.* (J. Strachey, Ed. and trans.) (Vols. 1, 2, and 3). London: The Hogarth Press and the Institute of Psychoanalysis, 1924/1955.

Freud, S. [*The complete introductory lectures on psychoanalysis.*] (J. Strachey, Ed. and trans.). New York: W. W. Norton, 1966. (Originally published, 1933.)

Friedman, S. B. The need for intensive follow-up of abused children. In C. H. Kempe and R. E. Helfer (Eds.), *Helping the battered child and his family*. Philadelphia: J. B. Lippincott, 1972.

Friedrich, W. N. and Boriskin, J. A. The role of the child in abuse: A review of the literature. *American Journal of Orthopsychiatry*, 1976, *46*, 580-590.

Gaddis, D. C., Monaghan, S., Muir, R. C., and Jones, C. J. Early prediction in the maternity hospital. *Child Abuse and Neglect*, 1979, *3*, 757-766.

Gebhard, P. H., Gagnon, J. H., Pomeroy, W. B., and Christenson, C. *Sex offenders: An analysis of types*. New York: Harper and Row, 1965.

Geiser, R. L. *Hidden victims: The sexual abuse of children*. Boston: Beacon Press, 1979.

Gil, D. G. *Violence against children*. Cambridge, Mass.: Harvard University Press, 1970.

Gil, D. G. *Testimony*. Hearing before the Subcommittee on Children and Youth of the Committee on Labor and Public Welfare, 93rd Cong., 1st session. Child Abuse Prevention Act, 1973. Washington, D.C.: U.S. Government Printing Office, 1973.

Gligor, A. M. Incest and sexual delinquency: A comparative analysis of two forms of sexual behavior in minor females (Doctoral dissertation, Western Reserve University, 1967). Dissertation Abstracts International, 1966, 27B. (University Microfilms No. 67-04588, 3671)

Green, A. A psychodynamic approach to the study and treatment of child abusing parents. *Journal of Child Psychiatry*, 1976, *15*, 213-224.

Green, C. P., and Pottzeiger, K. *Teenage pregnancy: A major problem for minors*. Washington, D.C.: Zero Population Growth, 1977.

Helfer, R. E. *Child abuse and neglect: The diagnostic process and treatment programs*. Washington, D.C.: U.S. Department of Health, Education and Welfare, Publ. No. OHD75-69, 1975.

Helfer, R. E. *Prevention of serious breakdowns in parent child interaction*. Unpublished paper presented at the National Committee for Prevention of Child Abuse, Denver, Colorado, 1978.

Hennepin County Attorney's Office. *Sexual assault: The target is you*. Brochure prepared by the Hennepin County Attorney's Office, Minneapolis, Minnesota, no date.

Herjanic, B., and Bryan, B. Sexual abuse of children. *Medical Aspects of Human Sexuality*, 1980, April, 92-99.

Herman, J. Father-daughter incest. *Professional Psychology*, 1981, *12*, 76-80.

Herman, J., and Hirschman, L. Father-daughter incest. *Signs: Journal of Women in Culture and Society*, 1977, *2*, 735-756.

Herrenkohl, R. C., Herrenkohl, E. C., Egolf, B., and Seech, M. The repetition of child abuse: How frequently does it occur? *Child Abuse and Neglect*, 1979, *3*, 67-72.

Johnston, M. S. K. The sexually mistreated child: Diagnostic evaluation. *Child Abuse and Neglect*, 1979, *3*, 943-951.

Jones, E. *The life and work of Sigmund Freud*. New York: Basic Books, 1961.

Jorné, P. S. Treating sexually abused children. *Child Abuse and Neglect*, 1979, *3*, 285-290.

Kempe, C. H. Sexual abuse: Another hidden pediatric problem. *Pediatrics*, 1978, *62*, 382-389.

Kempe, C. H. Recent developments in the field of child abuse. *Child Abuse and Neglect*, 1979, *3*, ix-xv.

Lenoski, E. F. Unpublished paper presented at the Seminar on Child Abuse, Denver, Colorado, September 1974.

Light, R. J. Abused and neglected children in America: A study of alternative policies. *Harvard Educational Review*, 1973, *43*, 556-598.

Lynch, M. A., and Roberts, J. Predicting child abuse: Signs of bonding failure in the maternity hospital. *British Medical Journal*, 1977, *1*, 624.

MacCarthy, D. Deprivation dwarfism viewed as a form of child abuse. In A. W. Franklin (Ed.), *The challenge of child abuse*. London: Academic Press, 1977.

Maisch, H. *Incest*. New York: Stein and Day, 1972.

Martin, H. P., and Beezley, P. Prevention and the consequences of child abuse. *Journal of Operational Psychology*, 1974, *6*, 68-77.

McGaghy, C. H. Drinking and deviance disavowal: The case of child molesters. *Social Problems*, 1968, *16*, 43-49.

Meiselman, K. C. *Incest: A psychological study of causes and effects with treatment recommendations*. San Francisco: Jossey-Bass, 1978.

Oates, R. K., Davis, A. A., Ryan, M. G., and Stewart, L. F. Risk factors associated with child abuse. *Child Abuse and Neglect*, 1979, *3*, 547-553.

Opton, E. M. It never happened and besides they deserved it. In N. Sanford and C. Comstock (Eds.), *Sanctions for evil*. San Francisco: Jossey-Bass, 1971.

Peters, J. J. Children who were victims of sexual assault and the psychology of the offenders. *American Journal of Psychotherapy*, 1976, *30*, 398-417.

Prescott, J. Abortion of the unwanted child: A choice for a humanistic society. *Journal of Pediatric Psychology*, 1976, *1*, 62-67.

Resnick, P. J. Murder of the newborn: A psychiatric review of neonaticide. *American Journal of Psychiatry*, 1970, *126*, 1414-1420.

Rush, F. *The best kept secret: Sexual abuse of children*. Englewood Cliffs, N.J.:

Prentice-Hall, 1980.

Sanford, N., and Comstock, C. (Eds.), *Sanctions for evil.* San Francisco: Jossey-Bass, 1971.

Scott, W. J. Attachment and child abuse: A study of social history indicators among mothers of abused children. In G. J. Williams and J. Money (Eds.), *Traumatic abuse and neglect of children at home.* Baltimore: Johns Hopkins University Press, 1980.

Sgroi, S. M. The sexual assault of children: Dynamics of the problem and issues of program development. In Community Council of Greater New York (Ed.), *Sexual abuse of children.* New York: Community Council of Greater New York, 1979.

Skinner, A. E., and Castle, R. L. *78 battered children: A retrospective study.* London: National Society for the Prevention of Cruelty to Children, 1969.

Spinetta, J. J., and Rigler, D. The child-abusing parent: A psychological review. *Psychological Bulletin,* 1972, 77, 296-304.

Steele, B. F., and Pollack, C. B. A psychiatric study of parents who abuse infants and small children. In R. E. Helfer and C. H. Kempe (Eds.), *The battered child.* University of Chicago Press, 1968.

Summit, R., and Kryso, J. Sexual abuse of children: A clinical spectrum. *American Journal of Orthopsychiatry,* 1978, 48, 237-251.

Taitz, L. S. Effects on growth and develoment of social, psychological, and environmental factors. *Child Abuse and Neglect,* 1980, 4, 55-65.

United States Department of Health, Education, and Welfare. *Child abuse and neglect: An overview of the problem,* (Vol. 1). Washington, D.C.: DHEW Publication (OHD) 75-30073, 1975.

Walsh, T. *Premature parenting and child abuse.* Unpublished paper presented at the Workshop on Teen Parenthood, Onondaga Community College, New York, March 8, 1977.

Wasserman, S. The abused parent of the abused child. *Children,* 1967, 14, 175-179.

Weber, E. Sexual abuse begins at home. *Ms.,* April 1977, p. 64.

Weinberg, S. K. *Incest behavior.* New York: Citadel, 1955.

West, J. E., and West, E. D. Child abuse treated in a psychiatric hospital.*Child Abuse and Neglect,* 1979, 3, 699-707.

Williams, G. J. Origins of filicidal impulses in the American way of life. *Journal of Clinical Child Psychology,* 1976, 5, 2-11.

Williams, G. J. Toward the eradication of child abuse and neglect at home. In G. J. Williams and J. Money (Eds.), *Traumatic abuse and neglect of children at home.* Baltimore: Johns Hopkins University Press, 1980.

Yudkin, M. Breaking the incest taboo: Those who crusade for family "love" forget the balance of family power. *Progressive,* May 1981, pp. 27-28.

PART III

Working with High-Risk and Low-Self-Esteem Groups

Introductory Notes

The depiction of human sexuality in the mass media overwhelmingly emphasizes the theme of an adult male pursuing and overtaking a young adult female. Both people are depicted as well proportioned, sexually attractive, healthy, and obviously in good physical and financial shape. Nearly always, too, they are portrayed as being affluent—in the video image or magazine fiction are luxurious physical settings, often including sleek automobiles or fast powerful boats, golf links, or mountains or beaches, swimming pools or ski tows. But in the real world people with strong sexual drives include persons who are physically handicapped, people who are aging and infirm, those who have suffered mild strokes and cardiac infarctions, as well as persons who are obese, people with bad teeth, black lungs, and other chronic diseases. Many of these people live in slums, urban and rural, and in blue-collar neighborhoods. They live in rooming houses and in trailer parks, in mobile homes and in ghettos; on reservations, on houseboats, and in cabins in the woods. They are in institutions and group homes, prisons and palatial mansions. In other words, sexual and affectional needs are present in nearly all people who are living and breathing and being human. Rarely does this broad range of people encounter sexuality modeled by those who are not "beautiful people." We learn sex roles from macho-men and the Dallas cheerleaders.

Some of these people have a higher than ordinary risk of having sexual problems and sexual frustrations because of their particular life-style, stresses, and handicaps. Examples of such handicaps include physical disability, chronic illness, damaged hearts, mental retardation. The papers in this section examine some of these specific high-risk populations and report on ways of reducing the sexual problems in these groups.

A widely accepted strategy in primary prevention emphasizes the importance of working with high-risk groups. Proactive efforts are aimed at building competence and coping skills, self-esteem, and establishing mutual support groups in order to reduce stress or to make coping with stress more effective. Groups at high risk for sexual problems and difficulties include persons who are "mentally retarded," including a large group called "slow learners," and a smaller group of the more severely intellectually handicapped. Gloria Blum is widely recognized for her success in teaching people who are mentally handicapped to feel good about themselves, to develop self-esteem, to learn to handle their sexual feelings, to channel their sexual behavior appropriately. During the conference, Blum demonstrated a whole series of techniques she has developed in working with these high-risk groups. Her paper contains examples of exercises that she has developed. Her written instructions are clear, but it is difficult to convey on paper the zest and enthusiasm that Gloria Blum brings to her training sessions. It seems safe to predict that persons working with these high-risk groups using these methods will have dramatic effects in preventing or avoiding low self-esteem, sexual problems, and sexual exploitation.

Blum's paper is overflowing with ideas for programs and exercises which help to promote high self-esteem, and the ability to say no. The difference between inappropriate behavior and feeling oneself to be an inappropriate person is also explored. The author's concept of public and private parts of the body and behaviors is developed in this light, and it is emphasized that repetition of such basic messages helps in understanding. Important information concerning human sexuality can be imparted in a similar format, in the context of love and a deep sense of caring which the author believes belongs in any classroom that teaches the disabled.

"Sex is a natural function. All people are sexual: the young and the old, the able-bodied and the disabled, men and women." This opening section from the paper on disability and intimacy by Sandra and Theodore Cole is an important, simple statement of rights. A person's response to disability, and his or her level of self-esteem, are viewed as components in the process of socialization. Negative images from the environment, and a negative bias in our culture toward imperfection, significantly affect how disabled individuals feel about themselves.

The psychological and spiritual assessment of the disabled indicates the pervasiveness of sexuality in all individuals. Ultimately, the loss of specific genital function or sensation does not mean a concomitant loss of personal sexual feelings or desire; relationships do not depend for success on genital interactions any more than self-esteem needs to be based on sexual performance per se.

Sandra and Theodore Cole work together in a department of physical medicine and rehabilitation where they have long observed and dealt with sexual problems of the physically handicapped and the disabled. Because physically handicapped persons frequently have especially serious problems with their self-image and self-esteem, sexuality for them can be a central concern, one which affects the quality of their life. The Coles' paper is concerned with the ways of helping to prevent or to reduce sexual problems among the disabled.

The special sexual concerns of cardiac patients are addressed by Sharon Satterfield in her paper. Typically, myocardial infarction (M.I.) patients are fearful of resuming sexual activity in the mistaken belief that orgasm will unduly stress the heart. Sex emerges as a major concern of these individuals; it is an area that is fraught with misconceptions, even among physicians and other professionals. The fact is that these patients need information, counseling, and affection, and especially family support. The great majority of M.I. patients can resume sexual functioning—there are few absolute contraindications.

Self-Esteem and Knowledge: Primary Requisites to Prevent Victimization

Gloria J. Blum

People who are diagnosed and labeled as "mentally retarded" are special and unique people. And they are also like other people. Working with such people requires acute sensitivity to both points. Once we learn from our slow learners what their special needs are, and provide for those needs, we can address their normal aspects, the parts that they share with the rest of humanity. Only then can they—and we—grow beyond their labels of "mentally retarded" or even "slow learners."

To improve the quality of life for people with disabilities, mainstreaming is becoming more and more common. Instead of institutionalizing our handicapped, hiding them, or overprotecting them, we are now working to prepare them to succeed within society. The intention of mainstreaming is to provide a sense of belonging, of inclusion in our society for people who have previously been excluded. The purpose of socialization programs, independent living programs, and independent learning programs is actually to reduce the amount of care that these citizens require by enabling them to take more care of themselves.

If we want people (e.g., immigrants) to join our society as contributors and not liabilities, we must teach them the social rules so that they can learn to succeed. In the same way, mainstreaming, socialization programs, and information programs (including academic skills, behavior awareness, and sexual knowledge) are designed to enable disabled citizens to catch up on what they have missed in previous schooling. With this assistance they can contribute to conventional society, as companions and friends, as teachers, as workers, even as taxpayers! Some do not get all the way right away. But many do, especially when provided with sensitively taught information. Then living becomes much simpler, not only for the disabled persons but also for those around them who no longer have to take care of them but instead can coexist and work *with* them.

In the process of working to incorporate slow learners into society, we must prepare them for all eventualities, including possibilities of victimization. People are often concerned about victimization of so-called normal people by other people who look and act differently. We tend to fear strange behavior. What is, in fact, more common is that mentally retarded people as well as other disabled people are victimized by the so-called normal members of society. Slow learners appear to be easy prey and are robbed, injured, and raped more often than almost any other segment of our population. Since they do not always tell us about it, we are not always aware of the extent of these problems.

Self-Esteem

Self-esteem is confidence and satisfaction with oneself. It involves learning how to give ourself approval, how to say, "I am okay." This is not something that comes automatically. It is something that must be learned.

Our first exposure to self-esteem comes early in life, through relationships with those who are close to us. If those people approve of and love themselves, our first learning experience is positive. Happy days and frustrating days, good times and bad, are part of living, for babies as well as for adults. With an underlying steady sense of self-esteem and self-acceptance, inevitable ups and downs become part of the process of living. Problems become situations that need solutions. Thirsts and hungers become opportunities to appreciate nourishments even more. Challenges, when successfully overcome, serve to strengthen both the child and the adult. When we experience a sense of completion, of productiveness and usefulness, we acquire a good feeling about ourselves. These good feelings are building blocks for gaining courage to take further risks, risks that allow us to grow.

Socialization Skills

Self-esteem, then, develops through the process of learning how to give ourselves approval. Social learning develops through the process of gaining awareness of outside approval or disapproval. We take it for granted that because we live among others, our behavior is subject to the approval or disapproval of others. We learn socialization skills by constant practice. When we are fortunate enough to have effective role models around us, we learn which behaviors are appropriate to our environment. Because there are so many different environments in our society, we learn which behaviors work in which settings.

Disabled people, however, have often been raised in a sheltered environment, such as a hospital or institution. They have had little experience in everyday social interactions. They often have little awareness of how they appear to others. The disabled person needs to learn how to act normally, namely, how to behave appropriately in public. Choosing what to wear, shopping in a department store, buying meals, or having correct change for the bus are not skills normally acquired in a hospital, a residential care facility, or in the overly protective home.

How to relate to strangers is one of the social skills acquired by practice and experience. Likewise, an understanding of sexuality and appropriate sexual behavior comes primarily from interactions within society. When these experiences have been limited or lacking, people will have to learn these skills in some way in order to function without risk of victimization.

Teaching Self-Esteem

The importance of self-esteem for slow learners lies in gaining a sense of inner strength and control. With repeated successes and completions, as well as lessons learned from mistakes, disabled people begin to see themselves as creative forces in their own lives. They feel less like victims and are therefore less likely to be victimized.

"Teaching" self-esteem may be too strong a term. But there are certain techniques that can foster a good feeling about one's self. These involve creating a safe, supportive environment, one of consistent and predictable acceptance. As teachers, we must aim to develop and reinforce attitudes and techniques of caring and loving (rather than those of confrontation and competition). We must make it easier for independent participation and risk taking, leading to the eventual assumption of leadership roles.

There are two important principles of self-esteem to keep in mind. The first is for the student, the second is for the teacher: each of us is special and unique *and* also like other people; the ongoing success of the participant is more important that any predetermined goals, objectives, or expectations.

Unconditional Appreciation

The first technique is a simple method of responding with applause to any contribution to the group. This demonstrates that it is not what you say that is necessarily special, but that you were willing to say it ("you" referring to the student). In other words, you do not have to be smart or to answer questions with the so-called right answers in order to be appreciated.

I. Clapping Warm-up (slow learners start with A; nondisabled start with C)

A. Leader says enthusiastically, "How many of you know how to clap your hands?"

B. "Okay, everyone, hold both of your hands in front of you; look at them; with the flat part of your hand hit the flat part of your other hand and listen to the sound you make."

C. "Now, all together, let's clap."

D. "Whenever anyone participates in the group, they will receive appreciation from all of us by clapping."

II. Other Methods of Expressing Appreciation (to be used according to the group's physical abilities)

A. Holding hands in the air, palms facing forward, and waggling the wrists or fingers (Tibetan applause)

B. Finger snapping

C. Any imaginative system, as long as it is used regularly and often

Affirmation

Another effective technique is to repeat certain statements to yourself or to your group which express a specific positive point of view. These usually concern your capabilities, or your positive attitudes toward yourself or others or to certain situations. These statements are affirmations. Reciting them individually or as a group and repeating them periodically constitute a valuable exercise.

Without knowing it, we create both affirmations and negations in our daily lives. For example, if we say repeatedly, "I can't do anything right," we may start to believe it. If it is reinforced in our environment as well as inside ourselves, it becomes our reality. This can also be applied to building strengths. "I can do things for myself" reinforced with "You sure know how to get things done" makes for a positive experience. Try it. Before you go to sleep say, "I will feel refreshed and happy in the morning" and believe it. It works!

Here is an example of affirmation. One time we were going around the circle in one of my classes. Each person said, "I feel good about myself," and each person received appreciation through applause. Then we came to one woman, Mary, who started to say, "I feel good..."but began to cry and said, "I don't feel good about myself and I can't say it!" I asked the group, "How many people here feel good about Mary?" Almost everyone in the group felt compassion for Mary and raised their hands, saying, "We feel good about you, Mary." Then Mary again attempted to say, "I feel good about..." and again began to cry. I said to Mary, "Sometimes people don't feel good about themselves. That's okay. Say 'I feel good about myself' anyway and start getting used to it!" Then Mary said, "I feel good about myself" about eight times, each time lightening up a bit until a sparkle appeared in her eyes. Several weeks later I received a letter from Mary's regular teacher thanking me for giving Mary permission to feel good about herself. She did not know it was okay to feel that way!

Experiment with your own affirmations. Become aware of signs of surfacing strengths and encourage their development. For example, Bill was labeled slow, and yet I noticed him remembering many details that everyone else seemed to forget and sequences in the teaching process. I would spontaneously say, "Bill has an excellent memory. He remembered to turn on the music at exactly the right time." I would refer to his successes during regular conversations as well as in class. The rest of the group gradually referred to Bill's good memory as a matter of fact and so it became a fact, and an asset to Bill's self-image. Even today, his memory for important details continues to amaze us.

YES NO Process

The specific techniques for the YES NO Process are explained later in this section. It consists of a series of exercises, procedures, and role plays that promotes a sense of ableness and assertiveness. It provides the tools needed for decision making.

I developed the YES NO Process while I was teaching a class at a sheltered workshop for developmentally disabled adults. I noticed that many of the clients seemed to be walking around with a lot of tension in their bodies. Their jaws were often held clenched and to me it appeared that they were saying no with their bodies though they may have been saying yes with their words.

We were discussing sex in our class and on one occasion a blind woman, 29 years old, came to me after class and told me that during recess from the workshop, she and another client were having sexual intercourse in the liquor store across the street and that she did not want this to happen. But the way she said it, "Well, I don't want it to happen any more," was in a very unconvincing little girl's voice.

I asked her, "What did you tell him [the other client] when he started to touch your private parts?"

She said, "Well, I told him I wanted to wait until we got married and then maybe we could have sex," again in the voice of a very shy little girl.

I asked her, "Did you say no?"

"Well, I think so."

"How did you say no?"

And she answered in child's voice, with the rising inflection at the end as in a question: "No?"

I said to her, "Say it like you really mean it."

"No?"

"Say it like you really, *really* mean it!"

Again the questioning: "No?"

We spent a lot of time learning to say no in that class. I noticed how many other people at the workshop would say no with a question sound to it, as if they were seeking approval.

YES NO Miracles

In normal development children go through a stage when they seem to say nothing else but no, and that is really a part of their own assertion that they are individuals. The no stage is actually the "I am" stage. Until you can say no adequately you cannot really say yes and mean it. This is the beginning of the process of decision making. Many of the people who are developmentally disabled have their decisions made for them as they are growing up, because it is assumed that they do not know enough to decide things for themselves.

It may be that when many slow learners went through their no stage, they were not adequately acknowledged. When we introduced the YES NO Process at the workshop, we drew out that unexpressed no and incredible things began to happen. People changed their names. People who never spoke started talking. The process is designed for nonverbal people also. If you can breathe, you can do the YES NO process.

A man named Al was in our class. He rarely spoke. Several months after he had started participating in the YES NO Process his mother relayed this story to me. She was getting ready to go out shopping with Al. She asked him if he wanted to come. He said no. Al had never said no to going out shopping before. He usually liked it. I asked her how she felt about his saying No. She was completely surprised, but she also liked hearing him take a stand. She said to him that he did not have to go since he did not want to. Shortly thereafter he decided to go.

His mother noticed a definite change in his behavior because he had succeeded in asserting himself. When he did go shopping, it was his choice. Sometime during the next month he changed his name to Robert, a name he had always secretly wanted to have. His family supported that change. Everyone at the workshop began to call him Robert. In a certain sense, he created himself anew. He had been practically nonverbal, and now he had not only chosen a new name for hmself, but also made sure everyone around him used that new name. He started to relate to other people, and in fact, he gained a girlfriend. They held hands. He became more verbal with her and with others. He became more helpful at his job. It was a fantastic change!

Another client at the workshop was named Jane. Although she was 30 years old, she looked 16, and most people called her Janie. Jane never spoke. But she did like to pretend to speak by whispering. She would often come up to me and whisper in my ear, "Spsspsspss."

When I taught the deaf, part of my philosophy was to respond to almost any kind of verbal expression. I would respond to Jane by shaking my head and saying, "Oh, how interesting." I was pleased to receive any type of verbal expression from her.

I had a private session with her shortly after we had taught the NO part of the YES NO Process. She came into the room and in a partly playful and partly serious way she started to shout no to me and then came toward me and hit me. I watched this with some amazement, because she had never done anything like that before. When she hit me (it was not very hard), I moved with the blow and fell to the ground. She was horrified. She had never before made anyone fall to the ground. As a matter of fact, she had rarely made anything happen before. Then she saw me laughing and she started to smile. She got down beside me and began to mother me. She cradled my head, snapped my snaps, buttoned my buttons, and helped me to get up. This is someone whose mother does everything for her: dresses her, takes her everywhere, and even buttons her buttons. Meanwhile Jane was acting as my mother to me, and I was loving it.

Several days later, Jane came up to me to whisper in my ear. I expected to hear the usual, "Spsspsspss," but instead heard something like "There's going to be a fire this afternoon." It was like hearing a ghost!

When someone who never talks says to me that there is going to be a fire, I hasten to tell someone about it! I went running to the education director: "You won't believe this but it's like the dead has risen. Jane spoke to me and said there is going to be a fire here this afternoon." The education director said, "Holy smokes!"

What had happened was that Jane had overheard people in the staff room discussing that someone was going to be fired that afternoon. Jane was always permitted everywhere in the workshop because she was supposedly nonverbal. It paid off for her to be that way. She enjoyed certain extra privileges not accorded to those who could talk. But somehow the forcefulness of the YES NO Process had brought out her own abilities to express herself.

Techniques of the YES NO Process *

The YES NO Process is a preparation for decision making. Its purpose is to promote a sense of one's power and identity, as well as a one's ability and assertiveness. These are the tools for basic communication, for expression feelings such as anger and joy, and for expressing yes and no with strength and meaning.

These exercises are designed for use with students who are slow learners. But, in fact, the same exercises are equally useful for nondisabled persons. Use them with parents when you are introducing this curriculum. Use them with other teachers in your school to demonstrate assertiveness training.

I. Preparing the Group

You want to wake up everyone—get the whole person involved. We will use breathing, moving, voicing, and expressing. Aside from its intended purpose, this is a wonderfully active way of being together. Everyone in the room, including other teachers, parents, aides, or observers, should participate, with an enthusiasm and energy that is catching.

Begin with each person seated on a firm chair, feet flat on the floor, legs not crossed, back straight.

II. Learning to Say No

A. Breathing

"Everyone breathe through your nose and fill your lungs with as much air as you can hold. Breathe through your mouth. Let your jaws relax into a partly open position. As you exhale, make a continuous voiced sound. Inhale through the nose and exhale through the mouth with the voiced sound as a group for ten minutes or longer."

B. Standing

"Everyone stand up in a circle. Plant your feet firmly on the ground about one or two feet apart. Give yourself a good solid base to stand on: Feel as if you are grabbing the earth with your toes, as though you are a tree, and your toes are your roots. No one can knock you over now. You are 'rooted'."

C. Voicing

"Breathe through your nose, filling your lungs as before. Push the air down inside you to your belly. Now as you breathe out, make a sharp, quick, low-pitched sound, like a vigorous grunt. Keep your mouth open as you bring out this sound." Use positive feedback to encourage everyone. Do it together. Then do it one by one with each client. It does not matter if it is not done perfectly. Cheer everyone on each time. You may be repeating this exercise for weeks, or months, so give them time. Encourage everyone to clap after each client's expression. Everyone enjoys giving support, and everyone enjoys receiving support.

D. Moving

"Remain 'rooted' in the circle. Do the same inhales and exhales as before. This time, punctuate the exhaled sound or grunt with a vigorous downward karate chop with one or both hands. Use the whole arm and shoulders to do this. Do it vigorously and dramatically like in the movies. This chop adds the power of movement to the voiced sound.

"Continue the process by adding a different hand motion: this time, as you inhale, bring your arms up with the fists clenched, and then as you exhale releasing the sound, bring your fist (or fists) down forcefully in a hitting action. You do not actually strike anything."

E. Expressing

"The next process is to transform the grunt into a vigorous statement of no. Bring the no up from the very deepest, lowest part of your belly." At first, you will be going around the circle one by one, giving each participant the chance to make their voiced sound, and their movement individually, as well as following it with the group doing it all together. And you will always be encouraging everyone with lots of positive feedback ("Great, Jim, that was really good. Mary, wonderful! Sally, didn't Sally do a great job? Really good!") and clapping and cheering.

III. Learning to Say Yes

A. Music

Learning to say no and to feel and mean it is far more difficult than learning to say yes. No is a conscious, hard decision. Yes is an affirmation, a rejoicing. To change the mood after the concentrated effort of saying no, put on some lively music (I use a tape of "La Bamba").

B. Moving

"Everyone shake your hands; shake your elbows; shake your shoulders; shake your heads. Dance! Shake out the no tension in your body. As you shake, rejoice with yes!"

C. Expressing

"Say it. Call it out! Yes to you. Yes to me. Yes to moving. Yes to breathing. Yes to being me. Yes to life!"

Now everyone should be livened up, feeling strong and present. The more we get behind our no, the more we support our yes.

IV. Pillow Hitting: Another Exercise for Saying No

Like everyone else, your client or son or daughter may have received a lot of mixed messages and rejection from the world around them. Unlike everyone else, they have far fewer opportunities to express that anger, resentment, or hostility, to say no, instead of okay or yes, as they are so often required to do. This offers a chance for them to express and get rid of that unstated NO!

A. Preparing the Group

The group can sit around in a circle. "Anyone mad? Someone bug you? Anyone angry? Here's how we can get it out."

B. Expressing the No

"Sit down on your knees and put a big pillow in front of you. Take a deep breath in as you rise up on your knees, arms overhead with clenched fists. Then start to bring your fists and arms down along with your shoulders and your back, with the rest of your body coming along. *Exhale* and *vocalize* no as your fists strike the pillow. Repeat it. No, no, no, no! Feel better now? Good!" The participant decides when they are finished and receives expressed appreciation from the group.

C. Parental Warning

Be sure to tell parents that you are teaching this method to their children. It is a good technique for them to use in the privacy of their own rooms to get out frustrations. But it can be frightening to the parents if they do not know what their son or daughter is up to.

YES NO Role Play: Saying No to a Stranger

I. Objectives

A. To introduce the concept of sexual harassment, i.e., unwanted sexual advances.

B. To reinforce the concept of stranger.

C. To develop an awareness of common sexual "come-ons."

D. To develop and teach behaviors for refusing a stranger's sexual advances.

E. To develop an understanding of the dangers of associating with strangers.

F. To increase ability to say no in appropriate circumstances.

G. To reinforce concepts of public and private body parts and places.

II. Preparing the Group

It is recommended that the leader prepare the group for this activity by warming up with some brief activity from the basic yes/no process.

III. Initial Discussion

A. Leader introduces activity by leading a discussion on sexual harassment. There are two approaches: one is to solicit actual past experiences from group members; the other is to pose a hypothetical situation. Suggested openings for discussion are: "Has a stranger ever come up to you and asked you to go for a drive? Has a stranger ever come up to you in a bathroom and tried to touch your private parts?' or, "What if a stranger came up to you and tried to touch your private parts? What if a stranger on the street tried to get you to go into the car with him?"

B. Leader facilitates discussion with the group, using brain-storming techniques: "What are some things you can do if someone tries to touch you, but you don't want them to? What can you do to get away from a stranger who is bothering you?"

C. Leader stresses the point that if a stranger approaches a student, the most important thing to do is to say no loudly and clearly and walk away.

IV. Instigating Role Play

A. Leader and coleader demonstrate the final point—saying no and walking away—in a role play. Leader approaches coleader and invites him or her to go for a drive or offers to show him or her something special. Coleader responds by saying no and walking away.

B. Leader reviews the role play with the class. "What did the stranger do? What did the coleader do? What should you do in the same situation?"

C. Leader and coleader do another role play, to exemplify what could happen if someone fails to assertively say no to a stranger and walk away. Leader repeats the previously demonstrated approach to coleader; this time coleader fails to respond and merely stands in place. Leader's advances become increasingly aggressive until coleader is bodily dragged away.

D. Leader discusses the above role play with the group: "What happened that time? What did I do? What did the coleader do? What do you think happened to the coleader after she or he got dragged away? Why is it so important to walk away from strangers?"

E. Leader and coleader demonstrate role play again and the correct way to reject a stranger's advances.

V. Leading Students in the Role Play

A. Leader asks someone in the class to come up and do a role play.

Leader again plays the part of a stranger, student plays the part of "victim."

B. Leader discusses the role play with the group. If student responded appropriately in the role play, discuss what she or he did right, and then zap her or him with applause. If student responded inappropriately, discuss what he or she could have done better and repeat the role play again. Keep repeating until student succeeds.

C. Role play continues in the manner outlined above. Possible variations are having two students participate in the role play or having students devise a new scenario, still along the theme of sexual harassment.

D. "Sometimes somebody you *know* will try to touch your private parts, and that is not right either. It is only right if you *both* want to, and the place is private and comfortable." This is another possibility for role play.

IV. Including Specific Techniques in Role Play

A. 'If a stranger grabs your wrists, remember that the thumbs are the most vulnerable part. Pull your fists away using the thumb hold [illustration needed]." Demonstrate this. Give each student a chance to grab someone's wrists and watch their grip release, and then be grabbed and break away.

B. It is not the intent of this program to teach self-defense techniques. But we are attempting to create the attitudes of correct defense. Depending on the sophistication of your group, it may be appropriate to invite a self-defense teacher (perhaps someone from the local police department) to speak to, or demonstrate to your group.

Sex Information

Sexual feelings are not learned. They arise in all human beings at one time or another. But resulting sexual behavior is learned. Each society has its own set of rules of acceptable and appropriate behaviors. When sexual behavior is solitary, for instance, masturbation, society teaches that there are acceptable (and unacceptable) times and places for it. When sexual behavior involves another person, there must also be agreement, or permission, with that other person, along with whatever societal conditions may exist.

The how, where, when, and what of sexual behavior are usually taught covertly to most of us. We get mixed messages, conflicting reports, and a lot of misinformation. We sort it out eventually and, since we do not share a lot of information about sex with our friends, we accept what we have and make do. Some of us are lucky and have satisfactory sexual lives. Some are not so lucky and have unsatisfactory sex lives.

Those people, however, who have some physical limitations to their mobility, or emotional limits to their socialization experiences, or intellectual limitations on how to deduce facts from the supply of contradictory information on sex that is publicly available, are handicapped until they do learn what is going on. They can be frightened by their own normal feelings; they can be victimized by other people's inappropriate behavior. Sex education provides the tools for them to make appropriate choices.

All people, not only disabled people, need to understand their own bodies and their parts and to understand what normal growth, both physical and emotional, means. In this way they can interpret their growth changes in adolescence as being normal. Fortunate teenagers will have resources from which to draw accurate information. These include parents, teachers, and friends—even data from the street. Slow learners usually lack a wide diversity of resources, and so it becomes even more important that the information they do receive is accurate and comprehensible.

One young teenager who was a slow learner had just started menstruating. No one had informed her that all women have periods, and she interpreted her monthly bleeding and physical changes as punishment. She buried her soiled underwear, fearful of being found different from other people. If this young woman had had an informed, approachable friend or relative she could have consulted, she could have enjoyed the feelings associated with the knowledge of becoming a woman, an adult like other people she looked up to, and having more in common with the rest of the human race. From a foundation of commonality she (and all of us) can build healthy and enabling self-concepts. We build on what we have in common as well as on our individual uniqueness, and then we get to share experiences of success.

The methods for teaching this material are essentially the same for slow learners as for persons with other disabilities. More repetition is required. Consistent use of simple words is required. Even after something is learned, it must be reviewed and described again months later. The slide curriculum *Sexuality and the Mentally Handicapped*, by Winifred Kempton, is especially valuable. * The *Sexual Exploitation Kit*, by J. Schupack † is also very valuable.

Occasionally when embarrassing moments arise during a sex education class, the group may dissolve into a mass of whoops and hollerings along with much laughter. There is nothing wrong with that. If you remember to use the unconditional appreciation applause activity consistently when people contribute to the group, that applause can refocus the group.

Teaching Environment

Just as the feeling of belonging to a group or family is so valuable for the development of self-esteem, it is also important for a teaching environment. It must be a safe, supportive environment where people can express themselves without feeling judged or compared.

Establishing a one-to-one relationship between leader and participant before they meet with the group can be helpful. The student has an opportunity to feel special in relation to the leader. Voiced breathing, the "feeling good playful question cards," or any other success-oriented activity can build positive feelings of trust. Because the environment must be one of unconditional acceptance and appreciation, the principles of expressing appreciation and affirmations are useful.

Another requisite of the teaching environment is total participation. We have no observers in our group. When visitors come to see what we do, they participate. The group becomes a supportive place for everybody.

The teaching group becomes a time and place to rehearse critical social situations. For example, you can practice how to say hello to someone of the opposite sex, how to ask someone to dance, how to ask someone out on a date. In response, there is a whole group of people that clap and say, "You can do it! You are really good!" If, on the other hand, someone's participation is not appropriate, that becomes a teachable moment. No one puts anyone "on the spot." Instead, you simply repeat what that person said and then ask the group, "What happens when you do that? What are the consequences of that action? Is there *another* way of doing it or saying it?" You then are able to seek a more appropriate response and thus

---

* Kempton, W. *Sexuality and the Mentally Handicapped*. Slide presentations available from James Starfield Film Associates, P.O. Box 1983, Santa Monica, Calif. 90406.

† Schupack, J. *Sexual Exploitation Kit*. Two-level curriculum with slides, available from Comprehensive Health Education Foundation, 20814 Pacific Highway South, Seattle, Wash. 98188.

creatively transform the situation into one that is a learning situation. This attention to self-esteem is a valuable part of the teaching environment.

Parental and Community Support

Since we need to create a safe supportive familylike environment in which to provide education and training, it is logical to enlist the support of parents and the community in this process. I find that when you approach parents with a wholistic view which does not focus so much on sexuality as on the whole person in a society, it is helpful to say, "I am interested in your son or daughter feeling good about themselves, getting to know themselves, becoming more and more independent and appropriate decision makers."

In addition, I present the concepts of enrichment and the concerns about victimization. I describe how we will be teaching their sons and daughters—our clients—ways to know the differences between strangers and friends, public and private touching, and the consequences of going off with a stranger, and how their sons and daughters can protect themselves by saying no and walking away. When the program is presented in this manner, parents gain confidence and then support the program.

Invite the parents to share with you their views concerning potentially controversial issues such as masturbation, dating, marriage, sexual intercourse, birth control, abortion, and sterilization in order for them to know that you want to be aware of their values. This is an opportunity to educate by clarifying misconceptions, myths, and fears, using factual information about bodily functions. *Not* talking about things that are already happening leads to easy victimization by so-called smarter people who *do not* know what is happening. When people recognize a sexually exploitative situation and what to do about it (like say no like you mean it, and walk away), they are better protected and can better prevent problems from developing. If a problem does develop, they can recognize it as a problem and are equipped to talk about it with a responsible adult as well as with their parents.

When you present a sexuality program attuned to the whole person, it is far more acceptable. It has balance to it. I think that many people become upset about a sexuality program if it only addresses the genitals and sexual acts. When it is brought into the perspective of other aspects of living, such as the privileges and responsibilities of adulthood, it then becomes a program that parents and communities want.

Repetition of Correct Answers

When you as teacher ask a comprehension question and the student does not know the answer, you should give the correct answer and then repeat the process if necessary. "Jane, are you a male or a female?" You are teaching the concepts of sex difference, and teaching the words *male* and *female*. Jane does not understand, or does not know the answer. "You are a female. Now tell me, Jane, are you a male or a female?" "Female." "Very good, Jane. You are a female." Of course this will be repeated many more times during the next days, or even months. But remember, this is not a test with right or wrong answers. This is teaching, to people who are slow at learning and who require a lot of repetition. And do not forget to reinforce correct responses right then and there: "Jane got that right! Jane knows that she is a female. That was very well done, Jane!"

Slow learners need lots of varied, simple repetitions, but without the process becoming boring. This requires some creativity on the part of the teacher. Concepts to be repeated can be emphasized at different times and opportunities during each day. Varying the pace of the lesson between high energy participatory activities and low key, less active times gets the messages across.

Appropriate Behavior

Slow learners need to know what normal behavior is, just as they need to have a safe place with trusted people around where they can rehearse these activities. Video feedback is extraordinarily valuable for people as it allows them to see how they appear to others and learn how they can improve their behavior, including their body language, dress, and communication skills. As they begin to *appear* more appropriate, they act and feel more appropriate.

Slow learners need to recognize which behaviors are considered inappropriate, without themselves being identified as inappropriate people. In class one day, I told my group, "I was in a Mexican restaurant last week and a family came into the restaurant and sat down at a table. All of a sudden everybody in the restaurant began to stare at the boy who was with the family. Do you know why they were staring at him?" My group guessed it. "Because he was so loud. He was speaking very loudly in the restaurant. And you're not supposed to speak so loudly in a restaurant."

A similar situation involved a 26-year-old student. Whenever he would get happy or excited he would clap his hands and rock back and forth (standing) in a posture of someone who was bowing repeatedly. We pointed this out to him and made suggestions for alternative behavior, and he had the chance to see his own behavior on the TV set. Several months later, he went out on his first date, and he came up to me afterwards, very pleased with himself. He told me about the date, and how he did not "act weird," and sat up straight and tall, and what a good time he had. Children and teenagers (and even some adults), whether disabled or not, are very aware of behavior, and whether or not it is "weird" or "funny" or just inappropriate for their peer group. What the slow learner often lacks is the ability or opportunity to observe in him- or herself the same "weirdness." The teacher or group leader can provide this feedback, especially using video. It is like the commercial advertisement for a mouthwash that says that even your best friend will not tell you. If your best friend will not tell you, how can you ever learn? If the best friend here is a trusted teacher in this safe environment, the student usually responds appreciatively to the information.

Just as a self-esteem program for adolescents must point out how normal we all are, how everyone goes through puberty with all its complex and confusing changes, a socialization program must identify what behavior is not appropriate, and what is appropriate.

Generalizations

Slow learners, or mentally retarded persons, are usually not good at generalizing concepts. Teaching by analogy is not usually effective. It is not a good idea to assume that because something has been explained and taught in one setting, it will be remembered and performed appropriately in another setting. For example, we use role playing quite often in teaching. One situation we practice a great deal is saying no to a stranger. "What do you say when a stranger offers you a ride in his car? You say no and walk away. What do you say when a stranger approaches you on the sidewalk and says, 'Come with me into the alley.' You say no and walk away." This may sound good in class but must be tested outside.

On one of our field trips to a museum we brought along our portable video unit. We asked a passerby at the museum to approach several female students individually and ask them to go for a ride with him in his car.

The first young women he approached said no appropriately and walked away. The second one though about it for a moment and then accepted his offer. And the third accepted right away and walked off with him. We learned that those last two students were not ready to go out on their own, and we told their parents so. Later, back in the classroom, we found it valuable to have the videotapes of that encounter to show to the students.

Public and Private

The most dramatically inappropriate types of behavior are usually those that suggest sexual activity. This includes sexual activity with oneself, such as masturbation, or with another, including the entire spectrum of public exposure from touching another to having sexual intercourse. The most valuable teaching guide for defining appropriate behavior is the understanding of public and private places, and public and private parts of the body.

A private place is where no one can see you. A public place is were there are other people around. The private parts of the body are those parts that we keep covered with our underwear. The public parts of the body are those parts that are exposed. Private parts of the body may be touched when we are in private places. We do not touch private parts when we are in public. Public parts of the body may be touched when we are in public. With this simple system it is possible to deal with a whole host of problems and situations that commonly arise with slow learners.

When teaching this concept to your group or client, keep the rules simple: private parts of the body are for private places; public parts of the body are for public places.

If someone is touching or exposing a private part of their body, simply remind them, "That's a private part of your body and this is a public place where people can see you. Private touching is for a private place where nobody can see you." This means that a private place must be available so that appropriate touching behavior is possible.

Remember that privacy has been a problem for most people growing up, whether disabled (intellectually or physically) or not. With the door closed, the bathroom or the bedroom (even under the covers) is usually available and appropriate for touching oneself. Institutions with public restrooms and dormitories may need to have doors installed in order to create a private space.

Attitudes to Develop

This paper has discussed in detail ways to encourage self-esteem and to give sexual information to the slow learner. One more point must be made.

A part of modeling attitudes is changing the way that we direct our communication to people with labels. If we use small words and "talk down," we reinforce that lower position. When we use a big word followed by a small word that clarifies it, there is a sense of talking friend to friend, rather than from high to low (and we teach new vocabulary at the same time). This concept also applies to the names we call our clients. Baby names are often inappropriate when we attempting to prepare people for adulthood. To refer to a 55-year-old man who may be mentally retarded as "Johnny" usually reflects the fact that his teachers or attendants think of him as a child and treat him accordingly.

I believe that no one is higher or lower than anybody else; we all have our lessons to learn and we are learning them all the time. Some of us are learning to walk, some of us are learning appropriate interactions in public, some of us are learning to deal with fear, some of us are learning how to get along with our in-laws. Let us hope that, as professionals, we go beyond the label, beyond the attitudes of limitation that we project on the people labeled developmentally disabled and mentally retarded.

To get beyond those attitudes, it seems to me that we are all responsible for finding out who we really are; and who our clients really are. The closer we come to knowing who we are, the more we are able to connect to that inner self in the person with whom we are communicating. And *that* is the part, that is the *able* part, where the miracles can happen. If we are attached to the role of "professional," we are also attached to the role of keeping the "helpless" helpless, encouraging the counterpart of that identity, the helpless one, to be manifested in our clients in response to us so that we will continue to be needed. But if we come from that part within us that really cares (but without the roles attached that have expectations), we can awaken that inner being in our clients and enhance that part in them. When we are being true to ourselves, we have a more direct experience of the person with whom we are connecting.

Inside every one of us is a wise person. If we did not believe that, we could not be in the learning and teaching professions. Inside every one of our clients is a wise person that we can reach, but only from that wise person within us. Tremendous expansion can take place within individuals and within the educational system if we all take responsibility for finding out who we are. I think that this is the basis of what must be looked at, especially in special education where we are dealing with people who have been limited and defined by labels. This extends to the entire world because we are all labeled and disabled in some way; the so-called retarded community is really a microcosm of the rest of the world. We all need more and more experiences of feeling good about ourselves. We all need to know it is okay to feel good about ourselves.

So many of us have been programmed to believe that if we compliment ourselves, if we nourish ourselves, something bad will happen. It is like inviting the evil eye. The opposite is true. It is okay to feel good about yourself. In fact, that is the only way that you will be able to guide the people you work with to feel good about themselves. It is okay to say "I like myself, I am okay."

Learn compassion with yourself, patience with yourself, so that you can love yourself. There is no chance that you can really love somebody else unless you love yourself. Often, a major shock to children when they enter school is the realization that their teacher does not love them. When I myself realized that, I never, ever, wanted to go back to school. I wanted to stay with my mother because she loved me. It is time now that we bring love into the educational system. It is not anti-intellectual to bring love, a sense of deep caring, into the classroom.

Disability and Intimacy:
The Importance of Sexual Health

Sandra S. Cole and
Theodore M. Cole

What emotional feeling do you experience when you think of the word *sex*?

What emotional feelings do you experience when you think of the words *disabled, crippled, gimp*?

What emotional experiences do you have when you combine these two concepts in your fantasies? Do the concepts of sex, sexuality, and intimacy become any less acceptable? Is there a paradox here?

Sex is a natural function. All people are sexual: the young and the old, the able-bodied and the disabled, men and women. Therefore, sexuality in the presence of disability is a central concern in the quality of life for individuals with disabilities. The presence of a physical disability, of course, may produce a physical loss of a sexual function, for example, genital sensation, orgasm, or ejaculation. However, genital sexual function may not be the largest part of an individual's sexual health and well-being. If the health professional is not prepared for the pervasiveness of sexual health or the subtle differences of how some disabilities can affect sexual health, the patient or client may not receive needed help (Green, 1975).

We attempt to socialize all people to recognize the normative values and behaviors of our culture. Families give their children an understanding of family values and the positive and negative principles upon which the family operates. Certainly, family values would arise around the concept of "imperfection" (Robinault, 1978). If an individual is perceived to be imperfect because of crippled or amputated body parts, inappropriate social gestures (arm flailing, irregular spastic movements, drooling, or grimacing), use of mobility apparatus (wheelchairs), or impaired speech, the cultural reaction is often repulsion. The result is that the individual is frequently regarded as asexual.

Sexual health is important to everyone. Concerns regarding appearance, grooming, hygiene, attractiveness and desirability are apparent in our daily behavior. These features are a large part of our personhood and our sexual socialization as mature men and women (Gordon, Scales, and Everly, 1979).

Awareness of one's own attitudes toward body image is necessary if one is to be sensitive about the so-called imperfections of such conspicuous disabilities as cerebral palsy, spinal cord injury, or multiple sclerosis. Sensitivity will not only increase one's awareness of the social values attached to disability but will also help one avoid contributing negativism to an already stressful situation (Comfort, 1978). The disenfranchisement experienced by one who is perceived as imperfect may result in social rejection and thus add a disabling stigma to an existing physical disability.

Another important issue relating sexual health to disability is the attitude of the disabled person regarding his or her own sexuality. This attitude will, of course, be a function of early sexual knowledge and experiences, especially if the disability had its onset before sex role development began. Since self-esteem and body image are important issues for able-bodied persons, they certainly will have a significant impact on how a disabled person sees him or herself as a sexual being. Will the disabled person be able to relate to others as a sexual person, desirous of and desired for intimate relationships? The presence of a disability will thus influence one's sense of masculinity or femininity, not only through the physical changes resulting from a disability, but also by influencing opportunities to have relationships with other desirable men and women.

The following are some of the issues which affect the self-esteem of a handicapped person. They should be addressed in the context of family life and environment of the individual.

What is the family like? What are the community expectations? What role did the individual have in the family, community, and in the geographical or regional culture?

Does the person view him or herself as attractive?

Did the person's role in the family, work place or community require an ability to influence or advise other people? Has the ability been jeopardized or limited?

Any lessening, or perceived lessening, of an individual's ability to contribute to society can be illuminated by assessing the individual's response to the disability. Self-esteem is always most vulnerable during illness, disease, or injury (Kaplan, 1974). Recognition of differences which could be regarded as imperfect or unacceptable can create a double-bind situation (Heiman, see this volume). These negative images affect self-esteem and contribute to disablement. Images which might further disable must be reconciled in order for disabled people to believe in positive ways about their potential opportunities in an able-bodied world.

The silent cost to personal dignity can be recognized and avoided if we reduce the negative bias or prejudice in our attitudes toward imperfection. It is important for the professional person working with disabled individuals and their families to recognize the tremendous emotional stress often felt as a result of a disability. Children born with a physical disability relate to the world as a different person from the moment of birth and cannot have the same set of emotional stresses which "normal" children experience (Calderone and Johnson, 1981). With the birth of the disabled child, the family experiences an "acquired" disability intruding on the intact family system. Furthermore, when an individual experiences an acquired disability, the disabled person and the family members simultaneously react and adjust to the disability. A kaleidoscope of human emotions may be experienced by all members in the family system. Such emotions include grief, sadness (death and dying emotions), denial, anger, guilt, frustration, rage, fear, anguish, confusion, hate, shame. Most individuals struggling to understand the event or to deal with loss are trying to redefine the present with some sort of realistic awareness (Bishop, 1980). There is no order in which a person necessarily experiences the gamut of emotional feelings, nor is there any particular time in the period of rehabilitation when these things occurs. It is extremely important to be able to know what is happening to the individual and the family as a result of the disability so that appropriate actions can be taken regarding sexuality and any aspect of rehabilitation and health care.

In assessing the implication of sexual health in a disabled individual, a physical examination is usually necessary to anticipate the specific physical dysfunction. It is important to know the neuromuscular dysfunctions associated with the disability so that specific loss of sexual function can be anticipated, evaluated, and integrated into the rehabilitation plan. For example, if there is a physical loss of sensation, we must assess whether or not sensation of the genitals has been affected, for if so, an alteration of the sexual function of the individual would be expected. Clearly, limitations in mobility or movement would indicate limitations of ability to physically participate in sexual activity, whether through masturbation or coitus (Kolodny, Masters, and Johnson, 1979).

When we assess loss of physical function, we must also make psychological and spiritual assessments. It is important to understand the individual's sense of self-esteem and relationship to the world in order to understand what role the disability will play in that person's own concerns—how the disability will ultimately affect self-esteem.

Next, we must consider at what point in maturation the disability is being experienced. There are several ways to classify a disability in order to anticipate how it affects sexual health. Generally, physical disabilities fall into a few categories. First, the disability may be defined as either congenital (birth or early life event) or acquired. Second, it is necessary to know whether the disability is acquired either before or after sexual maturity. A third category of determination is whether or not the disability is stable or progressive (Cole, 1981). Each of these classification categories has implications throughout the life-span and should be considered in relation to the specific sexual dysfunction.

As mentioned earlier, assessing the person, the disabilities, and the family is critical. Defining future problems enables affected individuals to gain the necessary coping skills to maintain their independence and to enrich the quality of their lives.

If the disabled person is also required to use equipment or apparatus for mobility or body functions (braces, crutches, wheelchairs, catheters, urine collection bags, prostheses, and so on), the apparatus must also be integrated carefully into the individual's current life. Will the apparatus add concerns of conspicuousness to the individual? If so, what are his or her abilities to "rise above it all"? What were the communication strengths of the person prior to the disability? We may be able to capitalize on the existing strengths and skills in problem solving, communication, and self-esteem in order to help a person understand a catastrophic situation or the concomitants of a disease (Cole, 1981).

Another essential component in the assessment of sexual function of an acquired disability is information about sexual experiences and knowledge prior to the disability. What sex education did the person have? How knowledgeable is he or she about sexual functions? What early sexual experiences occurred? Is there any evidence of early childhood sexual trauma or abuse? A comprehensive assessment such as this would be part of a general sex history (Munjack and Oziel, 1980).

Childhood Onset Disability

Persons whose disabilities began during their childhoods often become isolated from peers during the crucial years of sexual development. During childhood most people gain social skills through informal contacts with friends (Robinault, 1978). For example, language develops in the early years. An important part of the acquisition of language includes developing the language of sex. Disabled children may have limited opportunities to do such normal things as practice "sex talk" with friends, use grandiose and sensational terms, use sex words (whether or not the definition is known), participate in "show-and-tell" or "peek," and learn the natural body differences between self and others (male or female) (Blum and Blum, 1977). Remember that, by the age of 6, children have already learned that disability means imperfect and society views imperfection as asexual.

However, major concerns for all children in these critical developmental stages of maturation include such questions as: "Will I be able to have relationships?"; "Do I feel good about my body? My own genitals?"; "Will I be pleasing to someone else"; and perhaps the scariest question of greatest concern, "Would someone else want me?" (Hopper and Allen, 1980).

Sometimes peers or exploitative situations demand sexual expression or activity from the disabled child without the child's full understanding of vulnerability. The child may simply lack information, exposure, and decision-making skills. These occasions can happen with peers or adults who either tease them or respond to them sexually, assuming "real" sexual experiences will never happen. A child who is medically institutionalized during these early years will likely develop warped views of the world and how men and women actually relate. Much information about sexual values and behaviors is gained through the media without an opportunity to test and validate this information against real life experiences. The disabled child may become victimized by not having "normal" experiences to test this information with other people. The child may begin to feel and behave like a victim. He or she simply will not have the tools to measure life experiences. One of the most important lessons a disabled child can learn is the difference between appropriate and inappropriate touching behavior and the difference between public and private places for sexual expression. Sexual expression includes pleasurable touching of one's own genitals and learning the appropriate social touching of other people. A child with a disability may not be chronologically as mature as the same age peer. Therefore, the social, psychological, and environmental backdrop within which maturation occurs should be assessed, as should be the extent of knowledge the child has acquired about sexuality, from family, peers, and other sources (Gagnon, see this volume).

Several years ago, Havinghurst compared (Robinault, 1978) the concepts of disabled and able-bodied adolescents of preparation for marriage and family. The desires of both groups were the same. All of these young adults saw themselves as diligently preparing for adulthood with similar expectations. The disabled adolescents did not appear to have self-imposed limitations on this potential, suggesting that the limited potential is imposed from without.

Adult Onset Disability

If a physical disability is acquired after psychosexual maturity has been achieved, other implications for sexual health and function should be considered. The individual nature of the person's sexuality has already been established. If the physical disability is acquired after puberty, then a sexual preference toward heterosexuality or homosexuality may already have been established. Perhaps the individual has already experienced an intimate relationship with its rich rewards. Certainly, the individual has a highly developed awareness of self and, through experience, probably has an awareness of his or her genitals and preferences of sexual expression. When a physically disabling event occurs which interrupts "natural sexual function," one might understandably be reluctant to admit ignorance about sexual functioning or anxiety about body image and self-esteem (Trieschmann, 1980). Equally as important is the fact that disabled persons reveal that one of their greatest fears is that of being abandoned by people whom they love.

Several therapeutic principals should guide the helping professionals to become involved and to regard the disabled person in a positive way (Gordon, 1975). Be "askable" and create an environment wherein there is permission to discuss private and intimate subjects. Carry a low burden of guilt for another's situation and be able to pace questions and conversations appropriately. Disabled persons are not fragile, nor do they need to be protected from the real world. Training in social skills may help the disabled individual to be more independent.

In considering sexual activity we must realize the moral and spiritual values of the individual in relationship to the physical, sexual limitations. It is helpful to look at changes in behavior as goals or new ways of doing things rather than as compensating behavior. There are enough negative implications in being disabled without adding to the list. When we value and respect ourselves as individuals, our self-esteem is the highest. When our whole existence is negatively reinforced by society (Heiman, see this volume), our self-esteem is lowest. If we do not value ourselves, it is fair to assume that others will not value us and will continue to reinforce our own negative message to ourselves. As professionals we can also inadvertently reinforce negative self-image by being silent on the subject of intimacy and sexuality.

The P-LI-SS-IT system developed by Annon (1976), is helpful in organizing professional assessment techniques. This schema helps many professionals work sensitively with the sexuality without becoming more involved than their training allows. The first level of the PLISSIT model (P) encourages professionals to provide an environment of permission within which the subject of sexuality can be discussed in a nonjudgmental way. This helps to create an ambience of trust and confidence in working with private information. The second level will enable the practitioners to discuss sexuality and sex function and to provide limited information (LI) where there is misinformation, myth, or ignorance. Here, the chief function of the clinician is patient/client education. Information and validation alone will go a long way to assist someone to make physical adjustments. What are people really asking when they "bring up the subject of sex"? Perhaps they are really asking for validation and recognition of their concerns regarding sexuality and disability. Specific suggestion (SS) the third level of the PLISSIT system, implies (requires) that the professional has the ability to take a sex history and to provide sexual counseling designed to help the disabled individual and partner or family member work through personal and intimate concerns. The fourth level, intensive therapy (IT) requires deliberate therapeutic interaction with the patient/client. Advanced clinical therapy skills are necessary for the professional to work toward correcting the problem or dysfunction through specific retraining or therapy. Certainly not everyone, and perhaps only a very few individuals, needs such intense levels of therapy to solve or sort out their problems. If sex, sexuality, and disability can be viewed as natural health issues, most practitioners would probably be able to function quite comfortably at Levels 1 and 2 and occasionally find it necessary to move in and out of Level 3.

These guidelines may be useful in working with people's sexual concerns. If tactile feelings and sensations are absent, it does not mean that personal feelings have disappeared or have been discarded. If bowels or bladder have become dysfunctional and perhaps incontinent, it does not mean genitals cannot be used for sexual expression and intimate enjoyment. A functional relationship does not depend on genital function exclusively. Giving pleasure to experience pleasure is not restricted to one's physical ability to move. Desire does *not* stop when a disability occurs. Sexuality is not lost or forgotten if genitals are absent. Physical disability is not synonymous with sexual inadequacy and sexual enjoyment is not exclusively linked to functional movement. Feeling good about oneself is a health opportunity for all persons to enhance the quality of life and the celebration of living (Cole and Cole, 1976).

References

Annon, J. S. *Behavioral treatment of sexual problems.* Hagerstown, Md.: Harper and Row, 1976.
Bishop, D. S. (Ed.). *Behavioral problems and the disabled: Assessment management.* Baltimore: Waverly Press, 1980.
Blum, G. J., and Blum, B. *Feeling good about yourself.* San Rafael, Calif.: American Therapy Publications, 1977.
Calderone, M. S., and Johnson, E. W. *The family book about sexuality.* New York: Harper and Row, 1981.
Cole, S. S. Disability/ability: The importance of sexual health in adolescence: Issues and concerns of the professional. *Sex Information and Education Council of the U.S. Report,* May-July 1981, *9,* 1-2; 4.
Cole, T. M., and Cole, S. S. The handicapped and sexual health. *Sex Information and Education Council of the U.S. Report,* May 1976, *4,* 1-2; 9-10.
Comfort, A. (Ed.). *Sexual consequences of disability.* Philadelphia: George F. Stickley, 1978.
Gagnon, J. H. *On the sources of sexual change.* Chapter in this volume.
Gordon, S. *Living fully: A guide for young people with a handicap, their parents, their teachers, and professionals.* Toronto: Fitzhenry and Whiteside, 1975.
Gordon, S., Scales, P., and Everly, K. *The sexual adolescent: Communicating with teenagers about sex* (2nd ed.). North Scituate, Mass.: Duxbury Press, 1979.

Green, R. (Ed.). *Human sexuality: A health practitioner's text.* Baltimore: Waverly Press, 1975.

Heiman, J. R. *Women and sexuality: Loosening the double binds.* Chapter in this volume.

Hopper, C. E., and Allen, W. A. *Sex education for physically handicapped youth.* Springfield, Mass.: Charles C. Thomas, 1980.

Kaplan, H. S. *The new sex therapy: Active treatment of sexual dysfunctions.* New York: Times Books, 1974.

Kolodny, R. C., Masters, W. H., and Johnson, V. E. *Textbook of sexual medicine.* Boston: Little, Brown, 1979.

Munjack, D. J., and Oziel, L. J. *Sexual medicine and counseling in office practice.* Boston: Little, Brown, 1980.

Robinault, I. P. *Sex, society, and the disabled: A developmental inquiry into roles, reactions, and responsibilities.* Hagerstown, Md.: Harper and Row, 1978.

Trieschmann, R. B. *Spinal cord injuries: Psychological, social, and vocational adjustment.* New York: Pergamon Press, 1980.

Sexual Rehabilitation of the Cardiac Patient

Sharon B. Satterfield

Approximately once every generation a prominent American male dies of a heart attack, allegedly in the arms of a younger woman who is not his wife. Perhaps this has something to do with the universal fear of sudden death that occurs in patients following a heart attack. Perhaps as some patients report, it is the fear of losing control while having an orgasm. Perhaps it is fear or guilt of a spouse who fears that being sexual will result in another heart attack. For whatever reason, many Americans believe that sexuality, particularly sexual relationships involving orgasm are more likely to lead to sudden death than other forms of exercise. Although research done by Hellerstein and Friedman in the 1960s of men wearing cardiac-monitoring devices 24 hours a day did not bear this out, the fear has persisted, even among physicians (Hellerstein and Friedman, 1970). It is not uncommon for physicians to fear sexual activity on the part of their patients and without understanding the dynamics they warn patients to avoid foreplay or, in a case of erectile dysfunction following a heart attack, they tell patients, "Well, you did have a very serious heart attack. This is probably going to be permanent."

Although Hellerstein and Friedman reported that sexual activity is not likely to produce sudden death, they warned that extramarital sex can be fatal. This has become a common belief among physicians and was based upon a Japanese study of coroners' reports in which the instances of coital death were very low but most of the coital deaths reported were from geisha houses (Ueno, 1963). We forget that in going through coroners' reports we are only reading the cause of death as it is reported, not necessarily the circumstances under which it occurred. Although in the last 20 years we have become more sophisticated and concerned about coital activity among postmyocardial infarction (M.I.) patients, we still do not understand why so few people die during this period. Masters and Johnson documented up to a threefold increase in heart rate during orgasm, but Hellerstein found that the average increase in heart rate is only 117 beats per minute, and that this increase occurred several times a day in the convalescent patient.

Several studies have demonstrated that though patients are told that they can resume sexual activity, they do not do so immediately, and that approximately 50 percent report that sex is worse than it was before the heart attack (Olwen, 1974; Tuttle, Cook, and Fitch, 1964). A complicating factor is that drugs given to the cardiac patient often cause sexual problems in and of themselves, particularly the antihypertensive and beta-blocking agents. Another problem is that in cardiac rehabilitation programs patients are taught to measure the amount of exercise by metabolic equivalents that are expended during that particular exercise. Although patients are told that if they can walk up a flight or two of stairs, they can probably resume sexual activity, this is a very rough estimate and based upon empirical observation. The actual fact is that most of the physiological changes having to do with sexual activity occur for a few seconds at the time of orgasm and cannot be measured in the same way as sustained activity (Bartlett, 1956; Hellerstein and Friedman, 1969).

In working with rehabilitation personnel, the 6 C's of counseling the cardiac patient have been shown to be important for the professional team working with these patients. The first is concern: the awareness that sexuality is important in the life of a cardiac patient and also the awareness of anxiety, fears, and guilt that people have in discussing sexuality. The second is comfort, which is not only the ability to accept one's own sexuality and to recognize that in others, but to have the ability to talk about sexuality without embarrassment or judgment. The third is communication, which includes developing a language with which to communicate, developing communication skills, and the putting of information into the context of a patient's life. The fourth is curriculum, which means that we do have a discrete body of knowledge about the physiological response of the cardiac patient and that it is our duty to provide information including the do's as well as the don'ts about sexual activity. We recommend that written instructions be given to the patient to take home. The fifth is counseling, which is recommended following the PLISSIT model of Jack Annon (1976). This involves P: giving permission; LI: providing limited information; SS: specific suggestions; IT: the need for intensive therapy in only a few cases if the other steps are provided first. One of the major problems for cardiac patients before rehabilitation programs were started was the sixth C, or continuity, which meant in many cases the patient had a different doctor upon going home, or that someone would forget to include on following visits to ask about sexual behavior or to tell a patient when he or she could resume sexual behavior. Patients should also be given a number to call when questions arise because it is often later in the privacy of the home that they begin dealing with these problems.

Sexual Activity Following Uncomplicated M.I.

There are a very few absolute contraindications to resuming sexual activity. It has been demonstrated frequently to the patient that it is the physician's lack of knowledge or fears that inhibits their sexual behavior. An example is Mr. H., a 45-year-old man, who was admitted to a psychiatric unit for severe depression. He had had an M.I. about 3 months previously, during which time he had a cardiac arrest. He was resuscitated but was left with organic brain syndrome which meant he was unable to return to his usual work. During the history-taking process in the hospital, it was learned that Mr. H. was as concerned about his lack of erectile functioning as he was about returning to work. He and his wife both related that the cardiologist taking care of him had told him that this would probably be a permanent problem and was due to his heart attack. As it turned out in the course of therapy for his depression, some attention was devoted to sexual functioning and within approximately 2 weeks, he was having erections which enabled him to resume intercourse with his wife.

Many physicians feel that there are contraindications for sexual activity, such as the presence of arrhythmias, the presence of hypertension, or simply the fear that patients need to remain inactive for a prolonged period of time. Cardiac physiologists who have actually worked with these patients recommend that after an uncomplicated M.I. the patients can usually resume sexual activity to orgasm within 2 weeks. Since many physicians feel this is much too soon, it is recommended that the patient return gradually to their usual patterns of sexual functioning within 4 to 6 weeks of the infarction. It is unclear whether masturbation requires more energy expenditure than intercourse and obviously this varies from patient to patient. Another relative contraindication for sexual activity is the presence of acute congestive heart failure. Patients who have chronic problems with congestive heart failure should be individually counseled as to what sexual activity is possible for them. Patients and some medical personnel feel that arrhythmias are the biggest concern in the involvement of sexual activity. Most patients learn what irregularities are dangerous or which ones are chronically present. They should be specifically told in which cases an irregular heart rate is a contraindication for sexual activity and also which sexual activity is still possible.

Most patients have been told about physical exercise and have been warned about danger signals. They are usually warned to stop physical activity if the following symptoms occur: heaviness, tightness or pain in the chest, neck, arms or jaws, shortness of breath, severe exhaustion, nausea, vomiting, unusual weaknesses, some forms of irregular heart rate, dizziness, or fainting spells. Patients should be told very specifically that the presence of angina does not preclude sexual activity more than any other activity and should be told about taking medication during sexual activity as well as other physical exertion.

If one were to make a list of the things that should not be done during sexual activity, one might come up with the common laundry list of things to avoid in all forms of physical activity: fatigue, heavy eating, extreme temperature change, alcohol consumption, emotional strain and, as some people believe, isometric muscle activity. When one looks at this list, it begins to look like the factors present in a typical romantic evening, particularly when one goes out to eat, has wine, may or may not have emotional strain in relationships, and then uses the so-called missionary position which maximizes isometric muscle activity. Therefore, patients should be taught adaptations which will not interfere with their enjoyment of sex but will make them more comfortable and possibly will protect them from harmful sequelae.

There are several sexual adaptations that can be recommended for the cardiac patient. One of the first is that the patient should realize that he or she needs to communicate freely with his or her partner. Many people have developed sexual habits at a much younger age when there are more restrictions such as children in the house. When chronic illness or disability is present, people need to learn to communicate their needs and desires in a more direct way than they may have been doing previously. Many patients with disabilities report that with a small amount of sexual counseling, their lives are much more fulfilled than previously. It is also important to eliminate relationship issues. There may be guilt on the part of the partner or there may be a change in the roles when the patient returns home. Any illness usually puts some stress on a relationship. One adaptation that works very well for patients is to make sexual activity intermittent and possibly to include more variety. People need to realize that just as in walking or in other physical activity, they can stop and rest. The patient may wish to change positions of intercourse even though it is questionable whether this has an effect on the workload.

An important adaptation is to have the patient change the time of the day when sexual activity occurs. This is particularly useful to the person convalescing before returning to work and in minimizing the effect of fatigue: early in the morning or following a nap might be ideal. For the patient suffering from angina, it is necessary to remind him or her to have medication ready.

Counseling the Cardiac Patient

While the patient is in the hospital a brief sex history should be taken. In a recent survey of 45 patients, only two reported that this had been done (Satterfield, 1981). The main reason for doing this is that patients have said that sexuality is one of their major concerns after a heart attack. It also serves to give the patient permission to talk about sex and to realize that health professionals feel that this is important. Also, in the hospital, patients should be given a certain amount of information about not only their heart but about their sexual response, and how this is likely to be affected by their M.I. They should be told specificaly what is an optimistic picture for them in the future from the knowledge that we have available. They should also be warned if there are specific prohibitions such as not to have orgasms. Many male patients report masturbating while in the hospital "just to see if it works."

A specific activity which is very useful to patients in the hospital is that of providing a nurturing touch experience. The daily back massage given in some hospitals has a positive effect on patients. One man noted that it was the one thing that "kept me in touch." It is also important for future sexual functioning for the patient to be comfortable with affectionate touch. This is where the family can be part of the therapeutic team. It may make them more comfortable when they are in a setting where they often feel in the way. They are instructed to give specific nonerotic affectionate touch while the patient is in the coronary care unit. This is also a time when many people can practice receiving pleasure or being taken care of instead of always being the person who takes care of others. This is one of the basic tenets of sex therapy and is also important for a patient who may have been very active and may be suffering from a role reversal within the family.

Upon discharge from the hospital, all patients should receive a review of what they have been told previously since many of them report that they were very frightened or confused and cannot remember specifically what was said. It is important to inquire about feelings of masculinity and femininity, the changes in roles that may occur upon returning home, and their specific expectations for sex. They then can be told how long they should go without an orgasm and how long they should go without intercourse. At this point, the sensate focus exercises commonly used in sex therapy can be recommended, specifically nongenital pleasuring with the partner. These simple suggestions can overcome a great number of fears that patients had upon returning home. For instance, Mr. C., a 33-year-old man suffered a massive M.I. He and his wife were both extremely frightened by this and received little information about how they should resume their lives upon returning home. When Mr. C returned for a cardiac club meeting, he was asked about sexual activity. He reported that he and his wife were so afraid of any sexual response that they were afraid to sleep in the same bed together because they might brush against each other in the night, and he might become aroused. This fear can be quite debilitating and can interfere with a marital relationship.

It is also important to inquire about sexual activity on follow-up visits to the physician or rehabilitation team. This is where, in the past, continuity with the patient was often lost. At that time, one should ask about spontaneous erections, assess the amount of depression that the patient is feeling, and assess the willingness for adaptations of sexual activities. It is also important to reinforce the knowledge already given the patient and to review the prohibitions. At this time, it is likely that the patient can gradually return to normal sexual functioning. It is recommended that nondemand pleasuring exercises, including genital touching, can be resumed. This is similar to the protocol used by sex therapists in overcoming anxiety about sexual activity. The patient should be told that nondemand vaginal containment is an option that can be practiced before actually having intercourse. The next stage which is very important in the rehabilitation of sexual activity is to assess at about 3 months whether any changes have occurred, whether any drugs are having any negative effects, whether the patient's depression has lifted, if family relationships are stable, and if sexual functioning is back to the previous level. This is the time at which to assess very critically the sexual functioning, and if the patient is still having problems, it might be wise to recommend a sex therapist.

Most sexual rehabilitation has been aimed at the male patient. This occurs for several reasons. More males suffer from M.I. than females; also, male erectile dysfunction is a more obvious handicap than the lack of arousal on the part of the woman. It serves as more of a handicap in sexual functioning. Another problem of female patients surveyed is that many reported the unavailability of a partner. More attention obviously needs to be focused upon the sexual habits and needs of the female patient.

In summary, most patients who have suffered an M.I. are able to resume sexual functioning if properly counseled. As health professionals, we have underestimated their concerns for intimacy and for being sexual. This may require extra effort for the treatment team, such as taking a sex history or adjusting doses of drugs provided to the patient. Sexual rehabilitation can be easily incorporated into a cardiac rehabilitation program.

References

Annon, J. S. Behavioral treatment of sexual problems: Brief therapy. Hagerstown, Md.: Harper and Row, 1976.

Bartlett, R. G., Jr. Physiologic responses during coitus. Journal of Applied Physiology, 1956, 15, 469.

Hellerstein, H. K., and Friedman, E. H. Sexual activity and the post-coronary patient. Medical Aspects of Human Sexuality, 1969, 3, 70-96.

Hellerstein, H. K., and Friedman, E. H. Sexual activity and the postcoronary patient. Archives of Internal Medicine, 1970, 125, 987-999.

Olwen, J. F. Clinical sexuality for the physician and the professions (3rd ed.). Philadelphia: J. B. Lippincott, 1974.

Satterfield, S. B. Sexual rehabilitation of the cardiac patient. Presented at 5th World Congress of Sexology, Jerusalem, 1981.

Tuttle, W. B., Cook, W. L., and Fitch, E. Sexual behavior in post-myocardial infarction patients. American Journal of Cardiology, 1964, 13, 140.

Ueno, M. The so-called coition death. Japanese Journal of Legal Medicine, 1963, 17, 535.

PART IV

The Arguments for Sex Education as an Approach to Sane and Mature Sexuality

Introductory Notes

In the original plans for the conference on preventing sexual problems and fostering mature sexuality we carefully identified a number of topical areas we regarded as important and then selected experts whose daily work, clinical experience, and research activities had led us to believe that they would fit within our predetermined categories. The results of our planning produced some exceptionally interesting and stimulating papers, but their content did not conform neatly to our original scheme. Indeed, the reader will discover that a large number of the papers, in whole or in large part, deal with the important issue of sex education. We should not have been surprised, because one of the most obvious characteristics of our culture is the poor and haphazard quality of sex education of the young. Although most sex educators believe that the parents are the logical and appropriate persons to teach their children about human sexuality, parental anxiety, the lack of accurate knowledge, misinformation, and emotional discomfort around this subject often seriously impede this otherwise desirable process.

Sex education in the American schools is largely absent, and the little that does exist often is inappropriate or irrelevant. Yet our children grow up in environments that are saturated with sexuality. The mass media and the peer culture are major sources of information and misinformation, but our children also learn much from our own avoidance, anxiety, and obvious discomfort. Another subtle message is delivered to children in a great many ways, around the theme of sex roles—especially about the second-class status of women. Before puberty girls report career aspirations that include being doctors and pilots, police and fire fighters, truck drivers and farmers. But American culture has a way of shaping the children of the poor, especially, and the girls of a culture, into an awareness that many doors are closed to them because of their color, language, or sex. They see their mothers, and other women, in poorly paid second-class jobs, and they see the white male patriarchy holding the positions of power in the culture. This is sex education at a symbolic level and it has profound effects on female self-esteem.

In the final section we have brought together a group of distinguished national leaders in the field of sex education: Eleanor Hamilton, Mary Calderone, Nancy Hamlin, Mary Lee Tatum, Sol Gordon, and Albert Ellis. Each has achieved wide visibility in the marketplace and in the American mass media. They are bold spokespersons for social change. They all have appeared often on national television and radio, and their popular writing has reached millions and has drawn the ire and vicious attacks of the religious fundamentalists. During the conference, a popular TV program ("60 Minutes") filmed the keynote address of Mary Calderone, as well as a number of other speakers. Subsequently Calderone was shown on the program and her message was juxtaposed with the views of fundamentalist Christians. Similarly, Eleanor Hamilton has appeared on numerous media programs (such as the "Phil Donahue Show"), and Sol Gordon actually debated Reverend Jerry Falwell (on the "Today Show"). The books on sexuality by Albert Ellis have been read by millions. Nancy Hamlin and Mary Lee Tatum are widely recognized as leaders and advocates of sex education in the schools and the community.

Taken as a unit, the following papers argue that education for human sexuality has much to contribute to the primary prevention of psychopathology. In terms of enhancing intrafamilial communication and transgenerational relationships, few efforts can match these for potential effectiveness. A fundamental acceptance of one's sexuality incurs benefits in other areas of an individual's life as well.

Eleanor Hamilton's autobiographical sketch traces her own sexual enlightenment and involvement in the field of human sexuality. She asks a series of poignant questions: Why do people still suffer the effects of sexual ignorance and dysfunctions when help and knowledge are available? What are the origins of shame and negative attitudes toward sex? A look at childbearing practices and the paradoxical consequences of parenting styles alerts readers to the host of misconceptions which have passed from generation to generation. This chapter includes a series of moving anecdotes on the images of loving sexuality and creative energy. The last frontier in this field, the author believes, lies in solidarity in supporting the sexual rights and advances which have been hard-won battles in years past. Hamilton's chapter stands as a joyous affirmation to help combat the negative attitudes toward sex and pleasure which are growing stronger in American society.

Mary Calderone presents in her keynote address to the conference a summary of the knowledge she has acquired in a lifetime of experience as one of the nation's foremost sex educators. Her message is directed largely to parents, because she feels that the sexual attitudes of children directly reflect what they learn from the sexual attitudes of their parents. To interrupt the cycle of prejudice, misinformation, distortion, and anxiety she urges parents to understand that children are sexual creatures from infancy onward, that human sexuality is something to be celebrated, not suppressed, and that the more parents there are who learn these truths the more rapidly we will prevent the pathology that reflects the sexual insanity so rampant in our contemporary society.

Sexual concerns are addressed from the political vantage point in Nancy Hamlin's chapter on planning community-based sexuality programs. Ideally, human sexuality should not be a political issue, but since it is, it is with this reality that sexuality educators must wrestle. Hamlin writes that programs in this field must reflect the political, social, and cultural belief systems of the community, which must be involved in all stages of development. The author presents a 3-point design to be used in implementing programs which cover a broad range of sexual concerns. The design is conceptualized in terms of (1) the life span approach, (2) special population groups, and (3) points of stress and/or trauma which occur.

Hamlin traces the history of sexuality, power, and repression in the United States, and demonstrates how, against this background, contemporary programs have succeeded. The author's own work as coordinator of project PEOPLE (People's Educational Organization for Prepared Life Experience) provided pre- and postnatal education to unwed women and married couples. Hamlin reviews many other programs around the country working in these areas. Strategies are developed for bringing about change in climates often charaterized by anxiety and resistance; especially critical in this regard is the dismantling of past victories, such as the national human service system, and affirmative action. Preventive endeavors are stressed as a means to avoid such conflicts in the first place.

In her paper "Rationale for Sex Education in the Public Schools," Mary

Lee Tatum examines how public school systems have evolved as the dumping ground for unresolved societal problems. On the other hand, the omission of sex education from the curricula aggravates the communication gap between adults and pupils and makes a profound statement concerning communities' values and inhibitions.

Sex educators, Tatum argues, unequivocally believe that parents are the primary sex educators of their children. Including the subject in school courses elevates it to a position of serious academic consideration and makes it an intensely personal familial issue. Contributions from the media, as well as from peer groups, are detailed as being simultaneously positive and negative influences. Parent education programs now available in many communities assist parents in understanding these diverse forces, and in effectively educating their own children. Parental fears concerning school-based programs for children are explored, and focus is on the fear of the teacher's values being imposed on students and the fear of students experimenting sexually with knowledge gained in the classroom.

Sol Gordon, one of the editors of the current volume, has been lecturing and writing about sexuality for the past 30 years. Anyone who has heard him speak will agree that he is one of the world's great orators. His talks to teenagers about sexuality are greeted with wild enthusiasm, laughter, and understanding. He knows how to reach young people. His books, including comic books, cartoons, pictures with captions, and other devices, attract the attention of even those teenagers who are not much interested in reading. His work is distributed across the country. His paper is a transcription of one of these talks. It illustrates his thoughtful mixture of humor, seriousness, scientific data, and fearlessness. Gordon has an urgent message for teenagers and their parents. While he favors abstinence from sex by teenagers, believing them to be too vulnerable and too young, he notes wryly that they do not ask his permission. They often have intercourse with little knowledge of the consequences, and often when they (especially girls) themselves would really rather not. Gordon tries to teach them how to say no, if that is their wish. He helps them wait, if they feel like waiting. He helps young girls recognize the ploys, the lines, of the predatory teenage male: you would do it if you loved me! Gordon also places sex in perspective—in a continuing relationship between lovers it is number 9, still in the top 10, but following friendship, a sense of humor, and other bonds.

Albert Ellis is widely known for his books on human sexuality and as the founder and developer of Rational-Emotive Therapy (RET), and his paper explains how RET can be applied to the development of a sexually sane society. His position is that people are distressed, not so much by what happens to them, but by the views they take of these events. To be sane about sexuality as well as in other areas, people's belief systems must change—particularly their irrational beliefs. Ellis's position is quite similar to the themes expressed by many other authors in this volume: people's attitudes about what is right and wrong, good and bad, proper and improper, often cause great anguish and great distortion of behavior. Ellis's paper refocuses our attention directly on ways of thinking rationally about sexuality.

From the Past to the Future

Eleanor Hamilton

Today I find it hard to believe that when I entered college at age 16 my sole knowledge of the word *sex* implied the question "Is the person a male or a female?"

Luckily, mandatory attendance at a freshman course in personal hygiene erased that ignorance and at least I learned about the birds and the bees — the agricultural approach to reproduction. But the course also introduced me to the known facts about contraception and to the dangers of venereal disease.

I well remember commenting to my mother during a holiday at home "Now I know how I can keep from having babies."

"Oh, you do!" she snapped. "Then you had better know that both you and your brother were born when condoms broke."

Despite my mother's obvious antagonism to any discussion of things sexual, other than an emphatic "don't," my learning progressed rapidly after that. In defense of my mother, however, I must say that she was one of the original feminists who had learned the hard way that the sexual nature of human beings betrayed women, delivering them up to a life of motherhood, and what she considered to be slavery to men. Her ambitions for me were somewhat different.

At any rate, whether my parents willed it or not, a very illuminating book fell into my hands about then. It was called *Sane Sex Life and Sane Sex Living* by a man named Long. It revolutionized my life, for it offered me my first glimpse of sex as something beautiful and fulfilling (regrettably, it is now out of print, and I have no further information about it).

Another event changed things for me even more radically. My art professor fell in love with me. For the next 3 years he undertook my sexual education in a way that I would be happy to have my own daughter educated, with, I would hope, a few improvements based on better knowledge. He taught me reverence for male and female genitalia. Over a period of months, he also gently introduced me to sexual intercourse. I worshipped him but I did not come to orgasm. In those days not even this caring man knew of the role of the clitoris in female orgasm for some women. As for birth control, he still believed that withdrawal was an effective method.

The fact that I got pregnant during my senior year in college and was also the first woman president of a graduating class at that university led to my choice of a profession. For after trying in every known way to dislodge an embryo, such as swimming in the ice-cold mill-race and leaping from a barn rafter onto a haystack below, I climbed a mountain one night and prayed. The prayer went like this: "Dear God, I pledge my life to work for a better knowledge of love and sex. Please let me get through this ignorance of mine without disgracing my family and disappointing my professors."

On the way down the mountain that night I suddenly felt something warm and wet streaming down my legs. By the time I got to my room, it was apparent that I was in the middle of a spontaneous abortion.

My first job after college was with the Y.W.C.A. in California. There I instituted a course on sex education in the girls' summer camp. I believe it was the first of its kind in the country.

It was at about this time, 1930, that Paul Poponoe, a pioneer of his day, set up the first marriage counseling clinic on the West Coast while, in the East, Abe and Hannah Stone were founding one in New York City — also a "first."

But to go back to my personal story, it was not until 2 years after college, when I met and married my husband, Tajar, that I learned what an orgasm was like. This knowledge illumined my life. What a tragedy for womankind that the majority in those years did not have this blessed experience.

The first 20 years of my professional life were spent running a nursery school in New York City with my husband. There we had ample opportunity to observe children in relationship to each other and to their parents. It was soon apparent to me that 2-, 3-, 4-, and 5-year-old children were sexual beings. But in those days it was difficult for parents to acknowledge that fact. On the whole they turned blind eyes to it. If they saw a child's hand straying to underpants, they tended to say, "Do you need to go to the toilet, dear?" Today we know that we are sexual from birth to death and that there is some form of sexual expression that is healthy and good at every age and stage of life.

Many years later, when I gave up running a nursery school and devoted myself full-time to sex and marital counseling, I wrote my first book, *Partners in Love*. This occasioned a round of television appearances. In those early days, it was like running a gauntlet to discuss sexuality openly on the air. I well remember an instance in Boston, when a woman from the audience asked me, "What is the value to a woman of sexual intercourse?"

My response, quite spontaneously, was "It depends entirely on whether she is made love to or simply fucked."

This went out over the air and within minutes the studio phones were swamped. Before they were through, 3,000 calls had come in, not all of them complimentary by any means. Not only was the place Boston, but it was Holy Week. However, the vast majority of calls were pleas for help. The producer was so deluged, in fact, that she invited me back for a week to discuss various aspects of sexuality. I thought she must be either mad or exceptionally brave. I finally agreed—this time for a price—and the manager was at the door to greet me when I entered the studio. "Welcome to Boston," said he. "I hope you will enjoy your stay here." I couldn't resist saying "Thank you for inviting me. I hope I don't fuck up your show."

The poor man turned green with anxiety until he saw the twinkle in my eye.

Since that day I have been on scores of television shows, national and local, in Canada and in the United States. These have ranged from the "Phil Donahue Show," "Merv Griffin," the "Today Show," the "Tonight Show," and "Hour Magazine," to productions for less protected audiences who listen in the middle of the night. Little by little I have found that both hosts and audiences are losing their fear about discussing sexual issues. Furthermore, the managements have continued to encourage the interchange, despite the steady flow of protests from minority groups. In the beginning negative responses came in at the rate of 4 for every 4 positive responses. Today it is 1 in 20.

My old friend and mentor, Abraham Stone, were he alive today, might have less need to start his lectures with that classic statement, "The trouble with the garden of Eden is not there was a red apple in it, but a green pair."

Everyone today, through the media and through easily obtainable publications, has access to every known facet of sexuality that can be learned from the printed page.

But why is it not being learned? Why do sex education programs in schools fall by the wayside when attacked by a few sex negative attackers while, at the same time, it is known that 90 percent of parents want such programs for their children? Why are there still thousands of people in our own country who suffer sexual dysfunctions and neglect to get professional help that would eliminate these dysfunctions? Why do teenagers get pregnant before they either want or can care for a baby, and why is venereal disease so rampant?

To answer these questions requires consideration of several factors.

We must look at the kind of emotional education that most of our adults have been subjected to as children.

We must understand the nature of pleasure anxiety.

We must relate an individual's sexual development to that individual's capacity to love and to feel good about sexuality.

Let us look at psychosexual development first.

In about 1941 a number of research studies began to point up the fact that babies were born sexual; furthermore, many experienced orgasm in the first few weeks of life, most often while suckling. These studies also demonstrated that newborns breathe in a way that could be called "sexpositive." In other words their breathing is like that of the panting of a dog—with the accent on the exhale (which is the breath of pleasure and relaxation), rather than on the inhale (which is the breath of tension). With each breath, the baby's whole body experiences what Wilhelm Reich called "the orgasm reflex"—not the orgasm, but the orgasm reflex. And it appears to be pleasurable.

In fact, it was soon obvious to researchers that all physiological processes experienced by the baby appear to be pleasurable until interfered with by adults. Sucking, defecating, breathing, and body exploration were observed as joyful experiences. For example, when a mother changes her baby's diapers with a smile on her face and with warm and caressing hands, that baby coos and smiles and wriggles its body with unmistakable signs of pleasure. If, on the other hand, diaper changing is done with cold hands and an expressions on the mother's face of disgust and disapproval—that says nonverbally, "You're a dirty little baby"—that baby tenses and often cries. What the body is learning then, is that this part of the body is not acceptable to mama. Such experiences are, I believe, the beginning of our shame about what lies below the belt, in other words, the beginning of body guilt and shame.

Early studies also revealed that babies discover their genitals about as soon as they discover their noses, their eyes, their ears, or any other part of the body. Of course the discovery feels good.

If adults in the baby's life accept this pleasure as good, the child stands a chance of continuing to feel good about his or her sexuality. Many parents, however, fear that if they affirm their child's right to genital pleasure, the child will embarrass them by masturbating in the supermarket or when Great-Aunt Mary comes to call. But the fact is that children learn very quickly to distinguish between private acts and public acts and to confine each to its appropriate locale.

It is quite clear to psychotherapists today that a positive acceptance of self-pleasuring is one of the greatest contributions parents can make to their child's healthy sexual development. Of all the gifts that sexological science has made to humanity, I would rank the affirmation of self-pleasuring at the head of the list. Knowledge that auto-eroticism is healthy in young and old, both in and out of marriage, has probably taken more people off psychiatrists' couches than any other single finding.

Masturbation (a word I do not like to use, because it stems from Latin and means to pollute with the hand) is not, as Freud would have us believe, an immature form of sexual fulfillment. Rather it is one of the acceptable options for persons of any age, and its enjoyment has nothing to do with maturation unless it is used as an excuse for never relating to another human being.

Let us take another finding of the researchers. Early on, wise pediatricians, like Dr. Emmet Holt, discovered that babies (like all of us throughout life) have an intense need for body contact. In general, wanted babies get this need fulfilled. But from the time children go to school, almost the only body contact they know is aggressive, as in rough games, or through disciplinary action ("Shape up, Johnny—or else!"). Or it is specifically sexual, which is taboo. The joys of tender affectionate touch are completely left out of the educational scene.

But let us return to babies, for a moment, at least to the babies of the past. Their need for the kind of attention that they got while snuggling was so great that they let adults know in no uncertain terms if they were not getting enough. And here was where many of our present-day adults suffered the injurious experiences which, I believe, are responsible for what

I have found to be the deepest fear of adults today, namely, fear of rejection.

The early nursery scene went something like this. A mother, having fed, cleaned, and burped her baby (let's call the baby a boy), puts him down to sleep. Thirty minutes later, he awakens and wants more of those nice, warm sensations accompanying body contact. So he cries. His mother picks him up and says to herself that he cannot be hungry, because she has fed him so recently. So she checks his diapers, which are not wet. She burps him and he has no burp. And so she puts him back in his crib. But since what he really wanted was contact, he cries again. She may go through the same procedure once or twice more, but then, bewildered, she calls her pediatrician. In the past, quite typically, the busy doctor said something like this to her, "All your baby wants is a little attention. If you want to spoil him, pick him up. But babies can be little tyrants if you spoil them. So I suggest that you put him in the next room. Close the door and let him cry it out. It's good for babies to cry—good exercise for their lungs."

Why it should be good exercise for babies to cry alone is more than I can see, but the conscientious mother, rather against her instinct, did as her doctor recommended. The result for the baby was the equivalent of isolation cell treatment. All punitive systems through history have used isolation as a special kind of torture. In fact, we know today that isolation is what no person can stand without severe psychic stress. Indeed, you can brainwash anyone to do almost anything if you isolate him or her long enough. So this was what mothers were instructed to do to their babies, and the learning of the babies was swift and devastating. The basis of that learning was that "if you ask for what you want, something awful is likely to happen to you."

This learning is so persistent in adult life that there are few among us who can ask for the fulfillment of our physical needs for pleasure without some anxiety that "something bad" will happen to us if we do. So, in the course of the psychosexual development of most of us comes what I call "the great screw-up," the result of which teaches us not to trust the evidence of our own senses.

The screw-up works like this: We are born with a built-in mechanism that rewards us with good body feelings when physiological functions are proceeding naturally and without frustration. We experience discomfort when these are "disciplined" or interfered with. Unfortunately, child-rearing practices in the past have concentrated on rewarding babies when their bodies told them they were uncomfortable and punishing them when they felt good. In other words, babies were praised for emptying their bowels into a potty even when their musculature was too immature for comfortable control. They were called "good babies" when they learned to pay no attention to hunger needs until the hands of a clock stood at 10 or 2 or 6. And so it went. A bright baby, who wanted and needed mama's approval, quickly learned that its own physiology should be discounted in favor of mama's time schedule, for mama was the source of life itself. At a later stage in life, that same baby, now an adult, does not know how to trust good feelings. In fact, he or she is likely to equate good feelings with disapproval and rejection, and bad feelings with approval and acceptance.

This is, indeed, the great screw-up that sex therapists have to undo when they undertake to help rebuild a sex-positive attitude in their clients. And because it goes so deep—back to a preverbal level of learning—and because it seems to be lodged in muscle memory rather than in the head, sex therapists have had to devise relearning processes that involve the body, for example, such exercises as sensate focus. In our own training center here in Sheffield, Massachusetts, we teach our clients the art of massage, and we affirm their discovery that this is deeply pleasurable and that it is all right to feel body pleasure.

The sex researchers have also uncovered another factor contributing to positive sexuality. This relates to emotional mobility. The very word *emotion* means "feeling in movement." All primary feelings that a human being experiences involve movement, and the movement takes place in the body, specifically, in those organs of the body responsible for movement, namely in our muscles, in our temperature regulating mechanism, and in our breathing. Furthermore, each feeling calls forth typical body responses that regularly appear in all people. In anger, for example, we want to hit, kick, punch, scream, bite. In sadness, we want to cry or sob. In fear, we want to run or defecate, and, curiously, our hands and feet grow cold. In sexual attraction, our muscles of reach go into action: we want to hold, embrace, touch. The only way these movements can be stopped is by tightening the muscles involved in their movement and by limiting breathing.

Most child-rearing practices in the past have emphasized the "don't move" rather than the "how-to" move. Little boys have been told that "big brave boys don't cry," and little girls have had drilled into them that "nice little girls don't get angry." All children are told not to be afraid, and God help any child who expresses a sexual feeling. The result of this kind of "no-no" training is, as one might expect, a society of adults whose feelings are immobilized. They are what the younger generation call "uptight," and at another time were called "stiffs" or "cold fish." Obviously, they radiate no joie de vivre—no sexual energy—because mobility is frozen deep inside.

One of the crucial findings in sex therapy is that it is impossible to come to orgasm through the muscular blockade of held-onto anger. For instance, a woman whose jaw is set against a need to bite or scream, whose thigh muscles are tightened against a need to kick, and whose fists are clenched against a need to punch or poke, is not going to be able to allow her body to move in the soft and tender way that would permit her to feel sexual pleasure or to breathe so that she is carried into the ecstasy of orgastic release.

So, sexual therapists have had to learn that information, important as it is, is not enough. It will not produce an orgasm for an inorgasmic woman holding on to her anger, at least not until she is taught how to express that anger in non-destructive ways. Men and women who are uptight may also have to be taught how to laugh and cry and especially how to reach for physical satisfaction.

As sex therapists, we at our counseling center are discovering that we can hardly be sex therapists without also being love therapists. Most sexual dysfunction is not only a manifestation of disturbed body learnings but of inadequacies related to how to love another human being.

Just as we have inherited a host of misconceptions about what constitutes healthy sexual functioning, so have we also been the repository of a lot of misguided ideas about love. Such ideas for example, as that jealousy is a sign of love. Or that if love is to be honored as love, it must be for someone of the opposite sex.

I have come to identify four major love killers that so regularly diminish a love relationship that I have called them "the four horsemen of the Apocalypse." These are jealousy, possessiveness, perfectionism, and the need to control others.

On the other hand, there are identifiable love builders, namely, mutual appreciation, absence of negative criticism, praise, encouragement of the pursuit of individual goals, acceptance of a partner's imperfections, and the granting to the partner the right to personal freedom of action, as long as that action is not injurious.

Satisfying sex, then, is usually profoundly dependent on the presence of love builders and the absence of love killers. Therefore, sex therapy often becomes love therapy.

Perhaps one of the most revolutionary discoveries of the past 30 years has been the dawning awareness of sex as energy. Wilhelm Reich broke with his Freudian heritage, because he found that sex was a source of creativity—even a form of life energy—and was not, as Freud believed, a part of original sin.

I think we owe to Reich the demonstration and proof that sexual energy is indeed the biological source of love energy and creativity on every level. I first met Reich when the mother of one of our nursery school pupils demanded that we fire her child's teacher because that teacher was a student of Reich's. Since we did not hire and fire for such whimsical reasons, we suggested that the mother withdraw her child. Our curiosity was piqued, however, and we set out to find out who Reich was. On reading his book *The Function of the Orgasm* we were electrified, and both Tajar and I determined to study with him if we could. Thus began a long and rewarding relationship that turned our lives upside down, for Reich challenged the very roots of Freudian belief.

Personally, I believe that Reich was among the giants who lifted our concept of sexuality from the narrow confines of procreation on the one hand or pornography on the other, to a whole new level of awareness of the creative power of sex.

There were other giants also, as well as many sturdy pioneers who dared to follow in their wake and who risked being at odds with society as they began to utilize the information given them. If you want to know more about them, read Ed Brecher's book, *The Sex Researchers*.

For me, the giants who freed me to enjoy sex in new and wonderful ways, and to see it as integral to life itself, were Havelock Ellis, R. L. Dickinson, Wilhelm Reich, Alfred Kinsey, and Masters and Johnson.

The contributions of each are so well documented through their own writings that I will not elaborate on them here. But I do want to mention here what they have meant to me personally.

Havelock Ellis (1936) was a hero of my college days largely because of the records he left of his beautiful love affair with a remarkable woman, Olive Schreiner. But he was also a hero because through his *Studies in the Psychology of Sex*, he lifted the curtains from my eyes to the vast panorama and variety of sexual behavior.

R. L. Dickinson, gynecologist and artist, let me see the reproductive structure of women as beautiful. How wonderful was his ability to say to women of my mother's generation, "Do you know how exquisite are your labia, Mrs. Smith?" or "Mrs. Jones, your cervix is like a rosebud." And he said such things with a tone of admiration in his voice that transformed forever a woman's view of herself as "ugly down there."

I used to take my nursery school children up to his sculpture studio behind the stage of the Academy of Medicine. There he would show the youngsters a sculptured embryo inside the mother's womb, and then he would guide the baby down the pelvic bones and out into the light of day, getting the baby born. Not only were small children given these lessons, but so were practicing obstetricians. Dickinson's sculptures were the first three-dimensional previews that doctors got of the miracle of birth. For the first time in medical history they could see what they were doing when they ushered a new baby into the world before they actually had to do it.

One sad day Dickinson called me on the phone in despair, saying, "You will have to call a halt to the children coming to my studio for a while. I can't get any work done."

"What!" I exclaimed, for he had always seemed so happy to have the children there.

"I know, I know" he sighed, "I have loved having them, but now they are bringing their brothers and sisters, their mothers and fathers and their nurses and governesses, and they don't leave me any time for my own creative work. I tell you what I'll do, however. I'll make a special mother-and-baby sculpture just for your school. And then the children can get a baby born anytime they want."

Unfortunately, Dickinson died before he was able to fulfil that promise.

However, Dickinson gave me a new concept of beauty. His great gift to womankind was a safer way to give birth. He founded the Committee on Maternal Health. He also aided and abetted Margaret Sanger in her work. You might be interested in the story he told me of that relationship.

Margaret Sanger had come to him to request his sponsorship of her birth control clinic. Dickinson told her that he believed in her work, but that he had two daughters to put through school and that his sponsorship of her at that time would spell economic disaster for him professionally. How-

ever, he promised her that when his girls were through college he would
devote the rest of his life to the birth control movement, which is exactly
what he did. Eventually he was given a large studio in the Academy of
Medicine in New York City where he could create his sculptures and where
he could house his large collection of birth control devices that had been
gathered from all over the world. This collection, I believe, was willed
to the Kinsey Institute.

Perhaps this is the time to mention a pioneering woman whom I loved—
not a giant, maybe—but to many women a real savior. Dr. Sophie Kleegman was a remarkable gynecologist and also was one of the founding members of the American Association of Marriage Counselors. Sophie was the
scientist who identified monilia, which was, and still is, one of the banes
of a woman's existence, often completely destroying her pleasure in sex.
Dr. Kleegman not only identified monilia, but took the time and trouble
to cure her patients (which is more than can be said for most male gynecologists to this very day).

She is most remembered, however, for her work in infertility. I personally bless her for delivering my third child and then for staying up all one
horrendous night resuscitating that child, who did not breathe well in her
first 2 days of life. Thanks to Sophie, that little female infant is now the
mother of two husky youngsters.

Sophie also instituted courses in sex for medical students, and she was
one of the first to do so. Largely through her influence and that of a few
other stalwart gynecologists, this long neglected subject began to be taught
in medical schools throughout the country, though not in all of them, even
today.

I think that Helen Singer Kaplan, who has done such stunning work
at the Cornell Medical School in recent years, would be horrified to learn
that not so many years ago (and largely through Dr. Kleegman's and Dr.
Ralph Gause's insistence), I gave the only lecture on sex given to the third-
year medical students there. Even then, this annual lecture was regularly
scheduled for early Saturday morning before grand rounds. Such was the
relative importance of sex to other aspects of medical knowledge in those
days.

Both Dickinson and Kleegman sponsored the work of Kinsey, believing that he was the most promising researcher to carry forward their own
dreams of a sexually enlightened world.

I first knew Alfred Kinsey when he asked me to help him get the parents of nursery school children to be a part of his research study around 1945. It was inevitable, of course, that both my husband and I became part of his statistics.

Besides his other contributions that have been documented over and over again, I value him most for one single skill: he taught me to ask questions. It came about this way. When he had finished taking my personal sex history, I came away from the interview utterly astounded to discover that I had revealed material to him which I had revealed neither to my analyst nor to myself, yet this material could hardly have been called unconscious. When I mentioned this observation to my husband, he confessed that he had had the same experience. This fascinated us and we decided to ask Kinsey for another session to see if he could tell us his secret for eliciting so-called unconscious material.

"It's really very simple," he began modestly. "All I do is ask a thousand questions—it's a bit like mining—many of my questions yield only slag, but some yield pure gold. People's childhood sex experiences are not generally relegated to the unconscious, as the therapists of our time have seemed to believe. Rather it's that patients don't want to offend their poor analysts' sensibilities on the one hand, or they don't think these things are important on the other, so they just don't bring them up. How many people do you know, for example, who volunteer the fact that they masturbate, or that they have any other personal body habits, like picking their noses? But if, in a situation in which they are guaranteed confidentiality, they are asked a direct question about their masturbation, they will answer truthfully enough. The skill comes in knowing how to ask the right questions and in not being afraid to do so. And of course in not being judgmental when you get answers that differ from your own ideas of morality."

From that day forth, I obtained sex histories of every patient whom I saw. It was surprising how this process shortened what would otherwise have been long-term therapy.

Over the years, as it became known that I was good at solving sexual problems, a number of psychoanalysts began referring their patients to me for this specialized kind of help. Typically when I asked a patient how far he or she had gotten with the solution of any sexual problem in psychoanalysis, I regularly got the answer, "Oh, I've only been in analysis for a couple of years. We haven't gotten to that yet." What I had learned from Kinsey was that the careful taking of a sex history was not only therapeutic but provided a primary educational tool for teaching facts and breaking myths held by otherwise intelligent and educated people.

Then came the day that I first met Masters and Johnson. How well I remember that gathering of some 200 professional men and women, all members of the (then) American Association of Marriage Counselors, who heard and saw for the first time in human history motion picture, color films of what takes place internally in a woman during orgasm. This was mind blowing. Tears of appreciation ran down the faces of the audience, who included such brave pioneers as Lester Dearborn, Bob Laidlaw, Sophie Kleegman, and others, who had envisioned such a breakthrough of knowledge but whose courage had not led them quite this far. These two, Masters and Johnson, had dared to cross the threshold of verbal accounts over into the world of visual demonstration. This was a remarkable advance in the science of sexology, and every person in that room was acutely conscious of the historic importance of that fact.

Although marriage counselors had always been the professional group that had made it their business to help clients solve sexual problems, they had been handicapped in much the same way that gynecologists had been handicapped before the days of Dickinson and his teaching models. Words can go only so far. The next step is demonstration and intelligent guided action. Indeed, through them, the formalized notion of sex therapy, as an integral part of relationship therapy or of marriage counseling was born.

Today, of course, there is a lot of debunking of the Masters and Johnson research methods and of some of the accuracy of their findings. The world moves on, and no one is perfect. But I could wish that some of the debunkers had tried to practice sex therapy in the days before 1960 and Masters and Johnson, for no matter what the mistakes of the St. Louis team of researchers, they should still be thanked by their detractors.

Today one might imagine, judging from the books now available on every possible aspect of sexuality, that there are no more frontiers to cross. Today, because of those who dared, you who are sitting here are not ostracized for having sex books on your bookshelves, and you can send your son or daughter to a doctor for good contraceptive advice when this is needed. If these methods fail, you can get your daughter to an abortionist in a good hospital where her body will not be mangled by a half-trained money grabber on some back room operating table. Nor will you be awakened in the night by a knock on the door, as I was once, when a detective demanded the right to search my library for pornographic material. Nor do you get anonymous phone calls by the "moral minority" telling you that you are a witch who ought to be burned, as I received, only 12 short years ago after I had written *Sex Before Marriage* (1968). Furthermore, most of you can look forward to enjoying sex, male and female alike. You are women who are coming to orgasm rather regularly. You are men who are learning to be better lovers both emotionally and physically.

Those of you who have lovers of the same sex can find some places in this world where you can enjoy your sexuality without torment from biased homophobes. Those of you suffering from sexual dysfunctions can be helped to become sexually functional, often in a few sessions. Even sex education in some schools is a hoped for possibility.

But all this hard-earned progress is being threatened politically. We are, indeed, on the verge of a return to the dark ages of sexual freedom unless we watch out. The so-called Moral Majority, the right-to-lifers, the Bible-thumping born-again Christians, and other self-righteous interpreters of "God's will" and "God's Word" are on a rampage of destruction of our rights to privacy and sexual happiness.

Bills currently being presented to legislative bodies—and in many states, already passed—will make it impossible for you or me, for example, to have a sexual work of art on display in our own homes. We may be jailed as murderers for helping a pregnant girl or woman get an abortion. These legislative bills will limit our right to free speech and the right to control our own bodies and will prevent our children from having adequate sex education in our schools.

What is at the root of such a destructive campaign is hard to determine, but I think it is partly, at least, a result of that old bugaboo, *pleasure anxiety*. People who have been taught early on to fear that which feels good learn to repress feelings of warmth and to embrace discomfort as the rule of life. In order to support their endurance, they call on powers that they imagine are stronger than they are, such as legal sanctification or the authority of the so-called laws of God. These repressed people become the haters and the killers of all that is creative and good and joyous. Furthermore, it is my hunch that wherever throughout history there has been a repressed society, there has also been a dearth of creativity in other areas of life. It would be a tragedy now, if these haters and killers were allowed to take over the laws of our land, as they threaten to do.

It is my hope that enough persons like ourselves, of all ages and all sexual persuasions gathered here together, and thousands like us throughout the country who have been immeasurably enriched by the sexological enlightenment available to us, will not let this happen; that we will stand up and be counted in the fight for our right to enjoy our bodies, a right that has taken several generations to achieve.

May we all stand solidly behind those institutions that work to educate more and better sex educators, sex therapists, and sex researchers. Here and there, all over the country, training programs are evolving, such as, the Institute for Advanced Study of Sexuality, in San Francisco, where it is possible today to get a Ph.D. in sexology. Or like our own 10-day intensive training program on love and sexuality, held annually on Cape Breton Island, Nova Scotia, where professionals who already have some training in interpersonal relationship therapy can come for specialized training in love and sex counseling. Let us hope that such programs will multiply and develop leaders who can withstand the sex-negative pressure and can help make available to young and old the joyous fulfillment of their sexuality.

References

Brecher, E. M. *The sex researchers*. Boston: Little, Brown, 1969.

Ellis, H. *Studies in the psychology of sex*. New York: Random House, 1936.

Hamilton, E. *Sex before marriage*. Des Moines, Iowa: Meredith Press, 1968.

Hamilton, E. *Sex with love*. Boston: Beacon Press, 1978.

Hamilton, E. *Partners in love*. San Diego: Leisure Dynamics, 1980. (Obtainable from A. S. Barnes, c/o Leisure Dynamics, 11175 Flintkote Ave., San Diego, Calif. 92121.)

Holt, L. E. *The diseases of infancy and childhood for the use of students and practitioners of medicine*. New York: D. Appleton, 1922.

Reich, W. *The function of the orgasm*. New York: Noonday Press, 1961.

Childhood Sexuality:
Approaching the Prevention of Sexual Dis-ease

Mary S. Calderone

Through research in the past decade, new facts have come to light relating to the process by which children evolve the natural sexuality with which each is endowed at birth. This process is being called sexual socialization, a kind of behavioral/attitudinal programming that inevitably takes place from birth onward. By putting many old and new findings together, we can provide a clearer concept of the stages in sexual development from conception to puberty for health professionals than was possible heretofore. Those whose work brings them into contact with parents and/or children should be aware of these facts and their implications, because sexual socialization cannot be prevented—in one or another way it happens. It can, however, be weighted toward the positive or the negative. If we judge from what we see, in the past weighting must preponderantly have been toward the negative. Sexologists are now seeking to shift the balance toward the positive. The goal might be accepted as sexual wellness, that is, human beings who, at every stage of their life cycles, feel confident, competent, and responsible in their sexuality, and behave accordingly.

Sexualization as a Subset Process in Socialization

This is a complex process in which heredity, the sex chromosomes, hormones, and even more cogently, people, play roles: parents or their substitutes, as well as many others, influence the life and the sexuality of every child. A girl or a boy or a man or a woman are not automatically produced, nor do they function sexually *as such* , simply because they are born with certain sets of organs. Many influences can and do impinge on the growing organism in a multitude of ways that are different for every culture and individual. The result of the sexualization process is that human beings function sexually in an almost untold variety of ways; how they function sexually is the end result of the sociosexual programming, both direct and indirect, experienced by each individual from birth onward. Socialization that is sexual in nature would also appear to have different results from non-sex-related socialization: Byler, Lewis, and Totman (1969) found that here in the United States, as related to sexual interest and questions, children of all ages appeared to be about 2 years ahead of where their parents and teachers expected them to be. On the other hand, with regard to their capacity for reasoning toward making moral sexual decisions, Gilligan (1974) found that childen tended to be about 2 years *behind* their capacity for moral reasoning in *non*-sex-related dilemmas.

At the very outset of discussion there is a need to differentiate between two organ systems previously lumped together as one, related by organs held in common but that function differently in the two systems: the reproductive system that will not begin to function until puberty; the sexual response system that, like all the other organ systems, has already begun functioning during intrauterine life.

Prenatal Sexualization

The sex chromosome at fertilization has a single mission: to pass on the code that assigns the subsequent job of differentiating a male from a female to those pregonadal cells in the developing embryo destined to be testicles or ovaries. By the 8th week these pregonadal cells, in response to that code, begin producing the sex hormones that cause both sex and reproductive organs to develop as male or female. The testosterone or the estrogen thus produced is also considered to sensitize the sex center in the limbic area of the brain so as to predispose it toward later femininity or masculinity.

Postnatal Sexualization's Three Components

Gender Identity

At birth, the declaration of gender as boy or girl instantly crystallizes the attitudes and actions of the people most close to the baby. These then proceed to deal with the baby in such a way that, during the first 2 years, he or she learns clearly that he or she is a boy or a girl. A child's gender identity thus fixed is considered unsafe to try to change after the age of 3 to 5, even if gender assignment was incorrect.

Gender Role

At 2 to 3 the child begins to learn the kind of boy or girl that is desired. Parents tend to give cues to their girls to be "girlish," their boys to be "boyish," the definitions certainly differing from cultural group to cultural group. Green (1979) found that there is a special intentness on messages to a son not only to do "boyish" things, but in particular *never* to do "girlish" things, nor to play with girls. Heavy insistence on this may (and does) inhibit the capacity of males for later tender nurture of children. In the United States, fathers and children can both suffer from this incapacity. Furthermore it can be hypothesized that overemphasis on same-sex play might well serve to blur eventual development of wholehearted heterosexuality.

Childhood Eroticism

Sonograms during pregnancy have provided a surprise—that the sexual response system begins functioning *in utero* as do the other organ systems, as shown by periodic erections of the penis. It is also known that both male and female fetuses suck thumbs, and recent studies by Langfeldt (1980) have shown that the vagina of the infant girl lubricates cyclically from birth on with the same mechanism as it will later on in sexual responsiveness. Kinsey, Pomeroy, Martin, and Gebhard (1953) and others have verified that orgasm-like behavior is clearly apparent in very young infants: especially in girls, thigh pressure even in the earliest weeks may be accompanied by tensing of the body, flushing of and moisture on the skin, grimacing, rhythmic muscular contractions, then sudden relaxation into peaceful sleep.

Furthermore, the discovery of various parts of the body will inevitably lead a baby of around 6 months to discover its sexual pleasure area, the penis in the boy, the clitoris and vulva in the girl. Conscious self-pleasuring of these areas usually upsets a parent who has not been prepared for acceptance of its occurrence as normal, and this actually can and too often does lead to constant interference by well-meaning but uninformed adults who, because of their fear, do not permit children to "own" their bodies, and the pleasure that can be derived from them.

Blackman (1980) studied 3- and 4-year-olds and found that the area between the belly button and the knees appeared to exist for the children as "not-me." This leads to a curious and disturbing schizoid situation: the parents negate the existence of an area of the body that the child nevertheless almost daily experiences intensely. Here, present research would indicate, lies the greatest need. There is agreement by Blackman (1980), Langfeldt (1980), and Money and Ehrhardt (1972) of something pointed out by Martinson (1980) and others: the need for parents to accept the sexuality of their infants and children. They should do this in three ways and reinforce it by repeating it several times for the child between 2 and 5:

Identify the external genitals by correct names in both sexes. Small girls need help with a mirror and flashlight to find the clitoris, meatus, vagina, and anus as separate entities, each with a distinct function.

Affirm the pleasure functions of these, primarily of the penis and clitoris. In girls this should be accompanied by appropriate information on health safeguards: wipe the anus from front to back; wash the hands before touching the vulva; never insert anything into the urethra.

Link the sex organs to their future reproductive functioning, while emphasizing its elective nature.

Both boys and girls could hear something like this: "A boy has a penis for three purposes: to feel good; to urinate with; to enable him to become a father some day when he is grown up, if he decides that he would like to be one. A girl has three separate organs for these purposes: the part for feeling good is called the clitoris; the part for passing urine is called the meatus or pee-hole; and the opening between the pee-hole and the anus that is called the vagina is where some day when she is grown up, and if she decides that she wants to be a mother, a sperm can go in and travel up through the uterus to meet an ovum (egg), that will then grown into a baby in the uterus, and that will then come out, be born, through that vagina." In this way, the child of 3 can be given a clear, time-dimensional understanding of the acceptability of the genital organs and of their powerful feelings, and an understanding of their present and future roles in relation to these and to reproductive functioning. Such acceptance by parents is essential to assure a sense of self-esteem in children, confidence in the competence of their evolution and behavior as both male or female, and a better understanding by those who deal with children of the need for socialization attitudes that link appropriate privacy to all sexual matters, rather than "badness" or "sin".

It is obvious that such socialization for privacy should not be based on shame, fear, or punishment whether present or future, but rather on a sense of behavior appropriate in public or in other people's homes, as contrasted with what the family might consider appropriate within the privacy of its own home.

The parents should correlate such positive attitudes with similar attitudes about the drive to learn and know one's self and others as shown in the usual early childhood game of "playing doctor." The child with a clear-cut idea of his or her own genital anatomy and its functions and worth might be less likely to need and seek such knowledge directly with playmates; nevertheless, parents should be reassured that it can be expected that such seeking will go on simply because of the drive of all children for constant confirmation and reassurance as to their growth and competence, sexual and otherwise. Here again the attitude of parents should be to socialize for privacy rather than to punish or forbid. Nothing about childhood sexual interest, curiosity, or behavior should ever be labeled "bad," but simply not appropriate for time, place, or person. It is definitely appropriate for children to want to see and touch same-age children of the same or other sex. From time to time, nudity in adults is also desirable, but in this case touching is not. Here again parents should think and talk about together their own attitudes about sexual rehearsal play in their children, and their own feelings about nudity. The extremes of flaunting or repressing all nudity should be avoided, but it is reassuring and important for children to know clearly what they will look like when they grow up.

Other Aspects of Sexual Socialization

Pair-Bonding

There are other aspects of socialization which, when interfered with, have been shown to result in eventual sex-related difficulties. The classic research of Spitz (1965) proved once and for all that infants not only failed to thrive but often died when, though physically well cared for, they did not regularly receive nurturant mothering. There have been significant studies (Klaus, Jerauld, Kreger, McAlpine, Steffa, and Kennell, 1972) in which mothers and their newborn infants were placed alone in a room immediately after delivery and their first hours together recorded on videotape. All the mothers in this pair-bonding experience did exactly the same: holding the naked baby close to their bodies and fingering its toes, feet, legs, fingers, hands, and arms, they then gently but thoroughly massaged and caressed the body. Each mother cradled her baby's head in one hand so that its eyes faced hers and crooned and talked steadily to him or her as she gazed at his or her face. The intentness with which the tiny newborn's own eyes stayed fixed on his or her mother's was remarkable. Given the same opportunity, as they should be, fathers and infants reacted in exactly the same ways (Parke and O'Leary, 1975)—an opportunity that, with encouragement, might ultimately result in closer and more trusting father-child family relationships.

Condon and Sander (1974) slowed the speed of a similar film made at several weeks of age and showed the baby's body moving in a kind of cadence with the familiar rhythm of the mother's speech, but randomly when a stranger speaking the same words introduced a different rhythm. Such continuing parent-infant interactions, known as pair-bonding, are today considered to be the highly important initial links in a long chain of events at critical life stages that can serve to bind mother, father, and children together in an intimacy unique to each family, and to lay the foundations for capacity for intimacy in adult sexual relationships.

Separation Effects

The Harlows (1962) showed the devastating effects on monkeys of separation at birth from their mothers; these included pathological antisocial behavior and a total inability to copulate at sexual maturity. Infant monkeys raised in isolation were shown to have fewer mature cells in their central nervous systems than those raised in a peer-populated normal environment. And when females raised in isolation were finally induced to submit to copulation, they tended to ill-treat or kill their babies, particularly the firstborns. It is highly suggestive that, among children who have been abused, Fanaroff, Kennell, and Klaus (1972) found that as many as 31 percent of these had been born prematurely, in contrast to 7 percent prematures in the general population. No studies throwing light on these figures are yet available.

Pair-bonding can be looked at as a two-way process: a mother and father must bring to *social* life the baby they have called to *physical* life during gestation and birth. Play, interplay, and secure intimacy serve to accomplish this. But the baby also has a job to do: to create his or her own parents by his or her response to them. If such mutual experiencing of intimacy and trust does not occur in the very early days and months of life, the results can be emotionally underdeveloped children, damaged parent-child interactions, or diminished possibility of establishing a trust relationship during the critical early childhood years. Such specific preparation for the stormy days of adolescence is needed, so that then parents and children together can be in an already established close communication, instead of belatedly trying to establish something for which the foundations were never laid.

Language Learning and Sexual Learning

Money and Ehrhardt (1972), Gadpaille (1978), and others have drawn attention to the fact that the peak period for language learning coincides with one of the critical periods for sexual learning, between 2 and 5 years of age. But what a difference in our attitudes about these two fundamental, growth-related phenomena: how much we participate in positive ways with a child's language-learning experience, providing names for everything in sight, correcting a pronunciation, supplying new terms with a vision of ultimate intellectual attainment.

But supposing that, in our zeal, each word fluffed or mispronounced, instead of being greeted with amusement, was met with the instantaneous reaction of a slap on the mouth? Or, to go further with the simile, suppose we were so fearful that the children might precociously learn "dirty" words that we shouted at them or slapped their faces *every* time they ventured a new word? It could very well be predicted that we would fast become a nation of stammerers and stutterers.

Is the simile clear? I believe so, for what thrapists are seeing today in terms of sexual dysfunctions appear for the most part to be the results of interference with early childhood sexual drive and learning. In effect, we have been creating a culture of *sexual* stammerers and stutterers, whether in the form of premature ejaculators, or fetishists, or those who are impotent, or anorgasmic women with a certain proportion of nonconsummated marriages. Very seldom if ever is such negative sexual conditioning the result of lack of information alone. In other words, what we are seeing will not yield to any panacea of formalized school sex education programs, no matter how widespread. It would be quite unrealistic to expect *intellectual* learning to redress *social* learning that had been twisted and convoluted by the negative attitudes of the parental generation. Margaret Mead (1980), in Manus in 1928, found children who were the happy, carefree offspring of adults who were competitive and acquisitive of material goods for personal prestige. Twenty-five years later she returned to find that these happy, unpressured children had not continued in this way but had become exactly like their parents. She thought about this and wondered how it happened that a society's children could be cooperative and loving, and yet grow up to be selfish and profit motivated. Her recommendation for change was: "The cultivation in children of traits, attitudes, and habits foreign to their cultures is not the way to make over the world. Every new religion, every new political doctrine, has had *first to make its adults converts*, to create a small nuclear culture within whose guiding walls its children will flourish" (emphasis added, p. 154). Mead's thinking provides guidelines for giving priority to the reorientation and training of parents about childhood sexuality, instead of waiting for schools to rectify or supply what has been done badly or not at all by parents, something schools cannot accomplish.

Information Gathering: The Role of the School

Solnit (1977), director and professor of pediatric psychiatry at the Yale University Child Study Institute, and others have expressed the opinion that, because the prime years for acquisition of facts and information are between 5 and 12, this is especially the period for acquisition of solid information about sexuality as well as about other subjects. To wait for the adolescent years means that learning at that time about the very thing that is causing much of the adolescent storm becomes exceedingly difficult, especially if it comes from parents with whom no previous trustful intimacy has been established. The Sarrels (1979), codirectors of the Yale University Sexuality Services, have called their book *Sexual Unfolding in Late Adolescence*. They show that high school seniors and college-age freshmen are still in the same sexually evolving phase, at the very time that they are faced with the imperatives of separation from family, finishing education, and settling on a life occupation. Simultaneously they may also be choosing a partner with whom they must learn how to live in a new kind of pair-bond: sharing space, intimacy and possibly the care and nurture of children as well as each other. This is another critical period for which our young are poorly prepared. Communities, schools, and parents can cooperate to help their maturing young during late adolescence, before it is too late.

Solutions?

It is unrealistic to long for the "innocent old days" when children grew up looked upon as totally nonsexual beings, with no right to their own sexuality until marriage. (Read the Victorian and Edwardian literature for the real facts about these "innocent old days"!) Although we now know the grim and ugly results of ignorance, not just in terms of unwanted adolescent pregnancies and venereal disease, but also in terms of sexual dysfunction, today's situation has been heightened by the decreasing age of reproductive maturation. This is linked with the open sexuality and freedom that adults display and even promote before the eyes of our young people. "Do as I say, not as I do" does not solve, much less prevent, sex-related problems, but adds to them. Venality that leads to such openly blatant advertisements as steamy, blue jeans TV campaigns does a serious disservice to the developing sexuality of our children. These include the 5- and 6-year-olds who are fully conscious and aware of the adult world's obsessive preoccupation with sex, yet have no interpretations given them as correctives for their own sexual unfolding.

Approaches to Solutions

The extremes of sexual expression can have results that are as undesirable as the extremes of sexual repression. What the Sex Information and Education Council of the United States and other workers in the sexual health field are working toward is an approach to childhood sexuality that is open, that acknowledges its nature and dimensions, and respects and is conservative of these. By conservative I mean just that—conserving something precious and important as integral and normal to being born a human being. Today, there exist cohorts of scientists, educators, health and social workers, religious leaders, and others who are awakened to and aware of the need for this point of view—in truth, a desperate need—and in most communities they are eager to help parents help their children to move toward, into, and through adolescence with the knowledge, attitudes, sense of responsibility, and self-motivation that might, at the very least, result in a reduction in venereal disease and in the monstrous need for abortion. The silence of parents in the face of the seductiveness of the contrasting messages about sex that surround and assail children everywhere is perhaps the most destructive thing of all. Sexual silence, separating the child from the society and from the parents, worst of all separates the children from themselves. The silence says to a child: "This does not exist, you do not feel what you are feeling or, if you do feel anything, then this is bad and you must be punished for it. We cannot and will not talk about that part of you that is unspeakable and that we do not wish you to acknowledge." Figures from the Alan Guttmacher Institute (1981) tell us that more than one-fifth of first pregnancies in teenagers occur within the month after first intercourse, and half in the first 6 months; that 46 percent of all out-of-wedlock births are to teenagers—550,00 in 1978; and that 96 percent of the teenagers today retain their babies. This will require an estimated outlay of eight billion dollars per year of public support for these premature and immature parents, many of them carrying on in their single-parent homes. Increase in child abuse is also foreseen as one result—which will assure a rising toll of child abuse in the next generation as well.

Summary

The health professions seriously need to reinforce parental acceptance of their children as sexual persons from the moment of birth. They also need to defuse parental fears that sexual expression in children leads to irresponsible or pathological sexual conduct in adult life. Imagine a parent who can look at his or her child and be pleased with the sturdy growth of his or her body and the intelligent growth of his or her mind but is unaware that there should be equal pleasure in the child's evolving sexuality. Sexual responsibility in children can evolve out of a sense of the acceptance, enjoyment, and appropriate management of their own eroticism. Such an approach must naturally be based on parental knowledge, honesty, openness, and willingness to learn about the facts. Understanding responsible sexuality will also lead to understanding responsibility in marriage and in conception, which in turn can reduce the need for abortion. Health workers of any speciality who have been in touch with the 20 or so journals in the field of human sexualtiy will be aware of much of what I have condensed in this short paper.

You will draw your own inferences from the relationship between what I have only partially covered, and the development or prevention of sexual psychopathology. But, in closing, I am permitted to quote from the unpublished committee report of an interdemoninational and interfaith gathering of the clergy. Working informally with SIECUS on the question of parent education for childhood sexuality, they affirmed: "Parents should be taught to bless, honor, dignify, conserve, and celebrate their children's sexuality."

References

Alan Guttmacher Institute. *Teenage pregnancy: The problem that hasn't gone away.* New York: Alan Guttmacher Institute, 1981.

Blackman, N. Pleasure and touching: Their significance in the development of the pre-school child. In J. M. Samson (Ed.), *Childhood and sexuality: Proceedings of the international symposium on childhood and sexuality.* Montreal: Editions Etudes Vivantes, 1980.

Byler, R., Lewis, G. M., and Totman, R. J. *Teach us what we want to know.* (Report of a survey on health interests, concerns and problems of 5,000 students in selected schools from kindergarten through grade 12. Published for the Connecticut State Board of Education). New York: Mental Health Materials Center, 1969.

Condon, W., and Sander, L. Neonate movement is synchronized with adult speech. *Science,* 1974, *183,* 99-101.

Fanaroff, A. A., Kennell, J. H. and Klaus, M. H. Follow-up of low birthweight infants: The predictive value of maternal visiting patterns. *Pediatrics,* 1972, *49,* 287-290.

Gadpaille, W. Psychosexual developmental tasks imposed by pathologically delayed childhood: A cultural dilemma. In S. Feinstein and P. Giovacchini (Eds.), *Adolescent psychiatry* (Vol. 6). Chicago: University of Chicago Press, 1978.

Gilligan, C. Sexual dilemmas at the high school level. In M. Calderone (Ed.), *Sexuality and human values.* New York: Association Press, 1974.

Green, R. 'Sissies' and 'tomboys.' SIECUS Report VII/3, 1979.

Harlow, H. F., and Harlow, M. Social deprivation in monkeys. *Scientific American* 1962, *473,* 1-11.

Kinsey, A. C., Pomeroy, W. B., Martin, C. E., and Gebhard, P. H. *Sexual behavior in the human female.* Philadelphia: W. B. Saunders, 1953.

Klaus, M. H., Jerauld, R., Kreger, N. C., McAlpine, W., Steffa, M., and Kennell, J. H. Maternal attachment: Importance of the first post-partum days. *New England Journal of Medicine,* 1972, *286,* 460-463.

Langfeldt, T. Aspects of sexual development, problems and therapy in children. In J. M. Samson (Ed.), *Childhood and sexuality: Proceedings of the international symposium on childhood and sexuality.* Montreal: Editions Etudes Vivantes, 1980.

Martinson, F. Child sexuality: Trends and consequences. In J. M. Samson (Ed.), *Childhood and sexuality: Proceedings of the international symposium on childhood and sexuality.* Montreal: Editions Etudes Vivantes, 1980.

Mead, M. *New lives for old: Cultural transformation—Manus, 1928-1953.* Westport, Conn., Greenwood Press, 1980.

Money, J., and Ehrhardt, A. A. *Man and woman, boy and girl.* Baltimore: Johns Hopkins University Press, 1972.

Parke, R., and O'Leary, S. Father-mother-infant interaction in the newborn period. In K. Riefel and J. Meacham (Eds.), *The developing individual in a changing world* (Vol. 2). The Hague: Mouton, 1975.

Sarrel, L. S., and Sarrel, P. S. *Sexual unfolding: Sexual development and sex therapies in late adolescence.* Boston: Little, Brown, 1979.

Solnit, A. J. Sexual and gender development in the context of the family, school and society. In E. K. Oremland and J. D. Oremland (Eds.), *The sexual and gender development of young children: The role of the educator.* Cambridge, Mass.: Ballinger Publishing, 1977.

Spitz, R. *The first year of life.* New York: International Universities Press, 1965.

Planning and Politics of Community-Based Human Sexuality Programs

Nancy R. Hamlin

Human sexuality programs are needed throughout our lives. Our sexuality is continually evolving and is affected by the normal aging process. It is an integral part of our being. Sexuality involves our feelings, intellect, and senses, though sex is defined as the biological act of engaging in intercourse.

Sex education has become a political issue. Anti-abortionists have without fanfare won several key positions in the Reagan administration and launched efforts to alter federal policy not just on abortion, but on sex education, family planning, and world population control. Headlines are filled with news on the subjects of abortion, birth control, and the so-called Moral Majority's attacks on women's rights.

United States Health and Human Services Secretary Richard Schweiker is a longtime supporter of a constitutional amendment prohibiting abortion. In Washington, in his first briefing for reporters since his confirmation for the health policy-making job, he stated that he would lobby for such an amendment in his present post. He has also said, "I don't think the federal government should be in the sex education business" (Aborting Deformed Fetuses, 1981, p. 8). Edward N. Brandt, Jr., a physician and Church of Christ minister, who is assistant secretary for health in the Reagan administration, has been quoted as saying that he believes abortion should not be an option for a woman who learns that she is carrying a genetically deformed fetus, unless the woman's life is in danger (Aborting Deformed Fetuses, 1981, p. 8). Human sexuality should not be a political issue. It is unfortunate that the personal has become the political. People must have control over their bodies and their destinies. There is a desperate need for community-based human sexuality programs for all people. Regardless of moral views or political affiliations, there are programs which are helpful and informative in meeting basic human needs. It is essential to remember that these programs must match the political, social, and cultural belief systems of the community, and that there must be community involvement and ownership in all aspects of the programs.

In planning sexuality programs, a 3-point design is used. The overall program is divided into the following categories: life-span approach, special population, and life stress or trauma points. In the life-span approach, life transition periods such as adolescence, young adulthood, middle years, pre- and post-menopause and old age are the key areas for program development. Special population groups include the physically handicapped, the mentally retarded, and the mentally ill. Childbirth, divorce, death of a loved one, abortion, rape, and birth of a handicapped child are examples of life stress or trauma points. Specific, targeted, time-limited primary prevention programs are needed for the special population groups and the population affected by life stress or trauma points.

Sexuality, its myths and realities, is not understood by the majority of our people. Sexual problems are found throughout the population as a result of the lack of available and appropriate information. From youth to old age, there appears to be a consistent lack of directed information and education on human sexuality.

Although birth control and abortions are more available today than ever before, teenage pregnancy and venereal disease are in epidemic proportion. The National Center for Health Statistics reports the number of out-of-wedlock births doubled in the U.S. during the period from 1970 to 1976. There are now about one million unmarried teenagers giving birth each year with 9 out of 10 of them keeping their babies (Out-of-Wedlock Births Doubled, 1980). One study showed that even today, 85 to 95 percent of all parents with children under 11 years old have never discussed sexual behavior. Another study found that one-third of mothers and teenage daughters do not discuss sex or birth control with any regularity. Our sex-indulging and sex-denying society lacks adequate sex education programs.

Current literature supports the need for continued sex education, family planning, and human sexuality programs. A recent report based on a long-term study of the New York state experience with legalized abortion presents some interesting and impressive facts. The Alan Guttmacher Institute's report of the state's 10-year experience with legalized abortion showed that abortions improved the health of mothers, babies, and the general populace. Illegal abortions have been virtually eliminated, with the associated death rate dropping from 6.7 per million to .8 per million.

Yet, more than 75 percent of all U.S. counties currently have no abortion services. The imminent passage of new federal legislation to restrict all abortion services will leave few states with any hope of New York's achievement (Decade of Legal Abortions in New York, 1980).

Despite the United State's high standard of living, advanced medical technology, and sophisticated health services, the country ranks 14th internationally in terms of the infant mortality rate. Infant mortality is defined as the number of infants dying after birth and before reaching the age of 1 year. A startling statistic is the horrendous gap between the infant mortality rate of nonwhites and whites. It is 24.9 per 1,000 for nonwhites and 14.8 per 1,000 for whites (Wheeler, 1980).

The federal government is involved in family planning, at least for the moment. In 1980, the Office of Family Planning spent about 160 million dollars to finance 5,100 family planning clinics around the country to serve 4 million women of all ages. Another 7.5 million dollars was spent on programs to counsel pregnant teenagers. In addition, contraceptives are routinely purchased through Medicaid (The Feds and the Family, 1981).

Although progress has been made over the last decade, few programs exist to meet the special needs of the mentally ill, the mentally retarded, or the physically handicapped. The general population appears to fare no better. The future of sex education seems to be linked to the politics of our times.

I will discuss programs, paradigms, and strategies which have been used to develop community-based human sexuality programs and present a model which suggests strategies for bringing about change in communities and in institutions. It emphasizes that change is a slow, planned, and sometimes irrational process.

History and Politics

The history of sex education can be traced back to the Bible. Its teachings permeated the sexual attitudes, values, and behavior of the entire Judeo-Christian world. Until the 20th century, Judeo-Christian religious teachings dominated the sexual morality in the United States. The nature of sexual relationships between men and women in and out of marriage was, and is still, greatly influenced by religious teachings. The Bible leaves no question but that our foreparents believed sexuality to be deeply embedded in the human personality. In the Old Testament, sex is regarded as a gift of God. Genesis speaks of the creation of man and woman as sexual beings (Schiller, 1973).

How did the positive turn into the negative, "sex is sin?" Many New Testament scholars believe Paul was quoted out of context, "It is well for a man not to touch a woman," and followed through with the notion that sexual intercourse is the "original sin." Asceticism, virginity, and self-denial were widely regarded as the religious route to God. These ideas were supported by Augustine and later by John Calvin. The church is still active in our moral codes, attitudes, and legal system today. The Roman Catholic Church has been recognized by all parties in the abortion controversy as the strongest institutional force in the antiabortion crusade (Fishman, 1979). It is reported that Catholics comprise about half the membership of the national movement and support it with hundreds of thousands of dollars. The U.S. Catholic Conference, an official organ of the church, freely issues "pro-life" propaganda (along with propaganda on a host of other right-wing issues).

The Bishops' Conference, which receives at least 90 percent of its funds from the Catholic Church, has developed a "Pastoral Plan for Pro-Life Activities." It is the Bishops' Conference which has established the National Committee for the Human Life Amendment to push a constitutional amendment against abortion. The committee receives roughly 300,000 dollars annually from various Catholic dioceses throughout the country (Fishman, 1979).

The Moral Majority

The John Birch Society, the Christian Crusade, and the Moral Majority have attacked the Sex Information Education Council of the United States (SIECUS) since 1968. Their campaign charges that certain persons interested in SIECUS and educational programs were communist or communistically inclined. An attempt was made to link sex education with the "communist conspiracy" of the 1950s.

The Moral Majority seems to be linking sex education with the breakdown in values, morals, and family life. The following are excerpts taken from its January 1, 1981, newsletter written by Jerry Falwell (see Appendix A).

We have only begun to fight. If the liberals and advocates of pornographic sex education think that, by smearing me, they can stop the Moral Majority's campaign to remove offensive sex education meterial from our pulic classrooms...they have another guess coming. We cannot compromise our children's moral values because a small minority of people in America don't believe in the traditional moral principles this nation was founded upon . . . .

If you find obscene books, films, or other such material being used by our young people in schools, please advise us right away. We will then publish this information in our Moral Majority report newspaper and inform the public on our daily radio commentary. Then, you can politely, but firmly, take reasonable action where you live.

Human Life Campaign

The new right is trying to change the United States Constitution so that it will include the Human Life Amendment (HLA). This would outlaw some low-dose birth control pills and the IUD, and would destroy a woman's right to have an abortion by making it a felony to obtain or perform an abortion. Because this bill does not permit the use of most birth control methods and abortion, it seriously endangers the life and health of all women. The HLA bill, sponsored by Senator Helms and Representatives Hyde, Dorman, Asbrook, and others, forbids ending any pregnancy for any reason. Abortions for pregnancies resulting from rape or incest, and abortions necessary to save the life or preserve the health of the mother would be forbidden. All versions of the HLA would declare the fertilized egg, visible only under a microscope as a person, entitled to complete protection. The Helms/Dorman Amendment reads: "The paramount right to life is vested in each human being from the moment of fertilization without regard to age, health or condition of dependency."

The HLA would outlaw the birth control pill and the IUD; the rationale being that the pill and IUD can prevent the implantation of the fertilized egg, thus denying it the "right to life." Under the HLA some forms of birth control become equivalent to murder; moreover, if a woman should have a miscarriage or spontaneous abortion, she could be investigated to determine whether it was accidental or intentional. She could be subject to criminal prosecution. The HLA obviously denies the basic rights of all human beings to make decisions, not only about their own bodies, but ultimately about their own destinies.

The following are examples of what the Moral Majority consider objectionable material taken from *Our Bodies, Ourselves* (see Appendix B):

I confined my sexual involvement to heavy petting since the Catholic Church makes intercourse seem like such a sin. The day I left the church was the day I had an argument with the priest about whether having intercourse with my fiancé was a sin. I maintained it wasn't; he said that I would never be a faithful wife if I had intercourse before marriage. He refused me absolution and I never came back . . . .

It's exciting to make up sexual fantasies while masturbating or to masturbate when we feel those fantasies coming on . . . .

If you have never masturbated, we invite you to try it . . . .

Not until we have an economic-social system that puts people before profit will everyone be able to participate. (pp. 43-47, 113)

Power, Politics, and Repression

Yet another perspective was offered by Lori Bradford in 1980 in an article titled, "Evangelism: The Electronic Church and Conservative Politics." It provides a view of how technology is being used by the new right.

The Moral Majority under different names is infiltrating television networks, church groups and developing new concerned citizen groups throughout the country. Recently the conservative Christians have poured money into the creation of a Christian-owned and operated radio and television station, thus creating an "electronic church," which utilizes computer technology in its mailings and targeted membership drives . . . . Political lobbying organizations have been established as the political arms of the various versions of the "Body of Christ" . . . . The Moral Majority, Inc., is an offshoot of Falwell's "Old Time Gospel Hour" ministry based in Lynchburg, Virginia having 37 chapters nationwide . . . . The stated purpose is to "preserve biblical morality" and "to mobilize the grass roots of moral America." The Christian Voice is the lobbying arm of the American Christian Cause . . . . It compiled a "hit list" of 36 Senators and Congressmen with poor moral voting records calling for strong stands against anything anti-family; communal living, abortion, homosexuality, polygamy, child or wife abuse, abusive use of alcohol or drugs, premarital sex, incest, adultery, pornography, no-fault divorce and the ERA. (Bradford, p. 10)

Falwell is the director of the religious empire that employs 1,200 people, and has a budget of over $65 million. The mainstay of the organization is the "Old Time Gospel Hour," a program seen on 324 television stations in the United States, Canada, and the Caribbean. The Falwell conglomerate includes the Liberty Baptist College, and the "I Love America Singers," who performed at the Republican Convention.

In the May/June, 1973, edition of *The Humanist*, Lester A. Kirkendall offers the following list of right-wing groups besides the Moral Majority: the Ku Klux Klan and the John Birch Society, which are attacking sex education; American Council of Christian Churches; American Education Lobby; Association of Citizens for Responsible Education (ACRE); Christian Crusade; Church League of America; Citizens for Moral Education of Central Florida (CMECF); Concerned Citizens of Hawaii (CCH); Concerned Citizens Information Council (CCIC); Conservative Society of America; Friends of the (name of state) Schools; Illinois Council for Essential Education (ICEE); Liberty Lobby; Manion Forum; Mothers for Decency in Action (MDA); Mothers Organized for Moral Stability (MOMS); Movement to Restore Decency (MOTOREDE); Parents Opposed to Sex Education (POSE); People against Unconstitutional Sex Education (PAUSE); Sanity of Sex (SOS); and, the Citizens Committee of California Incorporated (CCCI).

The Evangelical Church encourages Christian businessmen to become involved. Behind the successful evangelical movement lies the expert advice of political experts, not religious leaders, Ed Ateer for example. Ed Ateer, a veteran marketing man for the Colgate-Palmolive Company, set up a nonpartisan, interdenominational group called the Religious Roundtable. Among its 56 members are most of the major television evangelists and the new right politicians. In a political rally in Dallas 15,000 faithful attended a rally. Candidate Reagan said, "I know you cannot endorse me but, I want you to know that I endorse you." The Moral Majority and the Christian Voice raised more than 3 million dollars to elect Reagan and other conservatives to office (Bradford, 1980, p. 10).

Ellen Willis in the February 4, 1980, edition of the *Village Voice* suggests that:

> The anti-abortion movement is the most dangerous political force in the country ... the cutting edge of neo-fascism, a threat not only to women's rights and to everyone's sexual freedom and privacy, but to freedom of religion and civil liberties in general. Right to Life propaganda leaves no doubt that abortion is only the immediate focus of a larger crusade. To crush women's liberation, sexual 'immorality,' birth control, sex education, and all other manifestations of 'Godless Humanism' which is the separation of church and state—in favor of patriarchal authority, the traditional family and 'Christian values' that is, Christianity at its most authoritarian, parochial and bigoted. (p. 8)

Members of the feminist movement suggest that the answer to why the new right is attacking women's rights may lie in Wilhelm Reich's theory that sexual represssion is tied to repressive governments. A special feature of right-wing political activity seems to be to develop a climate of hysteria around sexual issues such as abortion, equal rights, and sexually explicit information, and to create scapegoats such as Jews, women, blacks, labor, and so on. This tends to divert attention from what the feminist movement claims are the real issues: poverty, lack of jobs, and the military buildup. The right wing is on the offensive and the left is on the defensive. The activity is focused on financial cutbacks in "people programs" and an increase in defense dollars. It is important to remember that at the time when Americans are being asked to reduce, conserve and cut back, corporations are earning the largest profits ever, and capitalists and multinational corporations are in an expansionary spiral.

The Boston Alliance against Racism and Political Repression says it this way (Feinstein, Goldman, Hatch, and Wolpent, 1980):

> Blaming people who are not responsible for the worsening quality of life keeps us from attacking the real causes of these problems.
> Consider these examples:
> Oil company profits are at a record high despite their claims that hardship is causing them to raise gas prices to nearly $1.50 per gallon.
> Many factories are closing shops in the U.S., laying off large numbers of workers, and moving to countries where labor is unorganized and forced to work for lower wages. Corporation profits keep rising.
> The proposed federal budget for 1980-81 will cut important social services while adding even more to the military budget. (p. 8)

The Legal System

The judicial system also plays an important role in the politics of sex education. Ellen Willis, in the February 4, 1980, edition of the *Village Voice* states:

> Judge John Dooling's decision striking down the Hyde Amendment is heartening in a way that transcends its strictly legal impact: for the first time a federal judge has taken the offensive against the arguments and tactics of the right-to-life movement. The ruling does not contain a word of denunciatory rhetoric, yet simply by accumulating facts, it damns the movement as cruel, dishonest, and fanatical, devoid of decent regard either for the health and welfare of women or for anyone's freedom of conscience. (p. 8)

Personal Involvement

My own involvement in the human sexuality movement began when I gave birth to Rachel 12 years ago. Giving birth resulted in the realization of who I am, as a woman, as a mother and as a community person. I was young, uninformed about childbirth, poor, and isolated. I tapped into my own anger and resources about what happens to poor women and babies in childbirth. I discovered a deep desire to witness social change. I saw that I could experience the role of wife, mother, working woman, and still not be in charge of my own life.

Birth gave me an opportunity to learn about myself during a period of change and growth. The most critical discovery I made as a young pregnant woman was that in giving birth, I faced death. I view birth as a growth experience, and like Eastern philosophers, I believe that "life is a process and not an end-product."

Childbirth can be a life adventure and a woman's true coming of age. It is considered by some as perhaps the single most important event in a woman's life, at least for those who are free to choose to have a baby. It is also the birth of a new being, something very natural and beautiful. Many professionals imply that they are the only ones who know enough to make decisions for the good of the baby. Thus, many couples are denied their birthright by having professionals make the decisions for them. As a young, poor, uninformed, pregnant woman I found the system did not offer community-based prepared childbirth classes, unbiased information about breast-feeding, medications, or parenthood. The hospital-based childbirth system was geared to produce no-problem patients. Lie down, take a shot, and let us be the "miracle makers" seemed to be the basic philosophy, and it is to this day. Only a very few are permitted to "deviate."

I channeled this anger into a solid commitment to working in my home town of Lynn, Massachusetts, a poor, high-risk, multiethnic community. My work focused on creating a network of free community education services, offering free childbirth and parenting education classes to single women and poor families. The goal was to give women the opportunity to make informed decisions, thus gaining control of this natural experience.

Program Definition and Development

The planning and promotion of community-based human sexuality programs are complex. The planners and advocacy groups constantly change, whereas the professional medical opposition remains constant and persistent.

I am defining human sexuality programs in an educational context. Sex is a fundamental dimension of human awareness and development. It is innately a part of the ever present desire for personal expression and satisfaction. Life-styles reflect the manner in which individuals attempt to accomplish this goal, as well as the developmental stages at which people are functioning. Sex education takes into consideration that sex is at the base of our personality and identity. It incorporates our gender, anatomy, and physiology (Schiller, 1977, p. 133).

Human sexuality programs are needed throughout our life-span. Programs are essential for children, adolescents, adults, and the elderly. In planning human sexuality programs, this three-pronged scheme provides a conceptual framework:

life-span approach

special population groups

points of strees and/or trauma

Life-Span Approach

The task and scope of sex education are to develop the ability of the child, adolescent, and adult to cope with their individual sexuality. One often hears the term "sex education" and immediately focuses on the much needed and infrequently present school-based sex education program. However, human sexuality programs are needed throughout one's life-span. Programs are needed before, during, and after childbirth. Pregnant women and new mothers are plagued with myths and questions about their sexuality. How may times have you heard the myth that "women cannot get pregnant while breast-feeding" and that "having intercourse will bring on labor."

In 1972, a group of committed volunteers and I founded People's Education Organization for Prepared Life Experience (PEOPLE). The following is the mission statement:

Project PEOPLE, People's Educational Organization for Prepared Life Experiences, was developed by myself and a group of professional and lay people to offer free quality education to all people, particularly those of low socioeconomic circumstances in the greater Lynn area. It was felt that many people are not meeting life's experiences with the aid of information and support that would increase the probability of a happy, fulfilled life. Project PEOPLE is a group of concerned and dedicated individuals who have volunteered their time to offer seminars, workshops, and rap sessions in the areas of (1) childbirth education, (2) sex education, (3) early childhood education, (4) human growth and development, and (5) drug education, so that individuals would have the choice of planning and participating in the educational program.

PEOPLE'S classes were located at community schools and the Community Health Center, and the Lynn Girl's Club (Hamlin, 1972).

The purposes of the organization were:

to help unwed women and married couples attain a better understanding of childbirth and early parenthood in the belief that prepared, well-informed mothers can best experience the birth of a baby as one of the most meaningful and inspiring moments of life. Unwed mothers and expectant parents that participate actively in this program have an opportunity to have the optimum maternity experience;

to insure support for mothers who choose to breast-feed by the establishment of a Nursing Mothers' Telephone Council;

to provide essential information on the intellectual, social, emotional, and physical development of young children;

to offer people birth control and family planning information;

to help people understand drugs, their use, and their effects;

to provide all people, especially low-income people, with free, quality family life education;

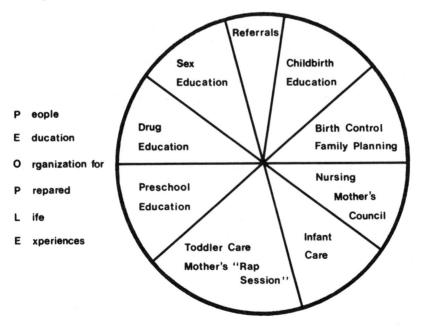

Figure 1. Project PEOPLE's Organizational Model.

to refer individuals in need of additional information or help to the proper agency.

The program was explained by viewing life as a continuum with sexuality, childbirth, and human growth and developmental issues integrated into the cycle. The following circle represents the PEOPLE model.

Project PEOPLE, which is free and nondiscriminatory, is a unique model for prepared family life experiences. The family or single parent began with prepared childbirth classes. Following the child's birth, the parents and child were invited to join a postpartum group to discuss the physical, psychological, and intellectual developments faced by the new mother. To give support to women who chose to breast-feed their child, a nursing mothers' telephone council was established which had an obstetrical nurse, a social worker, and a trained nursing mother on call. Birth control and family planning seminars were also given. A workshop in early childhood behavior was established to discuss topics such as discipline, behavior, toys, creative arts, planning and evaluation of preschool programs. Parents of preschool-age children had the choice of attending a child study "rap session" in which the group found its own subject focus. The goal of the sex education segment of PEOPLE was to provide parents and young people with an understanding of human reproduction and to encourage open discussion of sex. Our Bodies, Ourselves was both the name of the discussion group and the title of a handbook written by the Boston Women's Health Book Collective. The drug education component of the program was directed toward understanding the effect drugs have on the body as well as on the unborn fetus.

Community involvement was essential to the success of this program. From the outset, it was apparent that to succeed PEOPLE needed to reach individuals in need of services and insure their participation in the program. Equally important was an awareness and understanding of the needs of the community and of the learning process. Community people initiated the concept of PEOPLE and participated in all aspects of its development. In order to try to insure the continuance of PEOPLE, an interested community person, an "assistant," shared the responsibility with each group leader in the goal that each "assistant" would become the instructor.

Project PEOPLE had as its basic premise that parents were by far the most important positive influence in helping a child become socially, emotionally, physically, and intellectually mature. PEOPLE's position was that well-informed mothers would best experience the birth of a baby as one of the most meaningful and inspiring moments of life. Project PEOPLE hoped to begin a cycle that would produce informed, happy parents who would raise informed, happy children.

For 2 years, I coordinated project PEOPLE with all volunteers, teaching classes and training assistants. Ultimately funding was received from the Massachusetts Office for Children and then the Department of Public Welfare.

Another example of a life-span program is the prenatal and perinatal program sponsored by the Greater Lynn Community Mental Health Center. It offers weekly support groups for expectant parents and sponsors a monthly educational program. The new parents receive a "Pierre the Pelican" newsletter for the first 5 years of the child's life. The program was established to help parents cope with their problems and fears, to offer information on parenting, and to increase parents' confidence in their new role. Parental interaction, readjustment to a new life-style, and sexuality are key topics discussed.

Menopause support groups are another example of a life-span program. The physiological, sociologial, and psychological factors surrounding the second 40 years of a woman's life still remain a mystery for most women. For example, in Boston, a menopause support group exists for women to learn about menopause and to share their feelings, impressions, and fears about this new stage in their lives. Just the other day a 48-year-old widow told me of her expensive encounters with several well-known Boston clinics. Her concern was the changing quality and consistency of her hair. Not one clinic suggested that hormonal menopausal changes could have affected her hair. Menopausal and postmenopausal support groups are needed to help women develop a positive understanding and approach to this phase of life.

The elderly are not asexual. In California, Project SAGE works in nursing homes with senior citizens. Their program focuses on human sexuality, communication skills, T'ai Chi, movement, and relaxation.

Sex education programs can be offered through churches, universities, or the community. The Unitarian-Universalist Church has developed an excellent sex education program for teenagers and their parents. Boston University Medical School, Johns Hopkins Medical School, and the Greater Lynn Community Mental Health Center Training Institute offer programs such as "Sexual Attitude Reassessment" for professionals. Community groups can also provide networks for adults to share ideas and feelings about their sexuality. Women's liberation consciousness-raising groups and know your body courses are other well-known vehicles.

At a recent "Sexual Attitude Reassessment Course," which I attended, participants said, "The program helped me focus on my own sexuality," and "I learned to be more sensitive to the give and take in relationships;" also "I better understood and respected others sexual alternative life-styles." Other comments included, "I am better able to separate myth and realities regarding sexuality, I am better able to understand my partner's needs, and I am able to talk more openly about how I feel about my sexuality."

Special Populations and Sex Education

For the last 5 years, I have shared friendship and office with the founder of the Handicapped Peoples' Support Program (HPSP). This volunteer program based on the self-help philosophy believes that people who have successfully adjusted to their own disabilities are better qualified in relating to and understanding what the special needs are of others with similar handicaps. HPSP focuses on the social and psychological needs of people with physical handicaps through a threefold model of working with physical medicine, mental health, and peer counselors. This "triage" approach is followed by participation in mutual support groups. A readjustment to personal sexuality is integrated into the context of the program.

Attending a recent Boston conference on "Sexuality and the Handicapped," one of the HPSP volunteers, an amputee, stressed the importance of peer counseling in sexuality. She spoke of the intense feelings and anxieties which she experienced reengaging in sex after her operation and her need to have peer support.

Human sexuality programs are not limited to the needs of the "normal" population. Special human sexuality programs for institutionalized, mentally ill, and retarded patients are essential. For these patients, the problem of living in an institutional setting must be taken into account. From my own observations, even in the finest institutional settings for retarded citizens, the bathroom is sometimes the only place where a resident can find privacy.

Deinstitutionalization brought with it a whole host of exciting challenges. In Lynn, the Greater Lynn Mental Health and Mental Retardation Association addressed the issues of sex education and retarded citizens by offering a 3-day training program for parents and professionals. This program was followed by years of planning, involving parents, community agencies, and consultants. The outcome is an agency, community, family, and individualized approach to human sexuality including policies, programs, privacy, and respect for the basic needs and human rights of retarded citizens.

The program consists of educational groups, birth control counseling, and parental involvement. The groups are composed of seven clients and are run by cotrainers for 7-week periods. Client selection is based on the client's functional level of retardation, whether they are mildly or severely retarded. The curriculum depends on the level of the group. A well-functioning group may discuss feelings, relationship issues, and sexual intercourse. A less well-functioning group may focus on friendship, the parts of the body, how to avoid being taken advantage of and/or violation in the community. Since clients are at different levels of sexual development, birth control and family planning counseling are individualized. Clients are taught individual responsibility within the family, and agency staff reinforce the prescribed plan. Women are frequently counseled to use birth control pills or an IUD. The men are taught to take responsibility by using condoms.

The profoundly, severely retarded are not forgotten. A special consultant works with these clients in body movement, verbal and nonverbal communication, and getting in touch with their bodies.

Parents are an integral part of the program. They are invited to attend the groups and meet with the family planning counselor. Parents are encouraged to see their children's sexuality in developmental, chronological, and physiological terms, not simply in terms of the child's mental age. The philosophy of the program is not to foster or to discourage sexual activity, but to understand that sexuality can be expressed by retarded people. The goal is to help clients express their sexuality in positive, healthy ways. Parental consent is mandatory for participation, and the success of the program depends on parental involvement. When clients are living in group community-based facilities, it is essential to involve residential staff and case managers, who are seen in the surrogate parent role. Parents and community staff attend the program with clients. It does absolutely no good to train the mentally retarded client if parents and staff are not involved. Some parents enter a "Train the Trainer" program and are taught to help other parents. They often become cotrainers in the group. It is found that parents of mentally retarded people relate better to other parents.

Life Stress/Trauma Points

Divorce Education

Life is a developmental process. If we accept the notion that sexuality is at the core of this development, then all aspects of human life must be reexamined with our sexuality in mind. For example, with one out of two marriages ending in divorce, divorce groups and seminars must present people with an understanding of the changes brought about by new feelings, behaviors, and social mores. This knowledge can be catalogued under "anticipatory preventive education."

The Newport, Rhode Island, Divorce and Mediation Resource Center offers community forums, educational support groups, assertiveness training, and social effectiveness groups for the divorced and separated. Popular topics included in the community forums are: dating, being single in a couple's world, new relationships, and dealing with loneliness. (Sullivan, 1980).

An 8-week educational group provides time for members to establish peer support and work through the mourning process in which they are involved. The topics are similar to those of the community forum, but more specific and comprehensive. The curriculum includes:

introduction to the divorce process;

coping with loneliness and ambivalence;

handling guilt and feelings of failure;

children and divorce;

alternative ways of handling anger;

looking at emotional patterns;

new relationships;

saying goodbye and looking ahead.

Support groups are held in participants' homes.

Assertiveness training offers practice in communication skills to help divorced and separated people increase their effectiveness in new social, work, and family situations.

The social effectiveness training program is directed toward divorced, separated, widowed, and single adults. The purpose of the series is to help people meet affiliation needs. Many adults, after years of marriage, are anxious and ill at ease relating to the opposite sex in the single world. Some people marry early in life and never develop these skills. Skill training in this area is a preventative service which helps single people recognize the problem and develop strategies to handle it rather than withdrawing into further isolation.

Childbirth and Family Life Education
Family life education is a polite term coined to mean sex education, childbirth education, family planning programs, exercise classes, preparation for childbirth, and nutrition and postpartum education. All of these issues are either emotionally or politically charged. Sex educators working in schools are plagued with the nagging question of whether responsibility lies with the home or with the school. Many progressive parents would welcome the opportunity to discuss sexuality with their teenagers but need support and guidance.

Childbirth is often the first crisis one encounters in adulthood. If home birth and prepared childbirth offer the opportunity to promote self-help, self-care, and primary prevention medicine, then this life crisis allows for a key opportunity to affect a person's coping skills throughout life. The impact of this experience has ramifications on all aspects of both parents' and children's lives.

In the medical community, childbirth education has been controversial. It brings into play complex medical, ethical, and legal questions for practicing physicians and, to a lesser extent, for hospitals. The prepared childbirth movement of the 1950s, 1960s and early 1970s, whose goal was to bring fathers and significant others into the labor and delivery rooms and provide women with the opportunity to have natural childbirth, was followed by the home birth movement of the 1970s and 1980s.

Through the 1970s, I saw the prepared childbirth movement grow. I saw hospitals rapidly convert to family-centered maternity units with hospital-based classes. Some childbirth educators describe the 1970s as the "co-optation of the prepared childbirth movement." Childbirth classes became increasingly hospital-based. The philosophy focused on teaching women to be "good patients" who would accept the fetal monitor, medication, induced labor, unnecessary Caesarean section, intravenous feeding, and episiotomy.

In the mid-1970s, the home birth movement gained momentum. In Massachusetts, the Boston Health Planning Council and the North Shore Health Planning Council both grappled with this major political issue of home births. Many physicians flatly resisted the notion of individuals and physicians attending home births. On the North Shore there was discussion of outlawing home births because there was no emergency back-up system available. The compromise was that one out-of-hospital birth center was set up in a cottage next to the Beverly Hospital. The North Shore Birthing Center is staffed by nurse midwives, who are supervised by a physician. Women are screened carefully and only low-risk women are accepted. Emergency equipment is available, but out of sight. The hospital is present for any crisis.

Different models are needed to meet the needs of high-risk and low-risk births. Currently, many systems, as promulgated in state and national guidelines are based on a monolithic model of regional maternity centers. From a quality of care point of view, it is often argued that a sufficient volume of patients or procedures is necessary for staff to maintain a high level of proficiency. A single study by the American College of Obstetricians and Gynecologists (1971) suggested that units with less than 500 deliveries per year often lacked personnel, services, and equipment necessary for adequate maternity and newborn care. As a result of this one inadequate study, the quality of care is presumed related to the volume of service provided.

Results of recent studies show there is no basis in terms of quality care and the outcome for the arbitrary figures assigned as minimum numbers of annual births. Further research has also shown that there are no supporting data available which show the actual cost, much less the cost effectiveness of this system of care. Such figures as available are based on 1973 data from a Level 2 hospital in New Jersey. The figures are cited in Appendix C of a well-known document, "Toward Improving the Outcome of Pregnancy," which has been used widely in maternity care planning. According to Norma Swenson, founder of the Boston Association of Childbirth Education (BACE), past president of International Childbirth Education Association and coauthor of *Our Bodies, Ourselves,* there is no evidence which proves that a regional system of childbirth will improve the quality of the childbirth experience. In fact, low-risk mothers do not need the sophisticated technology of hospitals and highly trained obstetrical staff. They are well served by an out-of-hospital birthing center or a nurse midwife in the home with an emergency back-up system. It is a far more humane and cost effective approach. The North Shore Birthing Center's total fee is $800 as compared with the $2,300 fee for an inpatient maternity stay. If a woman is covered under comprehensive maternity benefits, Blue Cross-Blue Shield pays for either service (Cramer, 1981).

High-risk mothers tend to be poor; they receive late prenatal care and are nutritionally deficient. They need high technology care only because they do not receive proper care in pregnancy. These women are better served by a familiar, accessible community-based hospital, staffed by nurse midwives and physicians. Nurse midwives follow the pregnant woman prenatally in the home and hospital. This model can frequently change her status from high to low risk. A program model designed for high-risk mothers needs to include:

a nutrition program;

nurse midwives who follow the pregnant women prenatally in the home and hospital;

a team of nurse midwives and doctors working together;

prenatal and postnatal educational groups;

staff which is representative of the ethnic composition of the community.

The nutrition and outreach program will identify high-risk mothers early in their pregnancy. Prenatal care will begin earlier in order to prevent and reduce complications at birth.

Maternal and newborn services need to be reconceptualized and reorganized with the greatest emphasis on preventative primary ambulatory care utilizing nurse midwives, and implementing substantial food, nutrition, and outreach programs for high-risk mothers. This will reduce costs for all maternity patients. Prompt attention must be paid to the proliferation and expansion of high technology centers, and the development of birth centers must continue.

Birth has become a political issue because it involves money, and large amounts of money. If birth is treated as a normal, natural, and nonpathological experience, many people will stay out of the hospital, they will not use drugs, and will not bottlefeed their babies; altogether this will mean a loss of millions of dollars for the medical and baby industries.

The most important challenges facing childbirth in the 1980s is to help make it a creative growth experience for parents. Childbirth between now and the year 2000 must involve:

the development of out-of-hospital birth centers;

acceptance of home births and midwives;

establishment of community-based birth centers;

mutual support groups for pregnant women and new mothers;

greater cooperation between doctors and midwives;

food and nutrition programs for high-risk mothers.

Issues in Planning

Strategies for Bringing About Change

There are three strategies for bring about change. In creating new programs, organizers must remember that planned change is conscious, deliberate, and intended. Planned change utilizes knowledge as a tool for modifying patterns and institutions.

First, the *empirical rational strategy* assumes people are rational and will follow their rational self-interest once this is revealed to them. A change is proposed by some person or group which knows of a situation that is desirable, effective and in line with the self-interest of the person, group, organization, or community that will be affected by the change. Second, the *normative reeducative model* is based on the belief that norms from the basis of behavior and change come through reeducation in which old norms are discarded and supplanted by new ones. To quote Bennis, Benne, and Chin (1969) "Changes in normative orientation involve change in attitudes, values, skills, and significant relationships. It is not just change in knowledge and information or intellectual rationals" (p. 34). Emphasis is on experimental learning as an ingredient for all enduring changes in human systems (Bennis, et al., 1969). This system centers on the belief that "people technology is necessary in working out desirable changes in human affairs."

Third, *application of power* assumes the compliance of those with less power with those with greater power. When working within and without institutions, it is essential to understand the three models. At times, all three are factors in institutional decision making.

I believe, judging from my experience, that changing people's attitudes and values is the most important ingredient in the implementation of any new program. For this reason, I believe in a values-oriented approach to the training of people. Organizational change begins with people because people constitute the institution.

A normative reeducative model was used in developing a Comprehensive Rape Crisis Program at the Greater Lynn Community Mental Health Center (see Appendix C).

Taboo topics like rape usually bring out feelings of anxiety coupled with resistance. When dealing with any taboo topic, a values-oriented approach to training focusing on changing people's attitudes is essential to the success of the program. The mental health center staff and community advocates attended 100 hours of training over a 2-year period. The training dealt with the societal values, myths, and realities of rape; counseling victims; sexuality; "rap groups;" the legal system; and advocacy. The program is still functioning.

Because maintaining innovation is difficult, there is a built-in need for retraining annually. Goodwin Watson and Edward Glaser offer this warning:

Many an innovation brought in with great fanfare is superficially accepted, and months or years later things drifted back to the way they were before. Nobody may have openly resisted the change. Nobody revoked it. It just didn't last. (Cited in Havelock, 1973, p. 133)

Change Agents: Advantages and Disadvantages

Change agents is a term used to indicate people inside and/or outside a system who are planners and innovators. Over the last decade, I have functioned as both a change agent working in the community and as a change agent working inside institutions. There are advantages and disadvantages to both roles. The inside change agent has the advantage of knowing the system, speaking the language, identifying with the system's needs and aspirations, and being a familiar figure. Disadvantages facing the inside change agent include lacking perspective, not having adequate knowledge, having to live down past failures, not being able to move independently, and facing the difficult task of redefining ongoing relationships with other members of the system.

Advantages of functioning as an outside change agent include starting fresh, being in a position to be objective, being independent, and bringing in something which is genuinely new. The disadvantages faced by outside change agents are that they are strangers to the system, they may lack knowledge of the insiders, they may not care enough, and they may appear threatening to insiders.

Project PEOPLE, mentioned earlier, provides an example of a program developed by a group of outside change agents. The effect that PEOPLE's prepared childbirth class had on the local community hospital was to demonstrate a need for and to mobilize the institution to offer hospital-based and-controlled childbirth education classes. The PEOPLE's childbirth classes illustrated the effect that the national prepared childbirth movement had on hospitals throughout the country. Most hospitals now offer childbirth classes.

One solution for program planners is to develop a team approach involving inside and outside change agents. An example of this approach is the rape crisis program previously mentioned. In this program I served as an inside change agent representing the Greater Lynn Community Mental Health Center working with outside change agents, the Community Task Force, which is a volunteer group.

Freda Klein, who served as a consultant to the group, published an article on the experience entitled, "Developing New Model Rape Crisis Centers" (Klein, 1977). She described it this way:

Autonomy was a crucial question from the outset. Because the Community Mental Health Center funded the initial training and offered resources including meeting space, and typing and mailing costs, the Task Force's obligation became murky. After a long, sometimes tense process, we have developed a unique model: the Community Task Force, the Greater Lynn Community Mental Health Center and Union Hospital . . . three separate bodies working cooperatively to provide comprehensive services to rape victims and community education-preventive programs. This model is an outgrowth of the anti-rape movement, which won reforms from institutions. Since the Community Mental Health Center and the hospital must treat rape victims within a certain geographical area, there was no possibility for the community task force to become the only rape crisis center . . . .

We are without the burden of basic fundraising because the Community Mental Health Center provides a 24-hour hot line staffed by its Crisis Intervention Team members (calls are then referred to volunteer advocates screened and trained by the Task Force) . . . . Another trade-off concerns outreach. While the Community Mental Health Center has greater resources to conduct systematic outreach campaigns than do most volunteer centers, it is difficult to assess how many victims will avoid our advocacy services because of institutional ties.

The divergent practical conditions facing current anti-rape organizing and organizing of a few years ago are striking. But just as I'm longing for the good ol' days of political purism (and trying to ignore how steeped in privilege that model is), it becomes clear that our new predicaments can be turned into new bargaining positions of strength. (p. 10)

The new model did come with strings. It is incorporatd into a 4.5 million dollar mental health center. Its uniqueness and degree of community visability is married to a large diverse institution. However, in the 1980s many grass-roots women's health centers and rape crisis programs have been forced to close because of insufficient funding. The Greater Lynn Rape Crisis program with its institutional marriage is "alive and well." It has a life of its own, a 24-hour telephone hot line covered by professional counselors, and annual staff retraining programs.

Conclusion

In my 20s and 30s, I was involved in many causes including day care, antiwar, women rights, sex education, civil rights, education for parenthood, and affirmative action movements. My daughter used to play at writing agendas for meetings instead of playing house. It appeared that many battles had been won: fathers were allowed into the delivery rooms, a national daycare bill passed the House and Senate, the Vietnam War ended, *Our Bodies, Ourselves* was on the best-seller's list, abortion was legalized, and affirmative action was being taken seriously. Slowly, in my late 20s, things began to change. While teaching in a Massachusetts community college, I was struck by the apathy of students and the lack of social and political interest—there were no more protests. The aim of the students was to work hard, make money, and "play the game."

I am not yet 40, and I see the victories of my 20s erode. I see the National Human Service System which was assembled over the last decade being dismantled, I see race relations and affirmative action going "out of style." I saw the nation's daycare bill vetoed by former President Nixon and I am currently watching the Community Mental Health Systems Act being dismantled. The 1978 *President's Commission Report on Mental Health* cited primary prevention as one of the top priorities of the national community mental health system. Some ask the question, "Has primary prevention's time come and gone?"

Yes, many of us are fighting the same battle again, but this time we are no longer naive. In the words of Ellen Goodman, "It hits the generation that came into adulthood in the 1960s the hardest. They saw their piece of time as a straight line instead of a cycle. They saw progress as an arrow instead of a pendulum" (Goodman, 1981, p. 15).

I have learned that ground won in battle needs to be continually staked out and consciously held. The test before us lies in whether we can learn the lessons of the earlier activists who learned in lean times how to regroup, change, develop new strategies, and maintain their goals and energies over difficult times. We are fortunate that we have history to lean on and a new generation to join our ranks.

Today society faces a serious challenge. There are those who would wish to control the free dissemination of information concerning human sexuality. Special interest groups have begun to appear whose intention is to disrupt the advancement of study and sensitivity with regard to human sexuality. I feel strongly that we must protect our accomplishments as well as strive to improve the quality of our life goals in the future.

Powerful, knowledgeable people who have an understanding of the system must work together as change agents inside and outside and in coordination with systems to insure that all people receive quality human sexuality programs throughout their life-span. It is essential to work together toward this end to ensure freedom of privacy, freedom of religion, freedom of choice, and control of our sexuality and destiny. Perhaps it would do well to recollect the following passage written during the rise of Hitler by Pastor Martin Neimoller:

They came after the Jews,
    and I was not a Jew, so I did not object.
Then they came after the Catholics,
    and I was not a Catholic, so I did not object.
Then they came after the Trade Unionists,
    and I was not a Trade Unionist, so I did not object.
Then they came after me,
    and there was no one left to object. (cited in Gordon, 1981, p. 2)

As Edmund Burke once said, "All that is necessary for the triumph of evil is for good men (people) to do nothing."

References

Aborting deformed fetuses opposed by Reagan's top health advisor, would end pregnancy only to save woman. *Boston Globe,* May 28, 1981, p. 8.

American College of Obstetricians and Gynecologists, Committee on Maternal Health. *National study of maternity care and survey of obstetric practice and associated services in hospitals in the United States,* Chicago, Ill., 1971.

Bennis, W. G., Benne, K., and Chin, R. *The planning of change* (2nd ed.). New

York: Holt, Rinehart and Winston, 1969.

Boston Women's Health Book Collective. *Our bodies, ourselves* (2nd ed.). New York: Simon and Schuster, 1971.

Bradford, L. E. Evangelism: The electronic church and conservative politics. *Big Mama Rag,* December 1980, p. 20.

Cramer, D. Birth without doctors. *Boston Globe Magazine,* April 12, 1981, pp. 12-13; 24, 29, 30.

Decade of legal abortions in New York proves benefits. *Nation's Health,* December 1980, p. 20.

The feds and the family. *Boston Globe,* Feb. 2, 1981, p. 10.

Feinstein, R., Goldman, J., Hatch, H., and Wolpent, E. It ain't necessarily so. In *Myths and facts about racism and the Klan in Boston.* Docudrama, 1980, p. 18.

Fishman, W. K. *The right-wing attack on women.* Paper presented at annual meeting of the American Sociological Association, Boston, Massachusetts, August 1979.

Goodman, E. The second battle is the tough one. *Boston Globe,* March 5, 1981, p.15.

Gordon, S. Sexual politics and the far right. *Impact '80: Journal of the Institute for Family Research and Education,* October 1980, p. 2.

Hamlin, N. Project PEOPLE proposal. Massachusetts Department of Children, 1972, pp.1-3.

Havelock, R. G. *The change agent's guide to innovations in education.* New Jersey: Educational Technology Publication, 1973.

Kirkendall, L. A. The assault of sex education. *The Humanist,* May/June 1973, 13-14.

Klein, F. Developing new models: Rape crisis centers. *FAAR News,* July/August 1977, pp.9-10.

National Foundation of March of Dimes, Committee on Perinatal Health. *Toward improving the outcome of pregnancy,* 1976, pp. 30-33.

Out of wedlock births doubled. *Nation's Health,* November 1980, p.15.

Schiller, P. *Creative approaches to sex education and counseling.* New York: Association Press 1973.

Sullivan, P. Newport Training Institute: Prevention programs, community education and professional development. *Consultation and Education Models that work.* Springfield, Mass., 1980, pp.1-4.

Wheeler, W. H. *Developing and administering mental health services to minorities.* Staff College, National Institute of Mental Health, January 1980, Module 1, 5.

Willis, E. Abortion rights: Overruling new fascists. *Village Voice,* February 4, 1980, pp.8-9.

Appendix A

On a Moral Majority letterhead, showing a logo depicting the U.S. Capitol and an address at 499 S. Capital Street, and with "Confidential" stamped across the top in block capitals, the follow letter was received (dated January 1, 1981).

DEAR MR.— — —
We have only begun to fight!
If the liberals and advocates of pornographic sex education think that, by smearing me, they can stop the Moral Majority's campaign to remove offensive sex education materials from our public classrooms . . . they have another guess coming! We cannot compromise our children's moral principles this nation was founded upon!
Mr.— — —I'm sure you've read in your local newspaper there in— — —about our campaign to alert the parents of America to the insidious efforts of secular humanists to destroy the moral convictions of our boys and girls in some public schools.
Sometimes, they call it sex education — at other times "values clarification,"etc.
Perhaps you even received my letter where I gave you actual excerpts from a textbook so that you could see for yourself how offensive some sex education material is.
But now, we have discovered another book that has been used a reference book in several public school libraries that makes *Life and Health* (the book I mentioned last November) seem almost acceptable.
And that's why I say, we have only begun to fight!
The book is entitled *Our Bodies, Ourselves* and it was published in 1973 by Simon and Schuster. It is possible that material like that which is being used in this book may be found in many school libraries. I want you to help us obtain information on this matter.
Here are just a few of the book's chapter titles:

Living with Ourselves and Others: Our Sexual Relationships

In Amerika They Call Us Dykes

Our Changing Sense of Self

The Anatomy and Physiology of Sexuality and Reproduction

Venereal Disease

Abortion

I tell you, my friend—the little bit of this book that we have read is not only disgusting, it is shocking!

"Most of us were taught sex belongs in marriage. The linking of virginity and marriage often forces us into marriage before we are ready, before we know whether it's something we want."

"Those of us who grew up in religious families may feel that to lose our virginity before marriage is to have sinned."

"If you have never masturbated, we invite you to try. You may feel awkward, self-conscious, even a bit scared at first. You may have to contend with voices within you that repeat, 'Nice girls don't . . .' or 'A happily married woman wouldn't want to . . . .' Most of us have had these feelings too, and they changed in time."

Do you want your children or the children of your loved ones reading this type of immoral trash? This is out and out humanistic garbage!

The parents in Renton, Washington, thought so when they pulled it out of the 9th grade health class in their high school, and the people in Ludlow, Massachusetts, felt the same way when they removed it from their high school after this book had been used for one entire year.

I don't know what this country is coming to when some of our schools openly teach that premarital sex is not sinful—that the moral values that you and I grew up with are outdated and backward.

This is all part of the humanists' attempt to change our society. They realize that we will not endorse free love, free sex, so they are brainwashing our children.

Here are some of the humanists' basic beliefs:

They believe that there are no absolutes (no right, no wrong)—that moral values are self-determined and situational. Do your own thing, "as long as it does not harm anyone else."

They believe in removal of the traditional and distinctive roles of male and female.

They believe in sexual freedom between consenting individuals, regardless of age, including premarital sex, homosexuality, lesbianism, and incest.

So, my friend, if you don't know what books are being used in your public school systems in the sex education classes, I strongly advise that you find out today!

Moral Majority is trying to learn where offensive sex education books like *Our Bodies, Ourselves* and *Life and Health* are being used.

Will you help us obtain that information?

Examine your public school' libraries and textbooks for immoral, anti-family, and anti-American content. Arrange to see the films shown in classrooms. If you find obscene books, films, or other such material being used by our young people in schools, please advise us right away.

We will then publish this information in our Moral Majority Report newspaper and inform the public on our daily radio commentary.

Then, you can politely, but firmly, take reasonable action where you live, Mr. ———!

We do not oppose sex education when it is taught as a biological science. Reproduction, puberty, hygiene, and other such matters should be taught.

And, take into consideration, sometimes objectionable books and materials inadvertently find their way into good schools, where no one intentionally did this. Always be reasonable and gracious. Nothing is ever accomplished by being unkind, belligerent, or violent.

Across the top of this letter was "handwritten": "Please destroy this letter and the sheet I've enclosed immediately after reading them."

Another letter from the Moral Majority, to the same address, was sent in an envelope stamped CONFIDENTIAL - SEXUALLY EXPLICIT MATERIALS ENCLOSED—DO NOT LET THIS LETTER FALL INTO THE HANDS OF SMALL CHILDREN.

It contained the following letter and enclosures:

Any objectionable material should be taken to the principal. If he is unresponsive, go to the school board, state legislators, the governor, and U.S. congressmen.

Do you want your child to choose his values free from your influence and free from any standard of right or wrong based on issues like premarital sex, extramarital sex, homosexuality, lesbianism, and bisexuality?

Do you want books like *Life and Health* and *Our Bodies, Ourselves* being used to influence your child's decisions?

I say "no" Mr. — — —, and I will fight until my last breath to make sure that books like these two are removed from our public schools once and for all.

I'm not against sex education, when taught as a biological science, but I am against offensive sex education materials that distort and warp our children's minds and moral values.

But I need your help in this fight, and that's why I'm writing you today.

The Moral Majority is already working with several organizations to remove these harmful sex education materials that distort and warp our children's minds and moral values.

But I need your help in this fight, and that's why I'm writing you today.

The Moral Majority is already working with several organizations to remove these harmful sex education materials from classrooms. But all this takes money!

Your gift of $10, $15, or even $25 will help us fight to remove books from public schools like *Our Bodies Ourselves* and *Life and Health*.

In addition, Mr — — —, your gift will be used to help us publish our Moral Majority Report newspaper, produce our daily radio commentary, underwrite our large national staff and, in general, to help return this nation to moral sanity.

Believe me, you and I are slowly losing control over what our children are being taught!

And parents are legally responsible for the actions of their children, so it is only proper that they have an interest and a VOICE in what their youngsters are taught in the public schools and the textbooks that are being used!

So won't you help us remove sex education books that are harmful to our children once and for all?

Your gift to the Moral Majority today could make the crucial difference in a child's life!

I hope you will take a moment to look over the special sheet I've enclosed for you today so that you can see for yourself why it is so important that we remove offensive materials from our classrooms and libraries immediately.

Then I encourage you to sit down right away and write me a check for the largest amount you can possibly sacrifice and send it back immediately.

Please let me hear from you soon. Each day counts when a small child's mind and morals are at stake. I will be anxiously awaiting your reply.

Working to Save Our Children,
Jerry Falwell

P.S. Remember—our children's moral values are at stake! Please rush your special gift to Moral Majority right away.

I ask that you destroy this letter and the special sheet I've enclosed immediately after reading it so that it will not fall into the hands of an innocent youngster.

SPECIAL REPLY FORM

Jerry,

   I promise I will do everything in my power to help you remove offensive sex education materials that are being used in our public school systems.

_____
(Please sign here)

☐ YES! I will inquire in our local public libraries and let you know if "Our Bodies/ Ourselves" and/or "Life and Health" is available to our young people.

   Mr. _____

   _____

   _____

Dear Jerry,

☐ YES! I want to help! Enclosed is my special gift to help the Moral Majority continue its fight against offensive sex education materials and to help its other national programs!

Appendix B

IMPORTANT   ADULTS ONLY!

The following are actual excerpts from the book, Our Bodies, Ourselves:

PAGE 26   Photograph of woman using mirror to examine self plus advocating the use of a plastic speculum.

PAGE 39   Chapter entitled SEXUALITY—"When I made love with Jack I felt like he was feeding me. I felt full with his — — — inside me. When I wasn't with him I would feel hungry again. Often I didn't have — — —. I kept coming back to him, though it was an impossible relationship, because I needed to be fed. Later I realized he was mothering me. I was asking him to be my mother. That was a revelation!" Page also has photograph of a nude woman.

PAGE 41   Section entitled SEXUAL LANGUAGE—"I was dancing with a man I liked a lot. We were feeling very sensual. As we moved our bodies to the music I could feel his — — — and — — — pressing on me. He whispered in my ear, 'I bet your — — — is warm and juicy!'"

PAGE 42   Section entitled SEX IN OUR IMAGINATION: OUR FANTA-SIES—"I've had fantasies of having to drink — — — from a man's — — — while he was — — —."

"I used to have a recurring fantasy that I was a gym teacher and had a classful of girls standing in front of me, nude. I went up and down the rows feeling all their — — — and getting a lot of pleasure out of it. When I first had this fantasy at thirteen I was ashamed. I thought something was wrong with me. Now I can enjoy it, because I feel it's okay to enjoy other women's bodies."
I fantasize making love with horses, because they are very sensuous animals, more so than cows or pigs. They are also very male animals—horse society is very chauvinist."

PAGE 43   Section entitled VIRGINITY—"I confined my sexual involvement to heavy petting, since the Catholic Church makes intercourse seem like such a sin. The day I left the Church was the day I had an argument in the confessional with the priest about whether having intercourse with my fiance was a sin. I maintained it wasn't; he said that I would never be a faithful wife if I had intercourse before marriage. He refused me absolution and I never came back."

PAGE 47   Section entitled SEX WITH OURSELVES: MASTURBATION—"It's exciting to make up sexual fantasies while masturbating or to masturbate when we feel those fantasies coming on. Some of us like to insert something while masturbating. Some of us find our — — — or other parts of our bodies erotically sensitive and rub them before or while — — —. Enjoying ourselves doesn't just mean our — — —. We are learning to enjoy all parts of our bodies."

"If you have never masturbated, we invite you to try."

"It's this letting go of control that enables us to have — — —. If you do not reach — — — when you first try masturbating, don't worry. Many of us didn't either. Simply enjoy the sensations you have. Try again some other time."

PAGE   49 "... sometimes I — — — to get away from the tightness and seriousness in myself."

PAGE   36 "Marijuana is rumored to be helpful. If your symptoms are relieved by the heaviest flow of your — — —, try to have an — — — or take a sauna or steam bath, all of which can speed up the flow considerably." Section entitled THE UTERINE CYCLE : MENSTRUATION.

PAGE   51 Section entitled THERE'S MORE THAN INTERCOURSE—"We can — — — and — — — our partner's — — — to — — — or as a part of lovemaking that later may include intercourse. This is called — — —. With our mouths and tongues we can experiment with ways to delight our partners and ourselves. The — — — can be stimulated with — — —. The — — — is highly sensitive to erotic stimulation. However, it is not as elastic as the — — —. Be gentle and careful and use a lubricant (saliva, — — — such as K-Y Jelly) if you have — — — the — — — within the — — —" Note: No medical warning regarding the danger of using foreign object (slender object)!... "We can excite each other with *erotic pictures*, by sharing our fantasies, with the stimulation of a vibrator. Use your imagination. The possibilites are endless. For further suggestions see *The Joy of Sex* and *More Joy* edited by Alex Comfort." Editor's note: See *Washington Post* 9/10/77 - "Raymond Louis Urgo, a Georgetown hairdresser, convicted last June of involuntary manslaughter in the shooting death of his girlfriend at a sex and drug party at his apartment ... One psychiatrist testified yesterday Urgo possessed pornographic literature that gave him the idea of using his revolver—a 357 magnum—as a sexual stimulant by placing the gun's barrel in Miss Kisacky's mouth."

PAGE 113 "Not until we have an economic-social system that puts people before profit will everyone be able to participate."

PAGE 217 Section entitled HISTORY OF ABORTION LAWS AND PRAC-

TICE—"Last and perhaps more insidious, a highly moralistic group obsessed with banning 'sex for pleasure' struck up a campaign against both abortion and birth control."

PAGE 229 Photograph of girl having abortion in her street clothing and caption so notes the fact.

PAGE 233 Section discusses a COMPARISON OF SALINE AND PROSTA-GLANDIN ABORTIONS. Prostaglandin: "There is a likelihood that the fetus will be expelled with signs of life and not expire until shortly afterward—this is why the prostaglandin method is not often used beyond 20 weeks LMP"

PAGE 234 "With saline, the fetus is almost always dead. With prostaglandins the fetus often will show signs of life for a few minutes."

PAGE 243 Section entitled PARENTING IN A COMMUNE—"Communes are often attractive places for single or married parents to live in because child-rearing can be shared with others."

PAGE 353 Photograph—"The obstetrician-gynecologists' view of women."

Although this book is available at various places, we object to our tax dollars being used to provide this explicit, immoral information in our libraries and our schools. We are still "one nation under God."

Appendix C

COMMUNITY MENTAL HEALTH AND RAPE "THINGS TO THINK ABOUT"

1. Reassess your community.
2. What structure best suits your community?
   a. Feminist
   b. Hospital based
   c. Community based
   d. Combination of any of the above.
3. You can work with GLCMHC by coordination of:
   a. direct services
   b. consultation
   c. education
   d. training
   e. hot line
   f. space
   g. secretarial help
   h. information and referral
4. Why work with a mental health center
   a. longevity of service
   b. most # of victim served
   c. financial need
   d. coordination of services
5. Can you re-structure your Center without changing your philosophy?
6. If you don't integrate with a CMHC can you identify key consultants at the mental health center?
7. Why does a mental health center need grass-root groups?
   a. to fulfill their mandate to provide services to victims
   b. to fulfill their mandate of consultation and education

A Rationale for Sex Education in the Public Schools

Mary Lee Neil Tatum

To the chagrin of many educators, public schools often become the dumping ground for problems society has failed to solve. Certain individuals voice objection to sex education in public schools precisely because they feel the schools should not attempt to do what the family itself has failed to do (Thompson, 1981). While it may be true that many families have failed to provide effective sex education, this failure is not a rationale for the inclusion of sex education in the public school curriculum. Rather, schools should remain true to their basic mandate: to provide information, acculturation, and life skills for positive, responsible participation within society. Effective sex education does fit this mandate.

Public education is an important value in our society. Consequently, the omission of sex education from the public school curriculum makes a loud statement. Most school systems have no sex education program. Science classes often eliminate consideration of human reproduction and stop with diagrams of frogs. Health classes very often stop short of discussing sexual health or the romantic or sex-related aspects of relationships. Teachers are sometimes ordered officially not to talk about sexuality in class or in counseling.

To omit sex education creates many problems, not the least of which is the widening of the communication gap between adults and adolescents. Young people quickly begin to realize that adults know something they do not want them to know. For these young people the absence of any mention of sex education in the academic curriculum is a noticeable absence indeed, and can even cause the students to question the integrity of the school curriculum. A disconcerting question forms in their minds: "What is this great mystery that does not allow adults to discuss our sexuality wth us?"

Even in school systems that have no formal sex education, there is, rest assured, some form of informal sex education taking place. Skits in student talent shows, plays in the drama dept, and jokes in the athletic arena often contain subtle sexual overtones. The trouble is that these forms of sexual communication create an atmosphere of innuendo and imply that sex is a joking matter, not something to be taken seriously.

When we include education for sexuality in the public school curriculum, we are saying to young men and women that we think it is a valued part of life. When we elevate sexuality to the level of serious academic consideration, we are putting the concept of human sexuality in a place which is accessible to students. Once young people feel that the topic is approachable, we as educators can ask them to think creatively and to integrate their sexual thoughts, feelings and attitudes into their lives.

Parent-Child Communication

Sex educators firmly believe that family members—specifically the parents—are the primary sex educators of children. Primary sex education includes those things which the family does best: loving, caring, sharing, and displaying affection. Primary sex education can also include direct instruction on sexual matters and the relaying of sex-related information. However, many parents have difficulty in talking with their adolescent children about sexual topics because the parents themselves feel uninformed, ill at ease, and out of touch with their child's peer culture. Some parents shy away from discussing sexual concerns because they fear the emotional impact of sharing sex information with a son or daughter who is obviously becoming sexually mature. Still other parents experience awkwardness discussing sexual relationships between adults because they worry that their children will think that they are talking about themselves.

Even when parents do feel comfortable discussing sexual matters directly with their children, communication breakdowns can occur. For example, parents who act as specific sex educators have an emotional investment in the future behavior of their children. The child senses this parental concern, and this sometimes causes the child to question whether the information is slanted to support the bias of the parent.

All this is not to say that parents should not talk about sexuality with their children. They should. However, young people are also looking for objective, anxiety-free sources of information to clarify their thinking and deal with their fears. This is where the public schools can do the family the most service. The schools can serve the family well if they complement the home's basic sex education by offering the objective forum of the sex education class to students. Most families feel vasty relieved if information about menstrual cycles, pregnancy, contraception, masturbation, sexual responses, romantic relationships, decisions, and reproductive anatomy is being provided by knowledgeable sex educators. The students often feel more comfortable and confident knowing that the information is being presented by an objective instructor.

Music and the Media

The age of television has been commented upon so much that it is almost a cliché to say that the media perpetuate sexual and romantic myths. Television portrays sex without consequences and love without responsibility. Television's portrayal of romantic involvement is unrealistic and superficial. Rarely do television shows depict the real struggle or the deep commitment involved in sustaining interpersonal relationships.

Yet television should not shoulder all the blame for the pervasive effects that unrealistic dramatizations have on impressionable young people. In fact, the real damage to young people is probably due more to the lack of adult commentary on the media. Too often children and adults alike absorb unquestioningly the ideas offered by television. It is probably safe to say that the average family watching television does not comment critically on either the sexual innuendo or the sex-related content of a given production.

Magazines printed for erotic reasons are read by even very young children. Often these children read the magazines in the home, but almost never in front of the parents or with the parent's recognition. Unquestionably, these magazines disseminate misinformation that can be harmful to young people. The sexual content of erotic magazines is often erroneous, misleading, and not the way most parents want their children to learn about loving.

Films are another form of media which have strong influence on children. The film industry with its artistry often has an extremely important point to make about life. The focus or responsibility of the film industry does not center on responsible education for sexuality, nor should we expect it to. Yet families rarely attend the movies together and very often parents have little knowledge of current "in" movies which children or adolescents attend.

Popular music conveys a sexual and often irresponsible sexual message. Although young people protest that they do not "listen to the words," they can generally write down every verse without error if asked to do so. The covers of record albums imply that in the young adult world everyone who is "cool" is without sexual or social responsibility and is interested primarily in the mood of the moment.

The adolescent world of music and media is a cultural symbol for young people, their ticket to adulthood. The media attempt to define what young people should be doing, what they should look like, wear, drink, and smoke. And make no mistake about it, the media's punch packs a wallop. Young adults feel incredible pressures to conform to the images the media paint. Schools can provide a real service by helping students to develop their own critical awareness without telling them to reject—as the family often does—what is obviously an important part of this rite of passage. Serious peer discussion in the classroom about media messages is a more effective way of understanding the impact of these issues than is the typical parent comment. A teacher trained as a facilitator can elicit some general, honest feelings and opinions from teenagers about the ideas and pressures which come from the constant barrage of sexual suggestion. Such discussions help the students to think critically and to draw their own conclusions.

The Peer Group

Adolescents have a need to identify with and be a part of groups. In times past, the groups consisted of people living in rather homogeneous communities. To a large extent the individuals within a particular group encountered other individuals with similar backgrounds, life-styles, and aspirations. There was more sameness, more conformity, and there were more shared values.

Today adolescence is a very different time. Young people may find themselves a part of many different groups which represent varying, conflicting values. The sexual messages young people receive from these disparate groups are often myth-ridden, confusing and even damaging. It would appear that the best way to combat this confusion is to enable students to discuss their concerns within that peer group with a well-trained teacher or facilitator. Only the adolescent knows after all, the pressures and mores of the adolescent group. That fact can be used to great advantage in the classroom". The assumptions parents make about peer groups and teenage culture are often based on their fears and their protectiveness of their children. Children tend to discount those assumptions and opt to live in the atmosphere of peer involvement since that choice symbolizes their declaration of independence.

Parents are relieved to hear that over a long period of time the values which the family instills tend to prevail. However, experimentation is an essential part of growing up. Parents worry about judgment, negative experiences, and rebellion. Given the affluence and opportunity of this time in history, young people can indeed, do damage difficult to repair. In this area, schools can be more helpful in helping to explain the concerns of society and of the family to young people.

The public schools have an opportunity to encourage the group to critique its own behavior. A teacher who encourages expressions and discussions of peer pressure can enable students to evaluate behavior without the emotion so often involved in confrontation with parents. Decision-making skills should be taught within the context of the peer group since that is where these crucial decisions will be made.

In many enlightened homes parents do discuss specific sexual concerns and peer group behavior with their children and provide the information necessary for good decision making. Generally the parents in these homes favor public school sex education. Studies show that about 80 percent of any given community surveyed supports sex education (Kirby, Alter, and Scales, 1979). What the communicative home cannot do for its children is provide serious peer discussions of sexuality. Schools can do families a great favor by providing a forum which presents good, objective knowledge and is conducive to positive, healthy decision making.

The Classroom

Very often as students discuss philosophies and sexual behavior, girls and boys hear each other exchange serious comments about their feelings: "I think guys feel that they have to act macho, but lots of us really don't want to," or, "Girls are afraid they'll lose their boyfriends if they don't go along with everything, and sometimes things get scary, and it's no fun anymore." Comments like these are met with pensive silence, and perhaps a reevaluation of harmful stereotypes. The well-facilitated classroom discussion gives rise to this kind of learning. It is difficult to accomplish the same thing within the family.

Good information shared in the school classroom can relieve tremendous anxieties in children and adolescents. Sooner or later in a good discussion, the mythology surfaces, giving the teacher an opportunity to clarify misconceptions.

The adolescent rarely brings myth-laden fears to the family simply because the family is important in a way which often does not allow the child to ask questions which he or she worries will be misinterpreted. For example, an adolescent may want to know—out of sheer curiosity—when a woman can become pregnant. The child may not feel comfortable asking the parents for fear they will think something is amiss, that perhaps pregnancy is a problem.

In the classroom, children rarely express worries as traumatic as "does masturbation make hair grow on the palms of your hands?" But ideas about nocturnal emissions, menstruation, pregnancy, and growth patterns are commonly demythologized by a combination of peers and the teacher.

Perhaps more than any other concern, teenagers worry about their own growth and physical maturation. Growth, of course, happens at different times, at different rates, and in stops and starts. The reassurances of parents to a "late bloomer" meet with responses like, "You have to say that, you're my mother!" The objective presentation in the classroom comes across as nonmanipulative information, and hence it is much more acceptable and reassuring.

Of course, the most commonly accepted and strongly argued reason for having sex education in schools is the need for prevention of adolescent pregnancy. What we do not yet have is hard data which say that certain kinds of information or strategies will reduce adolescent pregnancy. However, there are many reasons besides pregnancy prevention for sex education to exist in public schools. It makes sense that whether or not adolescent pregnancy rates are reduced by sex education, our children should know that they have choices. Of course that knowledge can be shared within the family, but it most certainly should be reinforced in schools by both peers and teachers.

Another concept which can be shared at home but needs to be reinforced in the peer setting is that of being in charge of yourself, your own body. The question, "How do I tell my boyfriend I don't want to have sex when I don't really have a reason?" should be answered with a resounding: "She has a reason! She doesn't want to!" When that answer comes from peers, it is very influential.

Parent Education

Public schools have an opportunity to reach large numbers of parents with sex education. When children or adolescents are involved in a sex education class in school, a parallel course can be offered for parents to help them understand both what is happening in the classroom and how they as parents can enhance the curriculum. Experience has shown that communication between parents and their children regarding sexuality increases when parents are also involved in sex education classes.

The public schools serve more families with children than any other institution. The effort to educate both children and parents should be tremendous. Because of the pluralistic value systems served by schools, the classroom setting becomes a microcosm of what people, young and old, experience in the world. The issues brought up and discussed are the ones that most concern the parents, and the interaction between adult class members often gives evidence of very different value systems. Such exchanges allow people to test their own values in a close to real life setting. A well-trained instructor will help the group give people pride in their own values even though those values may differ from those of others. There are very few settings in which adults can find opportunities to discuss sexual concerns they have for their children or for themselves.

At the beginning of these classes, parents often feel isolated, as if they are the only ones experiencing trauma or concern over adolescents. As a result of the supportive network that forms among the participants, the parents are often reluctant to break up when the course is completed. The exchange of ideas about childrearing and the opportunity to express anxiety about sexual behavior make these course an important event in the lives of parents of adolescents. An additional value of these courses is the tremendous support gained in the community for sex education in the schools.

Reaching People

If we accept the premise that education for sexuality is a desirable goal for all people, we will look for the most effective ways to reach the most people. When a public school system begins developing a sex education program, protocol dictates the involvement of a number of parents, key faculty, administrators, and significant community leaders. This group will then consider course content and teaching methodology to insure that all aspects of the program are aligned with community values. The planning committee will also become the public's primary source of information and will receive community input. A committee so constructed should continue to exist after the program is instituted, and change membership often enough to insure wide citizen participation, and thus extend the school's outreach into the community.

Sex educators will recognize the familiar litany describing the beginning of a program within the community: parent preview, citizen input, teacher training, and administrative caution. Serious and important questions about the content of sex education programs are raised by careful parents, and the schools would be well advised to not only answer those questions directly, but also to educate the community at the same time.

Questions and Answers Regarding Sex Education in the Schools

Q. "Sexuality is a value-laden subject (at least decisions about sexual behavior are value laden); in a pluralistic society, whose values will be taught?"

A. Values are usually the result of total life experience. We are all influenced to some degree by the people around us, but the primary family is most influential. The primary value evidenced by the inclusion of sex education in the schools is that the community and the school value serious contemplation of human sexuality. Other values which are "taught" include:

manipulative, coercive behavior is bad;

supportive, caring behavior is good and enhances life;

knowledge is good, ignorance is bad;

teenagers should not have babies;

positive communication between friends and family is good;

well-thought out religious, philosophical, and family values are to be prized;

childhood and adolescence is an important and exciting time to be enjoyed but also to be taken seriously;

you are in charge of your own body;

you are unique and special.

Q. "What about the values of the teacher? How do I know what they are, and won't they be imposed on my child."

A. The teacher should be easily accessible to parents and should offer parallel parent education classes. The main value "imposed" on children by a teacher is that he or she considers it valuable to be in a sex education class. A well-trained teacher will focus on the students' comments and feelings and facilitate a positive discussion of those values.

Q. "Well what about abortion? How can you be neutral?"

A. It is not a question of the school providing answers but rather of the teacher providing information and facilitating peer exchange which help students to take pride in their own values and to recognize that we live in a society of many values. Young people tend to be conservative and thoughtful in consideration of life issues.

Q. "If you tell kids about sex, won't they try it?"

A. There is absolutely no evidence to support the contention that sex education increases sexual activity.

It is difficult to believe that in this society where sex is used and pushed as an object everywhere, that any child does not already know lots of things about sex. However, most of what they know is probably misleading, anxiety producing, and even harmful. Is it not a better idea for schools to provide both good information and a serious peer setting for young people to discuss their concerns as they mature?

Q. "Won't the sex education classroom encourage students to share private family matters?"

A. A well-trained teacher can avoid this situation and assist students in protecting themselves from revealing things they will have to live with later on. The point is to focus on adolescent groups, peer pressure, and being in charge of yourself.

Q. "If you talk about controversial subjects like masturbaton or homosexuality, aren't you saying that it is okay to engage in these practices?"

A. Good information on both of these subjects can help to relieve a great deal of anxiety in children. Homosexuality is myth laden and written about constantly in the national and local press, featured as the focus of movies and television shows, and the subject of erotic literature and pornography. Isn't it better to have a serious discussion about the obvious existence of homosexuality and to help destroy the myths about what homosexuality is, and how you "become one?" Reassurances that we are all who we are and that individual events do not change our basic personalities are important.

Masturbation can be discussed as not being acceptable in certain religious communities, but surely no one should object to destroying the anxiety-producing myths which surround masturbation.

Q. "If coed sex education classes are taught, won't students spend time thinking about sex in school?"

A. Yes. Whether they have been in a sex education class or not. The media blitz and their hormones will assure it.

Q. "How do you know children are ready to hear all about sex? Can't it be damaging?"

A. Public schools teach all subjects age-appropriately. It is especially important to do so in sex education. "All about sex" should mean responding to the curiosity, anxieties, and needs of the age being taught. Generally when there is too much information given, children become bored and write it off.

Conclusion

Public schools are vulnerable to public criticism. People who are frustrated with unreachable political institutions can reach the local school board. That fact makes it possible for a very few fearful people to control a school board, an advisory committee, and even an entire community. Therefore, when school districts begin sex education programs, they must plan with care, include the community in the process, select teachers wisely, train them well, offer parent education, and continue to relate to people as if they need always to "sell" the program.

In a final analysis of who should be educating for sexuality, one hopes the schools can answer affirmatively. The schools are certainly going to be making a loud statement to young people either way. A "no" will further shroud this serious issue in mystery and leave the family to fend for itself in a media- and peer-oriented world. A "yes" will add to the integrity of the educational system and give students the necessary knowledge and skills for dealing with life issues.

References

Kirby, D., Alter, J., and Scales, P. *An analysis of U.S. sex education programs and evaluation methods*. Atlanta, Ga. Bureau of Health Education Center for Disease Control, 1979.

Thompson, S. "Editorial," NASSP Newsletter, Reston, Va.: National Association of Secondary School Principals, April 1981.

The Politics of Prevention and Sex Education

Sol Gordon

I did not think I was that important until I began to read about myself in the press.

From a citizens' group in Nipomo, California: "All anyone needs to know about this workshop is that Sol Gordon is the most notorious of all sex instructors of children and the bane of good parents everywhere."(Citizens' Committee of California, 1980).

From *Christian Family Renewal*: "Gordon's books were banned in a N.Y. fair as obscene and his books have been removed from some schools because parents felt the promotion of bestiality and homosexuality was not proper for their children" (cited in *Sex Education and Mental Health*, 1979).

From *Social Justice Review*: "It is apparent that Sol Gordon as a leading secular Humanist proponent of the 'new morality' and the 'new sexuality' can only be understood in the context of the current rejection of the Judeo-Christian moral code by certain fashionable intellectual circles whose influence has penetrated educational milieus within the Catholic Church as well as other churches"(Likondis, 1975, pp.55-61).

I am a psychologist and a sex educator. I am married and a parent. I am a humanist. I am also religious and believe in God. I am proud to be associated with humanists who promote social justice and make personal commitments to changing the social order rather than leaving it to divine providence. My books are designed to promote responsible sexuality. They encourage egalitarian, nonexploitative relationships. They denounce sexism and the double standard, and unashamedly and unequivocally support the women's liberation movement, gay rights, and stable family life. I am conservative, pro-life, and pro-morality, but most of all pro the First Amendment (Bill of Rights).

But we are in trouble in this country. Book banning and censorship are on the upswing. Increasingly, small groups of extremists are establishing their doctrines, through the mechanisms of government and the media, as the credos of the general public.

Although I have been lecturing for 30 years in the United States without the cancellation of a single scheduled talk, 10 of my lectures have been cancelled— in Massachusetts, North Carolina, and California—in the last 18 months. I rarely discuss abortion, but each talk was cancelled because of pressure from right-to-lifers and supporters of the Moral Majority.

Faced with such situations, I fight. When Planned Parenthood in Dallas-Fort Worth, cowed by bombing and assassination threats from the John Birch Society there, tried to cancel a meeting, I insisted we schedule it and make it a free speech issue. The controversy, not the topic, drew 1,000 people and all the media. The people wanted to see the showdown. The media wanted to be there in case there was any "front page" violence.

I began my presentation by thanking the John Birch Society for making Sol Gordon a household word in Dallas-Fort Worth. "Now all my books have been sold out," I announced. Headline in the next day's paper: "Sol Gordon Thanks the Opposition."

A knot of John Birchers grew restless as the audience began to respond to my speech. Finally one of them shouted at me, "What's your religion?" If I had retorted with "What's your business?" or some other antagonistic question, I would have had to surrender the platform to him. Instead I answered curtly, "I'm Jewish. Is that all right with you?" What was he going to say, "No?" Then, to head him off, I added, "And besides, my religion is older than yours." A completely irrational, irrelevant response; it's the best way to deal with the opposition in such circumstances.

I was engaged to speak in Kansas City to the PTA and the March of Dimes, two "radical" organizations there. The opposition had mobilized an entire city, but failed to influence the national PTA president. "Don't you know that Dr. Gordon is America's leading child pornographer?" they asked. The PTA president didn't know that. She told them that since I was speaking to adults, people could make up their own minds about me. Forced to accept my presence, "they" were determined to modify my corrupting influence. So they tried to take over the platform, demanding equal time. Allowing this is a fatal step. Never hand them the microphone or let them step up to the platform; this takes control away from the legitimate speaker. *They* never give me equal time at any of their meetings. Instead, demand that they ask questions. Eventually, one asked: "With all your pornographic literature, with all your comic books, with all your pornographic films, do you really think you could reduce unwanted pregnancy?"

I paused for an impressive five seconds, giving it a lot of thought.

"Yes," I said, "next question, please."

I responded similarly in Fort Myers, Florida, when an outraged pastor demanded: "How could you say what you said about homosexuality? The Bible says it's evil. It's the grossest immorality the world has ever known." Without getting upset, I told him that I realized he did not like or agree with my position on homosexuality, and that was all right, too. A standing ovation followed.

Once I was on a Canadian television program called "Confrontation," along with six fundamentalists. I had made a point. "Listen," one of them told me, "What you say is your opinion, but what we say is fact." I then proceeded to ignore the fundamentalists and direct my discussion to the 1,000,000 people watching at home. One critic angrily accused me of being a showman. "Are you attacking me for being effective?" I inquired.

Another time, when 300 people at a PTA meeting had come to hear me, a woman rose from the audience, grabbed the mike and said:

"I will not allow Dr. Gordon to spread his garbage in this community."

"Who are you," I asked. "I didn't see your name on the program."

"It doesn't matter. I am here to prevent you from spreading your garbage in this community."

"Throw her out, do something, call the police," I said to the chairman.

"Madam, will you please leave?"

"Oh, no, I'm not leaving."

I approached her menacingly.

"Are you going to do violence toward me?"

"I might. You are violating my free speech," I said, and grabbed the mike back. Meanwhile, the audience was silent. Not one of those 300 said "Shut up!" or "We came to hear the speaker!" I turned to them, demanding that they support me. Every person in the room stood up. The woman? She sat down and took notes.

In every community in America there are five or six people violently opposed to sex education. Because they are fiercely vocal and visible, they are able to call themselves representatives of the general public, when in fact the public invariably believes in sex education. Aiding these small groups in their deception are the media; wave making always makes good press.

When I was invited by the school board and the March of Dimes to speak on sex education in Raleigh, North Carolina, those five or six marched down to the board of education. "There's massive opposition to Sol Gordon's coming here," they insisted. "He's controversial." The word "controversial" frightened the board superintendent. He immediately canceled my speech. Giddy with this victory, they made their next attack at the March of Dimes. This organization, too, withdrew its support. But when they called to cancel me, I told them they had better not. "I have a contract," I said. "I'm calling the American Civil Liberties Union; I'm suing." The next day an ACLU lawyer went down and reaffirmed my threat. Free speech—it's rather important. The meeting was held.

All six opponents were sitting in front. The local Catholic priest also attended; he was afraid there might be violence. After the speech, the priest rose and said I gave the best talk on sex education he'd ever heard. All six of my friends fainted dead away.

The problem with the rest of us is that we don't have 12 people to their 6 to march down to the boards of education to say what *we* think and feel.

In Oklahoma, I spoke to 300 people in an auditorium, while the press was busy covering pickets outside. "Sol Gordon is a friend of Planned Parenthood," "Sol Gordon favors gay rights," "Sol Gordon is a humanist," said the placards. And while Sol Gordon was inside espousing his views, the press interviewed the placards. Finally, excusing myself from the meeting, I appeared outside. "Hey everybody, I'm Sol Gordon." And the journalists—they have been taught in journalism school to take advantage of unusual opportunities—left the pickets and gathered around me.

"Hey, how do you feel about these pickets? They say you're for Planned Parenthood."

"Yeah, I am."

"They say you're for gay rights."

"Yeah, I am."

"What do you think about . . . "

I couldn't resist answering, "Listen, press. I want to tell you something privately. But please don't publish it. Every time there are pickets all my books get sold out. And I need the money." The next day, the headlines read: "Sol Gordon Needs the Money. Thanks, pickets."

Our most valuable remaining asset is our sense of humor; we have got to use it. A declaration of war has been signed by Jerry Falwell (among others), the leading bigot in this country and a guest at the White House. He and his troops are fighting pornography, homosexuality, socialism, and the women's movement. They are trying to take God away from us. They are trying to monopolize the family and the flag. They want "life" as their exclusive property. *We* are the people who are pro-family. We must use wit and our sense of humor to addle them. They will be unable to deal with such an approach because they are very nearly humorless. We have to say, "Listen, how can a 12-year-old who gives birth as a result of incest or rape strengthen American family life?" How, indeed, does an unwanted child born under any circumstances enhance the quality of life?

In Oklahoma, the pickets were shouting, "Leave our children alone!" "OK," I said, "You leave my children alone." These groups aren't just picketing, they're burning clinics and books, they're stomping on us. Moving past the pickets, I said, "God have mercy on your souls, because God will judge you." They can't handle God.

But sometimes we are our own worst enemies. We—proponents of choice, sex education, of equal rights for women, homosexuals, and minorities—have failed to get our message across. A group of sex education leaders talks about Sol Gordon: "Oh yes, he's funny, he's entertaining. But does he really teach anything?" There's a failure to appreciate that the use of humor reduces anxiety and allows us to have our messages accepted. Experts do research and discover that sex education doesn't affect teenagers' sexual behavior. How is that research done? The experts ask a student, "Did you have any sex education?" The student says yes. They write it down. Then they do fancy correlations. But the pertinent questions are not asked. How *much* sex education did this student have? Two classes on menstruation in the sixth grade? Were they classes on the "plumbing" (the relentless pursuit of the fallopian tubes)? Did the student learn anything?

Or, girls who are already pregnant are asked if they know about contraception. "Sure," almost all of them reply. Conclusion of the researchers: "Knowledge of contraception makes no difference." But when we asked about contraception in depth, we received answers such as these:

"I took one of my mother's pills."

"I had sex only during the middle of my period, when you can't get pregnant."

"I used foam after we'd had intercourse."

There is very little real sex education in this country. I can name very few schools that have valid programs. There are occasional schools, or occasional brave teachers (who, of course, do not want people to know what they are teaching because they do not have tenure yet). One of the greatest myths of our time is that knowledge is harmful. Opposition to sex education is based on the belief that young people who know about sex will have it. Yet valid research reveals that young people who understand their sexuality tend to *delay* their first sexual experience, and if they do have sex, tend to use birth control (Gordon, Scales, and Everley, 1979).

We proponents and experts are too far ahead of the general public, and this is one reason we cannot get our messages across. We are talking about clitoral pride. Three quarters of the population does not even know where the clitoris is! We are also unable to communicate that controversy is interesting, that it is the very soul of American democracy. Instead, one attitude, often based on bias, broad generalization, or scattered dramatic incidences, surfaces as the "truth" of a certain issue. That is what has happened to the women's liberation movement. Everywhere we find newspapers and research reports saying "Women are aggressive!" And the result of women being aggressive? Men are impotent. Impotent men wherever we go.

But for every man who is impotent as a result of the women's movement, tens of thousands have become liberated. Where did I get those statistics? I made them up. They make up theirs, I will make up mine. If assertive women are denied their legitimate rights, of course they become aggressive. We must communicate that this movement represents equal opportunities for leisure, for career choices, for decision making, and equal pay for equal or comparable work. We are not saying that men and women are the same; merely that they ought to be given the same chances for happiness. The blame foisted on women working outside the home for the destruction of the family is tragic. Liberation has little to do with working inside or outside of the home. Of the 1 million children abused by their parents yearly, of the 100,000 that must be hospitalized, of the 4,000 that are murdered by their parents, most have those abusing parents home taking care of them (National Committee for Prevention of Child Abuse, 1980).

I did not understand women's rights when I was growing up. I married a professional woman, and we both worked outside the home. Still, she did all the cooking and cleaning and shopping and child care. Me? I was busy, until the day she told me, "Hey, I'm busy too. How would you like a divorce?" It took me 5 minutes to rearrange my schedule. I still do not like to cook, shop and clean, but I am doing it now, because I have an assertive wife and I do not want her to become aggressive. I used to think that only women liked to clean. Now I know that women do not like to clean, and men do not like to clean. Even cleaning ladies do not like to clean. People who like to clean are preoccupied with dirt. And that too is a message of the women's movement.

Another myth concerns the propagation of bigotry as religion. Bigots, calling themselves religious, will say that if God wanted homosexuals he would have created Adam and Steve. Does that mean if God wanted black people he would have created Adam and Sheba?

We have entered the era of the "Bible Bigots"—the BB's. These are people who use the Bible to justify their own special brand of bigotry and animosity. God's word to all of us, and the message of the Bible, is "love thy neighbor as thyself." He did not say except blacks, except Jews, except homosexuals. The people using the Bible to attack gay people are the same ones who used it to kill Jews and justify slavery. People using the Bible to defend corporal punishment are the same ones who used it to legitimize the inferior status of women. This is not religion, but bigotry! But here again is a message difficult to transmit. These bigots can appear on Sunday television and rake in a million holy dollars a week. To fight them, we need someone on our side who can make a million dollars. But we do not have one preacher, one person, who can do that. We must be able to call this bigotry openly and freely and without fear. It is not OK to be antigay. About 4 percent of the population is exclusively gay. We do not know why, though we used to know. If a kid had a strong mother and a weak father, he was gay. But we recently discovered that 80 percent of American families consist of strong mothers and weak fathers. The only thing we know for sure about gay people is that they were probably born to heterosexual couples.

Another area of general confusion concerns the teaching of values. Many sex educators and parents believe that sex education is the objective presentation of anatomy and the reproductive process. But that is biology—not sex education. Our programs should focus on values, on moral education. Our society as a whole teaches values. In American social studies classes, we do not present communism, fascism, anarchy, and democracy as four equally good socioeconomic systems, and ask students to choose one. We tell them democracy is best. We do not teach that there are two acceptable kinds of pedestrians: one who litters and one who does not. We teach that littering is bad. And so with sex education; we all believe that teenage pregnancy and the spread of venereal disease are harmful and wrong. And we should say so. That does not mean we should not discuss certain subject matter.

Is it not naive to assume that teenagers will not gather information about birth control, masturbation, abortion, and homosexuality in their own manner—through gossip and secrets which propagate myths? It is incumbent on us, as adults, to discuss real problems young people face, such as sexism and the double standard. We must talk about choice, and responsible decision-making. Most of all, we must emphasize that people who feel good about themselves are not available for exploitation and do not exploit others. In a word, self-esteem. No one, we should tell young people, can make you feel inferior without your consent. On the merits of this type of discussion, there can be no dispute. As for subjects such as abortion, homosexuality, and masturbation, these too should be discussed, providing that the whole range of views is presented. Our first step must be to legitimize the discussion itself.

We cannot, however, create illusions about the impact of sex education. We have good reason to believe that by introducing valid programs we can decrease the incidence of teenage pregnancy and venereal disease by 10, perhaps 15 percent. But poverty, racism, and the double standard also account heavily for the alarming number of out-of-wedlock babies born.

There is a difference between being moral and moralistic, between using judgment and being judgmental. Moralistic or judgmental persons impose their own idiosyncratic or religious points of view on others. When we are moral we represent the universal aspirations of our democratic society.

As sex educators we must help young people put sex into perspective. Therefore, we should urge parents and religious leaders to stop insinuating that sex before marriage means no surprises in marriage; if that is the only surprise in marriage, we should say it is not worth it. On the other hand, we must show teenagers that adults can offer them more than reproductive facts.

I am one of the more conservative sex educators in this country. I do not think teenagers should have sexual intercourse at all. They are too young and vulnerable. They do not know that the first sexual experiences are usually grim. Very few girls will have orgasms during their early sexual experiences. The boys? They get their "orgasms" telling the guys about it the next day. I say this, and yet the righteous opposition thunders after my lectures: "Gordon says, if it feels good, do it!" I have never heard a responsible sex educator say such a thing.

But young people pressure each other about sex. It is necessary to help them understand that sex is never a test of love. We have all heard the line: "Oh, honey, if you really love me, you'll have sex with me." We know it is a line, but would we have known at age 15, excited by someone we had strong feelings for? In a Planned Parenthood study in Chicago, over 1,000 young men were asked: "Is it all right to lie to a girl and say you love her in order to have sex with her?" Seventy percent said yes (Syntex Laboratories, 1977). If boys are going to play such games, girls will have to get good at it too, until the time members of the opposite sex can relate to each other as human beings. A possible exchange:

"Oh, sweetie, if you really love me you'll have sex with me."

"Oh, sweetie, I really love you, but do you have a condom?"

"Darling, I get no feelings out of a condom."

"All the other boys I know get plenty of feeling out of a condom. What's the matter with you?"

"But darling, I'll go crazy."

Huh? No boy has ever died from an unrelieved erection. A girl's "no" is still the best oral contraceptive.

Every time I speak on "How can you tell if you're really in love" in a high school, some young person will get up and say, "Dr. Gordon, that's all well and good, but what do you do in the peak of passion?" No adult seems to know how to respond to a child's peak of passion. We have little chance of reducing the incidence of VD and unwanted pregnancy until we can suggest that young people masturbate, if they have reached a point of no return. I asked a mother: "Would you prefer your 16-year-old to have sex or to masturbate?" "That's not a fair question," she answered. Presumably, she wouldn't want to acknowledge that her child would do either. Children and teenagers don't get pregnant from "unresolved Oedipal fantasies"; they get pregnant because they have sexual intercourse. The boy knows he is having sex. The girl who gets pregnant may be more romantic; she is making love. But that is not love, that is stupidity. Until we can respond to our young people practically and maturely, they will continue to be damaged by our rationalizations and euphemisms.

We also must impress upon them that in the hierarchy or necessities for mature relationships, sex is not first on the list. Love and caring are. Sense of humor is number 2. Number 3 is communication, and number 10 is sharing household chores. Sex? That is number 9. Numbers 4, 5, 6, 7, and 8 I have left open—I would like to leave room for curriculum development. It may seem strange that there are 8 things more important than sex. But if we consider that there are 2,343 essential things in a love relationship, sex's rank in the top 10 is not too bad.

What does all this have to do with prevention of unwanted pregnancy and VD among young people?

As we enter a new decade, the "statistics" confronting those of us who care about strengthening family life are not encouraging. In 1980 there were 1,300,000 pregnancies among teenaged women. About 600,000 gave birth as teenagers. At the present rate, over one third of our 14-year-olds will have one pregnancy by the age of 20 (Alan Guttmacher Institute, 1981).

More than 1,000,000 cases of gonorrhea among teenagers are reported each year, with youngsters 10 to 14 years of age experiencing the greatest increase. Of the estimated 300,000 cases in 1977 among girls age 15 to 19, 45,000 developed into pelvic inflammatory diseases, leaving between 7,000 and 18,000 of the victims sterile (Center for Disease Control, 1980).

The majority of teenagers who have babies, even those who marry to cover the pregnancies, will have 90 percent of their lives scripted out for them. *Most* will drop out of school, will never be able to earn a decent living, will be on welfare for much of their lives, will be abandoned by the fathers of the babies, and will contribute disproportionately to cases of child abuse, delinquency, and the whole range of pathological conditions in our society. This is without detailing the medical and psychological problems associated with the unplanned, unwanted children (Gordon et al., 1979).

We, those of us who care, must stop playing games with this greatest of tragedies. People with little or no understanding of children are doing "research" and telling us that:

the majority of these teenagers want to get pregnant;

they suffer from Oedipal conflicts;

they need someone to love and to hold;

they cannot make responsible decisions because of their low state of moral development.

And there are those who can "prove" that

we are in a state of moral decay because of sex education in the schools and the Pill.

One can come up with these findings by asking already pregnant girls if they wanted to get pregnant and by making up everything else. If I had my way, I would spread these 10 rumors:

Girls get pregnant because they have sexual intercourse.

It is not romantic to have sex without birth control—it is stupid.

If someone says to you, "If you really love me, you'll have sex with me," it's always a line (Gordon, 1978).

Sex is never a test of love.

"No" is a perfectly good oral contraceptive.

Machismo is when you are man enough to avoid hurting and exploiting anyone because of your own insecurities.

People who boast about all the men/women they've "had" and how they need a lot of "it," basically hate the opposite sex.

More than 85 percent of all boys who impregnate teenage girls will eventually abandon them (Gordon et al., 1979).

People who feel they do not amount to anything unless someone loves them will not amount to much afterward.

Of the 10 most important things in a relationship, sex is number 9.

The goal for the next decade must be prevention. We need to get *our* messages across. First in importance is the realization that knowledge is not harmful; that young people knowledgeable about their sexuality tend to delay their sexual experiences, and, upon deciding to have sex, use birth control. Also, it is not just the promiscuous girl but the average girl who gets pregnant, the girl who, told by her parents not to have sex, "makes love" instead. Parents are the primary sex educators of their children, whether they educate them well or badly. To do it well, they need help and support. So far, sex education in the schools has not really been tried. Less than 10 percent of American schools have anything approaching a valid sex education program (Kirby, Alter, and Scales, 1979). Furthermore, we must keep in mind that sex education without values is valueless. We need to help young people make a distinction between moral and moralistic education. Moral education encourages self-esteem and nonexploitative behavior. Moralistic education seeks to influence children to accept a particular religious and personal point of view. Moral education represents the highest aspirations of a society.

The Salt Lake City schools of Utah have taken leadership in offering moral education in the area of democratic, ethical values. Here are some of their basic principles, which also could serve as the basis for a good sex education program (Council for Basic Education, 1980):

Each individual has dignity and worth.

A free society requires respect for persons, property, and principles.

Each individual, regardless of race, creed, color, sex, ethnic background, or economic status, should have equal opportunity.

Each individual is responsible for his or her own actions.

Each individual has a responsibility to the group as well as to the total society.

Sex education in the schools is essential. This does not mean that if it were introduced in all schools in this decade our problem would be solved (Gordon and Dickman, 1980). If we encourage young people to develop healthier attitudes about themselves, they can, if they become parents, be good sex educators of their own children. This would break the vicious cycle that forces each generation of young people to discover what sexuality is all about from their equally misinformed friends. But problems associated with sex will not be substantially eradicated unless we can reduce poverty, racial discrimination, sexism, and the pernicious double standard that exists in our society.

The sexual revolution has not started yet. We need one that binds intimacy with sex, for many people still use sex as an avoidance of intimacy rather than an expression of it. Let us prepare today's children for tomorrow's family by teaching them to respect themselves and the rights of others. If we want responsible children, we as adults need to provide them with models—not just critics.

References

Alan Guttmacher Institute. *Teenage pregnancy: The problem that hasn't gone away.* New York: Planned Parenthood Federation of America, 1981.

Center for Disease Control, Atlanta, Ga. Personal communication, 1980.

Citizens' Committee of California, Central Coast Chapter, January 15, 1980.

Council for Basic Education, Washington, D.C., 1980.

Gordon, S. *You would if you loved me.* New York: Bantam Books, 1978.

Gordon, S., and Dickman, I. *Schools and parents: Partners in sex education.* Pamphlet No. 581. New York: Public Affairs Committee, 1980.

Gordon, S., Scales, P., and Everley, K. *The sexual adolescent.* (2nd ed.). N. Scituate, Mass.: Duxbury Press, 1979.

Kirby, D., Alter, J., and Scales, P. *An analysis of U.S. sex education programs* (Vol. I., Center for Disease Control Report No. CDC-2021-79-DK-FR). Atlanta, Ga.: Center for Disease Control, July 1979.

Likondis, J. Sexologist Sol Gordon: A modern disciple of Pelagius. *Social Justice Review*, 1975, *68*, 55-61.

National Committee for Prevention of Child Abuse, 1980. (Obtainable from 332 S. Michigan Ave., Suite 1250, Chicago, Ill. 60604.)

Sex Education and Mental Health, 1979, *9*, (9).

Syntex Laboratories. *Family Planner*, 1977, *8*, 2-4.

The Use of Rational-Emotive Therapy (RET) in Working for a Sexually Sane Society

Albert Ellis

It may seem like extreme nerve—or chutzpah, if you will—for me to claim that rational-emotive therapy (RET) is a revolutionary method of changing individual and social sexual attitudes and of working for a sexually sane society. If so, let me be brash and nervy! For I do claim, as I have held for over a quarter of a century, that if you are looking for an effective and efficient method of changing your own sexual disturbances and enhancing your sex and love potential, RET is probably your best choice. If, moreover, you are seeking a means of helping to effect more global changes in amative and sexual mores and of working for sexual sanity, to what may you optimistically look? Again, to RET! A rash claim? Well, let me try to substantiate it.

First, in regard to effecting personal change and particularly in regard to helping people overcome their feelings of sexual inadequacy and their emotionally aberrant behavior, RET has an unusually good record. As a general form of therapy it originated in 1955 and started what has become the highly popular cognitive behavior therapy movement, which is now backed by literally hundreds of research studies supporting its clinical effectiveness (Beck, 1976; diGiuseppe, Miller, and Trexler, 1979; Ellis, 1982; Ellis and Grieger, 1977; Ellis and Whitely, 1979; Meichenbaum, 1977; Smith and Glass, 1977). Soon after its inception, RET began to be applied to the treatment of dysfunctional sex, love, and marital relationships (Ellis, 1957, 1958, 1960, 1961, 1962a, 1975, 1976, 1979, 1980; Ellis and Harper, 1961) and proved to be so useful that it strongly influenced the cognitive behavior movement that has become the center of modern sex therapy (Annon, 1974, 1975; Barbach, 1975; Kaplan, 1974; Leiblum and Pervin, 1980; LoPiccolo and LoPiccolo, 1978; Masters and Johnson, 1970).

How, precisely, does RET help people to effect significant changes in their sex and love lives, particularly when they are afflicted with impotency, lack of desire, orgasmic deficiency, obsessions and compulsions, and other forms of disturbance and dysfunction? By employing a large number of cognitive, emotive, and behavioral techniques, many of which are designed to ameliorate general and sexual insanity. A detailed outline of RET's multimodal methods would require more space than is available in this paper; but let me briefly describe one of the methods for which it is most famous, that of cognitive disputing or restructuring.

According to RET's basic theory, people are largely or mainly disturbed not by the things that happen to them (including the events of their early lives) but by the *view* or *philosophy* they take of these things (Ellis, 1957, 1962b, 1982; Epictetus, 1890; Marcus Aurelius, 1890). The A-B-C theory of RET holds that whenever activating events or activating experiences occur in people's lives (at point A) and are soon followed by emotional and behavioral consequences—especially, disturbed consequences—(at point C), A importantly *contributes* to C but does not directly cause it. Instead, people's belief systems (at point B) even more importantly and more directly contribute to our "cause" C. Therefore, if these people want to change their sex and love feelings and behaviors, they had better not only modify the activating events (A) in their lives but also give considerable thought and effort to changing their belief systems (B). RET teaches them, concretely and specifically, with cognitive and behavioral homework assignments, to acknowledge and get in touch, first, with C (their emotional and behavioral consequences or psychological symptoms); second, with A (the activating events that prelude or accompany these consequences); third, and especially, with B (their beliefs about A). Then it shows them how to scientifically challenge and dispute (at point D) their irrational beliefs (iBs), to surrender them, and to change them to E (a new set of cognitive, emotive, and behavioral effects).

To be even more specific, RET holds that people's irrational beliefs (iBs) that lie behind and largely (not completely) create or "cause" their severe problems mainly consist of absolutistic, rigid, bigoted, antiscientific hypotheses, and especially of absolutistic shoulds, oughts, musts, demands, and commands on themselves, others, and the world. If they recognize these unrealistic, antiempirical, *mus*turbatory beliefs, give them up, and instead stick rigorously to preferences, wishes, and desires, says the theory of RET, they will then strongly, appropriately, and even passionately feel and emote, but they will less often think, feel, and act self-defeatingly—that is, against their own and their social group's interest.

Enough of generalities! Let us see how an RET therapist, counselor, or teacher would help an individual with a fairly typical sex and love problem to retain—or regain—his or her sanity. Let us suppose that Joe S., a young male, is anxious about winning the love of Suzie Q., and that, consequently, he fails to get and maintain erections when having sex relations with her. At point A (activating event) Joe goes to bed with Suzie and at point C (emotional and behavioral consequence) he feels almost insanely anxious and needlessly fails at one of the sex acts he desires to complete with Suzie—sexual intercourse. He also tends senselessly to give up and thereafter avoid going to bed with Suzie (and other desirable women). Crazily, he seeks out much less desirable partners because he does not care if he fails with them.

As Joe's therapist, I use RET to assess his problem, at first to get only a brief history of his total life, and assume, on the basis of my clinical experience and much RET-oriented research, that he probably has one main irrational belief (iB) and three major derivatives that are also highly irrational. After asking him some questions and checking these assumptions, I find that RET rightly hits the spot (as it does not *always* do!) and that he indeed seems to have these iBs. I then proceed, in a typical active, directive (and some would say brash) manner to dispute (at point D) Joe's irrational beliefs and to teach him how to do this for himself, on his own. In brief summary, my teaching Joe the A-B-C-D-E's of RET goes something like this:

A (activating event): Joe goes to bed with Suzie.

rB (rational beliefs): "I want very much to succeed sexually with Suzie and to give her and myself real pleasure and thereby enhance our love relationship. It would therefore be very sad and unfortunate if I failed and helped ruin our intimacy."

aC (appropriate consequences): Feelings of concern and determination; active efforts by Joe to please himself and Suzie sexually and lovingly.

iB, no. 1 (irrational belief no. 1): "I *must* do well sexually and give Suzie complete satisfaction! I *have to* get closer to her and maintain and develop our deep relationship!"

iC (inappropriate consequences of irrational belief no. 1): Intense feelings of anxiety; failure to get and maintain erections; sexual avoidance of Suzie and other women.

D (disputing irrational belief): "Where is the evidence that I *must* do well sexually and give Suzie complete satisfaction? Why do I *have to* get closer to her and maintain and develop our deep relationship?"

cE (cognitive effect of disputing irrational belief no. 1): "There are no reasons why I *must* do well sexually and give Suzie complete satisfaction, though it would be highly *desirable* if I did. I *don't* have to get closer to her and maintain and develop our deep relationship, but I find it *highly preferable* to keep trying to do so."

iB, no. 2 (irrational belief no. 2): "It would be *awful* and *horrible* if I failed sexually with Suzie and thereby helped ruin our relationship!"

D (disputing irrational belief no. 2): How would it be *awful* and *horrible?*"

cE (cognitive effect of disputing irrational belief no. 2): "It wouldn't be *awful*—only damned inconvenient! If it were *awful* or *horrible,* it would have to be totally (100 percent inconvenient—when it obviously is much less than that. It would have to be *more than* (101 percent) inconvenient—which, of course, it cannot be. It would have to be more obnoxious than it *should be.* But however obnoxious it is or becomes, that (and no *more* than that!) is as obnoxious as it *is*; and it cannot be less annoying than it is. Tough!"

iB, no. 3 (irrational belief no. 3): "Since it *must* not be as bad as I don't want it to be, I *can't stand* failing sexually and emotionally with Suzie! I *can't bear* it!"

D (disputing irrational belief no. 3): "Prove that I *can't stand* it. In what manner can't I bear it?"

cE (cognitive effect of disputing irrational belief no.3): "I *can,* of course stand anything that happens to me, including sex and love failure, until I die and am then, and only then, incapable of standing anything! If I really couldn't stand or bear sex and love failure at all, I would die because of it—and that is most unlikely. Or, still living, I wouldn't be able to have any happiness whatever for the rest of my days—also most unlikely! Actually, I can practically always stand what I immensely don't like—and I'd better! If I don't like sex and love failure and I can't eliminate it, I can at least *accept* or *gracefully lump* it!"

iB, no. 4 (irrational belief no. 4): "Because I *must* not fail sexually or amatively with Suzie, and I have such deficiencies that I may well do what I presumably *must* not, I am an *incompetent, bad person* who doesn't *deserve* to get what I want in life!"

D (disputing irrational belief no. 4): "In what way do I amount to an *incompetent, bad person* if I am unproficient at sex and love? Where is it writ that I don't *deserve* to get what I want if I behave ineffectually in some important ways or areas?"

cE (cognitive effect of disputing irrational belief no.4):"I *am* not incompetent if I fail at sex and love relations but merely a *person who is failing in this respect at this time. A bad person* would *only* and *always* do bad or incompetent things, because he would have an *essence* or *soul* of badness. Virtually no one seems to be that bad; and for him or her to have a bad *essence* is unprovable. Even if I were bad in almost all my acts, how would that prove that I were *undeserving* of having my wishes fulfilled? It wouldn't!"

eE (emotive effect of disputing irrational beliefs nos. 1, 2, 3 and 4): Joe would most probably feel sad and disappointed about his failing with Suzie but not intensely anxious or depressed.

bE (behavioral effect of disputing irrational beliefes nos. 1, 2, 3, and 4): He would keep trying to succeed with Suzie; would not avoid sex and love relations with her (or other suitable women); and would work at continuing to overcome his feelings of anxiety and depression and his withdrawing behaviors.

If Joe learns and applies these A-B-C-D-E's or RET he will probably, as just noted, lost his anxiety and despair (but not his deep concern) about succeeding in his love relationship and will in all probability start succeeding at sex and more intensely enjoy his intimacy with Suzie. His new cognitive effect (cE) will lead him to feel and act less disturbedly. At the same time, since RET is a comprehensive or multimodal type of psychoeducational treatment, I, as Joe's therapist, will use a number of other cognitive, emotive, and behavioral methods.

Cognitively, for example, I may get Joe to use coping or rational self-statements, and to reiterate them and think about them many times until he begins to believe them—for example, statements like "I do not *need* what I *want!*" "I am a *person who sometimes fails badly* but never a *bad person!*" "It's *hard* for me to work at conquering my sex problems but it's *harder if I don't!*" I may also teach him cognitive distraction methods, such as Masters and Johnson's (1970) sensate focus or Jacobsen's (1944) progressive muscle relaxation method. I may use modeling and show him how, if I and other members of this therapy group accept him with his impotency, he can similarly unconditionally accept himself. I very likely will use bibliotherapy and have Joe read instructive books, such as Alex Comfort's (1973) *The Joy of Sex*, my own *The Art and Science of Love* (Ellis, 1960), and my well-known antianxiety book, written with Robert A. Harper, *A New Guide to Rational Living* (1975). I shall almost certainly give him some training in sexual imagery and (as noted below) rational-emotive imagery (Maultsby, 1975; Maultsby and Ellis, 1974). I may well use some humor to rip up some of his irrational beliefs (iBs) and to help him stop taking things too seriously (Ellis, 1977a, 1977b, 1981). I will certainly give him cognitive disputing homework, such as filling out the well-known RET self-help report forms (Ellis, 1974).

Emotively, I will again use several reliable RET-oriented methods with Joe, especially: (1) The use of very forceful self-statements, such as "I shall always be a very *fallible* person! I'm still human!"; (2) rational-emotive imagery, through which Joe imagines one of the worst things that could happen to him sexually and practices feeling appropriately sorry and disappointed instead of inappropriately anxious and depressed; (3) unconditional self-acceptance, in the course of which I show Joe how to accept himself *un*qualifiedly (and to love his aliveness and ability to pleasure himself) *whether or not* he acts well and *whether or not* others approve of him; (4) shame-attacking exercises, or Joe's overtly acting foolishly or ridiculously in public to show himself that, even under such stressful conditions, he never has to down himself or make himself feel ashamed (Ellis, 1971; Ellis and Abrahms, 1978); and (5) role playing, through which Joe is taught how to take chances with others and unangrily assert himself, sexually and otherwise, to get more of what he wants and less of what he does not want.

Behaviorally, RET invariably uses a number of behavior therapy techniques (Ellis, 1957, 1962b). So I will probably employ several of the most useful ones with Joe, such as: (1) activity homework assignments, especially *in vivo* desensitization, through which he may overcome some of his sex and love anxieties by deliberately doing what he is afraid of doing and by staying in unpleasant situations until he can tolerate them and often make them pleasant; (2) operant conditioning, whereby Joe rewards or reinforces himself contingent on his doing so-called dangerous or risky things (e.g., talking with Suzie about his sex problem); (3) penalizing, through which Joe contracts to give himself a stiff penalty (e.g., burning a twenty dollar bill) every time he does not do one of his contracted-for homework assignments; (4) skill training, in the course of which I, as his therapist, help Joe to acquire relevant skills that he lacks, such as assertiveness, communication, loving, and sex skills.

All told, then, RET provides people like Joe, who are thinking and acting foolishly or insanely in their sex and love affairs, with a theory and a multimodal practice that will enable them to think, feel, and behave much more sanely. At the same time, it has many social consequences and implications, and helps bring about a sexually sane society in several important ways.

RET vigorously opposes all absolutes, dogmas, and bigotries, including these irrational beliefs (iBs): (a) there is one invariant and right sexual morality for all the people all of the time; (b) there must not be any degree of individual or social sex and love experimentation, such as premarital sex relations; (c) when one needlessly harms others sexually, one should be denigrated and damned as a thoroughly rotten person; (d) one group of people who presumably are certain what are proper and good sex rules should have the power to make everyone in their community obey these supposedly fine rules; (e) sexual freedom always leads to promiscuity, illegitimate pregnancy, and other unwise acts and is therefore never to be allowed for anyone; (f) children and adolescents are too young and unknowledgeable to engage sensibly in sex acts and therefore should be almost completely restricted in this respect; (g) the widespread use of contraceptive methods only encourages promiscuity and therefore their use should be strictly curtailed; (h) fictional and nonfictional books and audiovisual presentations that contain explicit and direct sex material should be carefully censored and often banned; (i) many noncoital sex acts are disgusting perversions and people who participate in these kinds of acts should be apprehended and punished; (j) only heterosexual relationships are good and permissible and all forms of homosexuality should be banned and penalized.

By opposing these kinds of absolutes and by promulgating the theory that sex acts are rarely if ever wicked or disturbed in their own right but that, instead, the manner in which they are performed—e.g., sadistically or compulsively — may be immoral or self-defeating, RET notably strives for the establishment of a sexually sane society and attempts to minimize sex and love disturbances.

RET, by helping many people to be healthier and happier in their sexual (and nonsexual) affairs, and especially by showing them how to minimize their needless anxiety, hostility, and depression, frees them to share themselves with others and to work, individually and politically, for saner and more sensible rules and laws relating to sex, love, mariage, and family life.

By its educational pamphlets, books, cassettes, films, and other printed and audiovisual materials, RET helps spread sane thinking to millions of people who never undergo individual or group rational-emotive therapy, but who nevertheless are thus able to imbibe its messages and spread them to others.

RET, by helping people to give up their dire need for approval and concomitant conformity to conventional public opinion, has enabled a good many publicists—such as Sol Gordon, Robert A. Harper, Edward Sagarin, Warren Johnson, Janet L. Wolfe, and myself—courageously to speak up at talks, workshops, and seminars, over radio and TV networks, and in popular periodicals and books, and in the course of presentations to voice some highly unpopular sex views without flinching from attack and without going along with reactionary inanities and insanities. It is its risk-taking outspokenness and its teaching people not absolutistically to need mass approval that has helped spark much of the sex revolution that resurged in the 1950s and 1960s, and that is still under way (Ellis, 1958, 1960, 1961, 1962a, 1963a, 1963b).

Some leading politicians, such as the governor of one large American state and the mayor of a sizable city, have been directly influenced by RET and have consequently helped liberalize some of the sex and love laws in their communities.

RET is the pioneering therapy that is usually given credit for starting the cognitive behavior movement in psychotherapy; and it and the whole movement have now trained thousands of therapists throughout the world who have already treated tens of thousands of clients and helped them be more scientific and realistic in their sexual and nonsexual thinking. This therapeutic movement for sanity continues to grow apace and to combat the unscientific and rigid theories of several other systems of therapy, especially the Freudian system.

In considering RET's contribution to working for a sexually sane society, let me not exaggerate. All humans who think straightforwardly about themselves and others, and who are emotionally undisturbed, do not necessarily advocate or work for sexual liberalism. Some people, in fact, begin to enjoy themselves so profoundly because of their personal sex and love freedoms that they take little time to promulgate sane views and no time whatever to work politically for the acceptance of such views. I still, however, would firmly maintain the proposition that emotional health and sexual saneness are significantly correlated and that any theory and practice that helps people give up their absolutism and bigotry about themselves, about other humans, and about the world is both dirctly and indirectly responsible for increased social-sexual rationality. If so, RET is almost certainly of great use in helping people work for a sexually sane society. I truly hope so!

References

Annon, J. S. *The behavioral treatment of sexual problems.* 2 vols. Honolulu: Enabling Systems and New York: Harper, 1974 and 1975.

Barbach, L. G. *For yourself.* New York: Doubleday, 1975.

Beck, A. T. *Cognitive therapy and emotional disorders.* New York: International Universities Press, 1976.

Comfort, A. *The joy of sex.* New York: Crown, 1973.

diGiuseppe, R. A., Miller, N. J., and Trexler, L. D. A review of ratonal-emotive psychotherapy outcome studies. In A. Ellis and J. M. Whiteley (Eds.), *Theoretical and empirical foundations of rational-emotive therapy.* Monterey, Calif.: Brooks/Cole, 1979.

Ellis, A. *How to live with a "neurotic."* New York: Crown, 1957.

Ellis, A. *Sex without guilt.* New York: Lyle Stuart; and Hollywood: Wilshire Books, 1958.

Ellis, A. *The art and science of love.* New York: Lyle Stuart and Bantam, 1960.

Ellis, A. *The folklore of sex* (Rev. ed.). New York: Grove Press, 1961.

Ellis, A. *The American sexual tragedy* (Rev. ed.). New York: Lyle Stuart and Grove Press, 1962. (a)

Ellis, A. *Reason and emotion in psychotherapy.* Secaucus, N.J.: Lyle Stuart and Citadel Press, 1962. (b)

Ellis, A. *The intelligent women's guide to manhunting.* New York: Lyle Stuart and Dell Books, 1963. (a)

Ellis, A. *Sex and the single man.* New York: Lyle Stuart and Dell Books, 1963. (b)

Ellis, A. *How to stubbornly refuse to be ashamed of anything.* Cassette recording. New York: Institute for Rational Living, 1971.

Ellis, A. *Self-help report form.* New York: Institute for Rational Living, 1974.

Ellis, A. The rational-emotive approach to sex therapy. *Counseling Psychologist,* 1975, 5, 14-21.

Ellis, A. *Sex and the liberated man.* Secaucus, N.J.: Lyle Stuart, 1976.

Ellis, A. Fun as psychotherapy. *Rational Living,* 1977, *12,* 2-6. (a)

Ellis, A. *A garland of rational songs.* Songbook and Cassette recordings. New York: Institute for Rational Living, 1977. (b)

Ellis, A. *The intelligent women's guide to dating and mating.* Secaucus, N.J.: Lyle Stuart,

1979.

Ellis, A. The treatment of erectile dysfunction. In S.R. Leiblum and L.A. Pervin (Eds.), *Principles and practice of sex therapy*. New York: Guilford Press, 1980.

Ellis, A. The use of rational humorous songs in psychotherapy, *Voices*, 1981, *16*, 29-36.

Ellis, A. *Rational-emotive therapy and cognitive behavior therapy*. New York: Springer, 1982.

Ellis, A., and Abrahms, E. *Brief psychotherapy in medical and health practice*. New York: Springer, 1978.

Ellis, A., and Harper, R.A. *Creative marriage*. New York: Lyle Stuart, 1961. Retitled in paperback edition: *A guide to successful marriage*. Hollywood: Wilshire Books, 1961.

Ellis, A., and Harper, R.A. *A new guide to rational living*. Englewood Cliffs, N.J.: Prentice-Hall; and Hollywood: Wilshire Books, 1975.

Ellis, A., and Whitely, J. M. *Theoretical and empirical foundations of rational-emotive therapy*. Monterey, Calif.: Brooks/Cole, 1979.

Epictetus, *The works of Epictetus*. Boston: Little, Brown, 1890.

Jacobsen, E. *You must relax*. New York: McGraw-Hill, 1944.

Kaplan, H. S. *The new sex therapy*. New York: Brunner/Mazel, 1974.

Leiblum, S. R., and Pervin, L. A. (Eds.). *Principles and practice of sex therapy*. New York: Guilford Press, 1980.

Lopiccolo, J., and LoPiccolo, L. (Eds.). *Handbook of sex therapy*. New York: Plenum Press, 1978.

Marcus Aurelius. *Meditations*. Boston: Little, Brown, 1890.

Masters, W. H., and Johnson, V. E. *Human sexual inadequacy*. Boston: Little, Brown, 1980.

Maultsby, M. C., Jr. *Help yourself to happiness*. New York: Institute for Rational Living, 1975.

Maultsby, M. C., Jr., and Ellis, A. *Technique for using rational-emotive imagery*. New York: Institute for Rational Living, 1974.

Meichenbaum, D. *Cognitive behavior modification*. New York: Plenum Press, 1977.

Smith, M. L., and Glass, G. Meta analysis of psychotherapy outcome studies. *American Psychologist*, 1977, *32*, 752—760.

Contributors

Gene G. Abel is professor of clinical psychiatry, College of Physicians and Surgeons, Columbia University. His medical training was at the University of Iowa where he also did his psychiatry residency. He is a diplomate of the American Board of Psychiatry and Neurology. Abel has been a psychiatrist in the Air Force, and has been on the faculty of the University of Mississippi Department of Psychiatry where he was also director of research. He has also been professor of psychiatry at the University of Tennessee. His current research interests include the design and application of behavioral methods for measuring and treating sexual dysfunction and sexual deviation, as well as the evaluation and treatment of rapists and rape victims. He has published extensively in medical, psychiatric, and behavioral journals, and is the author of numerous chapters in scholarly books dealing with human sexuality, sexual aggression, and behavioral assessment.

George W. Albee is professor of psychology at the University of Vermont. He and Justin M. Joffe are general editors of this series of volumes on the primary prevention of psychopathology. In 1977-78, Albee was chair of the Task Panel on Primary Prevention for President Carter's Commission on Mental Health, and 20 years ago he was director of the Task Force on Manpower for the Joint Commission on Mental Illness and Health. His research and scholarly activities have been in the area of primary prevention, the psychopathology of prejudice, and human resources affecting the delivery of psychological services. He has been president of the American Psychological Association (1970), the New England Psychological Association (1980), and Division 12 (Clinical) of APA. In 1975 he received the Distinguished Professional Contribution Award from APA and in 1981 a similar award from Division 27 (Community) of APA.

Gloria J. Blum is a consultant for the development of disabled and nondisabled adults and children in the areas of social learning, self-esteem, and human sexuality, and an 18-year veteran in the field of special education. Blum is a fully certified teacher of nondisabled, hearing impaired, emotionally disabled, and orthopedically disabled people. Author of *Feeling*

Good about Yourself (with her husband, Barry Blum, M.D.), Blum trains teachers and professionals, and has produced a teacher training film, "Feeling Good about Yourself." Blum specializes in communication through presentation of the unique and experiential learning techniques that she has developed through her many years of experience.

Mary S. Calderone is widely recognized as a pioneering leader in the field of human sexuality. She is president of the Sex Information and Education Council of the U.S. (SIECUS), an organization which she co-founded in 1964 and for which she was executive director during its first 11 years. Calderone completed her studies in medicine in 1939 at the University of Rochester Medical School, from which she received the University Alumni Citation in 1968 and the Alpha Omega Alpha Honorary Alumnus Membership in 1978. She earned her degree in public health at Columbia University School of Public Health in 1942. She has received nine honorary doctorates and major awards from a wide range of organizations including the American Public Health Association and Planned Parenthood Federation of America. She is author, coauthor, and editor of many books about sexuality, including *The Family Book about Sexuality, Questions and Answers about Sex and Love, Sexuality and Human Values,* and *Manual of Family Planning and Contraceptive Practice.* Her contributions to medical textbooks, encyclopedias, and the professional literature are numerous.

Carol Cassell is currently director of education for Planned Parenthood Federation of America. She provides leadership to the education programs of 189 Planned Parenthood affiliates and contributes to other major national organizations' educational efforts. She is vice-president of the American Association of Sex Educators, Counselors, and Therapists, and a certified sex educator. She has been training manager with James Bowman Associates, providing training to family planning and public health agencies throughout DHHS Region 6. She has served as a consultant to health and social service agencies on community program development and human sexuality, and taught human sexuality at the University of New Mexico. She coauthored (with L. L. Doyle) "A Junior High's Sex Education Curricula for Rural Setting" and "Teenage Sexuality in Early Adolescence" (*OB/GYN Annual Edition,* 1981). Her research on the role of the stepmother has resulted in various publications. Cassell has given numerous papers on sexuality, working with adolescents, and sex education throughout the country, and has been a frequent participant on radio and television shows, including the "Tomorrow Show" and "60 Minutes."

Sandra S. Cole is an adjunct instructor at the University of Michigan School of Medicine in the Department of Physical Medicine and Rehabilitation and the Department of Psychiatry. She is director of the human sexuality sequence for the Inter-flex medical students at the University of Michigan. She is a trainer of rehabilitation practitioners on the subject of sexuality and physical disability. She has developed training curricula for Region 5 and has trained professionals all over North America. Six years ago, she founded the National Task Force on Sexuality and Physical Disability, an ad hoc liaison committee of the American Congress of Rehabilitation Medicine. She has published extensively in the area of sexuality and disability. Her works, often coauthored with T. M. Cole, her husband, include *Sexuality, the Practitioner and the Patient: A Problem or an Opportunity; Sex, the Handicapped and The Health Care System*, plus chapters in medical texts and articles in the scientific literature.

Theodore M. Cole has been chairman of the Department of Physical Medicine and Rehabilitation at the University of Michigan since 1977. Dr. Cole's academic interests have been in the areas of spinal cord injury, sexuality and physical disability, medical education, behavior modification therapy of chronic pain syndromes, and systems of health care delivery in rehabilitation. He has contributed over 40 publications to the medical literature in these related fields.

Edward I. Donnerstein is currently associate professor of communication arts at the Center for Communication Research at the University of Wisconsin. Dr. Donnerstein completed the Ph.D. in psychology at Florida State University and has taught at Southern Illinois University and Iowa State. From 1978 to 1981 he was a visiting associate professor of psychology at the University of Wisconsin. He has taught a wide range of courses in social psychology, media effects, and other psychological areas. He has done extensive research of human aggression, rape, violence against women, interracial relations, and media effects. He is currently the author (with various coauthors) of a number of forthcoming books including *Aggression: Theoretical and Empirical Reviews, Pornography and Sexual Aggression,* and *Social Psychology.*

Paula Brown Doress is a member of the Boston Women's Health Book Collective and coauthor of *Our Bodies, Ourselves* and *Ourselves and Our Children*. Interested in the process of affirming women's sexuality through sharing experiences, she has led numerous sexuality workshops, through the Collective, for women and teens. She holds an M.A. in women's studies from Goddard College and has taught women's studies courses at Emerson College and U. Mass-Boston. She is studying psychology and social structure at Boston College, where she has been especially interested in exploring why parents and children find it difficult to talk about sexuality.

Albert Ellis is executive director of the Institute for Rational-Emotive Therapy. He also holds an adjunct professorship in psychology at Rutgers University and at the U.S. International University. Early in his career he served as chief psychologist for the New Jersey State Diagnostic Center and subsequently as chief psychologist of the New Jersey Department of Institutions and Agencies. For more than 30 years he has been involved in marriage and family counseling, sex therapy, psychotherapy, consulting, lecturing, and writing. He has been president of the Division of Consulting Psychology of APA and has been a member of the APA Council. He holds fellowships in a dozen associations concerned with scientific and professional applications of his research. Ellis has published more than 500 papers and has been the author or editor of 45 books and monographs including *Sex without Guilt*, *A New Guide to Rational Living*, and *A Handbook of Rational-Emotive Therapy*.

John H. Gagnon is professor in the Department of Sociology at the State University of New York at Stony Brook. He has been visiting professor at the Graduate School of Education, Harvard University (1978-1980), a visiting scientist at the Institute of Criminal Science, the University of Copenhagen, Denmark, and he has taught at Cambridge University and Indiana University, among other academic appointments. He completed his Ph.D. in sociology at the University of Chicago and has published extensively in the literature on sexuality. He is the author and/or editor of a number of books including *Sexual Conduct: The Social Sources of Human Sexuality*, *Human Sexualities*, and *Life Designs*.

Paul H. Gebhard is director of the Alfred C. Kinsey Institute for Sex Research, Inc. at Indiana University where he is also professor of anthropology. With Kinsey, he is the author of *Sexual Behavior in the Human*

Female and senior author of the book *Pregnancy, Birth and Abortion*, and also a book called *Sex Offenders*. He did his graduate work in anthropology at Harvard where he completed the Ph.D. degree. As the director of a major sex research institute, he is known throughout the world as a contributor to this field.

Sol Gordon is professor of child and family studies and director of the Institute for Family Research and Education at Syracuse University. He did both his undergraduate work and master's work in psychology at the University of Illinois and received the Ph.D. from the University of London. Dr. Gordon is one of the best-known people in the sex education field, and is the author of a dozen books and monographs, including *The Sexual Adolescent, Parenting—A Guide for Young People, Facts about Sex for Today's Youth*, and *The Teenage Survival Book*. His articles, chapters, textbooks, and popular writings have reached millions. He is a frequent guest on radio and television shows, such as the "Phil Donahue Show," and the "Today Show" on which, as a target of the Moral Majority and other fundamentalist groups, he debated the Reverend Jerry Falwell.

Eleanor Hamilton is codirector of the Counseling Center at Hamilton School in Sheffield, Massachusetts. Hamilton is a licensed psychologist in New York and Massachusetts and a certified sex therapist. As author of many books including *Partners in Love, Sex before Marriage*, and *Sex, with Love*, she has also written 60 or more articles on love, sex, and marriage. A recent appearance on the "Phil Donahue Show" brought hundreds of calls and letters. She has received the annual achievement award from the Society for the Scientific Study of Sex. She did her graduate studies in psychology at Columbia University. She has appeared on almost every important national and local television station and is a frequent interviewee on radio shows. She participated in the segment of "Hour Magazine" which received the Maggie Award from Planned Parenthood. She and the staff of the Counseling Center conduct an intensive 10-day training workshop on love and sexuality for professionals on Cape Breton Island, Nova Scotia each June.

Nancy R. Hamlin is the founder and director of the Greater Lynn Community Mental Health Center's Training Institute, a continuing education program for experienced health and human service professionals. She has a private practice and is on the faculty of the National Institute of Mental Health's Technical Assistance Center, where she consults with individuals and agencies in the area of organized development, primary prevention, time management, burn-out, and training and development. Hamlin has developed programs focusing on human sexuality, family life education, and the prevention of rape, sexism and racism. Hamlin was featured on the week long channel 5, CVB-TV5 series on burn-out and stress in the workplace.

Hamlin has been the codirector of the New England National Institute of Mental Health funded multiethnic training program to retrain health and human service professionals in race relations and their effects on service delivery. In 1982, she served as the program chairman of the National Council of Community Mental Health Center' Conference on Prevention, Consultation, and Education, both nationally and in the New England region.

Julia R. Heiman is associate professor of psychiatry and behavioral sciences at the University of Washington in Seattle and is currently research coordinator for Harborview Community Mental Health Center. Between 1974 and 1980, Heiman was associate research director of the Sex Therapy Center at the Department of Psychiatry and Behavioral Sciences, State University of New York (SUNY) at Stony Brook. Concurrently she was also chief of the Laboratory of Marital and Interpersonal Problems in her capacity as research scientist with the Long Island Research Institute. She has a Ph.D. in clinical psychology from the State University of New York, Stony Brook. Heiman has published extensively on human sexuality with particular emphasis on sexual arousal, psychophysiology, dysfunction, and the interaction of sexual and marital problems. She has collaborated on research and therapy activities with LoPiccolo and is now finishing a book, *Patterns in Human Sexuality*, with Leitenberg. Heiman is a well-known speaker nationally and internationally, having given invited talks and workshops in Italy, Europe, Mexico, and Australia.

Harold Leitenberg is professor of psychology at the University of Vermont, director of the Ph.D. program in clinical psychology, director of the Behavior Therapy and Psychotherapy Center, and clinical professor of psychiatry. He has published over 50 research articles and chapters across a wide spectrum of topics, especially in the area of behavior therapy. He has extensive research and therapy experience in the area of sexual disturbance, and is coauthoring a new text on human sexual behavior with Jim Geer and Julia Heiman.

Joseph LoPiccolo is professor and director of the Sex Therapy Center in the Department of Psychiatry and Behavioral Science, School of Medicine, at the State University of New York, Stony Brook. He is also professor in the Department of Psychology. He has taught at the University of Houston, the University of Oregon, and the Baylor College of Medicine. He did his graduate Ph.D. work in clinical psychology at Yale University. An active research scientist, LoPiccolo has been involved in the assessment and treatment of sexual dysfunction, the enhancement of the sexual relationship in normal couples, and determinants of sexual function and dysfunction. He is on the editorial board of several journals in the area of sexuality and behavior therapy and has published extensively in these fields. He is an author (with J. Heiman and L. LoPiccolo) of a book *Becoming Orgasmic: A Sexual Growth Program for Women*, and with L. LoPiccolo, a *Handbook of Sex Therapy*.

Brian R. McNaught is a certified sex counselor, free-lance journalist, and lecturer. He received his degree in journalism from Marquette University in 1970. He has written for and edited a large number of publications concerned with sex education, religion, and gay civil rights. His syndicated column, "A Disturbed Peace," appears in a variety of gay newspapers. *A Disturbed Peace: Selected Writings of an Irish Catholic Homosexual*, published by Dignity, Inc. (Washington, D.C.) is a compilation of his work, including his Catholic Press Association award-winning article, "The Sad Dilemma of the Gay Catholic" (*U.S. Catholic*, 1975). He has frequently appeared on TV and radio shows and has lectured at over 30 colleges and universities. He was named one of the Outstanding Young Men of America in 1978 and 1979 and received the Margaret Sanger Award in 1979 from the Institute for Family Research and Education at Syracuse University for his contribution to the public's understanding of homosexuality.

James B. Nelson is professor of Christian ethics at United Theological Seminary of the Twin Cities, Minnesota. He received his bachelor of divinity degree at Yale Divinity School and his M.A. and Ph.D. at Yale University. In addition he has studied at Oxford and Cambridge Universities in England. Nelson has been a minister of churches in Connecticut and South Dakota and has had visiting faculty appointments at a number of theological seminaries and at the University of Minnesota Medical School. The author of five books and a number of articles on ethics, religion, and sexuality, his latest book is *Embodiment: An Approach to Sexuality and Christian Theology.*

Letty Cottin Pogrebin is an editor and writer at *Ms.* magazine, a nationally known lecturer, and author of three books, most recently *Growing Up Free: Raising Your Child in the 80s.* Her work has also appeared in the *New York Times Book Review* and on the Op-Ed Page, and in many other periodicals and anthologies. Her honors include listings in *Who's Who in America*, an Emmy Award for her editorial consulting work on "Free To Be, You And Me," and the Matrix Award for 1981.

Wendy Coppedge Sanford is a member of the Boston Women's Health Book Collective. She coauthored and edited *Our Bodies, Ourselves* (Simon and Schuster, 1973) and *Ourselves and Our Children* (Random House, 1978), both by the collective. Most recently she wrote three chapters in *Changing Bodies, Changing Lives: A Book for Teens on Sex and Relationships* (by Ruth Bell and others, Random House, 1981). She has a master's degree in theological studies from Harvard Divinity School, where she team-taught a course called "Sex Education as Ministry." For 6 years she led sexuality workshops for teenagers and young adults at the Northfield Religious Conference. She worked for 4 years as a counselor and trainer of peer counselors at the Sexuality Information Service of the University of Massachusetts, Boston Harbor Campus.

Sharon B. Satterfield is director of the Program in Human Sexuality at the University of Minnesota Medical School where she is also an assistant professor in the Department of Family Practice and Community Health and in the Department of Psychiatry. She is vice-chair of the Assembly Committee on Student Affairs at the University of Minnesota and other committees, including those concerning women and sexual harassment. She received her medical degree at the University of Michigan, did her residency at the University of Maryland, and is licensed to practice in both Maryland and Minnesota. She is a diplomate in child psychiatry and a certified sex educator and sex therapist of the AASECT. Dr. Satterfield has published extensively on the sexual problems of adolescents, on sexual rehabilitation for postcoronary patients, and on juvenile prostitution. She is editing a book entitled *Selected Topics in Family Sexuality* and has recently published a chapter on the sexual abuse of children.

Mary Lee Neil Tatum is a teacher in the Family Life and Sex Education Program at the Falls Church City public schools in Virginia. After study at the University of Washington and at George Mason University she became a certified sex educator, AASECT, and has developed training programs for teenagers and parents. In addition to publishing articles on sex education in the schools, she has filmed a model sex education program for television and has appeared on talk shows throughout the country. She is on the board of directors of SIECUS and the Center for Population Options, and is currently vice-president of the American Association of Sex Educators, Counselors, and Therapists.

Gertrude J. Rubin Williams is in private practice in St. Louis. A diplomate in clinical psychology of the American Board of Professional Psychology, she did her graduate work at the University of Southern California and at Washington University in St. Louis, where she completed the doctorate in clinical and experimental psychology. Williams has served as director and chief psychologist at the Child Guidance Clinics of the city of St. Louis, and has taught at St. Louis University, Washington University, and Webster College. She was editor of the *Journal of Clinical Child Psychology* for several years and serves on the editorial boards of numerous other journals. She has been president of the section on clinical child psychology of Division 12, APA, on the APA Task Force on the Rights of Children and Youth, and on the Children's Rights Committee of SPSSI. With Sol Gordon, she edited *Clinical Child Psychology: Current Practices and Future Perspectives.* Her articles have appeared in most child psychology journals. An active child advocate and crusader for the prevention of child abuse, Williams has been invited to speak and to appear in the mass media throughout the United States and Canada. Her most recent publication is a book (with John Money), *Traumatic Abuse and Neglect of Children at Home*, published by the Johns Hopkins University Press.

Name Index

Subject Index